MUD, SWEAT and GEARS

A History of the
British Cyclo-Cross Association

MUD, SWEAT
and GEARS

A History of the
British Cyclo-Cross Association

Ken and Maureen Nichols

Mud, Sweat and Gears

Copyright © Ken & Maureen Nichols, 2011

Published in 2011 by Mousehold Press, Norwich
For the British Cyclo-Cross Trust

Cover photograph: a National Trophy promotion by the VC Elan
at Maryon Wilson Park, Eltham, October 1995© John Coulson

ISBN 978-1-874739-58-6

Printed by CLE Print, St Ives, Cambridgeshire

Contents

Appendices

I would like to dedicate this book not only to the officials listed within, but to all those unsung officials, marshals, lap scorers, course layers, car park attendants and tea ladies. Without these dedicated helpers the British Cyclo-Cross Association could not have lasted so successfully for nearly 50 years.

Preface

I first became interested in this project when I heard that the Trustees of the British Cyclo-Cross Trust were looking for someone to research and write the Association's history. When Steve Grimwood asked me if I would like to think about writing such a book I decided to say yes, and have a go. From that moment onwards the next two years just flew by. I was completely unprepared for the task ahead of me. It seemed as if there were very few weeks when I was not busy researching, putting down facts, checking quotes or noting my own thoughts on the comings and goings of the Association.

Luckily, I possess a near complete set of Cycling in all its many incarnations, from the 1920's upwards, plus copies of other magazines which are now long defunct. Then there are the boxes of the B.C-C.A Archives, which consist of programmes, letters, association magazines and of course, most valuable of all, almost every handbook from the 1956/57 season onwards. Maureen then proceeded to spend her evenings sorting the various contents of the boxes into date order. These and other items would slowly migrate to our back bedroom where they remained piled up until I had scoured the likely copies for items of interest.

If ten different people were to write this history, the outcome would be ten differing approaches to the subject. Mine has been to try and put as much as seemed appropriate into the words of the officials, reporters, and of course, the riders themselves. Every age has its own way of describing events, from the polite gentlemanly words of the pre-war officials and reporters, to those who have always called a 'spade a spade'. I have not attempted to include reports on every major race but have included almost all National and World Championships. Many other details can be found in the various appendices listed at the back of the book

You may well ask what my credentials are for writing this history. I have always enjoyed riding 'rough-stuff' events which members of the Suffolk CTC introduced me to, way back in 1958. Both Maureen and I still ride tracks and byways when touring in Britain and Europe, and can rarely resist the opportunity to venture down a track that may go in the general direction in which we are travelling.

As regards my involvement in the sport of Cyclo-Cross, I can only claim to have raced in one event but during the 1970's I did promote twenty local cyclo-cross events. These were mostly for my club, the Wolsey Road Club, but I also volunteered to promote for the English Schools Cycling Association in the Ipswich parks. Being involved with these events, I discovered that both the riders and officials were some of the most dedicated and friendly in cycle sport. I well remember after events, riders covered in mud, and wet through, shivering with cold but still having the time and courtesy to come up to officials with a "Thanks, I've really enjoyed today." Recognising that we, the officials, had also been standing holding lap sheets with frozen hands, having to peer into bitter cold rain looking for the next competitor to appear. Afterwards there was the job of drying out soggy lap sheets and trying to explain to a group of mud covered riders why they had not finished as high up as they had hoped. One memory that does stick out is at an E.S.C.A Championships where Maureen was seated in the back of a very small van, frantically typing out the result sheets and squeezing over to print them out on a hand duplicator, so that the young racers could go away happy.

I have long admired seeing those skilful and brave riders pushing themselves to the limit over all kinds of terrain. I attended both the World Championships at Crystal Palace and Leeds during 1973 and 1992 where I really did become a fan of the sport.

After reading this history I can only hope that you are left with a greater appreciation of the amazing amount of work and dedication given by the Association's officials over so many years, to a sport they loved and believed in.

Ken Nichols

Introduction

There are many ways of writing the history of a body such as the British Cyclo-Cross Association.

I have attempted to show that the sport of cyclo-cross racing attracts every type of personality, from the cool, calm and carefully calculating rider, to the maverick who has no respect for either his body or his bicycle. Professional riders were often looked down on as a different breed of racer and even up to the nineteen sixties or later, amateurs were referred to as 'pure'. It is also interesting to note the many types of courses, clothing and equipment and how they evolved over the century since cross country racing began.

I would like to think that readers interested in the history of cyclo-cross will come back to this book and use it as a reference source. To be able to check on the champions, races or details of a favourite rider or event and for this reason I have shown every season as a separate section.

After reading this history, I urge you to turn to the appendix sections where you can really appreciate the dedication of the many officials who gave thousands of hours of their spare time to this Association.

You will see that when giving results I have tried to give full names of clubs and sponsors (or both sometimes) because I feel it shows how riders changed teams, or in some cases remained loyal to their first club, and how new trends in club names and sponsors came into the sport.

Spending so many months looking through the archives, I feel that at some point these boxes of papers, programmes and handbooks should end up being placed in the safe care of the National Cycle Museum or a similar archive for permanent preservation so that they can be available to researchers in the future, as they are a valuable part of British cycling history.

Acknowledgements:

This history could not have taken place without the help of many individuals, all of whom are listed below. However I apologise now if anyone has been accidentally missed from this list:

John Atkins, Ron Atkins, Chris Bevis, Jim Court, John and Wendy David, Rowland Ferris, Harry Gould, Steve Grimwood, Brian Kington, Phil O'Connor, Ted Saunderson, Lee Wardley, Chris Watts, Tony Wilkins, and the other members of the B.C-C.A Trust.

We would also like to thank Adrian Bell of Mousehold Press

I would also like to thank the publishers of the following books and magazines, and acknowledge the help that these publications have given in the research of this history

A Century Awheel – by Mike Rabbetts
A Wheel in Two Worlds – by Ron Kitching
Awheel – by Stan Bray
Coureur/Sporting Cyclist
Coventry Evening Telegraph
Cycling – which also includes all its various guises –
Cycling & Mopeds, Cycling & Sporting Cyclist, then finally, *Cycling Weekly*
Dancing Uphill – by Charles Holland
Fellowship News – published by Fellowship of Cycling Old Timers
International Cycle Sport
The Bicycle
The Birmingham Post
The Daily Express
The Daily Mail
The Daily Telegraph
The Evening Post
The Times
Three Peaks – Web page
Also local Association publications, such as –
North Western C-C.A Annual, Yorkshire C-C.A Crossways and Wessex Newsletter.

Every endeavour has been made to locate and acknowledge the owners of photographs reproduced.

I would also like to thank Maureen, who has had to put up with many piles of cycling magazines strewn about our house, and for her dedicated sorting of the B.C-C.A Archives. She has also had the task of reading all my rough notes and her help on the computer, and finally for her many good ideas and great support on this project.

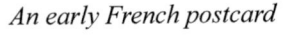

OFFICIER DE GUIDES. UN RENSEIGNEMENT.
GUIDE OFFICER. AN INQUIRY. K.1

An early French postcard

1

Soldiers and English
'Rough-Riders'

Going back to the early 1900's, before any cross-country cycle racing was organised, most roads were kept to a reasonable standard but many were in a very poor condition. In towns there were innumerable hazards for cyclists; woodblocks and cobbles could be very slippery when wet, and most dangerous of all were tramlines. In the countryside things were hardly any better, in summer the country roads could be rutted or with areas of deep sand, in winter or wet weather, lanes became more akin to ploughed fields with riders encountering wide and often deep fords. Even the most modest cyclist had to be very skilful to avoid carts, horses and the droppings they left in their wake or even the occasional automobile.

When and why did some riders want to race over tracks and through woods just for fun? Research seems divided about who was the founding father of cross-country racing. It appears that around 1900, a French soldier called Daniel Gousseau enjoyed riding his bicycle alongside his mounted general, covering various routes during Army exercises, including many rough cross country sections. Each winter they went out and the numbers joining them began to increase to 20 or 30, he even managed to convince the French Army to organise the events as part of troop training. Being young it was not long before they began competing with each other, at first with very basic ideas but later the events became properly organised. At this time, most European armies had Cycling Battalions and they would include in their manoeuvres, riding over rough countryside, through woods, scouting and observing other armies. Gousseau later became the Secretary-General of the French Cycling Union and in 1902 he and some friends became involved in organising the first French Cyclo-Cross Championship race, won by F. de Baeder.

Other researchers put forward the name of Geo Lefèvre, who in 1903 organised a race called the Cross Cyclo-Pédèstre at Ville d'Avray, a town just outside Paris. Although it has been pointed out that, as a winter sport, these dates could have been during the same winter season.

Both riders and spectators began to sit up and take notice of these offbeat events when Octave Lapize spoke out in favour of this side of the sport, after winning the Tour de France in 1910. He said he had only been able to suffer the difficulties of that Tour, because of the training he had done racing in cyclo-cross during the previous winter. Eugène Christophe recommended riding cyclo-cross in the off-season after winning the French Cyclo Cross Championships every year from 1909 to 1914; he was also the holder of the first yellow jersey in the Tour de France, winner of Milan-San Remo, Paris-Tours and Bordeaux-Paris.

Events were confined to France at first, although riders in neighbouring countries soon began to take up the sport. Belgium organised its first National Championship in 1910, which was won by Philippe Thijs, an amazing rider, who went on to win the 'Tour' three times in a row, this was followed quickly by a similar event in Switzerland in 1912. Some of these cyclo-cross events, which appear in photographs reproduced in the 1911 and 1912 issues of *Cycling* magazine, show large groups of riders starting off with great gusto, watched by crowds of animated spectators lining the course. The titles under these photos are certainly of their time: - "The start of a cross country cycle race near Paris. Even in winter the devotion to track clothing for road events is unshaken, and mudguards are scorned, although the road is saturated with rain."

Another reference in a January 1912 copy shows a similar picture captioned: - " Winter road sport in France: the start of a cross- country race outside Paris. In these events the toughest country is negotiated, including fields, woods and streams, the bicycles often having to be carried."

In England, one of several events being promoted around London during 1914 was the Catford Paperchase. Notable among the teams that entered, was one from the 25th Battalion County of London Cyclist Regiment. This event was run as a team event and was decided on a complicated formula where teams had to finish with five riders, and then time was deducted for every extra rider to finish. In these events a 'Hare' would be despatched with a bag of paper strips to spread along the course, then after a suitable amount of time, the 90 racers would be sent on their way. It is not recorded where the soldiers finished in the result, but the winners were the Etna C.C.

During the period of the First World War and for some time afterwards very little is recorded but it seems probable that some cross-country races did take place. Luxemburg held a National Championships in 1923 and by 1924 the sport was expanding to such an extent that the first international event was promoted in Paris with the title of 'Le Criterium International de Cross-Country Cyclo-Pédèstre'. This event had a feature called 'Trou de Diable' (the Devils Hole) where spectators would crowd to see the racers negotiate this obstacle. Some of the major figures to ride in this were; Eugène Christophe who finished fifth in 1925, Charles Pelissier winner in 1926 and 1927 and Sylvere Maes in 1933 who were both 'Tour' winners.

It appears that the French riders favoured the fixed wheel for this type of racing, because a photograph in *Cycling* shows the winner of the French National Championships in 1928, crossing the finish line with his legs hanging away from the free flying pedals and looking rather embarrassed in front of a large crowd of spectators. The caption reads "Winner of the French cross-country championship 'loses' his pedals at the moment of crossing the line."

Back in England a Cyclists v Harriers Race was held in 1922, when the Walsall Section of the Cyclists' Touring Club (C.T.C.) and the Bloxwich Harriers decided to hold a competitive event. It was such a successful promotion, with many clubs anxious to ride, that the next year it was thrown open to any Midland club wishing to participate. This event always attracted some of the most competitive cyclists and harriers from all parts of the Midlands, including Charles Holland (a Tour de France rider) winner in 1929, Percy Stallard (British League of Racing Cyclists pioneer) winner in 1933 and Albert Burman (cartoonist for *Cycling* and C.T.C Gazette magazines) winner in 1934/35/36.

In 1925 a report of an annual event between Midland harriers and cyclists, attracted 88 competitors and was described as "successful and thrilling". It was held over a 6½-mile course, consisting of fields, lanes and ditches. For the third year in succession, W.H.Genders, the well-known Wood End R.C.C. 'speed man' was first home. Above the report of this event in *Cycling* is a picture of a cyclist running in deep mud carrying his bicycle over his shoulder in a very modern way.

In the story of Charles Holland's life, *Dancing Uphill* by his daughter Frances, he describes riding the 1929 Walsall event:

I was delighted with the invitation to compete in the 1929 event, and more so when the November weather, though cold was dry, and so was advantageous to the cyclists. Quite big crowds gathered at the finish and at various vantage points on the course, and by using the faster roads cyclists could see the race at halfway, and beat the competition back to the finish. My track riding ability coupled with my time trialling stood me in good stead and I came in first. The crowd beyond the finishing line had closed in, funnel like and the cinematography news cameraman was right in the middle and being a fast finish I just couldn't help hitting him. I found out later at the cinema just how they managed to show objects seemingly coming off the screen and into the auditorium.

A long report in *Cycling*, November 1928, of the seventh joint Walsall Section of the C.T.C and Walsall Harriers A.C. race told of 80 competitors lining up for a 7¼-mile course. "The Swamp, a well known spot to spectators and competitors alike, was reported by the trail layers to be at least 2ft deep!" This did not deter too many, as 67 completed the course, did some perhaps have to swim? It was a great day for the cyclists, because the first harrier could only manage 17th place. 'Trail layers' were the men who started out ahead of the race to lay the course, with strips of paper and small flags or arrows, for the competitors to follow. The magnificent team shield is now preserved in Walsall Museum.

In Spain, the sport was getting more popular and they were the next to promote a National Championships in 1929 closely followed by Italy in 1930. In England, 'Rough-Rider' or 'Cross Country' events were taking place but were often regarded as light-hearted amusing sideshows held during the winter months, with reports in the cycle press certainly taking this line. However, the photographs with the reports indicate that there was fierce competition amongst the riders.

The Cyclists' Touring Club also promoted 'rough-stuff' events, one of which is outlined in the C.T.C. Gazette of March 1927. "Present day cyclists seem to have a penchant for cross country riding and when they are not pitting themselves in hopeless contests against harriers they hold paper chases and other competitions against themselves. The Northern Section of the Metropolitan DA have this winter been deciding on a series of Inter-club matches with the Welham C.C. The 'Welhamites' who are mostly 'C.T.Cites' gained the rubber for the second time in three encounters." – "It is not surprising to learn that the more experienced competitors had dry stockings and shoes at the finish."

By 1930 some ladies are recorded as taking part in these events. In *Cycling* of February 1930, a photo shows a pretty girl running with her racing cycle over the mud with the caption below: -

"Winter Sports Girls – The girls from "The Shows the Thing" company and Mrs E. Hamilton of the Delta R.C. had a practice cross-country bicycle race on Thursday of last week. The venue selected was the same as that employed by Thames Valley Harriers, starting on Hounslow Heath and the difficulties included getting over a hedge, crossing a stream, climbing over gates, riding through a gravel pit and a large amount of stubble. Men's bicycles were used and the girls, with two exceptions, did not employ free wheels. One started with plain sprint tyres but came to grief at a greasy turn. For costumes they wore running shorts and sweaters, and despite the intense cold they all thoroughly enjoyed the trial, and are arranging more outings of a similar description."

Stan Bray in his book *Awheel* (The Story of the Solihull C.C) says that Vic Pegg presented a trophy for the Club's Cross-country races, the first in 1930, won by Ivor Goodman; with the next recorded winner as Norman Lees in 1933, who also won in '34, '36 and '37. Cyril Lovegrove slipped in with a win in 1935, and Ken Topless in 1938 and 1941, proving that this was a well-established event.

Often *Cycling* magazine reported on Cyclo-Cross (or Cross-Cyclo as they sometimes called it) with amazement that the French racers competed in their summer racing kit, with such comments as "The French are a hardy nation, cyclo cross-country races are held every week-end and though there be snow on the ground summer attire is de rigueur."(January 1931). In February, this magazine returned to the subject of French racers with "French cyclists are a hardy breed. The professionals have their Tour de France, the most terrible endurance test of all sporting events in the world, whilst amateurs, not content with ordinary road racing, invent improvements such as the "cross-cyclo" in which competitors leave the road frequently in order to run across ploughed fields or ford rivers carrying their machines." Contrast this with a report on an English race, the next month in the same magazine, the Balham Rough Riders '25' held at Tatsfield, Surrey (known as the 'Alpine' course) has a full-page article that treats the event with ridicule and amusement and not as a serious race at all, despite the fact that the winner was B.A.Bevan of Highgate and the second placed rider was the great F.W.Southall of Norwood Paragon.

There were 100 entries, 90 starters and 75 finishers; a full third of the article seemed to be decrying the crowds on the road at the finish. The writer seemed to find it contemptible that there was a van complete with 'cinematograph' and 'talkie' apparatus reporting on the event.

It appears that the number of entries above were not unusual, as a report in *Cycling* March 1933, of the Centaur B.C Cross-country race over 14 miles was made up of 144 riders divided into 36 teams who were sent off at two-minute intervals. Other reports are from the North Herts 'Rough- Riders 13' and the Avon Road Club 'Rough-Riders 14'. These demonstrate great participation from riders, with reports and pictures showing the large crowds drawn to these events, almost all of the events were 'Entries on line'.

Cycling describes S.M.Butler winning the Balham 'Rough and Tumble 25.'

Emerging, rather unsteadily from a welter of dances and dinners, the London racing world crept out cautiously to the Surrey Downs, not too early last Sunday morning, to cast a somewhat bilious eye upon those enthusiastic young men whose pleasure it was this year to participate in the Prologue to the Racing Season. Rain, hours and hours of it had prepared the stage, but mercifully had practically vanished before Mr.J.T.Wells, the timekeeper, called upon the first of the players to begin. Thus began the Prologue – the annual rough and tumble trial held by the Balham C.C. each year since 1926. And for the fourth time in five years S.M.Butler, the Norwood Paragon crack, who holds the record for the course of 1.37.3, was the winner.

Some clubs even included rough-stuff time trials in their Best all Rounder Competitions. In an interview, in Dec 2006, with 90-year-old Ron Atkins, (a name that will crop up later) he remembered competing in the Longbridge C.C. competition where members had, during 1934, to ride four road Time Trials plus one over rough stuff. Ron also recalls winning the N.C.C Birmingham Centre 'Palmer Trophy' Cross Country event in 1938 (the trophy was donated by the famous tyre company).

Before the Second World War, the police were unconcerned when massed-start rough-stuff races crossed from one field to another, crossing roads in the process, as long as the organisers had permission from the farmers. These events were run with no controlling body, riders only knew about them by word of mouth, although some events did have notices put in the cycling press.

Robert Oubron the French winner of the International Criterium in 1937 '38, '41, and '42 was known as the 'King of Cyclo-cross', he pioneered a style that many would follow over the years. He took very short steps and held his handlebars tight to his shoulder, thereby preventing his front wheel from swinging or catching trees and bushes, he was also known as the master of the Sous Bois (undergrowth) technique. He later wrote a classic book on the techniques of the sport with Rene Chesal, called 'Cycle 100%, Serie cyclo-cross'. An item in the column 'News – Cyclo-cross training' in *Cycling* states "Leader in the Ile-de-France Cyclo-Cross championships Pierre Jodet trains for this arduous sport by running up flights of stairs carrying his bicycle and then riding down again!" Not something you see recommended by trainers these days

Sporting Cyclist 1964 has an article written by Neville Billington, recalling an episode in France just after the Second World War, which has both humour and danger. - "Reputed to be the fastest speed achieved by crossmen"

The veteran French crossman M. Duval claims it was achieved in a race in which he competed shortly after the liberation. The course went over an airfield and the group in which he was riding were horrified to hear a hail of bullets come whistling immediately over their heads! Every man rode for cover like the Devil possessed. 'We went through the sound barrier,' he claims. After the race it was revealed that 50 English soldiers were having target practice.

Even during the war years, sporting cyclists were continuing to show a desire to compete in cross-country events. *Cycling* in February 1940 featured reports of some of these events such as those promoted by the Kingsdale C.C and Northern Paragon, both described as 'Rough-stuff' races. This seems amazing, when in a later edition (July) there is a notice that the Cwmcarn Paragon had to abandon its '25' - "Due to the discovery of six unexploded bombs dropped by raiders a few yards from the road." In Ron Kitching's story, *A Wheel in Two Worlds*, there is a description of the Sheffield Roughriders event that he rode in March 1942.

In today's sport it would be called a cyclo-cross race. Then it was just a hard race for hard men ... I rode down that morning, the fifty miles to Bawtry, on my training bike, with mudguards. At the start, everything was frozen and we had to ride alongside a frozen canal, starting at minute intervals. We were told that if we overtook anyone we had to do it on the side nearest the water, so as not to push anyone in ... Halfway round my pedal disintegrated, but the axle was left on and I rode round on that and was surprised to find that I had won the race. Then I had to go back up the course to find the bits of my pedal, which I then put back together and rode the sixty miles back to Harrogate.

This sounds like quite a day, a 100 miles with a 25-mile cyclo-cross sandwiched in the middle, all this in freezing weather, they certainly were very hard men!

The first event of the 1944 season, the Wolverhampton R.C.C. cyclo-cross at Penn, saw a battle royal between two riders who became important names in British cycling. Ernie Clements of the Wrekin R.C.C who later became a top roadman and also the owner of Falcon Cycles, and Percy Stallard (Wolverhampton R.C.C.) a leading light in the formation of the British League of Racing Cyclists. Clements won the event with Stallard in second place.

With the war over, there were reports again in *Cycling* in 1946 recording several events such as the British League of Racing Cyclists (B.L.R.C) north east section 'Rough Riding Competition', showing that road racers were as keen on cyclo cross as their Continental counterparts. Among the best known was the Balham Rough- Riders '25' through the back lanes of the Kent/Surrey border. Other major events during this period were the promotions in Warwickshire and in 1946 the 'Tour de Blythe'.

Many clubs were starting up again as men and women returned from war service and they all had a great desire to get out and about in the countryside and start competing again. Cyclists v Harriers events as far apart as Gravesend and Oldham with another held at Royton and Rochdale were just a few of the new promotions.

Another quote from Ron Kitching describes an event this year, in which one wonders for the sanity of the competitors. Ron describes in his own words this dreadful day. "In March of that year the Yorkshire Cycling Federation organised a race that Ron just couldn't resist - a 'Rough Stuff' time-trial starting at nearby Collingham. While snowstorms were certainly not unknown in March in those days, a fall of three feet of the white stuff was a bit much for cycle racing. As a result, only twelve riders started and no one completed the first four-mile circuit in less than an hour, resulting in a number of retirements." - "But I had to live up to my hard-man image. I rode in shorts and ankle socks, with the result that my shoes were red with blood running down from shins cut by the top crust of ice. I think we ran more than we rode. I eventually finished third to J.D.Spink and my friend and club mate Jimmy Hibberd was second. We rode home to Harrogate pondering why do we do it?"

November 28th 1948 saw the Rugby 'November Handicap' where a certain Keith Edwards beat Ron Atkins, the next year Peter Shilton won this same event. It is interesting to see Ron Atkins's notebook itemising his use of various gear arrangements, sometimes he rode a three-speed derailleur and sometimes a 66" fixed gear.

The Annual Bagshot Scramble was watched by a large crowd in 1949, which was again promoted by the Ealing Manor Road Club and had 90 starters over a 10-mile course. "which included mud, sand and hills of up to 1 in 3." This description makes it sound more like modern courses, for they were now getting shorter and over a more compact area. During this period a certain Bob Thom attracted attention by riding cyclo cross, he was known as one of England's "most experienced and enthusiastic of all sporting cyclists." He had turned independent with the British League of Racing Cyclists in 1948, and was National Independent Champion in 1949, later known as 'Viking's Mr Biking'. Little did he know that 30 years later he would become the President of an association not yet formed.

2

Enthusiasts and Pioneers
Seasons 1950/51 to 1953/54

Cyclo-cross on the Continent was still continuing to develop at a fair pace, and in March 1950 the Union Cycliste Internationale (U.C.I.) approved the first World Championships. They were held just outside Paris, with the winner Jean Robic of France, who had won the Tour de France back in 1947 and was notable for always wearing a large crash helmet. Second in the event was his fellow countryman, R.Rondeaux with P.Jodet in third; the first non-Frenchman was Nelio Sforacchi of Italy in fifth place. According to *Cycling* magazine the event only became a World Championship at the very last moment and they did their best to play down its significance, as described in this extract. "By the decision of the U.C.I., made only two days before this event, this race, an early season roadman's training outing was officially earmarked as a championship of the world!"

Cycling couldn't seem to make up its mind whether the event was a 'French style cyclo-cross' or a 'Rough-riding event' as both descriptions appeared in the same report. What was clear however, was that the public enjoyed the event for the report continues: "The spectators who lined the whole course, were at times so dense as to make overtaking by riders almost impossible." With this event cyclo-cross passed a major milestone, being internationally recognised by having its own World Championships.

The sport was expanding in several countries within Europe, but in Britain there was no national organisation and most events were still being run as 'fun' events. Keen English exponents of rough stuff were reading about the standard of continental events and these riders yearned to sample the experience. Reference to this feeling is in a quote from a B.C-C.A leaflet from the 1980s. "In 1950 three Midlanders competed in an event near Paris, the first Englishmen with new ideas. From this moment onwards cross-country cycle racing became known as cyclo-cross on this side of the English Channel, but is frequently abbreviated by those involved to simply cross." There appears to be no other reference to this trip or what the outcome was.

In 1950, the January 12th edition of *Cycling* reported an event in Portsmouth where the cyclists were victorious over the runners, and the 'Forthcoming Events' list shows 'Rough-Stuffs' being promoted by both the Rickmansworth C.C. and Avon R.C. The same edition also has a picture of the second annual 'Sedgbourne Cyclo-Cross' with a large group of competitors running through deep mud with groups of spectators watching. Looking down the list of riders, there are two names to which we shall return to later during this narrative. Keith Edwards (Warwickshire R.C.) who came second and whose determined riding was described thus "when he crashed, he got up and crashed again" and Ron Atkins (Coventry R.C.) who was sixth. The winner of the event was W.Whiley of the Halesowen A. & C.C.

Many of the races were over shorter distances, for example, the Bagshot Scramble, a very descriptive name if some of the various reports of the event are to be believed, was held over 12½ miles during January 1950. It must have been run at a very fast pace, because the winner Arthur Kees (Ealing Manor R.C) finished in 29m 35s, on a 66" single freewheel. The report in *Cycling* (known affectionately at this time as 'The Comic'), describes the later stages of the race:

Despite the good conditions, however, there were many crashes and spills (in some cases serious) but these were no deterrent to the competitors. Biggest 'pile up' of the day was early in the race when on a 45-degree up and down 'switchback' at least 30 riders came to grief. Like sheep going to the slaughter they plummeted down to disaster. Surprisingly though only two lost interest in the race; one with a wrecked front wheel and the other unconscious. Despite falls, knocks and cuts it was voted by all to be a great success – especially for the trade repairers.

What an event this proved to be, with 139 competitors and 8,000 spectators!

The Bicycle of 22nd February this year describes three 'Rough-Riders' events. The Avon R.C event had 34 riders but the Rickmansworth C.C. had an entry of 75. Both these rides were of a very local nature, with almost all the riders coming from the surrounding area. The last event report shows a picture of a rider finishing under the eyes of a large crowd and the caption reads: "Only man to finish Saturday's 9½ miles Warwickshire R.C Cyclo-Cross was Keith Edwards, who organised the race. He covered the course in 50mins 15secs. All the other competitors lost their way!" A strange result indeed, but it's that man Edwards again!

The above reports show the very wide range of events that were being run during the early years of the 1950s. Some of these seem of a very amateur nature but a few were beginning to take on a more professional look. They were all popular with a certain type of rider, because it is a type of racing where team tactics play a very small part, as the riders are competing individually against each other. In the Bagshot Scramble, the mention of 'Primes' on the Saddleback Hill shows just how close these races were moving towards the road-racing model.

A picture of a young rider finishing the Worcestershire C.A. event in *Cycling* shows him wearing a rugby shirt, which was then a popular item worn by riders during the early 1950s. Purpose made cycle race clothing was really only available for track or road riders, and of course most 'crosses' were held during cold weather, so warm windproof clothing was always welcome. Equipment was basic too, with fixed wheels being popular, usually between 56"and 66", single freewheels and hub gears were often used, as early derailleur gears were very vulnerable to breaking or damage and therefore kept for touring or road racing.

Over the years there had been many 'Cyclists v Harriers' events and these were still popular during the early 1950s, providing great sport for the enthusiasts. On dry frosty winter days the cyclists would be to the fore, but on muddy days the runners could skip over the surface, while the cyclists were slowed by their wheels becoming gummed up with mud and leaves. Runners could also climb over any gates barring the way, whilst the riders struggled with their machines, runners could also descend faster down very steep slopes. These were usually run as team and points races, and over a shorter distance than cyclo-cross events.

In complete contrast to these exciting and sometimes wild events was the Road Time Trials Council A.G.M. report in *Cycling* "That all clothing must be black, except that an official panel, not exceeding 4" by 3", may be displayed on either arm with club colours or other flashes".

This demonstrates just how staid the R.T.T.C was at this time; still living in the early 1900s, while the other sides of cycle sport were becoming more colourful and outgoing. The National Cyclists' Union was also in flux, with the emerging British League of Racing Cyclists tugging at its coat tails like a persistent terrier.

More evidence of the spread of the sport in England, were events at Reading and Chesterfield. Many were still time trials with each rider being set off at minute intervals and with a timekeeper at both the start and finish of the course, the winner was not the first over the line but the rider with the shortest time.

John Bethell recalls in an article in the '87 North Western C-C.A. magazine Annual titled 'Thirty Six Years of Muddy Washing'. "It all started around 1950 when, as a junior in the Macclesfield Wheelers, I was conned into taking part in the local Cyclists v Harriers." Open events were very few in the mid-fifties, and John mentioned the infamous 'Circuit of the Claypits' at Flixton and that his own club ran the 'Rocky Road to Rainbow' course based on the Cheshire Hunt at Bollington, which had a 'Le Mans' style starts. "If you survived those events you could always ride at Lantern Pike, where if the bogs didn't get you, the clouds would. Several field gates were reduced to matchwood before the organisers realised it would be wiser to open them before the race commenced." He also remembered one young farmer who trained for rough stuff events by "regular stints on his bike, of course, rounding up the cows for milking!… Roy Comer was one of the first local riders to use lightweight equipment like Campagnolo gear mechs and chainsets, but Louis Renshaw swore by his Sturmey Archer hub gear and steel rims, riding them in the 'National' to the amazement of the Southerners."

Most events were, however, now turning to the 'Massed Start' formula, a term used at the time as a description of Road Races. The Worcestershire Cycling Association, formed in the thirties, was still promoting cyclo-crosses during the early months of 1951. These were being regularly won by Ron Atkins, with two being the "Segbourne" and " Chadwich" events, with Ron and Les Nock often in close competition for the main prizes. Ron Atkins did not however feature in the dramatic and controversial sprint for the line in a February event at Sutton Park, Birmingham, where the sprint between Les Nock and Keith Edwards was described in *Cycling* "Were so close together as they crossed the line after nine miles, that the Timekeepers could not separate them. The judges however gave the verdict to Nock by six inches".

Ron Atkins won a 'rough-stuff' event, which was sponsored by the Cyclo Gear Company, where Louis Caulis the owner, presented the prizes himself. Ron's first prize was a 'Cyclo' rear gear mechanism. (Remembering later in an interview, he gave the prize to a frame builder for a frame being built for his wife Edith, who would then go on to ride that same bicycle to success in many place-to-place Road Records including the Amateur Lady's 'End to End' in 1953.) This rough stuff event was still going strong in 1952, when Eileen Sheridan (the multiple place to place record holder) was asked to act as the event starter and W. Oakley (later to become the C.T.C President) was one of the judges. It was run off as a team event as well as having individual awards and it appears that these were cyclo-cross races in all but name but with harriers included.

Reports were coming from Ireland of Cyclists v Harriers events being held to a similar format as those in England, with an annual event in Phoenix Park, Dublin. But in Wales events were of a much tougher type, with for example the Cwmcarn Paragon R.C. 'Mountain Rough-stuff', which was described as "a six mile mountain massed-start rough-stuff event." All this activity proved that the sport was slowly expanding into every part of the British Isles.

The start and result sheets of most of these events appear to have been typed on ancient machines and perhaps hand duplicated on the cheapest paper, probably on kitchen tables, as was done by many clubs during this period. It must be remembered that a World War had not long finished in Europe; therefore all items, including food and paper, were hard to come by. The earliest race programme in the British Cyclo-Cross Association archives is from the Walsall's 19th Annual 'Cyclist versus Harriers Cross Country Race' held on 8th November 1952. Although this is two years before the formation of the B.C-C.A, it shows how some promoters of the 'rough-stuff' sport were already organising to a high standard. The programme was professionally printed, with adverts showing support from a wide range of advertisers, such as the Taylor Bros (cycle frame makers), Perrett's, and R.Russell, the brewers Highgate Ales and Stouts and even the Cyclists' Touring Club. The last named being a little surprising, as the C.T.C. was then thought of as a non-competitive touring club.

During 1953 the Universities C.U. held a cyclo-cross event with an amazing length of 43½ miles and it took the winner M.Foulger of West Ham 3h 26m 50s, a real endurance test for all. There was also a ladies competition incorporated, with their winner being B. Leith of the Rams C.C. There seems very little information available on separate events for ladies or prizes just for them, or how often females participated in such events during this period.

Snow featured in many events during this winter, with many hit badly by deep drifts, reports in February covered the difficult conditions riders were facing. Some of the *Cycling* quotes from this winter were: The Worcestershire C.A. event at Halesowen - "was held in snow with Keith Edwards winning on a bitter cold morning" and in the Stapleford R.C.'s event it was "deep in snow" and over at the Wakefield & Dis. C.A's race the conditions were "The snow had drifted deeply." Brian Haskell, the Huddersfield international was winning the Huddersfield C.A. event where "Deep snow made conditions so bad that riding was possible on no more than 1¼ miles of the 5 mile circuit."

The January 1st edition of *Cycling* carried a notice from the N.C.U. which would prove a major turning point in the sport.

ENTRIES FOR WORLD'S CHAMPIONSHIPS

The N.C.U announces that it can receive applications from riders both amateur and professional, wishing to compete in the World's Cyclo-Cross championship, to be staged at Onate, near San Sebastian, Spain on March 7, 1953. A maximum of six riders per nation can be entered, five of them comprising a team.

The N.C.U. was occupied with various problems at this time, including being in the throes of a financial crisis. They put the above advert in the press so that riders with enthusiasm for cross racing and who were also willing to pay their own expenses to the event could apply to them, as they were the only organisation recognised by the U.C.I. The team of super enthusiasts that resulted from the applications soon found its way en route to San Sebastian in far off Spain. These pioneers were Keith Brock (London), Keith Edwards, Ken Parrott and John Edney (Midlands) and Bill McAteer (Merseyside), the latter being the brother of the famous boxer Pat McAteer. Although there is a mention of Alan Winters (Solihull) riding, no confirmation has been found in the archives, perhaps he was only a reserve. This was all extra exciting as these five riders were on their very first trip abroad.

Cycling reported in their 12th March edition, the baptism of the five British riders at these World Championships:

On the first climb up a rough course hillside that reared 1 in 4 for 200 yards in the Cross-Cycle Pédèstre world's championship at Oñate, Spain last Sunday, there was a mass of 1,000 or more spectators whose chatter and acclamations echoed across the valley ... The French easily took the team honours with first place Rondeaux, second Bauvin, third Dufraisse and sixth Jodet. Jean Robic, also of France and champion in 1950, smashed his gear on lap 1 and had to retire.

After a description of the race itself, it continued – "Our best man Ken Parrott, Coventry R.C. aged 26 who has had three seasons of cross country racing, was three to four mins behind after lap 1.....Our 'Rough Stuff' king, Keith Edwards, who has raced in 55 such events in 13 yrs (he is 30 yrs of age), finished with great foot blisters, having to run more than his share because a brake failed on the first lap." Keith Brock also had problems, although of a different type: "He had smashed up his own machine in training and rode that of the team's manager Jock Wadley. It had the lowest gear range in our team of 45-80." Jock Wadley was later to become the editor of the classic cycling magazine *Sporting Cyclist* which is still revered in cycling circles for its outstanding articles and excellent photographs.

An interview afterwards with Keith Brock, in the same magazine, describes the San Sebastian course as being very intimidating. "The course included a sixteen-foot drop, so steep that it was like riding off the side of a house. Although most of the riders dismounted and slithered down, some hurtled down at full speed either putting themselves out of business completely, or gaining many valuable yards in the rush." Brock also tells of the hard competitive nature of the Continental riders.

On the first lap he was tearing down a steep track, alongside ex-world champion Frenchman Jean Robic. The track ran out through a narrow hole in a fence and as the pair sped nearer Brock felt Robic trying to force him off the path. He clung grimly to his course, and as they closed up to the opening almost leaning on each other, his knee clouted Robic's handlebars and the champion went slap into the fence. Brock went on, himself to crash a later lap, smashing his machine. In a daze, Brock ran along the only rideable portion of the course with his machine slung over his shoulder, until the team manager, Jock Wadley gently pulled him out of the race and took him off to hospital for treatment.

The honour of being the very first British rider to finish a World Cyclo-Cross Championship went to Ken Parrott, who finished in 30th place, 12m

15s down, J Edney came 32nd and K Edwards 33rd. There were 44 Starters but only 33 finished. These riders certainly had their eyes opened to the skills and speed of the continental riders. H. H. England demonstrates an interesting insight into the thinking at the time in this editorial in *Cycling* of March 1953:

The amateur definition is, the world over, becoming a joke. On the continent, with their own peculiar logic, the cycling Federations merely regard it as a classification of licence. If a rider holds an amateur licence racing is limited to certain types of events, and so on through other classes, which rank higher and provide better remunerations.

Even Britain, bulwark of amateurism, cannot hold out much longer. There is a continual cry for realism, for giving amateurs every support. It cannot be ignored, regrettable though the situation is.

Rather than make questionable relaxations, all sporting organizations (most of them already united under the British Olympic Association) should consider a fresh start on an open-to-all, paid-or-not, basis.

We should still have amateurs – those who wished to be and those not good enough to demand cash.

The large numbers of spectators turning out to watch the sport, were also a wake up call, showing just how big a sport cyclo-cross could be in Britain if all the existing Leagues joined together and concentrated their efforts towards one goal. When the riders who had ridden the World Championships returned, they were even more determined to bring the British Cyclo-Cross Leagues together as one association, as this would be the best way forward to a new future for this side of cycle sport.

It proved to be the spark to set things moving and by autumn of this year the momentum was gathering and those who wanted to push the sport forward had the foresight to realise its potential. It would need a meeting between the various associations and leagues who were running cyclo-crosses at the time, mainly in the Midlands but also north and south of London. Some of those forward thinkers were Keith Edwards, Ron Atkins and Keith Brock who arranged that a meeting of like-minded people should be called to discuss the main options available. The established Leagues knew they needed to get together to form a common set of rules and together they would get more press coverage, more support from the cycle trade and in modern speak 'a much higher profile'.

The big names faced each other in the Southern Cyclo-cross Association event at Biggin Hill in Kent during a January 1954 event described as "a good fun, off-season energy expender." 20-year-old Alan Jackson of De Laune C.C, who was also the Association's secretary, who had proved to be the new find of the 1953 road-racing season, came out on top after battling with Don Stone and Paddy Hoban. A description of the course appeared in *Cycling* magazine, "A good deal of the course lies over clay soil which when wet, makes riding a bicycle a very tricky matter. Besides the natural obstacles, like fences, ditches, rough land, brooks, woods etc" add to that, a field of 248 runners and riders, then it is plain that these events were not for the faint hearted.

Many better class events were being promoted by various clubs and among them were the Annual Mountain Cyclo Cross by Cwmcarn Paragon R.C. and the Ealing Manor R.C's annual Bagshot Scramble, which was won by Don Stone of the powerful 34th Nomads C.C. Although there were crashes as usual, *Cycling* had this to say on the subject: "Injuries to riders and machines were again numerous, with some competitors having to receive hospital attention. This hospital treatment was not confined to the participants in the scramble, for two officials of the event, crashed and both suffered concussion."

This number of crashes is emphasised by a photo of two St. John's Ambulance men looking nonchalantly the other way as a rider crashes with his bike in the air and hitting the ground.

The leading riders in the Midland C.C.A championship league in January, with five out of the seven promotions completed had G. Smith (Ivy Wheelers.) ahead of R. Bradford (Coventry R.C.) and J.Edney (Warwickshire R.C.) As can be seen by all this activity, the various Leagues were very keen to promote events and riders were enjoying the competition.

The first annual Cyclo-Cross Championships of the Midland Section was held on Hearsall Common on Sunday 31st January 1954, with the dressing rooms at The Butts Cycle Stadium (where these riders would later battle out sprints round the same track under hot summer sunshine). Race instructions included "The course will be marked with a paper trail and yellow flags, and will be adequately marshalled." Poor route marking was often a sore point with riders, sometimes spoiling good events.

The N.C.U. once more invited applications for selection to represent Great Britain at the 1954 World Cyclo-Cross Championship to be played out at Crenna di Gallarate, near Varese in Italy. Applications had to be in by 20th February, with the race on the 28th but the advert only appeared in *Cycling* on the 11th. This could certainly be described as cutting it fine.

Alan Jackson (De Laune C.C.) declined to submit an application to ride, despite being in dominating form when winning the Godiva R. & P.C event by over half a minute, on a course made "extremely treacherous" by rain on a surface of frozen ice. It appears he soon changed his mind, because, the riders picked to wear the Union Jack flags on their jerseys this year were listed as Alan Jackson, Paddy Hoban (34th Nomads) Alan Winters (Warwickshire R.C.) and Johnny Lawrence (Elsynge R.C.).

The French were once again far superior at the Championships with Andrea Dufraisse winning from his teammate Jodet. *Cycling* reported this World Championship with a very meagre amount of coverage, but included "...before 20,000 spectators Rondeaux, winner for the past three years, took an immediate lead at the fall of the flag, two laps later Rondeaux was 16sec. ahead, and looked assured of victory. But during the seventh and last lap he met disaster when his machine collapsed beneath him, letting Dufraisse into an immediate lead which he maintained to the end." Although this was not the full report, from what was written, you would never have guessed that any Britons were riding because their exploits were not mentioned in any way.

The mention of jerseys for the British team brings up the subject of winter clothing. The jerseys were made of wool, often with two pockets across the chest and three at the back, these were fine until it rained, when the two pockets would catch the water and expand like small breasts, leaving the rider to squeeze out the water whilst still racing. Woollen or leather gloves, cotton undervests, a racing jersey topped up with perhaps a woollen jumper were the training wear of choice. Below the waist it would be 'plus twos' fitting to just below the knee (closer tailored than plus-fours). Long woollen socks, gaily patterned and in bright colours would add a bit of flair. Shoes would be black leather lace-up (polished to a mirror shine) fitted with shoe plates screwed to their soles for grip. Sometimes a sheet of newspaper was tucked in between layers to protect the chest against the cold. All this was topped off with a zip-up cotton jacket and woolly bobble hat. This type of clothing did not change very much for the mainstay clubman, until the late 1950s when clothing designed by European companies produced just for cycle sport became available via specialist importers. A modern rider would despair to just to look at the winter training and racing clothes of the early 1950s

In the next chapter, we shall explore how the various Associations came together to try and make all the dreams and expectations came to fruition.

3

The Association is born
and Jackson becomes the first Champion

Season 1954/55

Those who wished to push forward the sport of cyclo-cross in Britain were certainly not superstitious, because they arranged a meeting to form an all-encompassing cyclo-cross body, for 13th October 1954, at the Cora Hotel, Euston, London. They hoped to coordinate all the different cyclo-cross leagues that had sprung up over the years into one national organisation. The three associations that attended this gathering were from North London, South London and the Midland Association and they chose 'British Cyclo Cross Association' as the name for this new body.

If the enthusiasm of Keith Edwards, Ron Atkins, Keith Brock and others had anything to do with it, the new Association's progress would be both rapid and successful. Unfortunately, no records of the early committee meetings appear to have survived, nor have any lists of those early officials. Most of these early freethinking pioneers have passed on and the memories of others have faded over the decades as to the exact details thrashed out at this early meeting.

The main recollection of this momentous meeting comes from an interview in December 2006, with Roland Atkins (always known as Ron), when he was then in his 90th year. He remembered travelling down to London by train, having taken the place of Keith Edwards as the Midland's representative. The reason for the switch was because Keith had to be at work on that day, and as the meeting was being held over a weekend, he could not get time off from his workplace. It must be remember that a 6½-day week was the norm in factories and offices in the early 1950s, and taking days off for sport related meetings was just not done.

At the meeting, Ron was voted in as President and was given the task of drawing up the constitution and rules of this new association.

Unfortunately copies of the first two handbooks, which Ron produced and typed out by hand, have disappeared over the years and as far as we know none have survived.

During 1954, the National Cyclists Union was the only official internationally recognised body for cycling in Britain. The N.C.U thought that it could take over this emerging side of cycle sport, but the new-born B.C-C.A resisted strongly, thinking rightly so, that it had the knowledge and the experience to continue to run a sport it knew best. An agreement was eventually reached, whereby the B.C-C.A. would affiliate to the N.C.U, but this meant that the N.C.U would have the authority to pick all the riders for the World Championships and other International events. This left the B.C-C.A as the governing body for all cyclo cross events in England and Wales, although the Scottish relationship is not very clear.

All this bargaining, shows how complicated the administration of British cycle sport was during this period. Perhaps an explanation of this situation is needed. In England at this time the N.C.U governed the trackside of the sport, massed start racing on closed circuits and the possibility of road racing. The other national organisation was the Road Time Trial Council (R.T.T.C), which governed cycling time trials on open roads. Time Trials were held at a very early hour, mostly at weekends, with the riders wearing black Alpaca jackets and black tights. This mode of dress was supposed to blend in with other road users, although anyone walking along a street could observe up to 100 black clad riders passing by at regular intervals, would guess that a race was taking place. Nowadays all this seems a nonsensical way to conduct cycle sport, but these conditions were imposed because of the heavy hand of the police at the turn of the century. Cycle sport bodies were therefore afraid that the police would ban all cycle racing. All these factions led to British cycle sport becoming a backwater, developing along very different lines to the rest of Europe and in fact from most of the world.

The B.C-C.A was unlike the other existing ruling bodies of cycling, who appeared to be led by rule-making officials, looking back to the days of their youth rather than forward to new ideas. The ruling bodies seemed wary, or even afraid of new ideas that could engulf their isolated side of cycle sport and even that the ideas were, 'not quite British'. The nearest organisation to the B.C-C.A could be likened to the emerging British League of Racing Cyclists, who had also seen the way cycle sport was run in Europe and desired a change of direction for their sport. The formation of the B.C-C.A was like a breath of fresh air, as the quote below from an early handbook shows a 'light handed' way of working:

From the outset the new body agreed to the mixing of categories in accordance with U.C.I rules. It also pledged itself to keep the pastime open to all cyclists irrespective of whether or not the participant was a member of other bodies controlling the Cycle Sport. This air of freedom has been our policy to leave the formation of rules, under which events are to be run, to the discretion of the promoter.

The spirit of the U.C.I ruling on Cyclo-Cross is that events shall be open to all classes or categories of riders. The sport is considered to be an athletic exercise and a form of training between the seasons for Road Racing as it requires thorough riding skills.

In some ways the cycling press, such as *Cycling*, colluded with the existing authorities rather than embracing the new organisation, it often made fun of reporting the early events. Perhaps because cyclo-cross has always been held over the autumn/winter months.

This statement appeared in *Cycling* during November:

Pending clarification from the N.C.U. the North London Cyclo-Cross Association have issued a statement regarding mixed amateur and Professional competition in cyclo-cross events. This states that there is a clause in the U.C.I. regulations to the effect that cyclo-cross is a pastime and not a sport and as such is not covered by the rule barring mixed racing, justifying the Association's policy of providing a ride for all.

An early London Association event was held at Flaunden, where it "Developed into a mud-bound fiasco rather than a serious struggle, a missing marshal resulted in the leading eight competitors taking the wrong path." After much discussion it was decided to award the result as a tie between A.W.Jackson (De Laune C.C.) and E.C.Gerrard (Barnet C.C.)

The Coventry R.C promoted the opening event of the Midland season and they needed to do hurried course alterations, which were necessary as floodwater in sections was too deep to negotiate. There were 72 entries including John Perks, a world championship road racer, who suffered a buckled wheel. Allan Winters proved to be fastest, with D.Smith

(Earlswood R. & P.C.C.) in second and R.Bradford (Coventry R.C.) who led home the winning team.

An article with pictures in the December 9th edition of *Cycling* stated: "The start of 'the race that wasn't,' the Southern Cyclo-Cross Association event at Green-Street-Green on November 21st Displacement of direction arrows along the course caused chaos in the big field, the second time this has happened around London this season." And then rather sarcastically: "The event will be re-run on December 19th – course marking permitting!" The first of two pictures shows a very large field racing away from the start, in the second, a group of bemused riders are shown milling around trying to sort things out. This proved that enthusiasm was not enough, if cyclo-cross was to prosper; much better organised events were needed. One of the main differences between this new Association and the existing ones, was that cyclo-cross and therefore the newly formed B.C-C.A allowed both the Independent and Professional categories to compete with Amateur riders. This led, later in the year, to a statement by the N.C.U and R.T.T.C, which said: "There is no objection to the mixing of categories of riders in cyclo-cross, so long as –

(1) This practice remains as a pastime.

(2) That professional and independent riders give an undertaking that their performances will not be advertised.

The January 21st. 1955 issue of *Cycling* has a photograph of G. Sinnet of the De Laune C.C bending over, trying to straighten a badly buckled wheel over his knee, something that was often done with rims at that time as a temporary measure. He not only had to straighten it once but also after buckling it again, he finished high enough to help his team to second place, persistence repaid. Cyclo-cross has always produced accidents, including the destruction of bicycles, with stories of snapped frames, handlebars, and wheels being written off were just run-of-the-mill happenings in many events, which was very good news for the local specialist lightweight cycle shops. Riders' knees, shins and bare arms were also very vulnerable to crashes and brambles.

While on the subject of accidents, this year's edition of the Bagshot Scramble held during January, seemed to have been more accident prone than usual. Don Stone (34th Nomads) won in the excellent time of 50mins 45secs from team mate Paddy Hoban, with B.Alexander (Westerly R.C.) in third, however, behind them chaos was breaking out.

During February this report appeared in *Cycling*, "Brian Haskell the Huddersfield R.C. International, recently back from the sun-baked roads of the Tour of Egypt, plunged into the snow and slush of the Huddersfield C.A.Cyclo-Cross on Sunday."

February 1955 was an historic date for the newly formed B.C-C.A. when it held its first National Championships at Welwyn Gravel Pits, Welwyn Garden City.

John David remembered this event in a 2008 edition of a 'Fellowship of Old Time Cyclists' magazine *Fellowship News*:

I was secretary of the North London Cyclo-Cross Association from 1956 to 1959. I was press-ganged into the job by Alan Emery, who was a club-mate of mine in the Marlboro A.C. and I helped him and Percy Lovell (Harrow & Rickmansworth C.C.) to run the first National Cyclo-Cross Championships in 1955 at Welwyn Garden City. This was held in the Stanborough gravel pits, on the site of which is now the flourishing cycle track, Gosling Stadium, and it was knowledge of this waste area which came in useful when I was involved in the creation of this venue.

John remembers Alan Emery as "One of the chief enthusiasts who brought serious cyclo-cross to this country. He was a completely all-round cyclist and first saw cyclo cross in Belgium and he rode several of the 'rough stuff' events that we had, including the Bagshot Scramble. He was the founder of the N.L.C.C.A. and its secretary for several years...Other N.L.C.C.A committee members included Mike Dyason (then Viking R.C) now widely known now in the cycle trade for his Ozzo mail order business." Yet another member of this committee was Stu Benstead (Archer R.C.) now well known as organiser of the Archer Grand Prix for 50 years.

With *Cycling* reporting: "This particular slice of history could not have had a more worthy figure to dominate this story. Right from the start it was a one-man show. That man was Alan Wharmby Jackson of the De Laune C.C. – for five weeks now 23098222 Pte. Jackson A.W. of the R.A.M.C. at present in forced residence at Crookham Barracks, Aldershot but taking advantage of the generosity of his sergeant-major and a special 48hr pass." This gives an insight into what young sportsmen had to face during the years after the Second World War. Even though the war had been over for almost 10 years in Europe, 'Call-up' was still part of a young man's life, whether sportsman or not.

The event was held with a deep covering of snow on slopes and thick mud lower down. 2,000 spectators watched the 73 racers battle it out in a bitter N.E. wind. Although Jackson gave the others a chance by crashing on the very first lap he dominated throughout, to win by 18 secs, although two professionals Mitchell and Scales did not start. B.B.C.Television covered the event with cameras around the course, with the film being shown on News and Newsreel that very evening. (Something we still yearn for over 50 years later!) Although Jackson was masterful at this time, things did not always go smoothly. This snippet from a report records that Jackson won on a 59" freewheel, he seemed certain to gain the victory until as *Cycling* reported: "He fell three feet down a ditch marked 'Two feet deep' he emerged with an unrideable wheel. A Good Samaritan was at hand, in the shape of Alan Emery, (Secretary, North London C.C.A.) who was almost a lap down. He sportingly proffered his machine." Alan Winters (Warwickshire RC) and Don Stone (34th Nomads) followed him home. The winning team on this historic occasion was the Coventry Road Club of M.Weston, I.Tovey and R.Bradford.

To illustrate how informal everything was during at this time, John David also remembers: "Alan Jackson was the winner, and later that day I had lunch with him in a cyclists' café in Welwyn.....There were events at South Mimms, (bikes and bodies washed in a stream)." Some of John's other memories when he was Secretary of the North London Cyclo-Cross League during the early days were:

> The main administrative debate I recall was about starts. Clearly, if you lined the buggers up in one line across a field and it looked as if the start was imminent, off some of them would go, flag, gun or no flag, whistle or gun. NLCCA (North London Cyclo-Cross League) experimented with what is termed a Le Mans start. Bikes were dumped in one corner of a field, riders set off from the diagonal corner on foot. Theoretically they picked up their own bike and trundled back the way they'd come. In practice there was always someone who snatched up the best or nearest bike, even if it wasn't theirs. Eventually we dispensed with a countdown (a regular disaster, as they all shot off on the 'five').

He continued with his memories on courses, mud and cleaning:

> Theoretically, too, all courses were on common land. Once or twice, when they were not, we had to deal with irate farmers who hadn't been asked for permission. We usually got away with it. It helped if there was a brook or stream, because this meant

there was somewhere to wash bikes if not bodies. I remember, at a Parkhill C.C. event, going back to clear up and finding a rider squelching around in deep mud at a farm gateway, trying to find a shoe which he'd lost. Hoards of following riders had trodden on the shoe, which became completely enveloped in mud; I don't think he found it. There never was any hot water. I remember the publican at the 'Valiant Trouper' in Aldbury, Herts, bringing out a half-dozen tin baths and keeping them topped up. I suppose it was in his interest, to keep some mud from his bars.

On the finance side he said: "Financially there never seemed to be a problem, since we offered little (no prizes) and only spent when things like AGM's came round."

Season 1955/56

Unfortunately, no handbook details have been found showing the officials or events for this season, so it must be assumed that they remained roughly the same as 1954/55.

One thing noticeable this season, was that top roadmen were more and more attracted to cyclo-cross, as was shown when Ray Holliday, who had distinguished himself in the Circuit of Britain, also won a Cyclists V Harriers event. Holliday was just one of many servicemen who raced after being 'called-up' to serve in the armed forces, he was a member of the R.A.F. cycling team but on this occasion was riding for his 'civvies' club of Wolverhampton R.C.C. Events, although well organised, still had 'gremlins' as the following report shows: "A lack of co-ordination between the loudspeaker vehicle and the starter, resulted in a number of competitors being caught 'napping' at the start."

By late November, Alan Jackson riding for the De Laune club, had knocked up his third successive win, and it was in the Belle Vue C.C's eight-mile event at Green-Street-Green, Kent, winning by half a minute from another top specialist. One of the 'Cyclists v Runners' events still being promoted was the Keighley District C.A. and this year the cyclists came out on top. C.J.Kennedy of St. Christopher's C.C.C. who was followed home by W.Holden (Keighly R.C.) at just over half-a-minute, with the first harrier coming in fourth.

Boxing Day saw Paddy Hoban (34th. Nomads) make the winning ride in the Welwyn Wheelers event. Among the small card of only 20 riders was Ted Gerrard, the International roadman, who finally finished eighth.

On New Year's Eve, the Ivy Wheelers race at Catherine -de-Barnes, had a large influx of London riders, many of whom did not appear on the programme, but this did not prevent a Londoner, Don Stone (34th Nomads) from taking the win.

During January 1956 Professional riders were approached by the N.C.U to ascertain whether they wished to compete in the World Championships in Luxemburg, and another big event to be held around Vincennes, Paris in conjunction with the U.C.I Spring Congress. No record of riders going to the Worlds this year has been found.

The first few days of the new year saw top cross man Alan Jackson (De Laune C.C.), have an amazing few weeks, exchanging the snow and cold winds of England for the sand and hot winds of Egypt. This was because he had been picked to ride in that National tour, having honed his form in the autumn cyclo-crosses. But by mid January, he had arrived back in this country far quicker than expected. The British team manager had withdrawn the whole team, due to a failure of the Egyptian organisers to pay the £93 excess baggage on the team's equipment. So he was back to battling through ice-cold puddles and down muddy lanes to win the famous Bagshot Scramble from 20 year old Mick Weston (Coventry R.C). The course included the scary 'Scramblers Menace' over the Saddleback hills.

Jackson retained his form and his title in the 1956 British Championship event held at Halesowen, on a course designed by Ron Atkins and Keith Edwards as a 'truly testing competition course'. His progress was not without problems, for when leading he had an unscheduled stop to "fix his shoe" this meant that D. Smith (M.C.& A.C) took the lead on the second lap. Smith then suffered an attack of cramp and Jackson proceeded to overtake him to pull ahead. The sun shone on the large crowd gathered around the course enjoying the to-and-fro spectacle. Choice of gearing was very much individual, when looking at the machines being ridden by the top three finishers. Jackson opting for a 58" freewheel, "which he thought a shade high", Smith went for gears with a 51" bottom, however M.R. Weston, who finished third, rode a 65" fixed gear. It is interesting to note that 86 entered, 72 started but only 51 finished. Billy Holmes (Hull Thursday), holder of the R.T.T.C Competition Record at 25 miles, was well up with the leaders on the early laps, showing that riders chose to compete in any type of cycling event, unlike today when everyone appears to be a specialist in track, road or cross. The event was being filmed once more as outlined in the race programme:

The Championship will be filmed by cameramen from a B.B.C. Television Unit, for inclusion in Sportsview on February 15th British Paramount News will also film the event for a Newsreel Story"

Season 1956/57

The B.C-C.A. produced its first National Handbook covering the 1956/57 season, at a price of 6d (2½p). It lists the President as Ron Atkins, General Secretary Keith Brock, Treasurer Keith Edwards and International Racing Secretary, A.E.Emery. It also has a list of six Area Officials D.Stone, A.Emery, A.Reynolds, Mrs E.Todd, H.Butcher and G.Goodwin. The list of promotions follows: North London C.C. Association promoting five events, Midland Association eleven, Merseyside three, Southampton & District four, Manchester & District eight and the Southern C.C.A. promoting six. There are also ten events listed as "Open Events not promoted by the B.C-C.A". It can be seen from the above that some areas of the country were very well served by races but others had none at all.

The small (now fragile) Handbook is printed on buff card with a few buff coloured pages, with adverts for G.B. (a cycle component maker), and these cycle shops: Tom Bromwich Cycles, Alan Shorter, H.E. Cycles, K. W. Brock Cycles and Holdsworthy Co.Ltd. (a cycle importer), helping to support this infant association. Unfortunately, as this is perhaps the only surviving copy, it is damaged, with missing pages, which may have shown entry fees and subscriptions. Of the events that are listed, three are shown as Time Trials, the others all listed as being Massed Start.

At this time L.Renshaw (Macclesfield Whls.) was proving almost unbeatable in the Manchester area, having won every event he had entered except one. The 34th Nomads' pair of Don Stone and Paddy Hoban were still also in good form, with Stone winning this year's Bagshot Scramble from Geoff Cross (Aylesbury C.C.) with Hoban in second and the 34thNomads taking the team award.

The Midland Counties event over Christmas 1956 saw an exciting finish, because two riders were locked together as they crossed a stream, only 120 yards from the finish, then one rider surged ahead up the grassy hill to the line and it proved to be Derek Tarbun of the Coventry Road Club, out-distancing Mick Weston (Coventry C.C.) At this time riders were still developing ideas on which type of gearing was best, for the first three chose fixed wheels, Tarbun riding a 60", Weston 65", and Winters, who was third a 66". But Barry Spence chose what was described as ' variable gears of 53-65ins.' although no other details were given.

In January the top North and South London riders clashed in the North London C.C.A. event, where the bearded Don Stone, described as "master of the mud" won by almost 1½ minutes. Meanwhile over at Sutton Park, the Warwickshire R.C event was won by Mick Weston of Coventry R.C, with the winning team of the Hull Thursday R.C. led in by W. Holmes, making their long journey from Hull well worthwhile.

The petrol shortage this month had a big bearing on the number of riders who could undertake to travel events. Those riders owning cars or vans had to choose their races carefully so as to eke out their meagre supplies. More and more clubs were now competing in 'crosses and this month the Wolverhampton R.C.C. joined the Midland Cyclo Cross Association so that they could have access to B.C-C.A. events.

Mud and water seemed to affect most of the events this season, and a picture in *Cycling* of the Kenton R.C's event in January, seemed to sum this up, it showed a large group of riders racing into what looks like a small river, then ending up carrying their bikes, with water up to their knees! The caption below the picture reads- "Riding, running –now swimming!"

About this time, Chris Bevis of the Gosport Clarion remembers riding a race held at H.M.S.Dryad, Portsmouth:

Up on the Downs, I sprinted into the lead, ahead of 'the stars', I then came to a path with a stream on my left and a copse to my right, and a notice stating 'Beware of Adders'. Needless to say I remained in the lead over this narrow path, as it was either fall in the river to the left or risk falling where adders may lurk! When back on the road section the 'Stars' took over once more. I was riding my work machine without mudguards, on 26"x 1¼" wheels with orange ribbed tyres and with a 56" freewheel.

During January of '57 the National Cyclists' Union (still the only organisation recognised by the U.C.I.) announced that they would send a team of four riders to the Criterium Martini Cyclo-Cross on March 3rd at the Bois de Vincennes, Paris. The race would be over a distance of 22 kms; most of the course was rideable, hopefully this would give the British riders a chance to pit their wits against the Continental experts. No riders would be sent to the World Championships this year, so this was at least one good chance to shine in Europe. Also the N.C.U Manchester Centre promoted their open cross "Thought to be the first in the area".

The question is, was this a ploy by the N.C.U to try to muscle in on the B.C-C.A?

Don Stone won the National Championship this year, held at Brands Hatch in Kent and Keith Brock, the National Secretary, quoted a senior official of the Brands Hatch Stadium in *Cycling* as saying "God man, they'll never do it, the Moto-cross riders gave that course best last week!" Brock wondered aloud "If the course does prove too tough my name will be mud" which was a premonition on the final state of the course. Behind Stone came Alan Jackson (De Laune C.C.) with Paddy Hoban (34th Nomads C.C.) in third. They led home the 80 starters, against an icy wind, and through masses of gluey, clinging mud. Stone also had the pleasure of leading his team-mates of the 34th Nomads, P.Hoban and R.Stevens as the Championship winning team.

Ted Saunderson a 34th Nomads team-mate of Stone and Hoban and sometimes a third team counter, recalls both the cycle equipment and lack of washing facilities at many events during these early days of the B.C.C.A. He gives an insight into riding these events during the mid 1950s:

Most of us only rode for the fun of it, although riding home in a jacket over wet and muddy racing clothes was certainly not much fun! If you lived not too far from the course, you would ride home and then clean yourself up after arriving home. My team-mates Don Stone and Paddy Hoban were in the top class of riders of the day, and as to our equipment, I remember we fitted football boot studs into the heels of our cycling shoes to provide more grip when running. We would also cut up a tyre and strap it between the top tube and seat tube of the frame, which then rested better on the shoulder when we had to run with the bike. I was one of those who wore crash hats, although there were no rules about wearing them, so it was just left to the individual. The woolly jerseys we wore soon became soaked and heavy when it rained, and the woolly shorts with chamois leather seats would sag down nearly to your knees when you got out of the saddle! Nobody rode in either arm warmers or tights, so we must have been hard! Sometimes cleaning yourself up after an event often meant just a bucket of cold water shared between many (another good reason for finishing in the top ten!). We had little idea about the best foods to eat, although we knew it was not a good idea to eat a plate of fish and chips before an event, everybody thought that you must eat lots of steak the night before.

Wendy David also remembers the old shorts with this story, "A tubby girl in an Essex event whose woollen road shorts were soaked and fell lower and lower each lap, but she got a much louder cheer when she finished than the winner!"

The crash hats mentioned above were made of filled leather bars crossing round and over the top of the skull, little changed since used by track riders at the turn of the century. Few people during this period had cars or vans, so it was just a case of riding to the event if local, taking a train trip to somewhere near to the event, or staying overnight at 'Digs' and then returning home afterwards. Travelling on a train with your bike was, of course, much easier because the Royal Mail postbags still travelled in large guards vans at the rear of the train.

At this time, it was still relativity safe to ride in groups on 'A' roads and many clubs would ride out to see cycle races in their area including cyclo-cross. They would then stand around the course at the best vantage points, encouraging all riders, but of course give extra loud support to their own club mates. Then they would start the ride home, perhaps stopping for a warm cup of tea, with other groups at a cycle friendly café before finishing their ride in the dark, with their sometimes 'dodgy' lights cutting through the blackness to get home safely.

The bikes being ridden by most of the riders, (except the top men) were standard lightweight machines, high bottom brackets were essential as was a fairly long wheelbase. The majority rode lightweight road tyres, although the top competitors rode Wolber or Hutchinson 'cross' tubulars and wheels with heavy gauge spokes. Clipless pedals were still a far off dream, so to ward off unexpected breakages, double thickness clips would be used and good quality leather straps held the feet firmly in position. Despite the top riders using some European tubulars, most of the equipment used was still from British manufacturers.

The wives of these racing lads were sometimes not too happy with their spouse's winter pastime, as this quote from *Sporting Cyclist* outlines, - "It is only T.V. for us on Saturday nights, never a dance and always early to bed. Then on Mondays the washtubs are inches deep in mud!"

Rowland Ferris remembering a race during this period in Fellowship of Old Timers Magazine, of June 2008, recalled riding at Daventry with this insight: "(it) included pig pens, ploughed fields and country tracks."

It must have been to his liking, because he finished fifth, "riding a Higgins road bike…there was a tin bath to wash in at the finish." Later he formed the Northants Cyclo-cross Association, which went on to promote events on a local motorcycle scramble course. In the same magazine Brian Kington also remembers his membership form of November 1956 being signed by K.W.Brock. He recalled having one win at cyclo-cross and many placings, and went on to organise and co-organise 32 events over a long period. He also recalls:

We used a piece of old tubular tyre taped to the top and seat corner, later on soft soldering a piece of bent and mitred tubing in place and we all tried a piece of padding under the shirt.

4

Briggs, Hoban, Spence and Stone all find success

Season 1957/58

Unfortunately no Handbook has been located for 1957/58, therefore reports in the press for officials and events will have to be relied upon for this season.

Sporting Cyclist gave this short but descriptive report of another in the series of the Walsall C.T.C. 'Cyclists V Harriers' events: "They awaited starters orders, for a blood-tingling, no holds barred plunge through some of the most glutinous mud in the Midlands. Among those competing were, Percy Stallard and W.H. Genders, who had been an Olympic rider." Another part of the report does a good job of describing the start, which could be the start of any big cyclo-cross event:

> The start was spectacular, like a Cecil B de Mille Hollywood crowd scene, a solid phalanx of humanity streamed across the fresh green of the football fields and funnelled down a narrow plank crossing a waterway.

This event was unique, in that it had been promoted since 1922, with only a lapse during the 1940s due to the Second World War. This year it was a very large entry with 166 runners and 144 riders. Afterwards cleaning up seemed rather a hit-and-miss affair, the above article being accompanied by a photo of two men washing, while sharing a bucket of water!

Some spectators were still finding it amusing to remove event direction signs during this period, and this problem raised its head once more in the North London C. C. A. event promoted by the Harrow and Rickmansworth club, which was held at Chorley Wood, during December. Luckily, race marshals saw the perpetrators and this allowed a private member D. Lee, to have a clear route to the finish, from J.Steed of the Barnet C.C.

Sometimes even top cyclo-cross riders are defeated by the elements as this snippet shows. Wet and windy conditions were to badly affect the result of the Merseyside Wheelers event where D.Greenall (Prescot R.C.) led from the start to finish, winning from P.Nowell (Lune R.C.) and S.Fraser (Yewtree Whls.) at Shaley Brow. With only eight riders managing to battle the elements to finish, and no complete team finished.

All the potential rivals for the coming National Championship were in excellent form at this time. Don Stone's form with only a week to go showed when he won the South of England Championships at Brands Hatch in Kent, even with mud clogging his wheels and having to stop often to clear them, nothing could prevent him from winning from Ken Knapman of the Southern Velo. Another challenger, Barry Spence the Wolverhampton Wheeler, put in an outstanding effort to claim victory in the Stafford R.C. event from Alan Winters (Solihull) and Dave Briggs (Saracen R.C.) who trailed in second and third. Meanwhile down in the New Forest Colin Lewis kept his unbeaten record with a win in the New Forest C. C's 10-mile event, finishing 40 seconds ahead of P. Hawker of the promoting club and F. Brew Southern Paragon who held on to third spot.

On the front cover of *Cycling and Mopeds* of 12th February 1958 was a splendid action photo of the wheel-to-wheel sprint for first place in the National Championships. The sprint was between the previous champion, Don Stone and 19-year-old Barry Spence. The picture shows two mud splattered men sprinting flat out, with a large crowd pressing forward into a narrow funnel, over a wet muddy surface, in fact it captured all the excitement of cyclo-cross. Stone and Spence battled it out to the finish with contrasting styles, Spence with daredevil descents against Stone's cool and skilful riding. Stone became Champion for the second time after this final sprint. Spence had had three wins this season, having had lots of trouble in other events he decided to change from tubulars to high-pressure wired-on tyres on this occasion. The event was held over one of the most famous cyclo-cross courses in the country used every year for the Bagshot Scramble. Paddy Hoban had overcome various handicaps, such as influenza earlier in the month and then on the very first lap he crashed, unable to avoid a falling rider in front of him. Another casualty was the record-breaking tricyclist, Dave Duffield (later to become famous as a commentator for Eurosport), who damaged his wheel early on and then had to change machines. Bill Radford (Elizabethan C.C.) at only seventeen, battled on to take third. The strong Solihull C. C thought they had taken the team award, but were in for a disappointment because later a revised result was issued for the National Championship by the promoting club, Ealing Manor R.C. now giving the 34th Nomads C.C. the team title, after a recheck.

After the event Stone, D.Briggs (Saracen RC) and D.Tarbun (Coventry C.C.) were invited by the N.C.U. to ride in a big international event, the 'Martini' in Paris. This race was regarded as the World Championship revenge match. Stone, regretfully had to decline at first due to not being fully fit after his bout of flu', Hoban also had to withdraw due to illness but Barry Spence accepted an invitation to take his place. Don Stone did ride the event after all by returning to full health, the bearded rider showed that he had both recovered from 'flu and his class, finishing fifteenth out of the field of forty-three. Spence finished 25th, Briggs 33rd and Tarbun 36th. The Italian Amerigo Severini won from André Dufraisse of France with another Frenchman Brulé in third.

Reading the race report in *Cycling & Mopeds*, by its Editor H.H.England, you would have thought the plucky British had had a very big influence on the race for he writes, "Don Stone was the British leader all the way " (when in fact he was only leading the British riders.) Italy finished as the winning team, with Britain in seventh place

Five Area Championships were held this season with Bryan Masters (Flixton C.C.) winning the Manchester & District event, Dave Briggs (Saracen R.C.) the Midland League event, Colin Lewis (Southampton Wheelers.) the Southampton & District race. But Don Stone would become a multi champion by winning both the North London Association and the Southern Association events.

Season 1958/59
Forty-eight promotions are listed in this season's small light blue Handbook, which has a mere 12 pages. R.Goodman is shown as organising the National Championship, with an entry fee of just 3/- (15p). The list of officials shows no post of President, but the 'Honorary Officials' are listed as Keith Edwards, General Secretary and Ron Atkins as Treasurer. There is no post of International Racing Secretary recorded but Keith Brock is the Chairman.

There is also a section appealing to the National Cyclists Union:

We shall continue to press for a team to represent this country in the World Championships, but at this moment this association appreciates that the National Cyclists Union is the only body in this country eligible to nominate riders for any type of World Cycling Championship. In the circumstances, therefore, we urge all N.C.U. members to press for British representation in the World Cyclo-Cross Championships, by taking resolutions from your clubs to your N.C.U. Centre meetings. There is no doubt that B.C-C.A. International Racing Funds would be used to help finance such representation.

Despite the very diplomatic words, you can feel the frustration of the emerging B.C-C.A. with the old national body, for the Association was waiting and wanting to use its newfound strength, within its own area of expertise. Membership of the B.C-C.A. could be either by an Association, a Club or as a Private Member, with Association membership being 3 guineas (£3.15p), Clubs could join for just 5/- (25p) and Private Members paid 2/6d (12½p).

British cyclists were at first pleased by the appointment of Ernest Marples as Minster of Transport, because as *Cycling & Mopeds* put it, -"An interview with Mr. Marples from which it was evident that he is an experienced, knowledgeable, discriminating and practising cyclist." It was hoped by all the cycling bodies that he would put his backing to proposals to help cycle racing of all kinds, although the hope seemed to fall on deaf ears, perhaps because he was involved in road building with his own company.

Don Stone (34th. Nomads) won the early season Bagshot Scramble from D.Carter (Aylesbury C.C.) and K.Knapman (Southern Velo). Afterwards he described the course in "unprintable terms" and "treacherous" when interviewed by *Cycling & Mopeds*: "It's the hardest race I've ever ridden in." It was a day of ice and frozen surfaces, with the enthusiastic crowd continually pressing forward, narrowing the course and forcing the riders to tackle the frozen puddles. Stone was to come a cropper; he then cleaned himself up and went to the local hospital to have his badly cut knee treated against infection, no personal coaches, managers or even First Aid boxes for help. What hard men!

Thirty-five clubs, made up of 81 riders were to contest the National Championships held at Bolton this year. It turned out to be a battle between Alan Winters (Solihull C.C.) and Barry Spence (Wolverhampton Wheelers.) The course included a strength-sapping climb of 63 steps every lap. Misfortune befell one contender, Neil Orrell (Manchester C.C.C.) as right from the start he fell damaging a wheel, then fell again when climbing the steps, again damaging a wheel that he proceeded to bend straight but when his chain derailed, it was all too much and he retired. Barry Spence finally proved to be the stronger, winning from Winters, with K.Knapman third and Bradford R.C.C. turning in the winning team of J.Whittam, C.Spaven and H. Bond.

The B.C-C.A had tried hard over these early years to gain the right to choose which riders should go to International events, but the N.C.U had always resisted any changes. On the 22nd of March 1959, Keith Edwards as the Association's Secretary sent this letter to the newly formed British Cycling Federation who now had the authority:

Dear Sir,
At the A.G.M. of the above Association held last Sunday, it was unanimously decided to approach the B.C.F with a view to affiliation.
The B.C-C.A wishes to retain control of cyclo-cross, but would like to have an official say in the selection of riders for international events, and in return would be willing to share in any expenses involved.
Our Executive Committee would welcome your representatives, if so desired.

This was an attempt to put forward feelers to this newly formed Federation. On the 13th April the B.C.F Assistant Secretary replied to the effect that they would be pleased to receive a deputation from the B.C-C.A on Sunday 26th of April at 2.30p.m at their offices to discuss the matter. This meeting carried the negotiations forward to October, when G.T. Bassett (the B.C.F secretary) drew up "A simple draft agreement." However by December letters were still passing between the two bodies attempting to sort out the fine details. Negotiations were slow and still dragging on into the next New Year.

The World Championships this year were held in Switzerland at Geneva. The Professional/Amateur winner was Renato Longo of Italy, who took the first of his titles, followed by Rolf Wolfshohl (West Germany) and another Italian, Amerigo Severini coming in to take the second of his bronze medals. No reference has been found to any British riders competing in this event.

But an insight into the British riders' experience of continental 'cross' racing is provided in this report by Paddy Hoban to the B.C-C.A committee, after a trip to ride the Martini International event.

Martini provided private transport to and from the airport. In order to ensure we had sufficient money, we declined to have breakfast in our rooms but purchased sufficient food and thereafter catered for ourselves, which we found to be much cheaper.

THE EVENT – the race was run upon hard dry ground in brilliant sunshine – Mr Keeler and Mr Barton served in two of the three available pits. (Areas where cycles can be exchanged)

TYRES – the tyres supplied by Dunlop, - No5s, were used by all members of the team. Needless to say we were the only amateurs in the event, all the others were either professionals or independents.

AFTER THE EVENT – We presented ourselves together with Mr Barton and Mr Keeler at Martini Rossi's Penthouse at the Champs-Elysées by appointment, to a cocktail party.

EXPENDITURE - £25 was handed to me to cover the team from Friday to the Monday.

All the hard work by Keith Edwards, Ron Atkins, Keith Brock and many others was now paying off. They had carried their vision into reality, good class events were now being widely promoted and riders were now regularly representing Great Britain in Europe. Those early enthusiastic pioneers could feel proud of their achievements. However, there was no time to rest on their laurels as much was still to be done if the standard of British riders was to improve and the cycling press needed to be encouraged to cover more events. Few among those reading this history will doubt their dedication to the task in hand, as the new season of 1959/60 loomed. The 'Swinging Sixties' were on the horizon and the B.C-C.A. had to show that it could swing into the tasks ahead.

Season 1959/60

There was a notice in the handbook for the A.G.M. to be held at Aylesbury, Bucks on the 13th March at 12 noon and also an appeal in this edition for more help with the International Racing Fund, as outlined below:

Sending riders abroad is a very costly affair, and while B.C-C.A. already have their own International Racing Fund, very special efforts will have to be made to raise money to pay for these representations. One way in which we expect to raise funds is to promote a National Prize Draw based on the National Cyclo-Cross Championship event, but B.C-C.A. would be most grateful for any contributions to their I.R.Fund. Donations to be sent to the Hon. Treasurer.

Percy Lovell had taken over as Chairman and Paddy Hoban as International Racing Secretary but Keith Edwards and Ron Atkins retained their positions. Now the B.C-C.A had three Trustees, R. F. Atkins, K. Edwards and P.H. Lovell, and two Auditors, E. Todd and Mrs. E. Todd. The price of this handbook had increased to 9d (4p) and was a very similar slim edition to that of last year, with the design remaining the same. For the first time there was an advert for B.C-C.A metal badges at a price of 3/6d (17½p) each.

It appears that there had been some dissent about a decision that the National Championships should be promoted on a Saturday. An explanation as to why the change had been made stated that better facilities would enable the promotion to be more fitting for a national title event. It should be remembered that during the 1950s and 60s, many factories still worked 5½ days every week, therefore getting a whole Saturday off might be difficult and car ownership was still low.

Six affiliated associations and leagues held their own championships and each listed its own rules in the handbook. The trophy which would presented to the winner of the Midland League event, certainly catches the eye, named as the 'Cyclo Opperman Shield', bringing together two famous names, a gear manufacturer and one of Australia's most famous racing cyclists, who also claimed British records.

September saw the first bicycle trip over the 'Three Peaks' walking route, the web page Three Peaks Cyclo-Cross History covers the story of how this came about. *The Evening Post* reporting, "The Three Peaks, the tough testing course for the Dales walker, were conquered yesterday by a 14 year old Yorkshire schoolboy – on a bicycle." The article went on to say that the schoolboy was Kevin Watson of Skipton, a pupil of Ermysted's Grammar school in the same town, how he had ridden and pushed his bicycle over the 30 miles involved, always complying with the accepted conditions of the established walk. Having planned to give it a try one day, he heard that some Leeds cyclists were also planning a similar expedition, so he decided to go ahead there and then. When the group from the Bradford Racing Cycling Club did attempt the route, the riders were all very experienced rough-stuff riders, with among them the British National Championship team of Harry Bond, Jeff Whittam and Colin Spaven. They encountered a variety of problems with Whittam puncturing; Spaven snapping a handlebar bolt and most of the ten riders involved being handicapped by not knowing the route. After this episode others including a C.T.C group also made a crossing by the same route. Not all cyclists agreed with the idea of cycle racing over such areas of wild land though, and there were protests in the local press from "dyed-in-the-wool" tourists.

Snow was the big talking point amongst riders and spectators during this winter; the showers swept south and affected both Midlands and South London events. However the top riders were still determined to show their undoubted skills to win despite the adverse conditions. Don Stone was to the fore in the white conditions of the Morden C.R.C event on the Shirley hills, winning by over half a minute from Ken Knapman of Croydon R.C, although the hero of the day was M.Garwood who, when his gear failed, was offered a cycle by a spectator and then passed rider after rider to finish a fine fourth. The arctic conditions also affected the 10 mile test that is the Bagshot Scramble, although the deep 'white–stuff' did not deter the crowds standing on the Saddleback Hills to watch the riders drop like stones. As the gradient swept upwards all dismounted to run up the incline to crest the top. A novel way to make sure riders continued to the finish in this event, was a prize list for the last four finishers, Dave Briggs however didn't need any incentive to make this his 12th win of the season. Yorkshire was not to be left out of these testing conditions for the Bradford event was run off in appalling weather; snow underfoot and freezing rain. Harry Bond defied the fact that at least half of each circuit was unrideable due to ice, by winning impressively. Two names of note who finished lower down the result sheet were John Rawnsley (later organiser of the 'Three Peaks') and Nim Carline, who would become a powerful force in long distance time trialling. In the Yorkshire Crossways magazine of 1992/93 an article looking back at the 1960's mentions: "Another early event was the Morley rough-stuff race round Nim Carline's rhubarb fields at Tingley."

The Hill Top C.C. promoted the Midlands title event in Sutton Park and it was held in relentless pouring rain. Dave Briggs turned up but mindful of the bad batch of 'flu he had caught the previous year, declined to ride. During the event, Alan Winters (Solihull C.C.) was the first to make an attack, followed by Bill Radford (Midland C.C.C). Then during the last lap Tony Quinton raced away, but his chain came off twice, and for the second successive week he had to run to the finish, this time for second place. Radford was to win making it a Midland C.C.C. one-two, with Winters in third. The next week *Cycling & Mopeds* had a full-page picture of Winters on its front cover, showing him riding through hub deep water while leading this event. The Southern C.C.A Championship was won by Don Stone with Ken Fuller in second and Ron Sefton in third. One of the favourites Paddy Hoban, broke a crank on the first lap and from then on was never in the hunt.

Dave Briggs had dominated most of the 1959/60 season and by the end of February had had his 14th win in front of the crowds at the Godiva R. & P.C.C. event. Dave was riding for the Saracen Road Club and only days before his 21st birthday in March, however he topped all this off by winning the National Championships, which were promoted by the Midland Cyclo-Cross League with Ray Richards as organiser. The venue was Baddesley Colliery, described as being 'near Atherstone on the A5'.

Deep snow also dominated this event, making surfaces even trickier than usual, with the faithful supporters standing in the freezing conditions all around the course. Second place went to Don Stone (now with the Croydon R.C.) at 2 minutes, with Alan Winters (Solihull CC) next at just over 3 mins. *Cycling & Mopeds* reported: "The race had attracted 113 entries, of whom 85 started and surprisingly enough 67 finished." The winning team was the Solihull C.C. of Winters, D.Mountford and A.Moss. Unfortunately the previous years champion Barry Spence, had taken to his bed with flu unable to defend his title.

The prize list included a first prize of a lightweight frame set to the winner's specification, although some of the other prizes would surprise modern competitors. Sixth and seventh prizes were dynamo sets, tenth placed rider won a pair of mudguards and an inflator (pump) then from 11th to 23rd place the prizes were also inflators. A glance at the list of clubs participating shows just how widespread the sport was developing over just the first six years. Among those listed, were the New Forest R.C.C, Yorkshire R.C, the C.C.Islington, and Barnett C.C. From Wales there was Abertilly Wheelers, Pontypool R.C.C, and then from over the Scottish border, Musselbugh R.C and Edinburgh R.C.

This year the World Championships were held at Tolosa in Spain, during February. Rolf Wolfshohl became the first German winner after his second placing the previous year, for although he was the strongest, he did not have it easy, crashed early on, and then punctured on the third lap. Young Arnold Hungerbühler of Switzerland was the surprise of the race, finishing second, having only been racing at cyclo-cross for four months. Robert Aubry of France was third for the bronze medal. A report on the race in *Cycling & Mopeds* makes no mention of any British riders competing, so unless other research turns up new information, it must be presumed that none were selected to ride this year.

The last major event of the season was the big 'International Martini' event held in Paris. Four British riders had been picked to ride, Barry Spence, Don Stone, Paddy Hoban and Dave Briggs, and this was yet another chance to match their skills with champions such as Longo, Declereq and the current World Champion Wolfshohl riding in his Rainbow jersey. The British riders were hit by bad luck when Spence had trouble changing up from bottom gear, having to reach back to lift the gear arm. Briggs fell on lap three losing time replacing a tyre, however the British team's biggest handicap was being geared far too low, as the entire course was rideable, except for a 100ft climb. Wolfshohl went on to win with Spence claiming 14th place, Stone was 20th, Briggs 30th and Hoban 34th. The moral being that foreign courses should be checked before the event, or a wider range of equipment carried.

For those of a technical turn of mind, below is the contrast between the gears ridden by the British riders and the Italian team in the Martini International event. The British team were equipped with – 82, 73, 65, 59, 51" gears, with 12oz tubulars. However the Italian team equipment was higher geared, with - 96, 78, 71, 64, 58" and with much lighter 9oz. tubulars. Note, there were only five cogs on a block (cassette) at this time. The above shows the power of the professional Italian riders and the type of fast racing they expected.

5

Atkins and Mernickle make their mark but snow dominates

Season 1960/61
The newly designed badge was placed firmly in the centre of the front cover of the new season's handbook. Percy Lovell had been installed as Chairman (a post he would hold for nine years), Keith Edwards, Ron Atkins and Paddy Hoban all retained their official positions.

A new race was proposed for this year, called the 'Team Trophy Race', for the 'Cyclo-Trophy' scheduled for Saturday 7th January 1961, at Baddesley Colliery. It had an unusual format in that only Association Teams would compete for it; each of the teams was to be composed of six riders, with the first three finishers to count for the team award. Two new areas were welcomed into the B.C-C.A. the Essex C.C League and the South Wales C.C. League. During this time, the Essex League was charging 1/6d (7½p) for advance entries and 2/6d (12½p) on the line.

Another interesting item included in this handbook, was a copy of the agreement with the newly formed British Cycling Federation. There was also a section on 'Recommendations for Conduct of Events', a few of which are printed below and just seem normal now.

1. In accordance with U.C.I. regulations, events are open to all categories of rider.
2. Covered changing accommodation with a supply of running water is essential.
3. Duration of events to be between 45 & 60 minutes
6. Where bridle paths are used it is advisable to post marshals to give warning to normal users that an event is in progress.
8. Events should be attended by at least one person qualified in first aid and having the minimum necessary equipment available.

Note that these were not called 'rules' but 'recommendations', demonstrating how politely things were conducted during this period.

The North of England title race was held as early as mid November, with Harry Bond (Bradford R.C.C.) the winner by 39secs from R.Comer (Westwood R.C.). It took place on a course that had been drenched by rain for 24 hours, producing massive floods, which all 81 riders had to negotiate. Early December brought even harsher weather in the Keighley R.C. event; it took the form of a howling wind straight from the Arctic with the added elements of icy rain, sleet and face stinging hailstones. None of this deterred a young man called Keith Lambert (Pennine C.C) who won from the acknowledged experts, D. Liversidge and Harry Bond. A fact which would not surprise riders of later generations as Keith Lambert went on to become a prominent Professional road racer and team manager, among many other achievements.

Racing cyclists were developing more and more as specialists; with fewer big named professional roadmen riding cyclo-cross than in the late 1950s. The exceptions at this time were Raphael Geminiani (a top continental professional) and Charly Gaul (a Tour-de-France winner and superb tour climber). Gaul it should be noted was also several times the Luxemburg Cyclo-cross Champion, declaring: "Cyclo-cross never did me any harm and running cannot hurt a rider provided he knows how." He must have enjoyed the sport, because he broke his collarbone no less than three times whilst riding cross races. Although he seemed to brush these mishaps aside with this remark reported in *Sporting Cyclist*: "It was all my own fault. I was too daring, there are some risks you can take in cyclo-cross and some you cannot, unless you want to end up in Hospital." Another reason for the lack of top names was that few events could afford to offer a big contract, the exceptions being National or World Championships, where a few stars could gain bonuses from their sponsors keen to gain more exposure for their products during the winter months.

In an interview with Arthur Wright in *Sporting Cyclist* Paddy Hoban outlined some of the changes in riders' attitudes since he first started riding cross races: "We took many liberties in the beginning of the sport, nobody bothered overmuch about training and went to parties most weekends but still managed to get placed. British organisers have always tended to overdo the rough stuff and there has often been little scope for bike-riding." Paddy goes on to say: "Lightness is another important consideration. Use as much alloy as you can. Remember – every ounce of bike has to be picked up and shouldered at sometime during an event. You start with a machine weighing say 26lb. Shoes are clean and you are fresh. But after a mile or two of picking up mud the bike can weigh 31 lb." He goes on to talk about the bike by saying: "I save as much (weight) as possible with alloy cranks, wheels and a plastic saddle, I even cut the spare from my spindles and chop off brake cables." Paddy was at this time at the top of his form, with 13 cross victories and several hill climbs already under his belt this season.

The Association continued to press on with their approach to the B.C.F, to be allowed to pick International cyclo-cross riders themselves. The Federation finally came up with a draft agreement in January of this year. A paragraph of note in a letter accompanying the Draft Agreement was from the B.C.F Hon. Secretary G. T. Bassett showing how the Government was playing its part in such a charter.

I have delayed it until now in the hope of obtaining clarification from the Ministry of Transport on the way they regard various types of competitive cycling events", and in another paragraph, "We hope that certain events such as map-reading contests, speed-judging contests, etc. will either be excluded from the scope of the new 'Cycle Racing on the Highway' Regulations or the subject of special and more lenient provisions. It is possible that Cyclo-Cross may be included among the events for special provision.

The draft agreement did include the main wording that the association had been pressing for:

The association shall be entitled to send two representatives at its own expense to any meeting of the racing committee of the Federation, when the selection of any International Committee of cyclo-cross teams is under consideration.

Most of the above may sound very worthy but it was a breakthrough for the B.C-C.A to be present at the selection of International teams and also gave the B.C-C.A much more prestige.

The National Championships this year could be described as the Championship of Youth as will become apparent in the race report. On Sunday 12th February, the De Laune C.C. were the promoters with K.Fuller as organiser and advertised as being on a 'South London course', which turned out to be at Chobham Common. The race took place in near perfect conditions for the time of year, with a dry, breezy mild day, so that those who looked forward to a mud bath were disappointed.

At the start it was chaotic, for the starter shouted "10 seconds to go" but most of the field only heard the word "Go" (or so they said afterwards) and off they charged, despite breaking the rules, they were allowed carry on with the race. The event was won by the outstanding youngster, 18 year old John Atkins (Coventry R.C.) with 17-year-old Mike Wilkinson (Southport R.C.) second and in third came Dave Briggs, who *Cycling & Mopeds* described as "discovery of the year." The winning team was Three Spires C.C. of Kerr, Brock and Wardle. Atkins was described in *Sporting Cyclist* as "A brilliant newcomer", this was indeed a prophecy, for within a few years he would dominate future championships and competitions. Afterwards Atkins was picked with Briggs, Hoban and Radford to go to the World Championships, although Radford had missed the Nationals due to a mix-up over his entry form.

This year would see British riders returning after a break of some years to battle with the top international riders in the World Championships to be held in Germany. Rolf Wolfshohl (West Germany) won in his home country, and became champion for the second time in a row. (Note there were two Germanys in those days). Previous champions Renato Longo and Andre Dufraisse came in second and third. The course was "spectacular" and centred on the Lower Saxony Stadium in Hanover.

The British team were again beset by problems, mostly outside their control, as the words of team manager Keith Edwards in his official report shows: "Fog prevented the team flying the Channel, and two incidents on the Autobahn caused by tyre trouble." All this caused delays, which resulted in the team not arriving at Hanover until 5a.m. on Saturday morning. Six hours sleep and a meal followed, then there was only time for the riders to cover a few laps of the course.

"A feature which caused trouble to our boys was the hurdles. 20 of which had to be negotiated during the race". Perhaps proving that once more the British still did not have very professional preparations for these championships.

The field of 40 riders covered two laps before having to encounter either the hurdles or the steep steps cut into a bank, on the third lap Bill Radford was in a fine fifth place but faded, and in the end it was Dave Briggs who would finish as the first British rider in 26th place at over 6 minutes down. Next was Radford in 31st then Hoban 36th with the young

Atkins in 38th and last, perhaps a place he would never occupy again. The top team was Belgium, with the G.B team ninth of the ten teams. *Cycling & Mopeds* described the G.B riders' experience as "The British team rubbed shoulders with the stars, as the Continental aces treated the huge enthusiastic crowd to an unbelievable display of acrobatic cycling."

The cost of the G.B team competing this year was £128.3s 0½d (£128.15p). Luckily, by a previous agreement, the B.C.F would pay one third of the costs (up to a maximum of £60), which helped the B.C-C.A to balance their finances.

Spring came early to Wales during mid February, where the riders in the Cwmcarn Paragon event saw Bob Jones of the (Malvernian C.C.) and Albert Moss (Solihull C.C.) fight out a wheel to wheel sprint for the line, with Jones being declared the winner by just half a wheel. T.Gunning (Pontypool) came in third, with the winning team being the promoting club.

It is hard to relate now to the cost of expenses in the1960s. For example, the cost of the airfare to the Martini event in Paris this year was - £4.19s.6d. (£4.97½p) each. Two hotel rooms, with two single beds, booked from Friday noon until Monday noon - £6.7s.7d. (£6.38p) Yes, that's 4 beds for 3 days, what value! The 'Martini International' held on the 6th March was won by Maurice Gandolfo (France). Our riders finished well down the field with Dave Briggs 23rd, Paddy Hoban 24th, John Atkins 35th with Bill Radford unable to finish.

Looking back at some of the winners of the Solihull C.C. 'cross-country' races, there are some very well known names amongst its winners, including, Harry Reynolds in 1951, Stan Bray in '54, Ray Richards (who became the B.C-C.A Chairman) in '56, Alan Winters in '59 and Barry Moss in '61.

The early days of struggles and setbacks experienced by the Association were now hopefully well behind it. Most of the principal movers were still in office, beavering away, burning the midnight oil on many occasions, all in a cause they believed in, the furtherance of cyclo-cross as a sport. With Percy Lovell as Chairman, Keith Edwards General Secretary, Ron Atkins as Treasurer and Paddy Hoban working with the international riders things were becoming more stabilised.

Season 1961/62
This season there was an impressive list of 74 events in the new handbook, The 'Three Peaks' is shown for the first time, also listed is

the Featherstone R.C. event known locally as the 'Circuit of the Alps', the 'Alps' being not beautiful snow capped mountains but tall slag heaps left after coal mining, with the winner being K. "Bas" Lycett, and prolific 'cross winner Harry Bond in second. One of the prizes listed, shows the offbeat friendly atmosphere of these events, presented for 'The Muddiest Rider'. Many were still using their 'winter irons', rather than spoil their expensive continental equipment and still preferred to use 26" wheels, which gave more clearance from mud and leaves, with both single speed and hub gears used by the majority. Photographers were beginning to realise that cyclo-cross produced some great action pictures, with cycling magazines printing some excellent shots, and in doing so bringing the sport to an even wider public.

For the first ' Three Peaks' race on October 1st there was still continued opposition from such as W. H. Paul (founder of the Rough-stuff Fellowship) who wrote to *Cycling & Mopeds* saying that he was dismayed to read that the "traditional home of the curlew and grouse is to be turned into another race route." John Rawnsley replied the next week by writing, "I have read with amusement the arguments put forward by Mr. W. H. Paul. ...a race which will be unique in the history of cycle racing, ... The police limit the race to 40 riders", he then concluded his letter with "every rider will be insured by my club at no charge, insuring them against damage to stiles, walls or animals in a sum of £50,000. In conclusion we would extend a hearty welcome to Mr. Paul to join the riders as our guest on Sunday, October 1, when perhaps with his experience of rough riding he may share some of the £30 or more prize money which we are giving in an endeavour to attract the top cyclo-cross riders from all parts of the country." Mr. Paul replied by declining the offer to ride and continued his attack on the event by saying "such routes are generally classified as footpaths and that it is legally an offence to wheel, let alone ride a bicycle on such." and "My regret will be for real lovers of rough-routes who may be restricted from using certain routes."

The Liverpool Echo during November, reported: "Such is the interest (in cyclo-cross) that it has been decided to try and form a Merseyside C.C Association, which will be affiliated to the B.C-C.A". Also a meeting was arranged between representatives of the North London C.C.A, South London C.C.A and the Essex League, with the declaration - "By joining forces we become a larger body which will place us on a par with the Midland C.C.A." This was an attempt to run all the three area events under one umbrella association.

Only sixteen, brave (or foolish), riders started in the Worcestershire C.A. event at the end of the year. Perhaps the report in *Cycling & Mopeds* describes it best: "From the start Briggs, Kerr and Atkins shot away to a 15 second lead and intently watching the icy surface on the only short stretch of road, they missed the turn with the route arrow hidden by the driving snow. ….no-one realized until another mile that the leaders were missing…..They appeared out of the snow and the race was restarted! ….All sixteen starters finished the course. The last rider was given a Christmas pudding!" Dave Briggs (Saracen R.C.) was the eventual winner from W. Radford (Wolverhampton Wheelers.) with M. Kerr (Three Spires C.C.) third.

A cover of *Cycling & Mopeds* carried a picture, which showed fully the dreadful conditions riders were battling against this winter. Three snow-splattered men were shown riding on a white carpet, against a snow filled sky. The leading two were D.Viney and P.Griffin, the event being the South of England Championships held in Surrey.

On the very first day of the New Year, John Atkins, Keith Mernickle and Ted Puckland travelled to Belgium at their own expense, only to encounter exceptionally bad weather and so only rode two events out of the three planned. At Klein-Vorst, John finished second, Keith fifth, and then at Knesslare, John and Keith finished 14th and 24[th.] This was, of course, all good experience at battling the continentals on their own ground.

In January the blanket of snow covering Britain featured in *Cycling & Mopeds* with an article headlined "CYCLO-CROSS ON TV" featured two pictures of television screens each showing the cyclo-cross event of the previous weekend.

"While the much publicized £100 a-week stars of football and the tough giants of professional rugby league found the bitter conditions were too bad … it was a great day for cycling, although the snow, ice and slush covering the country was said to have made it the worst-ever day for British sport. ….From the comfort of an armchair, the gay cavaliers of cycling and cyclo-cross men slithering in the snow looked like heroes." wrote John Matthews. T.V Commentator Peter West provided a brief appetizer when the Grandstand programme began at 1 pm. He emphasized it was "The first live transmission ever of cyclo-cross" (in Britain) and added, "I think you will find it tremendous fun." Thirty-five minutes later the cameras returned for the first heat held over four laps of a half mile circuit round the bleak waste of Rugeley Generating Station. Only 11 of the 12 teams entered started, with the presentation taking a total of something like 41 minutes viewing time. For example, each rider was interviewed in close-up before the start and the commentary was very accurate and well informed. The report went on: "But to keep Uncle George and Aunty Ada happy, cyclo-cross must provide more exciting viewing ….The first heat began to look so slow and unexciting that it was only saved when Ralph Jordan made a spectacular slide on his seat down a snow covered embankment." So it sounds as if the seat of Jordan's pants saved the programme!

Injuries and 'flu were to hit the 'cross scene during early January this year. The Midland Counties promotion lacked the following riders, John Atkins out with heavy cold, Ralph Jordan and Ken Fuller 'flu and Roy Comer broken ankle, but Dave Briggs (Saracen C.C.) had no problem in continuing his winning ways. Scottish Cyclo-Cross Champion Andy Kerr was seen riding a single 62" inch gear, he punctured twice on lap one, but strove on gamely to finished ninth. His compatriots didn't fair so well, all having travelled overnight by train from Glasgow, the effects of no sleep soon took its toll, with only one finishing. After this event the selection for the World's was made, with the large number of 12 names being picked to be in contention for places.

Yorkshire club, the Morley C.C, promoted the National Championships on 4th February with sponsorship by the Yorkshire Evening News. It took place on the Tingley Gas Works Circuit, which had the luxury of 'heated changing rooms and hot showers', another novel addition was that each rider was provided with a cup of tea and sandwiches, which was a boon for those having long distances to cover, (remember many still rode to and from such events by bicycle). 127 competitors tackled the course and the young John Atkins (Coventry R.C.) was the winner from M.E. Wilkinson (Southport R.C.C.) followed by Keith Mernickle (Middlesex Clarion). John Atkins was still only 19 at this event, but had his whole family helping; his father, mother and sister were all stationed around the course with spare bikes. The prize list for a National Championship seems very unusual today; the winner was awarded a Gold Medal, Jersey and a double bed size Philips Electric Blanket. Fifth place prize was an Electric Toaster, seventh to finish received a Table Lighter and both 13th and 17th won cycling capes.

A Women's event was held before the main championship and was won by Beryl Burton, who was riding in her own club's promotion. She already had three World Championships under her belt in different disciplines but could still mix it with other top ladies in the mud of Yorkshire. Beryl was to be followed home by Val Rushworth (Monkton C.C.) and J. Smith (Skipton C.C). *Cycling & Mopeds* headlined her win as "Beryl Leads Girls in Morley Mud-bath"

Luxemburg was the venue for the World Professional Championships this year, and the winner was the 1959 champion Renato Longo of Italy, with Keith Mernickle the top British finisher in 24th, on this tougher than expected course. Longo just sprinted away at the start and continued on his way to win by 2 minutes 20seconds from Maurice Gandolfo of France, with Andre Dufraisse also of France taking the bronze medal.

Cycling & Mopeds reporter Marcel Longchamp described how ill prepared the G.B. team were: "When the British team arrived on Friday night they were horrified to find a 300 yard hill of 1 in 5 and 1 in 7. Their lowest gears were between 48" and 51" while the Continentals, who had been training on the course for three or four days, were riding 36" to 40" bottom gears." Last year's champion Wolfshohl had been involved in a car crash only a few days before the big day and had to retire after the first lap. The other British riders finished close together, with John Atkins 32nd. Dave Briggs 33rd and Bill Radford 34[th.] *Cycling & Mopeds* also recorded the thoughts of the G.B. team manager Keith Edwards: "The lesson learned was to get over to the event four or five days beforehand. Next year, at Calais, we hope to do that."

Renato Longo also won the Martini International, which was held once more near Paris and Maurice Gandolfo followed him home. Britain had the pleasure of seeing progress in this event, coming fourth in the team race. John Atkins, gaining seventh place and led home Harry Bond 10th and Keith Mernickle 12th their winnings being 365 New Francs for their efforts. A note in the race report caught the eye, "Dunlop No 5s were donated and used on the front wheels, but individuals had to supply their own special cyclo-cross tyres on the rear wheels". Yet another sign of how Cinderella-like British cyclo-cross still was.

The Masseur's report by J. Robinson L.C.S.P. (phys) to the International Selection Committee is interesting as it shows a light on how top-racing men looked after themselves in the early sixties. He covered the physical condition of the riders in the World Championships this year:

Riders observed had good leg development, but all lacked development and build from the waist up. Also legs carry too much fatty tissue. Diet - from observations at meal times and questions asked of the team, more attention could be placed on a more wholesome diet. By this I mean more importance placed on unprocessed food, also calories. I also wish to thank Keith Edwards, who as manager, in my opinion, is a really first class man for the job and deserves all our help and thanks.

Season 1962/63

In July this year the Association sent a letter to Road Time Trials Council, proposing that the B.C-C.A should have control over all cyclo cross time trials. One paragraph outlined - " Over such events of a maximum distance of 15 miles which have 50% over un-metalled roads and rough-stuff." This shows yet another example of the complex way in which cycling in Britain was being controlled during this era.

The same hardworking dedicated officials were still leading the organisation onwards into the new season. The handbook had expanded to 24 pages, and now there were 103 races listed in England and Wales. Among the many events listed were promotions such as the Grand Prix of Cornwall, Viking Scramble, 'Mackeson' Cyclo-Cross, there was also the Rik Van Looy Birthday Cyclo-Cross organised by Velo Club Central, Grand Prix of Baddesley, Circuit of Tandle Hill, the 'Three Peaks' and a World Championship Selection Race. As is the tradition in cyclo-cross some of the biggest promotions had the most unusual names.

The Scottish Cyclists Union Cyclo-Cross Association listed five events, which included their Championships to be held on January 12th. Other Associations listed were Bristol & District, Merseyside, London, Manchester, Mid Devon, Portsmouth Command Royal Navy, South Wales and Yorkshire illustrating that the sport now well and truly covered all of England, Wales and Scotland.

On the back cover of this edition is an advert for a trip to Calais to see the World Championships; it was an 'All-in Week End Trip' by air from either Derby or Birmingham, or by coach and air from London, although no prices were indicated.

The Association wrote once more in October to John Davis, the National Secretary of the RTTC, enquiring about a joint agreement between the two bodies. One letter during the correspondence included this excerpt:

Cyclo-Cross is spreading rapidly, but we have yet to attain a sound financial backing. Despite what you have read in the cycling press, there are well over a hundred clubs affiliated at present, and each post brings more.

An outline joint draft agreement was drawn up for discussion but what the rumours in the press were, has not been discovered.

Sporting Cyclist covered the De Laune CC, Biggin Hill Scramble, with this sentence: "Starting at the top of the North Downs at the popular cyclist's rendezvous the 'Salt Box Café', near the immortal Biggin Hill R.A.F. Station." In this event good bike control was needed as riders were at their limit on the fast descent through the thick wooded slopes, forcing spectators back into nearby bushes as they swept past. 18 year old Keith Mernickle (Middlesex Clarion), proved himself the winner from M. (Ginger) Garwood (29th Wheelers) and D. Lyneham (V.C.Sacchi).

The very generous sponsorship by the Corona Soft Drinks Company meant that the spectators at two events this autumn had the excitement of seeing a very special visitor riding at both Halesowen and Rollswood Farm. The reigning World Champion, Renato Longo, had travelled to England to ride these events over one weekend. It turned out to be a Master-Class by the multi-champion, he pedalled gears two teeth lower than anyone else and showed his ability to pick the correct line over any surface. John Atkins, resplendent in his British Championship jersey, treated the crowds to the one-off sight of the two champions locked together as if on a tandem. However, the class of the man in the famous rainbow jersey gave him the victory in both events, although he remarked that he was sorry to see the young John Atkins retire during the Sunday race. He found the courses "the hardest he had ever ridden" (European courses included more riding) and he was unused to competing against so many, 130 compared with perhaps 40 or less at home in Italy. Longo was also used to racing before crowds of up to 50,000 so he found racing in English events very different.

Corona were just one of a gathering number of nationally known companies who were signing up to be associated with cyclo-cross. Some of these were Mackeson (Beer), Gilby Ltd (Smirnoff Vodka), Marston, Thompson & Evershed (Brewers). *The Daily Telegraph* perhaps the most high profile of all with David Saunders and his unmissable column on cycle sport, (many cyclists still remember buying the newspaper just for his cycling column). Another progressive step was the increased quality of the race programmes; more photographs of riders were appearing, many now printed in two or more colours on glossy or coloured paper.

Deep snow and ice, with freezing temperatures describes one of the coldest and longest winters of this century, snowdrifts blocked roads across the country, with even East Anglia being affected.

Despite these problems no sign of events being cancelled have been found, these tough men faced tough conditions, together with the organisers and marshals who had to keep the events rolling. A heavy snowfall caused problems for an event in Worcestershire; deep drifts had formed overnight covering direction signs. But the race set off and soon a breakaway group formed, however, when they turned up a cart track they were faced by the main group coming in the opposite direction! Everyone stopped and a discussion ensued, whereupon everyone returned to the start for clearer instructions.

The North of England Championships were held on 12th December at Houghton Dale, Denton. It was remembered in the North West C-C.A. magazine Annual in the 1989 edition by Neil Orrell. Harry Bond soon took the lead and continued onward to his third consecutive title. He described the course thus: "A steep drop through the trees to a stream, (which collected its quota of headlong tumbles each of the five laps), followed by a steeper scramble through thick loose clay pushed there by bulldozers, into which competitors sloshed more than knee deep-then half-made roads provided ultra rough riding ended with a plunge into hub-deep mud bath through a dark tunnel of thorns." But this was just bread and butter to a rider of Harry Bond's calibre.

During January a *Cycling and Mopeds* Editorial headline claimed "No Stopping Cyclo-cross" and continued, "In other parts of the country, cyclo-cross went on pretty much as usual. Yet this was on a weekend when hundreds of other sporting fixtures were cancelled because of the deep freeze that gripped Britain. Sport has never had it so bad, decided one Sunday paper, 135 professional football matches had been postponed. Amateur cycling, with riders floundering through deep snow for the fun of it, went on. What a pity the television sports programmes did not switch the unused cameras to carry the excitement of the tough, dare-devil sport of cyclo-cross to the fire-hugging millions of armchair sportsmen."

Almost a year after the correspondence passing between the Association and the R.T.T.C., a further letter outlined the reason why the Council could not approve a 'Grand Prix des Gentlemen' race. This type of event involves a time trial in which a professional or top class rider paces a retired champion or older rider:

Such an event could not be approved because the combination of two categories of rider in one team would constitute a breach of the amateur regulation. In this context, you will appreciate that an independent rider is a professional in the eyes of the R.T.T.C.

Independent riders were allowed to mix with amateurs or professionals in road races or 'cross' races but they were not full professionals although they could take cash rather than prizes.

The Viking Road Club promoted the National Championships in the Harlow Town Park, and (surprise, surprise) it took place in a snowstorm, with an icy wind making the riders struggle down into a gully through deep snow at one point. The event was won as described in *Cycling & Mopeds*: "Mick Stallard – 19 year old, 5 ft.10in. 11 stone, son of the man who finished sixth in 1934 world championship road race, stopped John Atkins from scoring his third national championship win in devastating fashion … it was his first event win of the season!" Keith Mernickle was in third spot, the first junior was J.Barnes of the Morden C.C. and Coventry Road Club won the team race. After all this endeavour against the elements, *Cycling & Mopeds* also described the prize presentation: "While Mick Stallard donned the champion's jersey and pocketed a voucher worth £20, a man from the sponsors placed a brightly coloured sash over his shoulders; a vivacious girl in an Eskimo's outfit kissed him." The generous sponsorship by Smirnoff Vodka giving the event a much higher profile than previously

The Times reported the event under the heading "Essex Course That Sorted 'em Out" and was covered by a Staff Reporter who set the scene well: "They came by bicycle, by tricycle, by car and by coach, and they came in hundreds, some from as far afield as Yorkshire. Many a car had a cluster of bicycles strapped to its roof, and in the white and wintry scene, with snow falling softly … There was never any question of calling off the ninth British National Cyclo-Cross Championship ('with people coming from all over the country, you couldn't cancel it'), but the course in Harlow Town Park, Essex, had been slightly modified at points where skidding competitors might intrude dangerously into heavier traffic. It would have been modified further said the programme, if the snow had been deep… On the starting line one rider, eyeing the bleak and barren landscape turned to a companion and said: ' Hey Len where's the course?'" Then came a good description of the atmosphere which could apply to any 'cross event, "They got off, plucked twigs from the wheels, shouldered the bikes and sprinted uphill, taking sundry rude remarks in their stride and giving a few in return. Then on to the next lap, gasping with effort and gently encouraged by such cries as 'Come on lad, you're not trying. Run!' Yet in little more than an hour it was all over." Accompanying the article was an excellent picture of six cyclists struggling up what looks a snow cliff, bikes over their shoulders, feet searching for footholds, and the silhouettes of the spectators looking down from the crest of the slope at this spectacle.

Cycling & Mopeds reported on John Atkins coming second in the Championships with "Soon afterwards, he had an x-ray and the doctors discovered a duodenal ulcer. He was too young for an operation, so he started a course of treatment, which kept him off his bike from September of that year until nearly the end of 1964" (this included 3 months off work). John then continues: "I was put on a diet, which excluded fats and alcohol, but since I rarely touched them anyway it wasn't too bad"

At the World Championships this year, Rolf Wolfshohl (W.Germany) gained a third victory having won also in 1960 and 1961. He dominated the February afternoon event at Calais almost completely. Renato Longo (Italy) came in second and third was André Dufraisse (France). *Sporting Cyclist* reported on the British team thus: "The selectors choice in sending such a young team is not just a policy of encouraging youth. For results back home had proved that in cyclo-cross the young ones are usually at the top of the tree anyway."

Two northerners, Dave Briggs of the Saracen R.C. and Harry Bond of the Bradford R.C.C. were the non-travelling reserves for the Worlds, both men being 25 years old. Mick Stallard finished 17th, Keith Mernickle 21st, William Radford 30th and John Atkins had to retire. Keith was the 'baby' of this British team at just a month over 18 years with William Radford the senior at only 22 years. At the Banquet afterwards the French team director, Robert Oubron was heard to say: "Your boys have courage, but they lack speed"

There was much controversy in the press about the course for this year's championship. It was said that it had been designed for the current French World Road Race Champion Jean Stablinski. The reason for the speculation was mainly financial, in that he would bring many extra supporters to the event. Although he had not qualified, he was no stranger to this side of the sport, as he had been Champion of Flanders in the past. There were also hints that he would receive 'start money', none of these rumours can of course be proved after this length of time, but over two thirds of the course was fast and flat, more suited to road riders than the British men who were used to mud and mire.

Keith Edwards produced a report after this World Championships, stating that in future, the Association should strive to have six completely equipped machines to be placed at the disposal of the B.C-C.A. "Using as much British equipment as possible, plus a comprehensive stock of spares". This was indeed the way forward if British cross racing was to progress on the international scene. For the technically minded, the strength of Wolfshohl can be gauged by looking at his gear range, he was riding 44/49 chain rings with a 14,17, 20, 23, 26 block compared with Mernickle and Atkins who were on a single chain ring of 46 teeth and a 14,16,18,21,26 block. Also on the subject of equipment at these championships, the Italians were seen with innovative light alloy chain guards on their machines, demonstrating that manufacturers were taking an interest in this side of the sport. Keith Edwards gave an interesting interview to *Sporting Cyclist*, with an insight into the training techniques used by the British team: "I figured that the biggest difficulty the boys would have, would be in jumping up to high speed on the roads after the 'rough-stuff'. I had them training mid-week behind a scooter. I would pull away from the corners fast, making them chase very hard to simulate race conditions."

The report by the masseur to the B.C-C.A. A.G.M. after this year's World Championships once more had some interesting insights into the riders of this period: "The physical condition of the riders, with the exception of John Atkins was good. The best in this respect being Mike Stallard." (This is not unsurprising, as John described himself in an interview as, "I was always the 8½ stone wimp"). The report continued: "It is my personal opinion that the diet provided for the team was most unsatisfactory for the riders" and "John Atkins was unfortunate enough to contract Bronchial Asthma and medical aid was obtained by the team manager." (he had to retire on the second lap). He then goes on to rebuke the Association's committee for not bringing forward his recommendations of the previous year. It appears he was trying very hard to drag the regime of diet, fitness and technique up to world standard.

Once more British riders were sent to the prestigious Martini International. Renato Longo was winner once again. However the British team of Mernickle (12th), Bond (13th), Stallard (22nd), came fourth, leaving top teams such as Belgium, Switzerland, Spain and Luxemburg behind. We are left wondering if the team could have climbed higher if John Atkins hadn't had to withdraw due to his illness at the World Championships earlier.

Prior to the Annual General Meeting, which was held on Sunday, March 10th, at Baginton Village Hall, there was a special road race promoted for cyclo-cross riders only. Keith Mernickle (Middlesex R.C.) won with John Perks (Independent) second and Hugh Porter (Wolverhampton Wheelers) in third place. The A.G.M. started at noon and there was an attempt to change the method of selection of riders for the World Championships, both the selectors and selected events but the proposals were unsuccessful.

Approaching its tenth birthday, the B.C-C.A had achieved a great deal over a very short space of time. Its next challenge would be to consolidate the successes and then move forward to new ventures.

W. J. Ewings, first of the Catford 'hares' to complete the full course. April 1914.

A competitor in the Midland Cross-Country Chase, March 1925.

Show girls taking part in a cross-country race, 1930

A rider in the Bagshott Scramble, 1948

Alan Jackson, De Laune C.C. 1954.   *Mike Weston, Coventry R.C. 1957*

Jean Robic on his way to winning the first World Cyclo-Cross Championship.

*Cyclo-cross riders
will know how Ted
Saunderson of the '34
Nomads is feeling as
he rides a Biggin Hill
event during the 1950s
– cold, wet, muddy and
just wishing it would
all soon be over.*

Ted Lees

Cycling Weekly

Riding, running and swimming – a Kenton R.C. event during 1957.

Handbooks from the 1950s.

Don Stone ('34 Nomads) lunges for the line to win the 1958 National Championship from Barry Spence (Wolverhampton Whls.)

The 1960 Championships were held in six inches of snow.

Cycling
Weekly

*Two designs of
badges used in the
1950s and 1960s.*

PAST WINNERS

John Rawnsley
1961

Ian Craig
1963

Harry Bond
1962, 1964, 1966, 1967

John Bell
1965

John Atkins
1969, 1970, 1976

Tom MacDonald
1968

Eric Stone
1971, 1977, 1978, 1979, 1982

6

Stallard to the Fore

Season 1963/64

Pink was chosen as the cover colour for this season's handbook, otherwise the format remained the same. Under the heading 'Introduction' readers were reminded that the Association was about to enter its 10th year and the programme outlined was bigger and better than ever. Another heading was 'Membership' where the Private membership fee is listed as 2/6d (12½p) per annum. There was also a warning that "associations, clubs and private members who have not paid by the 31st December of the same year, shall be deemed to have ceased membership and will not be re-admitted until a further official application has been made." G. Ingham was listed as the official for the newly created post of Membership Secretary.

Among the races listed in this year's edition, were four promotions by the Mid-Devon Road Club on Bovey Heath, each being nine miles in length, with entry fees of 3/- (15p) before event, 3/6 (17½p) on day or 10/- (50p) for all four events. An amusingly named event was the 'Bramble Scramble' to be held for the 10th time on Post Hill, New Farnley, Yorkshire. The Yorkshire Association also ventured into promoting an event at the York Rally, thus taking cyclo-cross to the famous Cyclists' Touring Club Rally held every year on the Knavesmire at York. The Cornish Cyclo-Cross League was kept busy promoting 14 events this year, including the South West of England Championships and the Larkhills & South Trekieve Omnium.

Some of the Leagues and Associations had their own colours, the Cornish colours were royal blue and yellow, the Midland's were racing in black, orange and red, and the Yorkshiremen in blue and white. A Mr. Morton wrote to the National Committee, indicating that a North Eastern C.C.A would be formed and he was asking for funds from Headquarters to assist.

In the B.C-C.A. archives there is a certificate produced for a National Schoolboys Championships for this year and a proposal that the event should take place during the following autumn. There is also a letter from the Birmingham School Sports Federation agreeing to promote this.

Portsmouth Command Royal Navy C A promoted their event in November in very stormy weather on England's south coast, where Keith Mernickle took his first win as an Independent for E.G.Bates Cycles. Mernickle won three of the four events, therefore securing the magnificent silver 'Sportrophy' which was inset with a gold medal of H.M.S Victory. A footnote to this event is that Keith Edwards rode one of these events, ten years after he helped found the British Cyclo-Cross Association.

A decision was made to have a trial run for the 1964 National Championship course this year and would be run off a month before the big event. All was going well until the Chief Constable decided that a small part of the course that covered a section of road could not be allowed, this came as a bombshell for the organising committee. When the organisers quizzed the Chief Constable, he could only give negative answers. The questions included: "How many people had been prosecuted?" and "How many complaints had there been from the public?" The answers were none on both counts. He therefore gave his permission for the course to encroach onto the public highway, after Percy Stallard (of B.L.R.C. fame), the Chairman of the Wolverhampton Sports Committee gave assurances that it would be covered by third party insurance and the section on the roadway would be neutralised, no racing over this part. This was a very important victory for cyclo-cross and cycle racing, demonstrating that they could not be banned without proper reason.

An excellent race programme was produced for the National Championships with 36 pages of colour printing and photos of the competing riders. Organised by the Wolverhampton Wheelers C.C. the event was held at Aldersley Stadium, Wolverhampton. After a race long tussle between Stallard and Mernickle, *Cycling and Mopeds* reported the decisive moment: "Then, anxious to get on the road, where the police controlled the traffic with walkie-talkie radios, the Southern rider pulled his foot out of the toe-clip and lunging forward fell heavily." Mick Stallard was therefore winner of his club's promotion, from Mernickle riding for Bates Cycles and Mick Ives of Coventry CC. 81 riders passed under the chequered flag with the winning team Edgbaston C.C.

Cycling and Mopeds proudly printed a photo of the World Championships this year above the caption: "Wire photo of the champ

Renato Longo racing to victory." at Grammont in Belgium. The course which included meadows, a stream, woods with slippery wet paths and a stretch of treacherous cobbles was described as the most beautiful course in Belgium. This year the British fans did have something to go wild about, when the nineteen year old Londoner, Keith Mernickle, raced into the lead after one and half miles and stayed there for another two miles. What a fine sight it was for the 70 or so fans who had made the journey from the snowy wastes of England to the grey drizzle of Belgium. It was a sight to warm every B.C-C.A member's frozen body as the Briton raced ahead of the riders from 11 nations. As the race progressed the big guns came to the front and the final result was the Italian Renato Longo followed by Roger Declercq (Belgium) with J Mahé (France) third. Mernickle finished 11th the highest finish yet by a British rider. Mick Stallard was 19th, Glyn Whitmore 30th and Roger Page 34th out of 44 finishers. Altogether a good result, as Britain finished sixth in the team race.

The differences between British and Belgian promotions could be plainly seen, by just looking at the lines of beer tents and souvenir stalls, some selling flags, all doing brisk business. There were signs, boards and banners proclaiming companies selling products such as beer, cigars and cigarettes all trying to catch the eye of the television cameras.

Six riders travelled to the 'Martini' this year, which was dominated again by Longo. Mick Ives was the leading British rider in 14th place, Mernickle, Stallard and Page were packed together in 23rd, 24th and 26th with Dave Wren 29th and Glyn Whitmore further back in 32nd. Great Britain was fifth team out of nine. A note in the report of the race to the Racing Committee recorded a loss of £6.5s (£6.25p). Keith Mernickle was also the winner of the season long Viking Trophy Competition this year with Mick Stallard second and the 6ft tall Roger Page third.

The early sixties marked the end of the first ten years of the Association and progress from those early days had been very impressive. The style of courses had changed; they were now more akin to the Continental style.

Season 1964/65

A new section called 'International Scene' written by Paddy Hoban, in the new season's handbook, describes the progress towards winning a Rainbow jersey: "Undoubtedly the most important step forward in the past international season was the sterling ride in the World Championships by the young independent K.Mernickle who led the field and when caught stayed with the leaders to finish eleventh."

It also outlined one way in which the sport was pressing forward. "Special evening classes for cyclo-cross riders were commenced in London last season. It is hoped that these are the forerunners of others to be started in various parts of the country and also the B.C-C.A. proposes to hold special training courses during the coming season at one of the C.C.P.R. (Central Council for Physical Recreation) establishments." This section closes with these uplifting words: "Bearing all of the above in mind there is no doubt that the future of Cyclo-Cross is extremely attractive."

After nine years the design of the handbook that dropped through the letterboxes of riders and officials had changed. Previously printed in different colours, it had now had a complete revamp with a white glossy cover and a purchase price of one shilling (5p). It would appear that the membership had faith in their officials by re-electing them all for a further year.

Things were also changing on courses, those with masses of quagmire mud and ploughed fields were being changed to faster grass sections and low hurdles or planks which could be 'bunny- hopped' or cleared with a smart dismount. A plea for this speed up was included in the handbook: "It is hoped that organisers will promote events upon fast rideable courses with not too much mud, etc. in an endeavour to attract perhaps some of the independent and amateur roadmen."

A letter from the R.T.T.C during November shows that the long extended correspondence between the two organisations over a joint agreement was still going on. It seems the wheels of the R.T.T.C at this time turned very slowly!

The Walsall Cyclists v Harriers race was still being held at this time and was fondly remembered by Jim Court in an article in the1995/96 N.W.C-C.A Annual: "I cannot recall whose rules the race was under (probably no-one's) but the event was always keenly contested between the local running and cycling clubs ... Thinking back, the race was also a wonderful excuse for competing along a course, which today would probably be totally unacceptable to the public with a fair chance of totally fouling up the local traffic ... This event was probably my cyclo-cross debut as a keen roughstuffer with the Wolverhampton C.T.C."

At the Three Peaks race this year, onlookers were kept in touch with the progress of the race with reports by the Territorial Army, who had radio contact with observers on various parts of the course. Harry Bond won, in a new record time of 3hrs 0mins 05secs. He had such a comfortable lead that he stopped to wash his face in a stream with only a few miles of tarmac to go. What his thoughts were when he found out after crossing the line, that he had missed going under three hours by such a narrow margin, is not recorded.

Neville Billington (later to become B.C-C.A International Racing Secretary) writing in *Sporting Cyclist* suggested that the aims of the B.C-C.A. should be: "(i) A rainbow jersey for a British rider, (ii) The World Championship race to be staged in Britain … and I think most observers would agree that (i) could surely be realised in the near future. With regard to (ii) The B.C-C.A. has the machinery, the flair and experience to pull off such a venture. The problems lie in the tremendous financial aspects of such an undertaking."

In another article in *Sporting Cyclist*, Billington lamented the fact that the World Championships did not include all the countries that have strong participation in cyclo-cross. The Russians were having major events such as the U.S.S.R. Cup, and races being sponsored by sports clubs such as Dynamo, Spartak, Burevestnik and Trud, although no records are kept of the number of crossmen racing cycling sections in U.S.S.R sports clubs had more than 1,100,000 members. The United States also had numbers of riders participating in cyclo-cross with their own championships being held in October.

The first National Schoolboys Championship was held in November with 80 competitors, at Four Dwellings School, Quinton, Birmingham with an entry fee 1/- (5p). The winner of this new Championship was Geoff Shaw (March End Sec.Modern), second M O'Connor (Lordswood Tech) and third Vic Fullard (March End Sec. Modern)

A race with a difference was by The Royal Navy, who promoted an event at 'H.M.S. Ariel', at Lee-on-Solent, Hampshire. It was held on December 6th and named the International Cyclo-Cross Championship. Extremely muddy conditions caused the organisers to reduce the distance of the race to 5 laps (14½ miles). The winning order was Stallard, Ives and Page. The race also incorporated the Area Championships, with the same three riders composing the winning Midland team, followed by London with Yorkshire in third place.

The Daily Telegraph sponsored the National Championships in Yorkshire, promoted by the Pudsey Owl Road Club at Roundhay Park, Leeds. The paper's investment raised the standard of promotion to a class above the normal. Amateur Mick Stallard showed the way home to two professionals Keith Mernickle riding for E.G.Bates Cycles and Harry

Bond riding for Ellis Briggs Cycles. Wolverhampton Wheelers won the team prize.

The World Championships was held at Cavaria, Italy with Italian Renato Longo winning the Rainbow Jersey for the fourth time, from Rolf Wolfshohl (W Germany) and Amerigo Severini (Italy). The British team consisted of M.Stallard (Wolverhampton Wheelers), K. Mernickle (E.G.Bates Cycles), M.Ives (Coventry C.C) and H.Bond (Ellis Briggs/ Simplex) with the team having to pay their own expenses. The report by the team manger on their performance makes enlightening reading. Two of the riders, Mernickle and Stallard did not agree with the training rides that were set out by manager, Keith Edwards, and this is reflected in his report. "There was in fact a British party in Italy, plus two individuals, Stallard and Mernickle." Both Mernickle (broken pedal spindle) and Stallard (loose gear lever) had mechanical problems. They finished in 13th and 20th places. Ives (in his first Worlds ride) and Bond were placed at 24th and 27th.

The report produced some scathing notes on Mick Stallard:

M.Stallard – Third appearance in World Championships, Equipment – Good and well presented, couldn't care less attitude affected the rest of the team, and his ideas on training prior to a World Championships are far too half-soaked in my opinion. This is his second successive failure in the Worlds, and if his present attitude persists, I can see little point in sending him on future occasions.

Pretty stern stuff, and very much to the point, did the selectors take any notice of his remarks?

Reg Ward writing in the North Western C-C.A's Annual of 1984/85, writes: "Back in 1965, our area secretary was Maureen Orrell and the Chairman, her husband Neil, with the money side being looked after by our Treasurer, then as now Ian Small." This is just a small example of the way at both Area and National level the B.C-C.A continued to benefit from the loyalty and enthusiasm of its officials.

7

Professionals and Amateurs
have their own Championships

Season 1965/66
This year started with yet more letters travelling to and fro between the Association and the R.T.T.C with still no sign of an agreement on the horizon. During July Mr E.Kings of the R.T.T.C was still saying, "My National Committee do not consider the draft agreement to be acceptable". So Keith Edwards B.C-C.A Secretary then wrote back:

Dear Mr. Kings,
I was extremely shocked at the contents of your letter dated 8th July.
In April of this year W.E.Baillie informed me that the only thing preventing the proposed agreement being accepted by the R.T.T.C was a definition of cyclo cross. I duly submitted a letter dated 5th May.
Negotiations concerning this agreement have been proceeding since July 1962, and I consider that your brief letter terminating these negotiations without a word of explanation, singularly lacking in courtesy.

Stern stuff!
A reply from Kings stated how sorry he was about his lack of courtesy, but that the agreement was not acceptable, so three years of negotiations came to an abrupt end.

Mike Dyason was the only recorded change of officials in the handbook, taking over from Paddy Hoban as International Racing Secretary, which Hoban had held for the past six years. The first event listed was the York Rally Exhibition Cyclo-Cross on the Knavesmire, on 29th August. Then on September 12th there was what was described as a 'Conducted Tour of the Three Peaks', which was a taster for the fifth real event to be held on 26th September. The handbook also had ten pages of promotions, one of which was an advert for the 'Circuit of the Cliffs', which sounded pretty scary. Among others was one at Friday Wood Farm, Colchester, showing the spread eastwards and this event became a regular fixture in the East for many years.

Looking through the Association rules, five catch the eye.

No 2 – The private membership fee is 2/6d (12½p) per annum; sponsors of Independents 10/- (50p) per rider per annum, all other affiliation fees 10/- per annum.

No. 12 – Complaints regarding riders or officials actions shall be referred to and dealt with by their local Associations

No. 21 – Six weeks shall elapse before a rider changing clubs can count in his new club's team.

No. 25 – Should foot and mouth disease or similar infection break out in the locality of a course, the event must be cancelled unless an alternative course is readily available and the conditions imposed by Rule 13 are complied with.

No. 28 – No rider is to cover any part of the course without his machine.

More riders were taking the opportunity to become Professionals (or the 'Cash-ranks' as some sections of the press still sarcastically called them!). The move to the Professional side meant that they could earn a good living by riding for cash during the summer months on the road, and cross events during the winter.

Cycling commenting on Mick Stallard's change of category said: "Mick Shows His True-Blue Colours. ....Mick Stallard was in such complete control of Velo Club Central's cyclo-cross on Saturday, that he even had time for a smile at spectators and shouting rude statements to Cycling's representative. Riding in his new Falcon colours, he was away to his usual fast start, from a jostling field in Hadley Stadium in the heart of industrial Smethwick, on an ideal spectators course."

The National Schoolboys Championship (no schoolgirls yet) in December was held at Shirley Hills, Croydon. Geoff.Shaw of Bilston College (Wolverhampton Wheelers) was Champion for the second year running, second was Vic Fullard, March End Secondary Modern (Wolverhampton Wheelers) and third was Colin Browning, Cardinal Newman (Velo Club Central). Of the 53 starters there were 49 finishers after a tough race and it showed how these young boys were already established in racing clubs.

Featherstone Road Club promoted the North of England Championships and some of the prizes on offer make interesting reading 40 years later because then, as now, organisers had a struggle to obtain prizes. The top prizes were good, with a pair of G.B.brakes and £2.00 for the winner but lower down the list they were perhaps slightly less impressive, eighth spot was a 'carrying handle' and last place had a touch of humour, a rear light!

Over a weekend in the New Year, four riders decided to try their luck in Continental races near Ostend, Gent and Rotterdam. Eric Stone (Matlock C.C.) on his first racing trip abroad said: "It opened my eyes a lot, they were so much more professional in their approach." and he was surprised to finish five minutes behind the Belgian winner. On the Saturday in Ostend, Mick Ives (Bantel/Mercian) claimed ninth spot, Roger Page (Solihull C.C.) was tenth and Martyn Baker (V.C. Central) 21st with the Dutch champion Hub Harings (good name for a cyclist!) being the winner.

A headline in a February Cycling highlighted the continuing theme running through the press and backed up by many cyclists in Britain, who thought that riding for money was not quite the thing a true racing cyclist should do, harping back to the old days of 'pure amateurs'. "A Stallard-Atkins Cross Struggle?"

Will Great Britain have its first Professional Cyclo-Cross Champion after this Saturday? In the only branch of the sport where it is permissible for 'pures' and cash men to ride against one another, it looks likely that a professional will come out on top. For three of the country's top mud boys ride in trade jerseys.

We have to wonder what the writer of this article would think if he could see even schoolboys today riding in sponsored jerseys. The article notes: "Hugh Porter Wolverhampton Wheelers is determined to gain championship honours in yet another phase of the sport." Hugh Porter is, of course, still involved in commentating on major cyclo-cross races over 40 years after this article was written.

A splendid poster in the Association archives announces that *The Daily Telegraph* was presenting the National Cyclo-Cross Championships on 5th Feb. at Kings Heath, Birmingham. One big bonus of having a national newspaper involved was that David Saunders, a great supporter of cycling trailed the event for several weeks and days beforehand, in his column in the sport section of the paper.

Another paper *The Birmingham Post* covered the event in a friendly way: "Welcome back, king John Atkins duly won the National Cyclo-Cross Championships at Highbury Park, King's Heath Birmingham. But it could have been oh-so-different had our own Edgbaston boy Roger Page, not slipped after nine laps when holding a hard fought 20 second lead." Page was second and Dave Wren (Edgeware R.C.) took the bronze, Page led the winning team of Edgbaston Road Club with Briggs and Florence. After the event the riders for the Worlds were announced as Atkins, Page, Stallard and Nie.

The February 19th Cycling announced the result of its 'Go-To-Antwerp' competition. The winner was a 15 year old from Foxwood School, Gerald Richardson and the magazine carried a picture of him competing in the Pontefract 'cross in deep snow. Presumably Richardson was much warmer when enjoying his prize at the Antwerp 6-Day later in the month. His winning letter was a scathing appraisal of how British cycle racing was seen as a "struggling minor sport."

Eric de Vlaeminck became the first Belgian World Cyclo-Cross Champion, in Beasain, Spain. In second place was Hermann Gretener of Switzerland and the tough previous champion Rolf Wolfshohl of West Germany third. The British team were disappointed with their result. John Atkins (Coventry R.C) was 21st, Mick Stallard (Falcon Cycles) 26th, David Nie (Dragon R.C.) 27th, and Roger Page (Edgbaston RC) 29th after being lapped. It is interesting to note that Great Britain was listed as 'England' in eighth position. Cycling magazine of March 5th was rather sympathetic: "The course was the toughest the team had ever seen, one for true specialists. Eight times round a 3,000-yard circuit 40 per cent road, 35 per cent cross country and the rest uphill running. Two 3ft 6ins hurdles, 100yds apart, in front of the stands cut sharply into the longest stretch of riding. All the British riders agreed that if they had known the course was going to be so taxing, they would have done more training on foot." Dave Nie was very unlucky when his frame broke at the seat tube, just below the lug, going down a steep descent. He was lucky in that the spare Falcon bikes were nearby and he lost no more than five places.

The final result of the season-long London C.C.A League Championship was a win for Dave Wren (Edgware R C) - 116 points, Dave Nie (Dragon R C) - 115 points, Keith Mernickle (E G Bates Cycles) - 97 points. It appears that the London boundary net was spread very wide, as riders in the league came from as far away as Guildford, Brighton and Luton and even included nine riders from the Colchester Rovers C.C.

Season 1966/67

The new season handbook showed Ron Atkins taking over the posts of both Membership Secretary and Treasurer, the Handbook Secretary was now R.Hesling, John Rawnsley the International Racing Secretary with Keith Edwards moving seats, from General Secretary to President. An article in the press indicates that Mr. Edwards was to be the Association's 'first President' however research shows that Ron Atkins had been listed as President during the 1954/55 and 1956/57 seasons. It therefore remains a mystery as to why Mr. Edwards was thought to be the first. Another big change this season was Ray Richards to General Secretary and in doing so became only the third person to hold this post. Keith and Joan Edwards were both made Life Members this year, with Cycling commenting: "Both put a tremendous amount of work in for the 150 affiliated clubs." There was a proposal this season to make a new large area region and if agreed, it would cover Cumberland, Westmoreland, Lancashire, Cheshire, North Staffs, North Derbyshire and North Notts.

The Three Peaks held on 1st October was won by Harry Bond (Bradford C.C./Ellis Briggs) recording a new course record of 2hrs. 57secs. 21secs. He was so dominant that he finished a clear nine minutes ahead of the next rider J. Bell, who was followed by John Rawnsley both of the Bradford C.C. However, this is not the whole story as Jeremy Fell recorded in the pages of *Sporting Cyclist*: "Within yards of the start of the race, in a rough line leading to the summit of Pen-Y-Ghent, Harry Bond was off his machine, unable to avoid a sudden eight man pile-up and injuring his wrist and a leg. A pedal of his machine was slightly bent, but it continued to spin, and he soon became accustomed to hearing it catching the crank." This mishap only delayed him catching the leaders and going into the lead himself. Fell continues: "Then Harry Bond went ahead and that pile-up at Horton turned out to be his only major misfortune. Once clear he concentrated on a fast time." The first history of this event started way back in 1887, when two schoolmasters used the course as a walking test taking 14 hours, the challenge to cyclists competing on the route has been covered in an earlier chapter.

At this time Welsh cyclo-cross promotions were gaining in stature, with Cycling reporting one such event thus: "Bevan's Welsh Win, Bob Bevan (Risca C.C) had no difficulty in running away with the Acme

Wheelers/Rhondda C.C. event. ... Only those who know the Rhondda valley can really appreciate the hazards of this course, with its one-in-three gradients and narrow tracks over grassy slopes where only top bike control kept riders from slithering and tumbling over the side."

A December headline "Coventry Wizz- Kid" heralded the winner of the National Schoolboy Championships when fifty-eight schoolboys started, out of an entry of 62 and an impressive 53 finished. Barrie Elson (Wolston High School/ Coventry Road Club) was the winner with R. Russell (Velo Club London) second and R.Pinder (Coventry C.C.) third. Prizes went down to 20th spot, with prizes for both the under 14's and under 13's.

On New Years Day the course instructions for the Hornsea Trophy sound novel, even for a cyclo-cross: "Start at 2.00 on the beach" with other instructions for the riders: "Below the Public Shelter, along the sand and over first groyne, along the lower promenade, and cross the stream dyke by the planks." All this demonstrating that even the seaside can be turned into an exciting cyclo-cross course.

The end of January saw the saga of 'The Fourth Man', which sounds like a title of a spy thriller, rather than about who should fund Dave Wren to the World Championships. It may be a lot clearer to just reprint the saga as it was recorded in the pages of Cycling, then you, the reader, can make up your own mind just what was going on.

"WREN LATEST – Cycling received on Monday the following letter from the B.C-C.A. President, which we construe as an attempt to prevent us printing something which two million Daily Mail readers had seen that morning."

I understand that you contacted the B.C-C.A. International Racing Secretary John Rawnsley and kindly offered to take Dave Wren to the world championship if he was nominated as a member of the Great Britain team.

Mr.Rawnsley agreed but in doing so he overlooked a decision made at the executive committee meeting held on January 29th at which he was present.

The entry of Wren is not an official one, and the matter will be discussed at the next meeting of the committee, which will take place on Saturday, February 11.

In the meantime I would suggest that it would be best for all concerned if this matter was not mentioned in the press. No doubt you will be able to advise Dave Wren of the position.

Keith Edwards (President B.C-C.A.)

On the same page was this report:

"B.C.F racing secretary Wotton telegraphed to Zurich at the last minute to get Wren's nomination in, no other body has this authority. He did so after speaking to Rawnsley, who on Monday said to Cycling 'The matter of the fourth man was discussed at the executive meeting but never put to the vote; when you brought it up on behalf of Wren needed a quick decision, and I as the International Racing Secretary, made it'."

Keith Edwards, asked by Cycling if he wished to withdraw his letter after Wren's week-end win, said: "Certainly not; the question of the fourth man paying for himself was discussed and rejected. If we let one pay for himself, others might object on their own behalf. Go ahead and publish the letter so long as you leave in the fourth paragraph." When Cycling referred to Wren "as one of the best men in the country" Edwards only reply was, "according to whom?"

As you can see, some hot words were being exchanged over this matter. In Cycling of 11th February this appeared as the Editorial"

HAPPY AUGUARY– One of the signs of a man is that he can make his mind up and then, if circumstances change, be big enough to change his mind with them, to fit the new conditions. This is what the British Cyclo-Cross Association has just demonstrated, with a magnanimity, which, coming at the beginning of a new season's racing, might well serve as a pointer of the way to behave. Officials of the Association said they had little money with which to pay for Wren to go to Zurich, but were planning on 'mortgaging' next year's budget in order to allow this young rider to represent his country. Those who have been shouting loud and long – and we have heard them – for Wren to go to Zurich, might well bear this in mind and perhaps put their hands in their pockets showing the same kind of magnanimity.

The national press picked up this dispute with *The Daily Telegraph* headline on its sports page: "Selectors Red-Faced After Wren Storms Home". This report by the good friend of cyclo-cross, David Saunders, continued: "Wren, not considered for the forthcoming world title event in Zurich, stormed over the 14 mile course, leaving the amateur champion John Atkins gasping more than half minute in arrears."

Keith Mernickle now with Ryall-Weldwork won the Viking Trophy Series taking home the gilt medallion and £10. John Atkins picked up the silver medallion and £6 for second place, with Harry Bond taking third and a bronze medallion plus £4. The final event of the series at Highbury Park, Solihull, was a very slippery affair with the surface frozen hard with ice. The ice claiming many hard luck stories, Atkins and Ives each had two falls, Page one fall, and Wren was brought down by Page falling, which makes it all sound more like an ice dancing event! *The Daily Express* printed a picture with the caption. "Atkins failed by half a wheel to catch Keith Mernickle, the London Cyclo-Cross Pro, in the Solihull race yesterday." The photograph shows it was more like three bike lengths; even the official result was given as two lengths! This was yet another event organised by the ever-energetic B.C-C.A General Secretary Ray Richards.

Three new Championships were created this year, with the first for Professional riders only, promoted by the Featherstone R.C. with a separate Amateur Championship to be held later in the season. The Professionals were to race on the course called the 'Alps Circuit'. Unfortunately only five professional riders lined up for this new event, these few pioneer contenders were K. Mernickle (Ryall-Weldwork), M.Ives (Mottram/ Simplex), E.White (Mottram/Simplex), G.Halls (Viking-Trumans Steel) and M.Coward (Witcomb Cycles) with the winner being Keith Mernickle. Also held on the same day and over the same course was the new Junior Championship. With a win for Phil Norfolk of the Bradford R.C.C and the V.C. Central rider David Cartwright coming in second, with Crabwood CC's Mike Girling third. David Cartwright's name also caught the eye for his sheer persistence in a Cycling report about a race in Wales which took place on February 4th : "A snapped gear cable, two punctures and three bike changes could not stop National Junior Championship runner-up Dave Cartwright (Velo Club Central) from winning the Risca C.C. cyclo-cross after lapping all but two of the rest of the field." Another headline in Cycling from Wales during this period was: "Crowd Puller Mick Romps in Welsh Mud" recording the win by Mick Ives (Mottram/Simplex) in the Newport Phoenix C.C. event. A record number of 40 riders had competed in front of a good-sized crowd from South Wales.

The B.C-C.A archives have a programme from an event in Holland from this period, which clearly shows the difference between European and British programmes. The Dutch one is printed with three colours on the cover and 28 pages, but the main difference is the numbers of advertisers, 53 in all, were happy to buy space in this production. It may have been a smart programme but John Atkins outsmarted all the Dutch riders to win, with Maurice Broadbent 10th although Roger Page was not able to finish. Then the next day, John Atkins was seventh in another event at Wassenaar in Holland.

"Foot & Mouth Halted" reads an unidentified newspaper headline now held in the B.C-C.A archives. During this season the Midland Area Championships were called off, although those in the North and South still went ahead. However, the Foot and Mouth outbreak swept south and after weeks of preparation by the organisers all came to nothing for the new National Amateur Daily Telegraph sponsored Championships. A disappointing day for both the Royal Navy, Portsmouth and particularly David Saunders of *The Daily Telegraph* who had planned this event for the 4th February. It was also disappointing for the 81 riders who had their entries returned, although there was still hope of restaging on February 11th

The Championships were indeed restaged and John Otway writing in *Sporting Cyclist* presented some statistics of the ride by John Atkins in the National Championships that were to have been at H.M.S. Dryad near Portsmouth. The course was changed to Highbury Park, Kings Heath, Birmingham. John won from Dave Wren with John Barnes (Morden C.R.C) third, but these plain facts do not show the underlining skills, which John Otway goes on to describe: "During Atkins winning ride he covered 22 laps in 55 minutes and he had to deal with an amazing 132 obstacles. His lap times show he was riding like a metronome; he covered all but one lap between 2m.38s and 2m.50s so to cover 21 laps, all within 12 seconds is breathtaking in precision..... The dense crowd were treated to a fine display of bike handling as Atkins bobbed and weaved his way, lapping rider after rider." Thanks for the quick change in venue was due to the dedication and energy of Ray Richards B.C-C.A President, David Saunders of *The Daily Telegraph* and the Birmingham Parks Dept. who completed the adaptation in such short time. There were many moans from the riders about the course being too small, both before the event and afterwards. The course, specially designed for live T.V. coverage, was only 800 yards per lap and the smallest ever used for a championship.

Over this period, various riders such as Atkins, Wren, Page, Shakespeare and Mernickle went on raiding parties to France and Belgium, unfortunately with little success. They put it down to gaining experience against the numerous excellent riders and different courses in both these countries.

This season the World Championships were also divided into Professional and Amateur Categories for the first time. Cycling's editorial staff were not happy with the result of the Amateur World Championships this year, producing this banner headline: "PROS WIN BOTH PURE AND PAID 'CROSS TITLES".

They went on to cover the races by praising Renato Longo as an "acknowledged Professional" but described the winner of the Amateur race as - "Michel Pelchat, a French senior amateur riding for Kamome-Wolber and one of last year's pros, he proved far too good and experienced for the amateurs." Further on, the magazine lambasts the UCI with this piece: "The dithering and dallying at the UCI seems to continue in this business of professionals, senior amateurs and amateurs, with the Frenchman Michel Pelchat holding the limelight in Zurich as a glaring example of a 'shamateur.' Riding as a professional in last year's Cross season, he reverted to senior amateur when everything was changed around; a licence which gives him the best of both worlds – he can ride against pros or amateurs". The castigation of the U.C.I went on: "This was Saturday night, the day before the championships, and the deliberation of the so-called wise ones was lengthy indeed. Eventually the answer came through that the protest had been turned down and that he was classified as an amateur, a more ridiculous thing one could not imagine."

West Germany, Switzerland and even the French amateur members were unhappy with this UCI decision, with the Swiss commentating: "He got 600 francs for riding an event at Hanover only two weeks ago." So no one was very happy at the result, least of all the British press.

But when it came to the result of the Professional event Cycling praised Longo's ride as "you could run out of superlatives to describe his smooth, almost effortless performance over this terribly hard quagmire of a course." Longo won the Professional rainbow jersey with Rolf Wolfshohl in second at a devastating 3 minutes 49 seconds and even further back in the bronze medal position was Hermann Gretener at 9 minutes 14 seconds. Mick Ives was the first of the British riders in 19th position and Keith Mernickle 20th the last two to finish, although in their favour many other riders had already retired. Their places do not tell the whole story, for Mernickle had to make an amazing number of 32 bike changes, being continually clogged up with the sticky mud, his leg was deeply cut, which only stopped bleeding because of the mud covering the wound. The all-engulfing mud covered both of the G.B. riders up to their eyeballs andcontinually clogged their gears.

The Amateurs also had to face heavy rain and a biting wind as they battled the same course. Pelchat won the Rainbow Jersey, (as previously mentioned), and was followed home by the Belgian J. Van den Haezevelde for silver, with the Swiss P. Frischknecht in third. Once again it was a tale of woe for the British, with Atkins in 20th place having to run the last mile with his gear in shreds. Our only other rider to cross under the finish banner was Dave Wren, 13 minutes after Pelchat finished. Roger Page was beaten by the course, which was two-thirds ankle deep in mud, and was beset by other problems. Maurice Broadbent having pushed himself to the limit collapsed with exhaustion and was carried off the circuit, no more could be asked of a rider than to ride to his limit for his country. Dave Wren did at least prove his worth as a team member after all the previous controversy and his inclusion had been worthwhile. A footnote to this result is that the British team came 10th out of 15 teams, beating such as Holland and Poland, but were listed as "England".

As a last comment on this season, there was a noticeable increase in cyclo-cross coverage in the cycling press. It can best be illustrated in copies of Cycling during the first nine weeks of 1967, where the sport dominated the front covers, with either full-page photographs or several photographs and a race report. These were indeed heady days for cyclo-cross in both words and pictures. Would the British riders also up their standards during the last part of the 1960s?

8

'King' Atkins reigns, as the Association fights for recognition

Season 1967/68

In August the sport would hear of a tragic accident, which was reported in The *Coventry Evening Telegraph*: "Young Cycling Star Dies after a Coventry road accident. Barrie Elson, one of Britain's most promising racing cyclists died in the Coventry and Warwickshire Hospital today. Barry became Schoolboy National Cyclo Cross Champion last December. In August 1966 Barry was acclaimed in Dutch newspapers after he won the 'Tour of West Brabant' – he was captain of the team that won the team event." The sport had therefore lost, not only a present champion but also a star of the future.

The new handbook priced at 1/6d (7½p) had a plain black and white cover, but otherwise was of the same familiar style and contents. John Marshman was elected to the post of Membership Secretary, K.E. Bonner became Handbook Secretary and Neville Billington took on the task of International Racing Secretary. Race programmes were taking on a more professional look, with many including photographs of prominent riders, such as the South of England Championships that had four pages of photographs.

Bob Mansell, an energetic promoter, staged this year's Schoolboys Championship round the playing fields of Oldbury Technical School. This took place on December 3rd and among the 141 entries were no fewer than 17 from Foxwood School. Jeff Clayton, their schoolmaster, had entered them but much of his hard work came to nought, when one of their buses broke down on the way to the event. It is not clear whether all the boys lined up in a mini 'light brigade charge' to start the event or in age groups. A fine photograph in *Sporting Cyclist* show the boys lined out across the starting area charging over the first grassy hill. The winner, Alex Hook of Daventry School, was a prominent force throughout.

John Atkins (Coventry R.C) was dominating the headlines in both the cycling press and national papers, here are just a few - "Atkins Again 'Cross Master" - "Atkins Clinches Viking Trophy" - "John Atkins is Undisputed King of British Cyclo Cross" - "Little John Caught Big Roger" - "Who Else But Atkins?" He didn't have everything his own way, although it is certainly true that the Midland riders were dominant at this time. Roger Page often being his nearest challenger, as this excerpt from Cycling shows: "After 14 laps, all of them at the front, 30 year old Page forged ahead on the last lap, when Atkins failed to get his feet in the toe-clips to give his father, who was watching, a fine birthday present." It was not only Midland seniors who were dominating, for by November this year 15 year old Chris Dodd had already won six schoolboy races.

John Otway reported in *Sporting Cyclist* during December: "Energetic organisers like Neville Billington, and Ray Richards in the Midlands and Ralph Jordon and Johnny Morris in London, have worked hard to put on events that make interesting and equitable competition for the contestants … Neville Billington opened the season proper at Bromsgrove with his Beacon R.C.C. race that attracted a team from the Cologne Police Sports Society. Although these visitors hardly set the race alight."

Ralph Jordon promoted the Edgeware Two-Day, (three stage) race, which included a 36-mile handicap stage on Saturday; Sunday morning was a three-mile Time Trial and Sunday afternoon the final stage. The whole weekend of racing took place in appalling weather conditions and after this endeavour Keith Mernickle won by only 24 seconds.

Falcon Cycles based at Smethwick presented a new trophy for the Schoolboy Cyclo-Cross Championships. A paragraph from a letter in the archives outlines the reasons:"We, ourselves, are extremely pleased at this venture and feel that by sponsoring these young boys we have some champions of the future in the making."

"Since the inception of a cyclo-cross title for the Junior ranks there could hardly be a more convincing champion than 16 year old Chris Dodd of the Coventry Road Club, for the manner in which this lithely-built youngster used his strength all the way through this eight-mile championship was truly remarkable". This was the description of the winner's performance given by Cycling in January. Another remarkable fact was that Dodd was also a team-mate of Senior Champion, John Atkins and this meant that for the first time both Junior and Senior titles were held by the same club.

New sponsors were coming forward, some were more interested in sponsoring road racing but others were happy that their riders would get exposure in cyclo-cross. Companies showing their logos on jerseys in cyclo-cross at this time were; Ryall-Weldwork, Carlton/BMB, Broadhurst Biscuits, Bantel/Mercian, Falcon Cycles, Young Cycles, and Fred Baker. The A.T.V. cameras were out in force to record Trevor Bull winning the Staffordshire Grand Prix, his first event in the colours of Sun Cycles. Well known names also riding this event were Arthur Metcalf (Carlton/BMB) a Tour de France finisher and Six-Day rider Billy Holmes, just back from racing on the boards of Montreal and London.

In the very last edition of the influential magazine *Sporting Cyclist* there is an article on the 1968 Amateur National Championships. It recorded John Atkins winning the white jersey with the red and blue bands across the chest for the fifth time. He also led his club team (Coventry RC) to an outstanding win, when they packed three into the first six. Darryl Brassington was placed fifth and junior Chris Dodds was sixth. Second overall was Roger Page of the Edgbaston Road Club, with Dave Wren coming in third, riding for the Edgware R.C. The event was organised on the Crystal Palace circuit by the energetic Johnny Morris.

The second Professional Championships brought this comment: "Ives success was something of a surprise but even more unexpected, was the relegation of last year's champion Keith Mernickle (Ryall/ Weldwork) to third place by 'Goz' Goodman (Carlton Cycles) who, riding in only his third cyclo-cross event, finished second." This was how *The Daily Telegraph* saw the struggle for the top three places in the Professional Title race. Mick Ives had therefore added yet another victory to his growing list of palmarès, having already gained successes in Grass Track, Pursuit, and Team Pursuit.

The riders picked to represent Great Britain this year at the Amateur World Championships in Luxemburg were John Atkins, Roger Page, Dave Nie and Dave Wren. Roger De Vlaeminck (Bel) won, followed by the Swiss rider Peter Frischknecht and third was Cornelis van der Hulst from Holland. The British placings were John Atkins fifth, at only 14 seconds (still the best ever placing by a Briton in a Senior World Championships), Roger Page 14th, Dave Nie 31st and Dave Wren unable to finish. Afterwards, Atkins was picked to give a sample at the dope control. Keith Edwards, the team manager, described Roger Page's ride as "The ride of his life", because he was riding very strongly until he had mechanical trouble on the last lap so losing places.

A clean sweep of the weekend by the De Vlaeminck brothers came when Eric won the Professional event on the Sunday. Eric was completely dominant throughout, winning from previous champion Rolf Wolfshohl (W.Germany) and Herman Gretener (Swiss). The Pro's were lapping a minute faster than the amateurs. Mick Ives finished in 23rd place, Keith Mernickle 27th with Mick Coward 28th. Coward was also picked to report to dope control and both Atkins and Coward were declared clean in the results. It is interesting to reflect on the team manager's report on the riders' behaviour: "The morale, humour and discipline of the team were exemplary at all times, and I had no cause to complain about their disposition or conduct. Mernickle went to bed when he was told, and Wren even asked permission to go shopping." An aside to Mick Ives's performance is that his father had died just an hour before the team manager collected him. However he put his mind to the task of representing his country to good effect after the first 24hrs. The manager was Ralph Jordon, with mechanics (three Pits)- Ken Banner, Ralph Digges, and Dick Braderick.

As indicated before, the sport of cyclo-cross has always had a reputation for some strange race titles, but this year some were very strange indeed. For example 'The Tour of the Deanery', 'The Circuit of the Duckpond', 'Tour of the Sinderland Woods', 'Circuit of Nico Ditch' and last but not least, 'The Fisheries Do'.

Season 1968/69

The season started with a Schoolboys event at Halesowen in September, also on the programme was a senior event and a mixture of grass track events from 220 yards to 10 miles, although none of the grass track riders appeared to take the opportunity to try the cross races or vice-versa.

More changes in officials were outlined in the new handbook, top of the list was that Joe Dickenson became Chairman and Johnny Morris took the new post of Press and P.R.O. The handbook had for the first time a photograph of a rider on the cover, National Amateur Champion John Atkins. The price had increased to two shillings (10p) but it was still a very modest production at 32 pages.

Still organised by the inaugurator, John Rawnsley, The Three Peaks remained a uniquely hard event. Riders still had to scale the peaks of Whernside (2,414ft), Pen-Y-Ghent (2,273ft) and Ingleborough at 2,373 ft. Although these may be the highest peaks, also thrown in to sap the strength of the competitors were Horton-in-Ribblesdale at 750ft, Chapel-le-Dale (777ft) and Ribblehead a little higher at 1,000ft. Such an awesome challenge is this event that competitors were instructed: "Competitors who retire from the race MUST report to the nearest marshal."

A new publication, *International Cycle Sport*, devoted four pages to this race entitled "Follow the leader over the Three Peaks. ....This early winter classic of the cyclo-cross brigade has gained a fearsome reputation for toughness in its eight years of existence – and after watching the 1968 version I agree that it is in a category on its own. You can imagine how rugged the 26 mile route is by the fact that winner Tom McDonald (Keighley S.C) took over three hours, while the last of the 35 finishers went round in over 6 hours!" Tom McDonald actually took 3 hours 7 minutes 51 seconds, with Brian Hawes (Hemsworth Wheelers) nearly four minutes back, after a close finish with multi-winner Harry Bond at one more second. This year there were 60 entries of which 46 started and only 35 completed the course. Keighley Velo rider D. Horsman was the oldest finisher at 40, and the first team was the Bradford R.C.C. of H.Bond, J.Rawnsley and Harry's brother Sid Bond.

In September John Atkins finally turned professional, with Marsh & Baxter gaining his signature. He only had to wait until October for his first win in the Beacon R.C.C. event held at Chadwick Grange, he also had the added pleasure of being the conqueror of the top class Belgian visitor, Rene De Clerq, in the process.

On 6th October the Beacon Roads Cycling Club, promoted a special race to commemorate the 100 years since the running of the very first cycle race, which was held at Saint Cloud, Paris, in May 1868. Incidentally, on that same day in the very next race (the second ever), James Moore of Paris (although he was born in England at Bury St. Edmunds in Suffolk) became the very first Englishman to win a cycle race. It was the Beacon Roads seventh annual event and involved yet another newspaper, The Bromsgrove Messenger. The programme listed the competitors as: "Schoolboys, Juniors, Non-Experts and Experts."

On December 2nd *The Times*, no less, printed four large pictures of the National Schoolboys Championship held at the Scouts Association, Gilwell Park, Chingford with the headline "Mudlarks At The Schoolboy Cyclo-Cross." One of the excellent photos showed boys laughing at a rider who had tumbled from his bike into a ditch full of mud, while other competitors raced past. Longslade School of Newbury were delighted with the result for not only did their Peter Williams win the event but they also won the team award. Fifteen year old Williams won the National jersey after having only ridden four other 'cross events and didn't even own a pair of cycling shorts. Once more the coverage in the cycling press was excellent, with *Cycling and Sporting Cyclist* having almost two full pages and four photographs covering this event. There were so many entries, 154, that there was a need for three heats and the surviving 60 riders went on to contest the final, from which Williams emerged the winner. Eric Smith of Beauchamps School rode to silver, while Neale Jauncey of Arden High took the bronze. *Cycling and Sporting Cyclist* reported that his schoolmaster ran up to him at the finish shouting: "Now they can't ignore cyclo-cross at school. We're going to hang your National jersey in the school hall, cross is going to be the sport at Longslade!" In a different vein, this year cyclo-cross was chosen as one of the sports for boys in Approved Schools. Two schools had fielded teams with the boys riding a motley assortment of machines and an appeal was made for club people to donate spare equipment.

The Solihull C.C. were in trouble for cancelling a time trial without notifying the R.T.T.C (Midland District), and were suspended from promoting any events. They appealed against the ban, because as it was so complete, the Club could not promote either road races or cyclo-crosses. The Club's Chairman, Ray Richards told Mike Price of *Cycling and Sporting Cyclist*: "We have admitted the offence, but we are fighting the severity of the sentence." The club were due to promote the final race in the Viking Trophy Series on the same day as the appeal hearing but Richards managed to get the date of the appeal moved, so that the event could continue without the threat.

During December, the County of Suffolk saw a wide mix of cycling talents come together at the Bungay (Godric CC) event on the 'Broom Course'. The winner Vaughan Read (East Anglian C.C.) and his team-mates were also the club's 12-hour Roller racing team. Other competitors were Brian Harper (Godric C.C.) who had only been beaten in this event once in six years and Tony Calver (ex Tour of Britain rider).

North of England events in December continued to be dominated by Harry Bond (Bradford R.C.C.) In the North of England Championships, it was Bond who produced yet another win in this event, which was held on the tough Cliffe Castle Park Circuit in Keighley. The promoting club, the Keighley St Christopher's CCC was supported by their main sponsors *International Cycle Sport* magazine. It was Bond's sixth win in nine years; he also led the winning team with the Rawnsley brothers to the outstanding result of nine consecutive wins. Behind Bond came T.Wignall (Southport R.C.C.) and in third place P. Farnworth (Horwich

C.C.). Other Championship winners this year were John Atkins, Midland Champion, who by Boxing Day had topped up his professional wins to nineteen. Down south it was Keith Mernickle who recorded a second hat trick in the Southern Championships.

During Mid December, Alan Gayfer, the editor of *Cycling and Sporting Cyclist* published a scathing attack on the B.C.F in an article entitled "Growing – but bogged down".

> There is much talk at the moment of a decline in the sport … Yet we are in the middle of a period of staggering growth, for one association of cyclists can hardly keep pace with events, with overseas travel, with its own growth – and gets ignored into the bargain! It's the British Cyclo-Cross Association of course, which is doing all this, and which has just seen its chances of organising the World Cyclo-Cross championships at the Crystal Palace in 1970 go by the board without a B.C.F voice lifted to save them. As CYCLING understands it, despite assurances and insistences that the BCF would continue to press for the cyclo-cross to be in Britain in the same year as the road and track championships, when the crunch came Britain's name was simply not put forward to the UCI congress which met in Geneva a week or two back. The B.C-C.A could not of course put its own case, since the BCF is in sole charge of all these international goings-on and apparently did not really care about the issue at stake, so long as its "own" championships, those on road and track were safeguarded. … All of which seems scandalous in a world where cyclo-cross is becoming a more and more effective means of propaganda for our sport, and a very good way of introducing youngsters to it. In granting the B.C-C.A £400 more for the running of the sport, the Government recognised its place in British cycling, but insisted that coaching work should be done through the national coaching scheme.

It took over a year for the BCF to give in to the principle that Keith Edwards could sit on their coaching committee. Then the B.C.F decided that they would change the rules after he had attended only one meeting!

The article goes on to outline that B.C-C.A had 240 clubs signed up, making about 2,000 members, enjoying cyclo-cross: "'We don't need to publish expensive advertising pamphlets to push our sport,' says Ray Richards, the live-wire Secretary of the Association. 'The kids just seem to love it, and come running'." So it turned out that the B.C-C.A could not get on the Cycling Council of Great Britain, only the B.C.F, R.T.T.C and the C.T.C were invited, despite the fact that the B.C-C.A ran events from September through to March every season. He then continued: "For six years in the B.C-C.A constitution they've had written in a paragraph (p.275 B.C.F Handbook) saying that the Association representatives were entitled to attend meetings of the B.C.F racing committee when the selection of an international cyclo-cross team or any of the significant matter concerning cyclo-cross is under consideration - six years in which they've been invited to not a single meeting. Frankly we find the B.C.F backward in its thinking throughout, only too ready to jump on our bandwagon just when we seem to be exciting the interest – how can we make real progress like this?" So from this we can deduce that the B.C.F were quite happy to have cyclo-cross bring many newcomers into the sport of cycling, so long as their officials did not want to rise above themselves and join in making the rules or decisions.

International Cycle Sport carried an interesting advert for cyclo-cross equipment by W.F.Holdsworth Ltd. Their advert declares: "Follow the lead of Dave Nie the Holdsworth Cyclo Cross Expert". This was next to a picture of the rider looking rather muddy after an event. There then followed a list of specialist 'cross' equipment such as Kowalit tubulars at two qualities, 50/- (£2-50p) and 39/6 (£1.97½p) Campag Special Cross Chain Sets, Lyotard Alloy (long thread) Pedals, Barum 'T' Tread and Studded Tread Tubulars and Patent Leather Crash Hats for 33/9 (£1.70p). Demonstrating that more and more companies were manufacturing products for the expanding 'cross' market.

On Boxing Day ice and snow played a big part in the racing, as every rider had to pick the correct place to attack. *Cycling & Sporting Cyclist* noted the slippery conditions thus: "Spectators suffered as much as some competitors on the ice, and often a shout of 'rider up' would be followed by a cry of 'spectator down'." But the ice did not stop John Atkins picking up his 19th win in the colours of Marsh & Baxter, tall Roger Page came in second, with Keith Mernickle (Ryall- Weldwork) slipping and sliding into third.

Even top class professionals, such as Keith Mernickle, can have spectacular spills. One of these was in the Becontree Wheelers event in early January, as this report in *Cycling and Sporting Cyclist* records: "Expertise, though, didn't protect him from the swampy ditch when he, bike and a little yellow hat parted company and landed in reverse order in the mud." However despite this mishap Mernickle's class meant that he recovered sufficiently to win by 2 mins 16 secs

This winter the Inter-Regional Team Championship was held at Saffron Lane, Leicester. 41 riders were divided into seven teams and raced for the honours on a new "Continental style course". Spectators had an elevated walkway and refreshments were served throughout the day (a new concept), this proved ideal for families and spectators alike.

The face of John Atkins seemed to be a regular feature in the press, smiling out from the front covers of Cycling almost every week during January this year. He well deserved all the praise he received, for he clinched the Viking Trophy Series yet again. Although cyclo-cross has and hopefully never will be, just about the big names and events, important as they are, at grassroots level the races go on. Some of the winners at this time being Mick Florence (Edgbaston R.C.) at the Cwmcarn Paragon event, John Rawnsley (Bradford R.C.C.) won the Sheffield Highgate C.C. race in South Yorkshire, then up in Renfrewshire a heavy snow fall cut the numbers and Tommy Church (St. Christopher's C.C.) was to sprint home just 3 seconds ahead of last year's winner, Jim Leek of the Glasgow R.C. In Wales, it was Tim Gunning (Newport Ph.) who produced a home win for the Principality in the Abercynon R.C. event.

Meanwhile back in England, National Junior Champion Chris Dodd retained his Junior Title at Hessle, which was promoted by the Humber Velo, with the promoting club's duo of Dave Goddard and B.Dixon riding to the silver and bronze medals.

John Atkins (Marsh & Baxter) suffered a rare defeat to Roger Page (Solihull C.C.) and Mick Ives (Bantel-Mercian) in the South Pennine promotion at the Scout camp at Little Eaton, Derbyshire. The course was not to Atkins liking due to the absence of obstacles, added to that he slipped on the first lap, which threw him against a wall, then he also punctured, so it was just not his day this time.

For the first time both the Professional and Amateur titles were sponsored by *the Daily Telegraph* and they were held on the same day, Saturday 1st February, at Allesley Park, Coventry. 18 professionals were on the start sheet showing that more sponsors were coming forward, keen to have their names in front of the cycling public. Some of the pro's listed were wearing the names of these new sponsors such as Larry Rose (Stimson Cycles), Barry Davis (Sports Motors), John Aslin (Carlton-Truwell-Campag), Roger Newton (Holdsworth-Campag), M.Curtis (Whisker Cycles) and a rider well known from the road race side of the sport was Albert Hitchin (Falcon), there were also two unsponsored riders Brian Sandy and Fred Gardiner. Ron Atkins, the organiser, was well pleased with the professional entry judging by his remark in *Cycling & Sporting Cyclist*: "Still, the critics said we wouldn't even get six to ride."

The Professional winner was John Atkins (Marsh & Baxter) his first win in this category, despite a broken hand! Second was Keith Mernickle (Ryall-Weldwork) and in third place Mick Ives (Bantel-Mercian). Cycling described the race thus: "It had been threatening to rain all day and then just as the professionals rode the last lap it tumbled down, but nobody noticed as they and Coventry had experienced a well organised, excellent day of 'cross racing. After the racing had finished, the selectors met to pick the team for the World's at Magstaadt in West Germany. It was then they discovered that John Atkins had a broken hand, and so although he was selected he was unable to take part." Disappointing for Marsh & Baxter, who had had the idea of sending him to Belgium for three weeks, to train and race in preparation.

A headline in *Cycling and Sporting Cyclist* early in the New Year shouted: "Handbrake on World Championship". It told of the misfortune that had happened to John Atkins, the picture accompanying the article, shows a smiling Atkins with his hand in plaster. "I am still managing to train at the moment, but of course I cannot tackle hurdles." This put doubts as to whether he could take part in the World Championships this year.

Of the 80 Amateurs, the surprise winner was Barry Moss (Solihull C.C), with team mate Roger Page following him over the line to take second and Eric Stone (Matlock C.C.) taking the bronze medal. Solihull C.C. took the team award with third counter D. Boyle. In the race programme Keith Edwards praised sports writer David Saunders for all his newspaper columns, as a cycling T.V. and Radio commentator and how he had worked hard to bring about the B.C-C.A/Daily Telegraph alliance.

An interesting press cutting in the B.C-C.A archives, by Barry Moss, recorded his view of the above Amateur Championships (there is no attribution to the source of the cutting) partly reproduced here.

I anticipated that the Mayor would drop the flag after Ray Richards had finished broadcasting us our last minute instructions, but he delayed and I lost my balance and had lost valuable yards when the flag finally dropped - I didn't pass anyone on the run but remounted quickly and passed Roger and several others during the next 200 yards of the first hurdle...running was the one thing which was likely to go against me for selection so I decided to demonstrate that my hill running had done its work. I swept past Roger, remounted quickly, rode hard to the hurdle ... I had dropped the race certainty! I felt sorry to rob Roger of the championship which he so richly deserved but I had a few disappointments myself during the past seven years racing... I entered the finishing straight and crossed the line arms aloft in jubilation.

This snippet from the article gives an insight into how the top riders thought, for although each wanted to win, they felt great respect for each other's abilities.

The headlines covering the report of the World Championships this year in *Cycling & Sporting Cyclist* sound very upbeat: "Unawed by Continent, Mernickle fights back: Stone and Baker try so hard they need a doctor!" These were not the thoughts of Johnny Morris, the G.B. team Manger, for he came out at the finish with these statements: "They saw they weren't going to get the places they dreamed of, and became dispirited – and that doesn't make a rider into a world champion. ... For next season, we should train harder and try harder, I think you have to train for this as though for a kermesse, and keep all-round fit."

So no medals once more for the British, Eric De Vlaeminck (Belg.) won from Rolf Wolfshohl (W.Ger.) with Renato Longo (Ita) third. Keith Mernickle got the worst of all starts, when another rider's pedal caught in his wheel and lifted him and his machine off the ground, but Mernickle fought back to such good effect that he was finished 12th. Atkins could only finish a brave 19th still suffering from his broken hand.

In the Amateur event it was left to the trio of great Belgians to show just how it should be done, with Rene Declerq winning from Roger De Vlaeminck, although in a cyclo-cross race nothing is certain until it's over, for with just 500 yards to go De Vlaeminck 's chain unshipped and he was left to watch his team-mate take the laurels. In the bronze place came Bert Vermeire. The British amateurs had their own tale of woe, for although the British Champion Barry Moss showed his colours when in third spot near the head of the race, over the first rise he faded and finally abandoned. Roger Page fared no better, never keeping with the fast pace set by the Belgians and could only finish 34th. Martyn Baker and Eric Stone were now our only hope but despite trying hard, they both collapsed after crossing the line, a doctor was rushed to help but they soon recovered. So despite the gutsy effort by Mernickle it was to be another blank day at the World's.

Soon we will leave the 'Swinging Sixties' behind and move into a new era, the B.C-C.A. was now strong, with a large number of affiliated clubs. The professional class was established and very active, and there were now championships for Professionals, Seniors, Juniors and Juveniles, and the standard of promotions had improved ready to face the new decade.

9

Into the 1970s

Season 1969/70

As we approach the new decade the handbook remains a modest production with only 40 pages. It has a new style cover with the title and B.C-C.A badge, white out of black, with a picture of a rider racing towards the camera. Membership Secretary was R. Bull, and John Marshman moved jobs to become Handbook Secretary. Very few adverts were included but each was directly related to the world of cycling. One suspects they were placed more as support for the B.C-C.A, than for purely commercial reasons. It was a welcome sight to see the number of events increasing this year to a very substantial 130.

A quick look through the rules shows that Annual Affiliations remained the same and entry fees still included a minimum levy of 6d (2½p) per rider. Rules worth mentioning - "The entry fee for National Championships shall not exceed 5/- (25p)." Rule 29 was slightly changed to tighten up on advertising, "Amateur riders, as defined by the National Joint Council of the B.C.F and R.T.T.C. will not be allowed to display advertising on their racing attire." Under the title 'Drugs and Stimulants', the same three lines of rules continued to be used, "Riders are warned that action will be taken by the executive committee under Rule 16 against any rider found guilty of taking substances likely to affect his competitive performance". The reference to Rule 16 is not at all clear, as that rule covered such things as: "The law of the land relating to Road Travel", and "Road Race regulations of the Road Traffic Act 1956." Maybe it just shows how it was thought unlikely that any British riders would cheat by using artificial help.

During November, Eric Stone was asked to appear before the B.C.F. racing committee to answer charges that his photograph had appeared in a Derby newspaper wearing advertising for Dawes Cycles. There had been rumours for a time that the Matlock C.C. rider would turn professional for that company. After the meeting, the B.C.F. recommended that he should be declared 'a professional'.

This month the Bantel rider Mick Ives had his sixth and seventh wins from only eight starts, with two in one day. The first was in the Molyneux event at Newton-le-Willows where, after battling for the whole race against Barry Davies (Sports Motors/ Manchester) and V.C. Central's Martyn Baker, he came out the winner. He then made a high-speed dash over the Pennines to compete in the Huddersfield Star Wheelers race at Castle Hill, where he won again, this time from Eric Stone, still Matlock C.C.

Velo Club Electric, backed by The Evening Chronicle were the promoters and sponsors of the November edition of the Viking Trophy, which was held at Wallsend. It was advertised as having a £90 prize list with a very fast course. An event that continued in the old tradition of 'Cyclists v Harriers' was the annual promotion by the East Surrey Road Club. Held during November, the winner this year was a cyclist Tony Barlett (Tooting B.C), the first cyclist to win this event since 1965.

An unusual advert in Cycling from Keith Mernickle's sponsors announced, "Keith Mernickle now rides for Chris Barber - Go and see Keith and go and see The Band." A report in the same magazine about the Forty Hall Scramble detailed some of its more interesting course details: "With 33 river crossings on the eleven laps of this fast North London course, it is no wonder that the crowds come to gasp and cheer. This year the Wembley and Enfield Road Club, who promote the event will be adding a short run-up to make it still more spectacular."

Other reports included "Coventry amateur Daryl Brassington joined an elite band of crossmen, 'The Atkins Beaters', when he won the first Viking Trophy race." The second report covered an award to Ron Atkins, "Another national honour has come the way of Coventry's famous cycling family, the Atkins. This time it is Ron, and not his son John, who is on the receiving end. He is one of nine people selected to receive an Olympic Style Torch Trophy for sport at club level over many years. Ron Atkins, who joined Coventry R.C. 35 yrs ago, has been a rider, official and promoter for most of his 52 years. His last big promotion was the 1969 Cyclo-Cross Championships, and he is a founder member and treasurer of the B.C-C.A." Said a modest Ron "It is particularly happy for me that the sport of Cyclo-Cross has got this award."

Another unsung worker for the B.C-C.A. could be seen shaking his collection box at events this season, for the 'World Championship Fund'.

This was Ralph (known as Digger) Digges, a Division coach and member of the Crescent Wheelers; the result of his efforts was that he collected £8 for the fund at the Beacon event.

International Cycle Sport magazine produced a batch of posters to give away free to organisers, they featured a photograph of cyclo-cross riders with the ICS advert on the bottom with a large space for organisers to advertise their own events. These posters were seen pinned up on trees advertising the event at Shirley Hills. The magazine sent reporter Arthur Wright to this race, on a very cold day in November. His report gave the real flavour of a cyclo-cross event:

> They'd got up a good head of steam at the café by the time we arrived. It was hissing from the tea-urn with the force of a power station exhaust. Brisk business was already being done. In the tidy car parks a variety of transport was drawn up with military precision and the crews were unshipping frames and wheels from the roof racks. Near at hand, event official Harry Lancaster stood by his table in the open like a man with a stall in Kingston Market. … Little boys in racing caps and mini track-suits, wives and girl friends in mini-skirts, tufted poodles in coats, all part of Sunday morning at Shirley. … Sharing my tree-trunk were Redmon men Bill Hens and Ed Warner. Cycle mechanics, both of them. They worked really hard this Sunday morning, straightening handlebars and brake levers and picking up fallen riders for the fun of it. Bill pulled a buckled alloy sprint into something like wobbly truth, bending it over his knee.

Arthur was vividly describing what had been happening at cyclo-cross venues up and down the country from the mid 1950s onwards.

Another article looked into the problems of youngsters riding against top competition. "Pity the schoolboy with a 16th birthday part way through the season. One week he is riding in an event against his own calibre, lasting twenty to thirty minutes! Seven days later he faces Atkins in a race that could last an hour or more."

Neil Orrell remembered this year's *International Cycle Sport* Trophy (in the N.W.C-C.A Annual of 95/96) with the following description: "Stone laps the field, leading from start to finish, Eric Stone (Tower Cycles) won Sunday's Pignut Hill Cyclo-cross. …From 40 starters he took an immediate lead with Barry Davies (Denton CRC) Mick Shakespeare (Solihull C.C) and Ray Barker of Bantel. …With three miles to go he had lapped the field, and finished with a little less than a minute and a half lead."

The wide experience of Keith Mernickle was to prove decisive in the Bagshot Scramble, which he won by a clear 30 seconds. However the Smirnoff Scramble this season was to fall for the first time, to multi-winner John Atkins (Marsh & Baxter). In doing so John had to hold off the challenge of Vermeire, the Flemish rider, who the previous year had finished third in the Amateur World Championships. The riders were not the only ones tested at this event, for the promoters and their helpers were hit by a cloudburst while preparing the course and as they struggled to dismantle the same course, were attacked by freezing showers of sleet, demonstrating that a marshal's job is not always a happy one.

Young amateur Chris Dodd appeared on the front cover of Cycling magazine twice within a few weeks, first on Nov 29th where he is shown racing ahead of both Harry Bond and John Atkins, then, in another edition, racing alone. The professionals proved to be the top riders in the Area Championships, by winning all the titles over the first weekend in December. The Midland edition was won by the almost unstoppable John Atkins (Marsh & Baxter) with Coventry riders Mick Ives (Bantel) and Daryl Brassington (Coventry R.C.) in second and third; this result would have graced any national title race. The promotion was generously sponsored by Berry-Magicoal, which enabled the race to have an excellent programme, with black and white photographs reproduced on good class paper, a real step up from the old style programmes. The Northern title went to Barry Davies (Sports Motors-Tower Cycles) ahead of amateurs Harry Bond (Bradford R.C.C.) and Tom McDonald (Keighley St.Chris.) For the Southern title Keith Mernickle (Chris Barber-Sun) won from fellow Professional Dave Nie (Holdsworth/Campag.) and top amateur Dave Wren of the Edgeware Road Club. Sixty-three entered for the Midland event and fifty- six for the Northern race showing that these events were still popular with the riders.

An event at Bungay, during December, produced a letter in Cycling under this headline: "Undercover!"

Reading Mick Gambling's report of the cyclo-cross at Bungay, it struck me as significant that this event was not listed in the B.C-C.A. handbook nor published in your 'What's on' yet a fair field seems to have started. I can see only two clubs mentioned who are paid up members of the B.C-C.A, which leaves seven non-member clubs. Is there a rival underground 'cross organisation in Norfolk?"

John Marshman (Membership Sec. B.C-C.A.)

This letter brings a smile, as Norfolk got the blame for this promotion by the Bungay club, which is in fact a Suffolk club!

The New Year saw 75 juniors line up for their championships at the Wolverhampton venue of Aldersley Stadium for a 55-minute race.

"Junior title looks open – but Barry Dixon could have edge" was a headline in Cycling magazine the week before the Junior Championships. But another rider had other ideas, as *The Daily Telegraph* pointed out, the new winner of the National Junior Championships, "Peter Williams (Longslade School C.C) became the first rider to take two major cyclo-cross titles of different categories". After being the schoolboy champion last year, he was now the new Junior Champion. Williams was followed home by the pre-race favourite B. Dixon (Humber Velo C.C.) and B.O'Hare (Birchfield C.C.) who took third place. The Wolverhampton Wheelers promoted the event and despite a very hard fast race, 49 youngsters finished.

A Cycling article by Johnny Morris, the B.C-C.A. Press & P.R.O, championed the cause of racing abroad thus: "For anyone living within fifty miles of the ferry it's almost as easy to go and race in Belgium as it is to travel to the other side of England. Certainly from London it's no further and only a little more costly to race abroad than it would be to drive down the Bath Road to Bristol or South Wales."

He went on to tell of a trip with three others to ride events near Ghent in Belgium. Describing the challenges these events posed he said, "The difference lay in the riders, who would fight for every inch of space rather than let you pass." and this is one of the courses he describes. "This time the course was more what we had expected to find in this land of Eddy Merckx. It went through a farmyard, a cabbage field, a turnip field, and along a bit of road then through another farm and along a road to the finish." However in this event they were disqualified. Why? Because the judge told them –"Gentlemen, on Belgium territory you may not ride without a crash-hat!" The moral of this story must be to check race rules in other countries before leaving these shores.

Mick Ives took full advantage of John Atkins suffering a bout of 'flu during December, when he won the Raleigh Invitation race at Kenilworth Common on Boxing Day. His contract with Bantel was coming to a close and he showed his full potential to any prospective new sponsor by a fine win ahead of a strong field. Declaring it: "My biggest win since I took the National Professional title in 1968." A notable non-starter for this event was the Northern champion Barry Davis (Sports Motors- Tower Cycles) whose car had skidded on ice during his journey to the race and although he was unhurt, "his transport suffered badly." Ives then went on to prove he had also the speed to take the Bristol Road Club Aston Court Scramble, winning this time from Ollie Nagle (Coventry R.C.) over the 10 laps.

Dave Nie (Holdsworth-Campagnolo) also took the opportunity to excel in the Guildford Phoenix event, while Atkins was out of action over the Christmas period, and then added the Bagshot Scramble to his palmarés. However all was back to normal when Atkins returned to good health at the end of January. On the 20th there was a report in Cycling that Marsh & Baxter were to terminate their sponsorship with John Atkins, due to budget cuts. John replied that he "had great hopes he would be riding for a Belgian based team in the future." He had produced a great deal of publicity for his sponsor over the two years they had been together, winning 45 races during that period.

By the time the National Championships came along on the London, Crystal Palace circuit in February, Atkins was back to his best and retained his professional title and his seventh national in total. His old adversaries Keith Mernickle (Chris Barber-Sun) and Eric Stone (Tower Cycles) finished second and third, from the 15 starters. Chris Barber/Sun also produced the winning team on the day, with K.Mernickle, R.Newton and R.Pannell.

The Amateur Championships saw Ollie Nagle (Coventry R.C.), sporting a fashionable full, dark, Mexican style moustache. He triumphed in the battle with his team-mate Daryl Brassington and Roger Page (Solihull C.C.) with the winning team also coming from the Coventry R.C. with the help of seventh placed Chris Dodd. *The Daily Telegraph* sponsored the event, and in the week before, produced this description of the course: "From the top of the climb there is a sharp descent to the main finishing circuit, completing the two mile lap. Each lap will have six run-ups and looks (the most) dramatic championship course of recent years but also one of the toughest." The photographs which appeared later in the press, certainly reinforce the above comments.

It is interesting when looking down the list of organiser for this important event, just how many were also National Officials. A few of which were: Organiser Ray Richards, Director of Course Johnny Morris,

Chief Judge Keith Edwards, Recorders J.Marshman and R.Bull, Barriers Ivan Dodd and the hard working ladies who handed the Competitors numbers – Mrs M.Marshman and Mrs. J. Morris. Added to them was that firm supporter of Cyclo-Cross, *The Daily Telegraph*'s David Saunders on the microphone, as the race Commentator.

After the event, riders were chosen for the coming Worlds, the first three were automatically picked, plus Barry Davies (Sports Motors-Tower Cycles) as an additional professional, and Chris Dodd as the extra amateur. The World Championships this year were held at Zolder in February.

In the archives is a single edition of Newsletter, which was produced by the Association edited by Reg Ward and includes some interesting items. One described a trip to the Cyclo-Cross World Championships in Zolder, with the purpose of trying to encourage more supporters to travel to such events. Reg Ward was lucky enough to travel this time with the Great Britain team, there were fourteen in the party, and they left Enfield at 6.45 a.m. Travelling in a convoy of four cars, finally arriving after a Channel crossing and driving on to Zolder, Belgium at 7 p.m. He went on to describe mixing with the riders and the scenes after each race: "Truly amazing with press and spectators frantically pulling and pushing. ... and the T.V. cameras having great difficulty in getting near the winners." Then it was back to the hotel and next day (Monday) the departure for home. The return crossing took four hours and then the last part of the journey home, where they arrived back in Cheshire at 2.30 a.m. on Tuesday. Proving that to have a great time as a cyclo-cross supporter you needed to have plenty of stamina as well.

The British were hoping for a good showing and John Atkins produced a ride to be proud of, finishing seventh in the Professional event despite a broken gear cable, leaving him with only top gear. Even then Atkins was not satisfied, as this comment to Cycling revealed: "But it's not good enough – I'll just have to do better in future." John Atkins may have been disappointed but his ride still stands today as the best by a British professional at the World Championships.

The Professional winner for the third time running was once more the senior de Vlaeminck brother Eric, with his compatriot Robert Vermeire making it a Belgian top two, by winning the Amateur Championships. The races were held on a damp day, after two days of rain had soaked the course. At the finish the crowd was allowed to swarm across the finishing line, with the Police unable to hold them back. The riders barely able to get to the line through the narrow gap left for them.

The podium riders for the Amateur Championship were Robert Vermeire (Bel), J.M.Basualdo (Spain), N.de Deckere (Bel). The British riders result was Ollie Nagle 17th at over 4 minutes, then Roger Page 24th at another minute, Chris Dodd in 29th having to change bikes due to being over geared, at over 6 minutes and Daryl Brassington in 30th spot almost 7 minutes down.

The Professional podium read: Eric de Vlaeminck (Bel) Gold, Albert van Damme (Bel) Silver, and Rolf Wolfshohl (Ger) Bronze. The British riders finished with Atkins 7th, Eric Stone 20th at just over 6 minutes followed by Keith Mernickle 21st at 1 lap and Barry Davies 23rd also at 1 lap.

The season long Viking Trophy competition was won by John Atkins (Marsh & Baxter) with 46 points, from Chris Dodd (Coventry R.C.) with 34 points followed by Daryl Brassington (Coventry R.C.) with 27 riders gaining at least one point but it was disappointing that only five professionals qualified.

With the 1969/70 season now over, the Executive Committee held their meeting on the 21st of June at the home of Ron Atkins in Coventry and several momentous changes were made, as the minutes record:

The appointment of R.Fowler to replace J.Morris as International Racing Secretary was confirmed.

The Secretary reported that Government Travel Grants for International Teams had been increased to $66^3/8$%. (Strange amount!)

The Secretary read a letter from our President concerning not standing for election

The Secretary reported that the official application for the 1973 World Championships had been submitted.

The Secretary drew attention to the B.C.F. circular concerning advertising on race clothing, and a letter from J.Rawnsley referring to advertising in the Three Peaks event was discussed, and it was agreed "that the Bradford R.C.C. team would not be mentioned in advertising."

Treasurer Ron Atkins, reported that the International Racing Fund stood at £290, then explained that tax problems had arisen with the Inland Revenue and therefore he tendered his resignation, which was accepted with regret. R.Bull was appointed to take over from Mr. Atkins as treasurer as soon as could be smoothly done. "It was agreed not to publish the

1969/70 accounts until we had taken professional advice."

On a lighter and more optimistic note, a new Area Association would be formed, as ten events had already been fixed for the Bristol area, and a new Association could be justified. There was also a suggestion that an East Anglian Area Association be established.

Season 1970/71

September 1970 saw an article in Cycling that provided an insight into the behind-the-scenes workings to get the World Cyclo-Cross Championships to Britain: "Big hope of the winter men in late 1968 was that we would stage this winter's championships, a neat parallel at Leicester. But when the crunch came, the B.C.F. who had repeatedly assured the B.C-C.A. that it would push its case, raised not a voice at the U.C.I. congress in Geneva."

Ray Richards commented: "By the time the congress came up we reckoned we probably would not get them. We suspected this when we were not asked if we had found ourselves a sponsor for the world championships-to-be; after all the U.C.I. won't work for nothing and we presumed that we would have to have some sort of sponsorship. But nothing was said, and we thought that perhaps our ideas were being taken lightly. Obviously they were."

This new decade brought more development in clothing and equipment at the top level and club riders soon cottoned on. New materials enabled brighter colours to be used for race clothing with a smarter and more professional look for all competitors. Cotterless chainsets and quick release wheels were now almost universal, although black leather shoes were still the only type of footwear.

There was a break with tradition when the new edition of the handbook appeared with a picture of Robert Vermeire, the Belgium amateur on its light blue cover. The previous governing officials remained in their posts although R. Bull now combined Treasurer with Membership Secretary; R. Fowler took over as International Racing Secretary and R.Ward the Coaching Advisor. The four Life Members were Joan and Keith Edwards, together with Ron Atkins and Percy Lovell.

This season's Midland C.C.A. programme listed an encouraging number of 33 events, with the first starting on Sept. 6th and carried right on through to mid February. Top midlander John Atkins competed in road races pre-season to be in good form for his new sponsors T.I.Carlton

Cycles. His fitness showed early when he won the awe-inspiring Three Peaks race on September 29th with Harry Bond (Bradford R.C.C.) second and C.Wilkins (Keighley St. Christopher's.) third.

The *International Cycle Sport* series was much improved with counting events at Mastiles Lane (Yorkshire Dales), Pignut Hill (Cheshire), and then in November it moved to Wakefield, December saw it at Glossop (Derbyshire) with the final event at Cliffe Castle (Keighley). The notes about the prizes on the start sheets show how they were totalled up and the wording was certainly of the period: "All prize money stated, does not include any entry fee, - entry fees will be added in the manner, to increase the prize list. ... Each event will carry a first prize of £10.00 except the first – which will be £15.00." Hopefully this is quite clear!

The distinctive red, white and light blue jersey with a castle tower on it crossed the line in first position at Pignut Hill, worn by Eric Stone, (Tower Cycles). Eric was winning the second edition of the *International Cycle Sport* Trophy Series. Behind him was Barry Davis, who was unsponsored at this time, with third over the line Mick Shakespeare of the Solihull C.C.A. A note in the report by Noel Henderson praised the hard working Jim Court for his part in the proceedings – "with announcer Jim Court doing as fine a job of labelling and race commentary as most of those present can have heard for a long time." The defending champion, Harry Bond, was forced to retire after both he and Bill Whitworth aimed at the same narrow water crossing where only one could get through. Bond suffered a buckled wheel and a broken pedal in the collision and retired with grace. Barry Davis, however, after colliding at the very same spot with a lowly placed rider, "hurled himself and bike melodramatically off the path before treating spectators to a totally unnecessary stream of abusive comments." Those looking on probably realised that it was only his frustration in the heat of battle. Meanwhile, up front, Stone had time to puncture in both wheels and still win comfortably.

An unusual headline appeared in Cycling declaring: "Pat Pepper for Smirnoff". Pat was a member of the Colchester Rovers and a top International road racer; the cutting went on to say that she would not be the first girl to ride this event, because Beryl Burton had ridden previously. Pat was just one of those listed on the massive entry of 130 who hoped to ride the main event, but it was more likely that she would ride in the overflow race.

Ralph Digges produced two full-page articles in the same magazine during November, describing how training at 'Woodlands' had improved young riders under the eye of the good coaching. He ended his article with a plea, that with the possibility of the World Championships coming in 1973, there should be training weekends and evening sessions with the national squads. There were also many new riders coming forward this year to challenge the established top men, including Brian Davison (Nearside Wheelers) who had just become a junior and who showed his true form when he won the Houghton C.C. event ahead of the previous three winners of this race, Colin Lewis (Northern Velo), Harry Donnelly (County Wheelers) and Derek Dawson (Cleveland Wheelers)

Top cross riders, such as John Atkins, filled their weekends so full that their activities make the armchair supporter feel weak just reading about them. One weekend in November justifies this, with Atkins riding on a Saturday in Belgium, finishing a fine sixth behind the current World Champion Eric de Vlaeminck, and ahead of ex Champion Rolf Wolfshohl. Then it was car and ferry to return home at 1a.m. and later the same morning he was off again to ride and win, the third *International Cycle Sport* Trophy event at Wakefield, against the top British riders. None of the other riders were going to give Atkins an easy ride though; with Eric Stone (Tower Cycles) and Barry Davis (unsponsored) both determined to win, but Atkins would complete his very active weekend by taking the first prize.

During December there was an interesting insight at the drugs issue in a report on the 'Whippendell Woods' race at Watford. Keith Mernickle won but Dave Nie was forced to quit. The report in Cycling revealing: "Forever plagued by bronchial trouble in damp weather, the Holdsworth man was grabbing for breath, heaving his lungs painfully until it was impossible to continue. ….My doctor has given me some medicine, but I'd be a naughty boy if I took that while I'm racing – it's full of Ephedrine!"

Amateur Champion, Ollie Nagle had a disappointing start to his championship year, as it was not until Boxing Day that he gained his first win of the season. Things had just not gone his way, for he wrecked four sets of gears before finding out that his frame was out of track. Then no less than eight punctures during previous events had dogged his results, making it hard to find the form he wanted.

Not all promotions were a success, as illustrated by the Dulwich Paragon event, which had to be cancelled due to lack of entries. The event was due to be put on at Shirley Hills, despite having put in an order for 350 programmes, a good line up of prizes and hoping for an excellent event they had opted for a closing date. After all that work, they were very disappointed when they received only 12 senior entries by the final date. The club declared: "Unless riders keep to the closing date rule (as Time Trial and Road Racers have to) sponsors and advertisers would not continue putting money into the sport."

A cutting in the archives describes an unusual handicap event at the Meadowbank Velodrome, Edinburgh. The Lothian C.C. turned the area around the stadium into a course but the judges must have had a complicated job, because the cyclists had to complete 10 laps, but the harriers only ran 5 laps. This did not deter cyclist Joan Tome (Dunedin C.C.) from winning.

The B.C-C.A. must have looked enviously at the English Schools Cycling Association promotion of their Cyclo-Cross Championships. 129 riders lined up in seven races, with all the girls' team races won by Bungay High School. The winner of the under 12 years boys event was a C.Wreghitt of Loughborough; whose progress we shall follow with interest over the next few years.

Tony Summerfield became the first Veteran National Cyclo-Cross Champion at the age of 35, and the Elizabethan C.C. rider achieved it on a frame he had been riding for 20 years. These Championships were held at Alexandra Palace in North London on December 19th. Summerfield won from a midland rival, Mick Florence (Solihull C.C.) with Jimmy Blankly (Calder Clarion) third and Johnny Morris (Wembley R.C.) the first of the southern rivals, in fourth. Morris also led home the winning team, which included the race organiser Ivan Dodd. B.C-C.A official, Keith Edwards was press-ganged into riding this first Veteran Championships and did so, despite riding his bike all the way down from Knowle to London.

A novel place to hold an event was found by the Marlbro A.C. when they planned a course behind Rayners Lane Tube Station in London. Keith Mernickle completely dominated the event, lapping every other rider, and as Cycling reported: "The previous days rain had indeed left its mark on this intricate little loop and turned the 'watersplash'- a six foot wide river which should have been about a foot deep, into a knee-deep bath. ...The only way across was to jump into the middle and grope to the opposite bank. The fortunate ones still had their shoes when they reached the other side." Perhaps this is one of those times when even tough cross men think they could be a tiny bit unhinged.

January 1971, saw talented schoolboy Tom McDonald (Keighley S.C.) win the Sheffield Schools C.A. event and strengthened his grip on the Yorkshire C.C.A. Championships. The defending champion Harry Bond (Bradford R.C.C.) had his work cut out in his attempt to win the title for an amazing eleventh time.

The schoolboys had to travel down to Southampton for their title contest. Dr. Horace King M.P. the speaker of the House of Commons set the large mass of boys on their way. Looking at the start sheet of 118 riders it was very noticeable that some schools had large numbers dominating the sheet. Longslade 14 riders, Gleneyre 11, Shirley Warren 9, and Forest Hill 6. However, the winner Geoffrey Williams came from Brook Comprehensive. The event was held in terrible weather. This year Ron Kitching put up a monthly award for the 'Most Outstanding Achievement each month' and Geoffrey Williams took the first of these awards for his winning ride.

Described as both "whippet-framed" and a "surprise winner" by Cycling, Jeffery Morris (Polytechnic C.C.) led from the first lap, to run out an easy winner of the National Junior Championships held at Aldersley Stadium, Wolverhampton. At only 16 years, he was an outsider, although he was certainly not lacking in confidence if these quotes are anything to go by, for as he stood resplendent in his National Championship jersey he declared: "I didn't really want the lead at the start, but I found myself at the front and just kept going. ...I told my parents on Saturday that I would win." Second was Andrew Jones (Royal Sutton) and third Phil Allison (Sheffield Phoenix). Only one girl, June Pearce of the Elizabethan C.C. tackled the Championship course.

Because of a national Postal strike, there had to be a novel way of informing the riders about the Senior National Championships. This prompted the organisers to have a special 'Competitors Instructions' section in Cycling the week of the race. It outlined the start time, where to collect numbers and even how to find the course! The promoters had to trust that all the competitors read Cycling. It must be remembered that there were no web sites, texting, mobile phones or e-mails then and many people had no telephone in the house.

John Atkins was chasing a 'hat-trick' of professional titles and his eighth title at *The Daily Telegraph* sponsored Senior National Championships in Heaton Park, Manchester. With only seven Professionals entered, they would have to ride at the same time as the 80 amateurs. A pre race report in the same newspaper is rather illuminating: "There are only seven pros, which is the main reason for holding both title races at the same time. The lack of premier-class riders, though, is not due to a decline in the sports popularity. Atkins and his six challengers have set such a high standard that the normal racing men would stand no chance." One late entry in the Pro race was the Six-Day track star Tony Gowland (T.I.Carlton) who signed on with the words: "If the De Vlaeminck brothers can mix racing so can I." The race had a very surprising ending, which developed because Atkins and Daryl Brassington, who were Coventry R.C.C. club mates, broke away, yet neither could drop the other. A Cycling report quoted the reason for the result thus: "With two laps to go Atkins turned to Brassington and suggested that as he was first for the Pro title and Brassington just as sure of winning the Amateur title, they didn't bother to sprint for the line but cross it together. Brassington agreed, but these things are easier said than done, and at the finish his (Brassington's) wheel was inches ahead." Eric Stone (Tower Cycles) finished second Professional, but his day could have been so different, as this report explains: "On the third lap Stone was leading when, splashing through a stream, he knocked one of his pedals on the root of a tree and snapped it right off. He had to run back up-hill to collect another bike, crashed twice more and finally, after going through two more bikes put in a brave finish on the one he started with. He was to finish third overall, but the second Professional home, his guts raised the biggest cheer of the day." The sport of cyclo-cross is littered with such hard luck stories, which are not reflected in the cold list of results decades later. Third Professional to arrive was Keith Mernickle for Chris Barber.

Roger Page despite riding into second place in the amateur event heard that he had not been selected for the World Championship team. Page, now 33 years old, had ridden six previous Worlds and was told that the decision had been made to give younger riders a chance. The bronze medal for amateurs went to Chris Dodd (Coventry R.C). The full team selected was Professionals – Atkins, Stone and Mernickle with Ray Barker as reserve and the Amateurs – Brassington, Nagle, Collyer and Dodd with two reserves Tony Lyne (Ross-on-Wye) and Geoff Shergold (Southampton)

The site of this year's World Championships was Apeldoorn, in Holland, named "The mountain in the woods". The Belgians dominated once more with winners in both categories. Cycling's report was scathing about the British performance: "For Britain it must be described as a disaster day, the steady progress over recent years undone, with only Chris Dodd's sixth place in the amateur event any cause for joy; and the former British Junior champ certainly saved us from complete despair." Although the event was held in sunshine, the bitter cold early on had frozen the soft surface the riders trained on the day before into treacherous ruts. In the Amateur event the eventual winner, Robert Vermiere (Belg) just put on the pressure until no one could follow his wheel. West German Deiter Uebing was his closest challenger, with Jan Spetgens (Hol) coming third. Other British riders apart from Chris Dodd, were Daryl Brassington in 34th at over 6 minutes, Ollie Nagle at just over 7minutes in 37th and G.Collyer coming 46th. Britain's eighth placing in the team awards was due almost entirely to Dodd's fine efforts.

Eric de Vlaeminck the Belgian multi-champion, would copy his amateur compatriot by completely dominating all the professionals with his two team-mates Albert Van Damme finishing second for silver and Roger De Clercq claiming the bronze. The British riders who had started with such high hopes could only finish with John Atkins 10th although still a very good placing in such company, Keith Mernickle in 13th and Eric Stone 15th. There were large gaps between the riders showing the murderous pace set by the three Belgians. A novel idea of trying to start fairly was an electronically controlled bar dropping down in front of the riders. In interviews after the event de Vlaeminck said: "I had just one challenger, Van Damme – but though he stuck close to me was never a real threat. …That's why I decided to hold to the pace, though without taking any risks, for it would have been foolish to try to increase my lead. I have been called a cowboy, but I also know my capabilities." All these reports were in Cycling, who gave this comment themselves: "Eric certainly confirmed his easy strength at Apeldoorn, giving the impression of someone out for a pleasant Sunday afternoon ride in the park." That comment wouldn't have helped the morale of the British riders one bit.

Ray Richards Annual Report at Rugeley Power Station highlighted the application for the 1973 World Championships and the 40 per cent increase in promotions, with membership unchanged. He also reported a disastrous drop in Annual Draw profits, which were due to the Postal strike. Two proposals put forward were that the executive committee wished to have no heats for the schoolboy championships and the Midland area proposed that heats be held at least 28 days before the event.

Good news arrived from the Union Cycliste Internationale Congress later this year, giving approval for the B.C-C.A. to promote the World Championships during February 1973.

10

Britain looks forward to
promoting the World Championships

Season 1971/72
The theme of putting a Continental rider on the handbook cover continued with a photo of the Belgian World Champion Eric De Vlaeminck. The price was now in decimal at 15p, and those with an eye for such things can see that the price had increased by one third. In most ways the handbook retained its traditional look, both in size and number of pages.

This year the I.C.S Trophy series was spread throughout the country and consisted of five events. The first was in October, the Newcastle Evening Chronicle event, in November there would be two, the Smirnoff Scramble and the Halesowen Pro/Am. In December it was the Solihull/ Tower Cycles Pro/Am race, then in January the riders had to battle it out in the Keighley Final Cross, making it a very hard series of events from which to find a worthy winner.

On October 10th a strong Dutch team was booked to ride the first of these events. This was a big step, for by inviting Continental teams it was hoped to give the British riders top class competition. These were not just any Dutch riders, as they included Jan Spetgens and Gertie Wildeboer, who were third and fifth in the previous year's World Amateur Championships. This Wallsend event was an excellent promotion if the picture in Cycling was anything to go by, for a massive crowd lined the finishing straight as Daryl Brassington (Sun) crossed the line, hands held aloft. The final touch to this class promotion was a programme with a full colour front cover.

On November 7th the British National Veteran Championships were held and the main sponsor was Ansells the Brewers, the winner being A. Winter (Solihull C.C.) with J.Blankley (Calder Clarion C.C.) second and T. Summerfield (Elizabeth C.C.) third. Although there appears to be no record of the number of starters it must have been good, for the result shows there were 46 finishers.

Jeff Morris retained his Junior Championship title on Sunday 16th Jan at Cleethorpes, but this year he was followed home by Steve Atkinson (Calder Clarion) and John Metcalf (Halesowen C. & A.C.). It was interesting that several of these riders were representing the R.A.F. C.C.

"Edwards Champ!" was the large caption under a cover picture in Cycling showing a schoolboy riding cyclo-cross. It related to the win by Paul Edwards, who was pictured, the son of Keith Edwards, (the B.C-C.A President). The magazine covered the race report with the headline: "A Tribute to his Dad" and continued: "Keith Edwards a tireless worker in the furtherance of cyclo-cross, was rewarded for his years of effort when his son, Paul, won the National Schoolboys' Championship at Sutton Park, near Birmingham on Sunday." To the delight of the Edwards family the event was organised by the Royal Sutton C.C, which was founded by the Keith Edwards. Seventy-two boys finished the tough course in a relentless biting wind. After Edwards received his jersey from John Atkins it was Charlie Jackson who stepped up to receive the silver medal. But as Martin Springer stepped forward, John Thompson protested to the officials that he was third. This caused bewilderment, as Thompson persisted, so an investigation of the lap scores was called for, with Springer being declared third and leader of the winning Glen Eyre team.

The Smirnoff Scramble had developed into a whole day of events. There was a World Hour Roller Record attempt, a Pram Race, a Pig Roast and a Tug-o-War, making it sound like a very lively day out. On this occasion the champion Atkins (T.I.Carlton) was in dominant form to win from Freddy Nerts the top Belgian. Nerts would return with a vengeance for the third edition of the ICS trophy series, to win from Atkins. The I.C.S December 4th event saw Freddy Nerts again having far too much power in the muddy conditions. The course included a slippery bridge that claimed many victims, including Dave Koryczan who crashed headlong into the stream below, losing his spectacles, leaving him to appeal for a chauffeur to drive his car back to Luton. The spectators took pity on him and sportingly made a collection to help buy a new pair of spectacles.

The New Year saw Eric Stone give a very honest interview to Cycling; he had been riding with success during this season in the blue and gold colours of RBM Otley. He said he needed a "rest and rethink" after a racing trip to Belgium with several of the top professionals. "Our trip was a waste of time. Although I think we made a small profit, we didn't do very well. ...Over here you can only get so good. You are only as good as your opposition, and abroad they are on a much higher level." His mood at this time he described as, "a bit cheesed-off with things. ...It's great being backed by an organization like RBM, but the problem is that you have to live up to their support." He was soon to put all those doubts behind him, to win the very next week at South Manchester, beating John Atkins in the process.

Haverhill in Suffolk was the venue for a new Eastern Area Championship course with a champion's vest, trophy and a combined prize value of £12.50, but there was only a very small entry of just nineteen. Chris Gooch (Colchester Rovers) was listed as the pre-race favourite of the seniors and Lee Wardley (Wolsey R.C.) riding the 'boys' event was trying to maintain his 100% record of winning every 'cross he has ridden, in his own style with straight handle-bars and a hub gear. Gooch did live up to his billing, by becoming the first Eastern Area Champion and Wardley kept his record by a tyre's width from Gerry Taylor of the promoting club.

Jeff Morris (Polytechnic C.C) took his second successive Junior Championship title at Cleethorpes, during mid January. The race was promoted by the Lindsey R.C. with the start a headlong charge along the sea front, then it was out to the hurdles and the sand dunes, where the young riders had to battle against chilling cold and gale force winds. The race favourite Morris was away and clear on his own, with Metcalf in second and Atkinson third. However, in the final result Atkinson gained the silver medal by outsprinting Metcalf in a close lunge for the line. The East Bradford team were first declared the winners, but were disappointed to find that after a recount it was the Humber Velo who were the new team champions. Morris declared afterwards in Cycling: "In future it will be road racing for me" because he had been having disc pain and had had to give up his job as a painter and decorator.

Cycling produced an unusual cover on February 5th, two pictures of riders, both with their arms spread wide in triumph as they crossed finish lines in two British championships. They were John Atkins (TI/ Carlton) taking his ninth win, and Chris Dodd riding for Otley C.C, taking his first senior title. Atkins was also winning his fourth consecutive Professional title when he passed the chequered flag 1minute 28 seconds clear of the chasers, Daryl Brassington (Coventry Eagle/Tighe) last year's amateur champion, and his old rival Keith Mernickle (Chris Barber/Geoffrey Butler). The combined races took place at Temple Newsam Park, Leeds, and were once more sponsored by *The Daily Telegraph* on a day of cold snow showers. The fourth rider home was the delighted Dodd, followed by Roger Page (Solihull C.C) and then the bronze medal amateur winner Vic Barnett (Welland Valley Wheelers) arrived in 7th spot. 'Mister consistency' Roger Page was taking his fifth silver medal in six years, and also led home the winning amateur team of himself, Travers and Winters.

The snow and bitter wind blew so hard, that David Saunders said that he and David Duffield, who were perched high up in the commentators tower, would never ever forget this bitter cold day. Riders were then told who had been picked to go to Prague for the World Championships, the professionals being - Atkins, Brassington, Mernickle, and Eric Stone and the amateurs were Dodd, Page, Barnett, Tony Lyne with the reserves Dave Miller and Graham Collyer.

It was to be the Belgians who made a clean sweep of both the Professional and Senior Amateur Championships, with Eric de Vlaeminck and Norbert de Deckere. Once more the British had to rely on John Atkins to gain the only respectable placing by finishing in 12th spot. Barnett did have a reasonable excuse, having crashed on city cobbles on the Thursday before, reopening an old wound. The morning amateur race resulted in a win for de Decker, from the home country's Milos Fisera and then Wolfgang Renner of West Germany. Chris Dodd was the top G.B finisher in 42nd with A. Lyne 45th, Roger Page at one lap in 49th then the struggling Vic Barnett last in 52nd. The afternoon saw Rolf Wolfshohl of West Germany take the silver medal from Hermann Gretener of Switzerland. Atkins in the Cycling report is described as "Our one rider in the pro event." This is not clear, as Mernickle and Stone had also been picked to travel.

Next year would bring the B.C-C.A a great responsibility with their biggest promotion yet, the World Cyclo-Cross Championships fought out on English soil. A small insight into the background of planning a World Championship can be gauged by the following quotes from a Ray Richards interview in Cycling:

> In fact it took many hundred hours of work over four years and cost more than £500 just to have the championships allocated to Britain. It will cost a further £10,000 to organise. A tender fee at £1,000 and a further £800 towards the costs of medals and UCI expenses has already been paid. I will be acting as organiser with Johnny Morris as Course Director. The final member of the committee will be Len Unwin, Secretary of the BCF. ... The championships will

take place on a 3,000 metre circuit at Crystal Palace. ...Medical arrangements have been placed in the hands of Maggie Saunders, who has considerable experience in this field both with the Milk Race and the Leicester World Championships. The medical centre at Crystal Palace is equipped to motor racing Grand Prix standards, and this should easily be able to cope.

He followed up with another insight into club life.

Recently at the end of a week in which I had travelled some 1,000 miles on cyclo-cross business on top of my full-time job, I took an hour off to go to my own club for relaxation. I was soon greeted by a remonstrative voice, which said, 'You haven't been out on the runs lately. Have you lost your keenness?' I slowly counted up to ten.

Season 1972/73
Dark green was the overall colour for the handbook with a faint picture of riders in black. Joe Dickenson was still the Chairman, Ray Richards the General Secretary and R. Bull remained as Treasurer, Ivan Dodd was Handbook Secretary but a new name added to the list was Barry Moss as Coaching Adviser.

This is still in the age of separation between Professional and Amateur codes, therefore the prize list for the *International Cycle Sport* series is interesting in the light of the prize lists of today. The overall winner's prize list was declared as £25, with £50 minimum prize list per event with "Cash for the Pro's and vouchers for Amateurs" and "For this season, vouchers will be awarded for the Amateur prize value to enable Amateurs to purchase a prize of their own choice". Two adverts in the handbook stand out for different reasons: the Ron Kitching advert includes the details of his specialised 'Cross bike', which included T.A. 'cross' chainrings, 'cross' front tubulars were Wolber at 280 grams with their rear 'super cross' ones at 290 grams. The other advert was for the Wearwell Cross event described as "Exacting – Exciting – Excruciating and Rewarding", but the words that really caught the eye were "Christmas Eve", (one of four held that day). Perhaps the advert should also have said that the riders could 'Recuperate' the next day! One of the promoters on that day, Neil Pears, (Colchester Rovers) would have a busy Christmas because he was also promoting on Dec. 27th as well. The National Scout Cyclo-Cross Competition was outlined in the handbook, with an impressive five regional finals taking place during September. The final on 16th October with age races for 11 and 12, 13 and 14, and 15 to 16.3 months. Entry forms were only obtainable from the Headquarters of the Scout Association.

It was now five months to go to the British promotion of the World Championships and the Organising Committee met for a progress report. It recorded that the estimate of £10,500 would be required to promote the Championships had remained unaltered.

On October 20th the Zodiac CRC promoted the Tandle Hill Cyclo-Cross, which was held as a Time Trial. Barry Davies sponsored by Ron Kitching was the fastest over the 10 mile course, with 1hr 5min 32 seconds. Paul Loftus (Bronte Wheelers) came in second at 2 minutes 8 seconds, in third place came Jack Kershaw of the Oldham Century at a further 3 minutes 58 seconds. November saw the fourth edition of the Veterans National Championships being won by Roger Page riding for the Solihull C.C. with John Rawnsley (Bradford R.C.C.) and Mick Florence also of the Solihull C.C. taking the silver and bronze medals.

The third event in the *International Cycle Sport* magazine trophy series held on the banks of the river Humber was "A long road section followed by a tricky descent into a disused limestone quarry, followed by an equally tricky winding path through trees, just one bike wide, made even more problematical by the rain that had fallen generously all over the area in the week before the event." Colin Willcock giving that description in the sponsor's magazine report on the event. John Atkins would make it three out of three wins but only after a superhuman effort, when he was made to show his true class, after a puncture and a slow wheel change left him one minute down on the five leaders. However, he made contact on the slippery section after the bell had been rung. "Had it not been so serious, that final lap could have been straight out of the Goon Show. Down the steps into the quarry and Davis came a real cropper, falling, never to get back on terms with the front. With the pace white hot the remaining leaders came onto the path". ... "Brassington and Dodd were the next to go down as their machines lost traction in the slop." so ran the gist of the I.C.S report. Atkins was the only one to remain upright and went on to win a race that he thought he had lost, only one lap back. *International Cycle Sport* magazine, was becoming a very important sponsor to cyclo-cross, by not only sponsoring five events for the I.C.S. Trophy, but printing in-depth articles and reports in the magazine with excellent black and white and colour photographs.

The Consett Wheelers provided the National Junior Champion this year, in the form of John Fenwick. He led throughout the race promoted by the GS Barossa on the Bagshot course. Second and third were John Metcalf (Halesowen C & A.C) and Paul Edwards, Royal Sutton C.C. Several riders had their bikes smashed in a big pile-up at the start including eventual fourth placed rider Glenn Longland of the Crabwood C.C. who led the winning team with his 14-year-old brother Adrian and Peter Brookes.

A stylish programme was produced for *The Daily Telegraph* sponsored Amateur and Professional Championship at Sutton Park, Sutton Coldfield with Chris Dodd the previous year's Amateur Champion featured on the cover. In the programme B.C-C.A Secretary Ray Richards expressed. "sincerest thanks are due to them (Daily Telegraph) for their support for our sport", this being their ninth sponsorship of these Championships. Once more it was a joint Pro/Am race as there were only ten professionals entered, although more sponsors were coming forward such as Everwarm, Bob Jackson and Researched Building Materials, others had withdrawn.

Last year's victors, Chris Dodd and John Atkins, retained both their titles. It took just seventy minutes for them to take their victories in this combined race. Atkins (T.I Carlton) was followed home at 39 seconds by Keith Mernickle (Chris Barber/Geoffery Butler) and then came Eric Stone (RBM) to take the top three Professional awards. Chris Dodd (Coventry R.C.) finished in fifth place to take the Amateur National jersey. In eighth spot was Graham Collyer of the GS Barossa the next amateur home for the silver medal, with Richard Travis just one place behind to take the bronze. The top team was GS Barossa out of the 72 finishers. Afterwards Atkins was asked by Cycling how long he could carry on at the top level and he replied: "Well Roger Page gives me a few years, so I reckon I'll go on a while yet."

Richard Brock reported in *International Cycle Sport*, an unusual fact that only came to light after the end of the fourth race in the I.C.S Trophy series. It was discovered that the three Czechoslovak riders Milos Fisera, Jiri Murdych and Vojtich Cervinek had left home with little funds having "Eaten practically nothing on their two-day journey to England. The first real food coming at breakfast time on the day before the event." Today's riders would find this hardship just amazing. However, this did not stop them from excellent performances with Fisera finishing second to the winner, John Atkins, and his compatriots coming in sixth and ninth. Brock also reported: "The Redhill's sound organisation was rewarded with fine weather and a very large crowd. Getting on for two thousand found their way to this normally quiet backwater of Dorking." Atkins took a commanding lead in the series with 120 points, ahead of Dodd and Mernickle both on 107 points after this event.

The big day of the World Championships was looming, with a meeting of the World Championship Committee held at 5, Copstone Drive, Dorridge, Solihull, (the home of the Ray Richards) on the 5th. January. The minutes included some serious comments from Len Unwin (B.C.F) who said he had been advised by the U.C.I that the level of prize money for Championships had been raised to a figure that would cost the organisation over £200 more. It was agreed that Unwin should write to the U.C.I Treasurer indicating that he could not accept the higher figure for 1973. No provision was made in the contract signed for the prize money to be increased. He should also mention in the letter that if finances allowed he would arrange to pay the riders the higher figure.

Under the Course Director's Report, J. Morris indicated that he had requested all the marshals he needed, including a number of people who could speak various continental languages. The Finance report noted that the decision by the British T.V companies to cover the events live had given no room for error. Therefore the organiser had to prune the original budget and to urgently seek other income. The Government Grant had been finalised at £1,667 and there had been an improvement in the offer from Thames T.V, who were to show 10 minutes of coverage. "Although the fee of £100 is small." Raleigh Industries would provide £250 worth of banners and pay for a further 1,000 flags with their name on. It seems amazing that these items were still in a state of flux at this late stage, with less than two months to go to the event.

Ron Atkins received another letter dated 15th January from Wally Leonard stating that he was willing to be the starter for the World Championships. He finished his letter by saying that he had enclosed a stamp-addressed envelope for a reply, (not everyone had telephones at home). Obviously everything was still not in place and now time was now running away with little over a month to go to the big weekend.

The weekend of 23rd/25th of February 1973 at Crystal Palace, London, will remain as a landmark in the history of the B.C-C.A. The importance of this event is brought home on page one of the race programme, where there was a photograph of Prince Phillip, Duke of Edinburgh with a letter of encouragement, which is reproduced here:

International sport is not without its problems, but these are far outweighed by its merits. The most important consideration is that every detail of the organisation should be properly prepared and efficiently managed.

I have no doubt that the British Cycling Federation and the British Cyclo-Cross Association will do every thing possible to make the first World Cyclo-Cross Championships to be held in Britain a major success. I am also certain that every visiting competitor, official and spectator will receive a very warm welcome in this country.

Philip

The event was to be spread over three days, starting 9a.m Friday with the opening of the headquarters and ending Sunday evening with a banquet at 8 p.m In the archives for the Championship is the menu for this Banquet, which was held at The Selsdon Park Hotel. It is printed on a silk like material, and resembles a small banner. On it are printed the toasts. Starting with: 'Her Majesty the Queen' which was proposed by A.Campbell (President of the B.C.F), the toast 'International Sport' was proposed by Dr. Roger Bannister (Chairman of the Sports Council) and 'The Union Cycliste International' proposed by A. Campbell, (B.C.F) with the response by Adriano Rodoni the U.C.I President. Then it was Joe Dickenson the Chairman of the B.C-C.A, who proposed the toast to 'Our Sponsors'

International Cycle Sport magazine reported this first promotion of the most prestigious race in the cyclo-cross world under bold headlines. "Exhibition at the Palace." N.G.Henderson outlined the event thus:

What did it matter that De Vlaeminck joined the illustrious ranks of the other septuple champions, Meredith, Scherens, Mapes, Reyners and Burton had already been crowned seven times but their triumphs had been seen only by the faithful few Britishers. What did it matter that Eric De Vlaeminck took his seventh title in London, after a processional championship of unrelenting brilliance. ....There was tragedy as well as triumph, tragedy for the delegates from South Africa, one white and one coloured, who came to London to seek representation at the U.C.I. and who brought with them highly impressive publicity folders which revealed that South Africa has more tracks of championship quality in one town than there are to be found throughout Britain.

Henderson also goes on to describe the calmness of the B.C-C.A. General Secretary:

One could, and must, talk of the magnificent organisation headed by the immovable Ray Richards. I don't recall ever seeing Ray sweat or hurry. He never loses his temper and he has an answer for everything. It was the devotion of Ray Richards, more than any other single factor, which made the 1973 World Cyclo-Cross Championships such a resounding success.

Thanks to the generous support once again of *The Daily Telegraph*, and other sponsors, the event only needed 3,000 paying customers through the gates to make a profit. This was despite the fact that British television had refused to cover the event live, so that the expected revenue from this source was not forthcoming. The supporters did turn up in swelling numbers, and what supporters they were too. London had never seen anything like them and nor had the dyed-in-the wool British supporters. Belgians with their enormous flags, caps and banners were outdone by the Swiss, who swaggered around with giant cowbells, slung from their waists, and rung with great gusto and noise whenever one of their riders came into view. Ron Atkins remembered the crush of spectators trying to get in: "The traffic was built up to such an extent, that the Police ordered the organisers to stop taking gate money, to ease the traffic jam, this meant that the event lost a great deal of money, however due to good sponsorship, this was not the disaster it could have been." Music was provided by that great supporter of cyclo-cross, Chris Barber, who entertained the jolly international crowd in the winter sunshine. The Welsh Guards followed him and then the U.C.I. President Signor Adriano Rodoni cut the tape. The teams were all lined up behind Boy Scouts, who came all the way from Coventry to proudly hold the names of the competing countries on placards.

The Amateur event started with a whoosh, as the riders took off down the long straight a few seconds before the official starter was ready. Unable to hold back the mass of riders any longer, he was seen to shrug his shoulders as they got away. The first bend saw several riders crashing; twelve soon broke free and were joined by Thaler (West Germany). Meanwhile at the back of the race, the jerseys with the stars and stripes were very prominent. Commentator David Duffield pointed out that the course allowed the teams to use road race tactics and this just what the West Germans did, by protecting Thaler. At halfway distance, it was Vermeire (Bel) and Thaler leading, with de Deckere (Bel), Teichreber (West Ger.) and Zweifel (Switz.) at 55secs. The British were fading from the leading groups, with Chris Dodd now out of the first twenty. Vermeire had by now led for nine tenths of the race with Thaler content to follow. On the road section of the last lap Thaler was away; he was fresh and now was not to be overtaken before the line. Near disaster was just averted as the riders finished, many photographers pressed forward to get the best shot, leaving no room for the speeding riders. The winner Thaler was able to swerve, but the disappointed Vermeire collided with the 'snappers' head on, being lucky to get up with only a few scratches. Much further back the novices riding for the U.S.A only saved the G.B. team from being last. This Amateur Championships were the first to have both Americans and Australians competing.

Henderson's report on the Professional race in *International Cycle Sport* magazine, mentioned the little known fact, that despite the strength of Belgium as a cyclo-cross nation, " yet it is strange that this should be so, for there are only ten professional cyclo-cross riders in Belgium, and only the de Vlaeminck brothers and Rene de Clerq have no winter jobs." The hope for a top sixth place by John Atkins evaporated at the very first bend where he could only emerge in twelfth place; Keith Mernickle started well but was soon overtaken by a determined Atkins. Henderson again relates the race progress,: "Across the road at the back of the circuit came the steepest of the climbs, and here it was that de Vlaeminck gave an indication of why he was, and still is, World Champion, as he rode smoothly up the hill while everybody else either walked or ran .... By the end of the lap a leading group had formed, consisting of de Vlaeminck, Van Damme both of Belgium with Wolfshohl, and the one surprise, Andre Wilhelm, the slightly built French rider is not a new discovery, for Wilhelm is aged thirty." Stone and Brassington only featured near the rear of the field, with their team mates finding it increasingly hard to get up to the leading groups. Stone was riding with an injured ankle that happened in training. Henderson then continues: "Over the microphone came the sudden announcement that the first puncture victim of the race was Rolf Wolfshohl. It was known that the German was seeking only a medal, trying to be the first cyclo-cross rider to win twelve medals." De Vlaeminck would soon attack Van Damme, and then the crowd's attention turned to Wolfshohl who was riding to his limit, passing first Wilhelm, then caught and passed Van Damme. A great cheer went up as it was announced that Wolfshohl had caught the champion and then attacked him. He was, of course, a winner by nature having won the Tour of Spain, Paris-Nice and been second in Milan-San Remo, so knew the tactics of a top Professional. However, it would be de Vlaeminck who would power on to win. Photos of the race show the massed ranks of the crowd leaning forward cheering on every rider as they crossed the finishing line. After crossing that line, John Atkins did an interview with Noel Henderson in which he gave some strong opinions: "As for de Vlaeminck, he's like I am in the Nationals, he knows what it's like to be champion, Van Damme doesn't know. Nobody beats him; nobody beats me in the National. I'd stop riding World Championships right now if there were four riders good enough for the places in the team, and I wish there were, but I'll go on riding until there are four better – probably another five years." Nineteen Professionals started, including two riders who had crossed the cycling disciplines, Karl-Heinz Kunde who like his countryman Rolf Wolshohl, had had the honour of wearing the Tour de France yellow jersey.

Once more looking at the list of race officials the same hard working names crop up. Organiser Ray Richards, Chairman Joe. Dickenson, Treasurer R.Bull, Course Director Johnny Morris with Assistant Commissaires – Mick Ives, Keith Edwards, Neil Pears and Jim Court. Ceremonial arrangements were in the hands of Ron Atkins and Transport Manager was Dave Wren.

The event could, of course, not have gone on without the assistance from Len Unwin and the B.C.F. as acknowledged in the race programme. On a personal note, thumbing through my own programme, with its large format pages and full page colour photographs, brings back all the thrill of standing on the course on a Sunday in February as the famous names and heroes swept by within inches, running up slopes like gazelles and descending at breakneck speed.

The top ten in each race, plus the British finishers are listed below,

Professional	Amateur
1. E. de Vlaeminck (Bel)	1. K.P. Thaler (W. Ger)
2. A. Wilhelm (Fra)	2. R. Vermeire (Bel)
3. R. Wolfshohl (W.Ger)	3. E. Teichreber (W. Ger)
4. A. Van Damme (Bel)	4 N. de Deckere (Bel)
5 M.Baele (Bel)	5 A. Zweifel (Swi)
6. P. Frischknecht (Swi)	6. M. Fisera (Czech)

7. J. Atkins (GB)
8. J.M.Basualdo (Sp)
9. Van Den Haesevelde (Bel)
10. K. Mernickle (GB)
16 E. Stone (GB)
18. D.Brassington (GB)

7. F. Livian (It)
8. D.Uebing (W. Ger)
9. K. Jordens (W. Ger)
10. G.Scheffer (Hol)
29. C.Dodd (GB)
42. G. Collyer (GB)
44. D. Miller (GB)
47. R. Travis (GB)

So the big weekend promotion had been a resounding success, and all those hundreds of hours that the people behind it had put in, had been well worthwhile.

The final round of the *International Cycle Sport* Magazine Trophy series was held at Highbury Park, Birmingham on the 11th Feb. John Atkins was yet again the winner and the winner of the series overall with 150 (maximum points) followed by Keith Mernickle (Chris Barber/ Butler) with 134, Chris Dodd (Coventry R.C.) was third with 130. For the coming season John Atkins was to join T.I. Raleigh together with other top British road racers to make a very formidable team, with all the publicity that such a cycle giant as T.I. Raleigh could provide.

Season 1973/74

Neil Orrell recalled the Three Peaks event of this year in the North West C-C.A Annual, with, "The old adage 'If at first you don't succeed' proved right for Ron Kitching pro Barry Davies on Sunday, when he won the Three Peaks cyclo-cross at his fifth attempt, crossing the line almost seven minutes clear of the field at the end of 25 gruelling miles in a gale force wind." Davies was followed home by P.Walkinton (Lancaster C.C.), then T. McDonald (Bronte Wheelers). In eighth place was Phil Norfolk of the Leeds Wellington, who later became the B.C.F Coaching Development Officer.

A red was the background colour used on the cover of this year's handbook. Inside, the list of National Officials show that the only changes were R. Fowler who would give way to Johnny Morris and Mick Ives took over from Barry Moss. Two more faithful servants to the B.C-C.A., Ray Richards and B. Richards, would be honoured by being made Life Members.

Looking a little closer at the handbook, it shows that not one of the 147 events made any mention of 'Ladies' or 'Girls'. Although they were mentioned in the rules in 'Promotion of Events' and 'Competitors' but only as regards entry fees and that girls were not to ride with seniors. Sometimes promoters would give prizes for the first female, but often they just competed on equal or rather 'unequal terms'.

A circular produced by Co-ordinator Barry Moss, declared "The B.C-C.A are pleased to announce greatly increased status for the *International Cycle Sport* Trophy League. ...The sponsors of the overall competition I.C.S. Magazine are increasing their sponsorship by an amount sufficient to guarantee one European team of three riders to ride in each of the five races, thus providing a challenge to home riders." Round One being in October, the 'Smirnoff International Scramble' at Harlow, then in November, the 'Berry Magicoal International' in London, the 'Crescourt Conversions International' would follow this during December. In January it would be round four, with the 'Burton Grand Prix International' in Leeds, and finally the 'Courage Grand Prix'.

The first round winner was John Atkins who appeared with arms aloft in the sponsoring magazine in his T.I. Raleigh colours. This Smirnoff Scramble had Continental representation from both Belgium and Luxemburg. The organisers did not use the usual course, near to Harlow Sports Stadium, because Ron White, the organiser, had moved the course nearer to the Town Railway Station, where some day the Harlow Cycle Track would arise. An organiser's lot is not always an easy one and this was proved correct on the morning of the event when at 9.30am a Road Safety Team arrived expecting to use the same area. Ron White had to then contact the Chairman of the Council to intervene, so that the event could continue. Atkins triumphed ahead of Daryl Brassington and Keith Mernickle with the three Belgians taking the next three positions.

Saturday 27th October was the last date that that the Walsall C.T.C. Cyclists- V-Harriers cross country event was to be held. It was the 39th edition of this famous race, first promoted way back in March 1923. Only the Second World War broke the sequence until 1950. The overall result was amazing, Cyclists–18 wins, Harriers–19 wins, with one race tied, however the cyclists won the last event, therefore making the final result after all those years of endeavour, a draw!

Meanwhile back in the big league of events, Raleigh and Carlton sponsored a 2 day International event during November, promoted by the Hebden Valley C & A.C. John Atkins upheld the Nation's honour and pleased both his and the race sponsors, by winning from a clutch of three Belgian and three Dutch riders who were close on his heels.

This autumn Leo Mason travelled to Belgium with a group of British riders, who were looking for experience and glory. He recalled in *International Cycle Sport* that "Team Manager Johnny Morris, himself still an active competitor in mud-plugging circles, was the very epitome of the new-found sophistication of approach, picking us up in his well equipped, spacious American station wagon, an ideal team car." Local hero Roger Vermeire disappointed his fans by not leading on the first lap, which covered some of the tracks on his father's own land. The rain became a torrent and Van Damme turned the on the pressure to win with Mernickle sixth, young Jeff Morris 11th and Ian Jewell 19th out of the 40 finishers. Mason continues his piece with a description of the next day's course: "The circuit ran through a dense, dank forest. The light was appalling; at two in the afternoon it was more like dusk. With the freezing rain making conditions very difficult, the course was the cream on a rather unappealing cake, containing several descents of fearsome proportions which were nearly unrideable as the inexperienced juniors found to their cost"..... "With half the race run and conditions deteriorating and the very real prospect of some serious accidents ensuing, the organisers very wisely cut the distance by one lap." West Germans came in first, second and third with Mernickle in ninth and Morris 12th after such horrific race conditions they were very creditable rides. Mason concludes with: "After dropping Jeff Morris off in Ghent where he was to join John Atkins for a race on Christmas Day, we caught the ferry from Zeebrugge and spent Christmas Eve on the North Sea getting somewhat inebriated along with members of the ship's crew."

"Dodd's Boxing Day triumph" was the New Year headline, because he had beaten John Atkins into second place in the Coventry R.C.'s promotion at Kenilworth Common. He attacked Atkins at a spot that *Cycling* described as "a narrow tree-lined descent where a slip either way could have meant violent contact with the trees. It was a move that bordered on foolhardiness on such a dicey drop where members of the Red Cross usually station themselves ...just in case"

During this time the Viking Junior Trophy League result could not have been much closer. Lee Wardley (Wolsey R.C) led the series with 24 points with Peter Brookes second only one point behind, and Bob Arnold just another point behind, after three events. After the last event Wardley won by just 5 points from Martin Springer (Crabwood C.C.) who pushed Peter Brookes down to third place. Dennis Donovan in *Cycling* reported on the rise of Lee Wardley with: "Known as 'carrotcruncher' to the international youth squad, Lee Wardley, Wolsey R.C, is the exciting young find to emerge from the cycling backwaters of East Anglia. Schooled with ESCA and a love of cycling gained at club level, Wardley was a 58 minute man at the tender age of 15."

Looking at pictures of the Burton Grand Prix after 30 years, the length of hairstyles, sideburns down to the chin and with many competitors sporting drooping moustaches, certainly shows how fashions have changed. Four visiting Frenchmen pleased the large crowd who had made the effort to turn up to watch them but the lack of appearance of the Dutch team disappointed the spectators. They had failed to arrive after their top man, Hans Streekars, found he had pulled a hamstring. The crowd were kept warm by the closeness of the racing, with John Atkins eventually emerging as the winner from the young amateur Jeff Morris (Polytechnic C.C.) The French Amateur Champion Jean-Michel Richeux lost out when he snapped a gear cable with less that ½ a mile to race. So the crowds and the sponsors, Burton Tailoring Group, went home happy having seen a good race on a cold but sunny day at Temple Newsam Park, Leeds.

Sefton Park, Liverpool, was the venue for the 1974 Professional and Amateur National Championships, the 20th edition of these championships, but the first to be held in the Merseyside area. Only eight Pros were down to race but 82 amateurs.

There was an unusual start to the Senior event as the oganiser brought in the Hussars to start the race with a cannon. Unfortunatley the riders watched the gunner and as he lit the touchpaper, they set off. The field was allowed to go and the cannon went off after half a lap of racing.

Roger Page and Dave Linehan were riding for their new sponsors Hereford Rebores/Brian Wilkins Cycles. David Saunders recalled many years later in *International Cycle Sport*, that the wind and rain had frozen him: "Oh! How it did rain that day and I was struck on top of a 15-foot tubular steel tower, which swayed about in the wind. I was so cold that even after a meal on the train and a few wines I still had not completely warmed through when the train reached Euston."

19 year old Jeff Morris not only took his first Amateur title but was good enough to also beat professional champion John Atkins by a couple of lengths at the chequered flag. Atkins had been coasting to the finish even freewheeling down the finishing straight when Morris came roaring up from behind to pip the multi champion. Atkins was not too concerned as he was already 40 seconds clear of his nearest rival Daryl Brassington (Falcon-Tighe) and Keith Mernickle. Next came Chris Dodd who arrived

to take silver medal spot for the Amateurs with A Williams (Archer RC/ Cutty Sark) taking the bronze.

A request by Mick Ives through Cycling magazine for help with the coming World Championships had resulted in offers of a Tom Bromwich frame, Shimano gears sets from Middlemores, freewheels from Harrogate's Ron Kitching and both shoes and shorts from R. Reynolds, Northampton.

During February 1974, several G.B. riders were racing in an International event at Lanarvilly in Finistere. The programme showed Dodd, Morris, Jewel, Shergold, Davis and Atkins as being listed amongst the 26 riders, all the other riders appear to be French Area Champions. The number of advertisers in the programme would come as an eye opener to British organisers, with 26 pages of adverts.

The 1974 Worlds were held on 24th February in Vera de Bidasoa, Navarra in Spain. Photographs of both President Franco and the future King of Spain, Juan Carlos de Bourbon were in a very attractive race programme. Only six countries sent professionals, Belgium, Spain, France, Holland, Switzerland and Great Britain. The four British picked were John Atkins, Keith Mernickle (down on the starting list as 'Kernickle'!) Daryl Brassington and Barry Davies. Fourteen national amateur teams were to contest their championship, with Great Britain sending six riders, Chris Dodd, Jeff Morris, Ian Jewell, Alan Williams, Geoff Shergold and Vic Barnett.

Most cyclo-cross riders at the age of 34 do not expect to win a World Championship, however no one had explained that to Albert Van Damme, the muscular Belgian racer who had twice been in the silver medal position. David Saunders reported in I.C.S. magazine describing the course thus: "Never can there have been such an awful nightmare of a course as the one dreamed up and put into reality by the Spaniards. Certainly I have never seen anything worse and this was the 13th World Cyclo-Cross Championship that I have covered. True, it was the same for all the competitors but one is entitled to expect a fair quantity of fast riding and not the terrible uphill slog that the course proved to be." This does not truly describe the full profile of the course, for it was estimated that the Pros' climbed over 2,000 feet which included several 1 in 4 and even 1 in 3 ascents in the 13 miles they had to cover.

Despite the fearful mud and mire only two men retired, last year's silver medallist Frenchman Andre Wilhelm and Britain's Daryl Brassington.

Albert Van Damme ended this adventure into the mire, by taking the gold medal and Rainbow Jersey at last, with Roger de Vlaeminck the silver and Peter Frischknecht taking bronze. Barry Davis and Keith Mernickle were both outclassed on such an energy-sapping course, but John Atkins once more saved the British hopes a bit, by coming in 12th despite a puncture on the second lap.

The Amateur Championship saw last year's top men not in the hunt, Czech Milos Fisera second in Prague and the 1972 champion de Deckere were bogged down in the mire. Others including Jeff Morris at 14th had to fight for their places. The winner in the mud was Bert Vermeire of Belgium, with West Germans, Klaus-Peter Thaler in silver and third Ekkehard Teichreber. Out of the seven riders lapped, were two British, Chris Dodd and Alan Williams and two Americans. Ian Jewell managed to avoid being caught by the leaders, and finished 38th.

The 1973/74 A.G.M. was held at Newton Village Hall, Silver Street, Newton, Warwickshire on Sunday the 3rd March at 12 noon. All members were allowed to attend but only National Officials and delegates from Local Associations were allowed to vote. Each Local Association was allowed one vote for the first six clubs and then they were allowed one extra delegate for each additional four clubs. The list of votes allowed were as follows – London C.C.A. 15 votes, Midland C.C.L. 12, Eastern C.C.L. 8, Yorkshire C.C.A. 6, North Western C.C.A. 6, Wessex C.C.A. 3, South Western C.C.A. and North Eastern C.C.A. both with 2 each, and South Wales just 1.

Chairman Joe Dickenson's report outlined some interesting points, such as, "our policy of encouraging schoolboys and juniors is beginning to show results with new names challenging the established stars.... The administrative side of the Association has not been without its difficulties this year and if our administration is to keep pace with the rapid growth of the sport a serious overhaul of our procedures must be a priority of the new Executive Committee. ...Whilst I am all in favour of keeping our rule book as simple as possible oversimplification can only result in confusion for riders and officials alike. ...In my opinion our rules and recommendations are, in some cases too vague and open to various interpretations resulting in inconsistencies in different areas of the country. ...My particular thanks to the members of the executive committee who, despite differing opinions, have in the main, placed the good of the Association first, and personal opinions second." This may give a hint of the differing attitudes at committee meetings.

Ray Richards in his General Secretary's Report, raised the question of the standard of courses: "Many promoters are doing a great deal to raise the standard of events but a great deal more needs to be done by some organisers. The Executive Committee have not been happy with some courses used for major events and will be looking more closely before approving such events for the 1974/75 season". Other items he touched on were, "The National Squad has continued under the control of M.Ives who has put in a great deal of work. We have been able to take advantage of a Government Grant for World Championship Training of just over £500." He brought up the subject of Insurance cover with this item "It has been found that some Local Authorities were demanding cover of £250,000 and this can be arranged with the same insurers for clubs requiring this." Mick Ives as National Coach and Team Manager reported: "I have appointed several sub-coaches and have appointed full coaches in Wessex – G.Greenfield, Liverpool – D. Linehan, Bob Ainsworth and assisting me with Midlands, Mick Shakespeare. All of these Coaches have attended and been involved with coaching weekends for the National Squads." He also outlined that there had been talks in Grimsby and Leicester, and weekends at Lilleshall, Chigwell, two at Coventry, and one at Penistone, Yorkshire that had to be cancelled due to the 'power crisis'. Next year more work will be done in neglected areas, Colin Lewis has asked me to come down to the West Country for a weekend and get something going."

R. Ward gave his report on Press and P.R.O. and it shows the work put in behind the scenes. "Again I have to report a good response to the advance details forms which were returned enabling me to present the Press, Radio and Television with Press Releases of which over seventy-five are sent out each week."

In the 'Proposals' for changes to the rules was one by London C.C.A. for a new rule covering the length of courses and that Judges be allowed to reduce races if there is adverse weather conditions. And another by Yorkshire C.C.A. "That all riders, other than actual competitors competing in the particular event, shall be banned from the actual course during the duration of that event to prevent obstruction to competing riders." It seems amazing that this rule was not already on the books.

As this chapter closes, we look back to the success of the first promotion of the World Championships in England the previous year and forward to the end of the seventies. Machines were becoming lighter and riding techniques were being perfected, but the international opposition continued to remain many steps ahead of the British riders. Could the B.C-C.A narrow that gap or would Britain always be trying to play 'catch-up'?

Bob Thom, BCCA President 1981–94

*A field of 35 riders starts the first 3-Peaks
cyclo-cross race in October 1961.*

Paddy Hoban

Highbury Park, Birmingham, 1967.
(l to r) John Barnes (3rd), John Atkins (Champion), Dave Wren (2nd).

Dave Nie leaps a barrier in the 1968 Smirnoff Scramble.

The Atkins family (l to r)
John, Edie and Ron.

The GB team waiting to start the 1966 World Championship –
(l to r) Mick Stallard, Dave Nie, Roger Page and John Atkins.

Mick Ives –
National Champion 1968,
Veteran Champion six
times.

Programmes

Phil O'Conno

Robert Dane, first British rider to gain a medal at a World Championship –
Silver 1984

Stuart Marshall
World Junior Champion 1986
British Juvenile Champion 1982/83

World Championship logo.

Chris Wreghitt,
National Champion, 1978–82.

PAST WINNERS

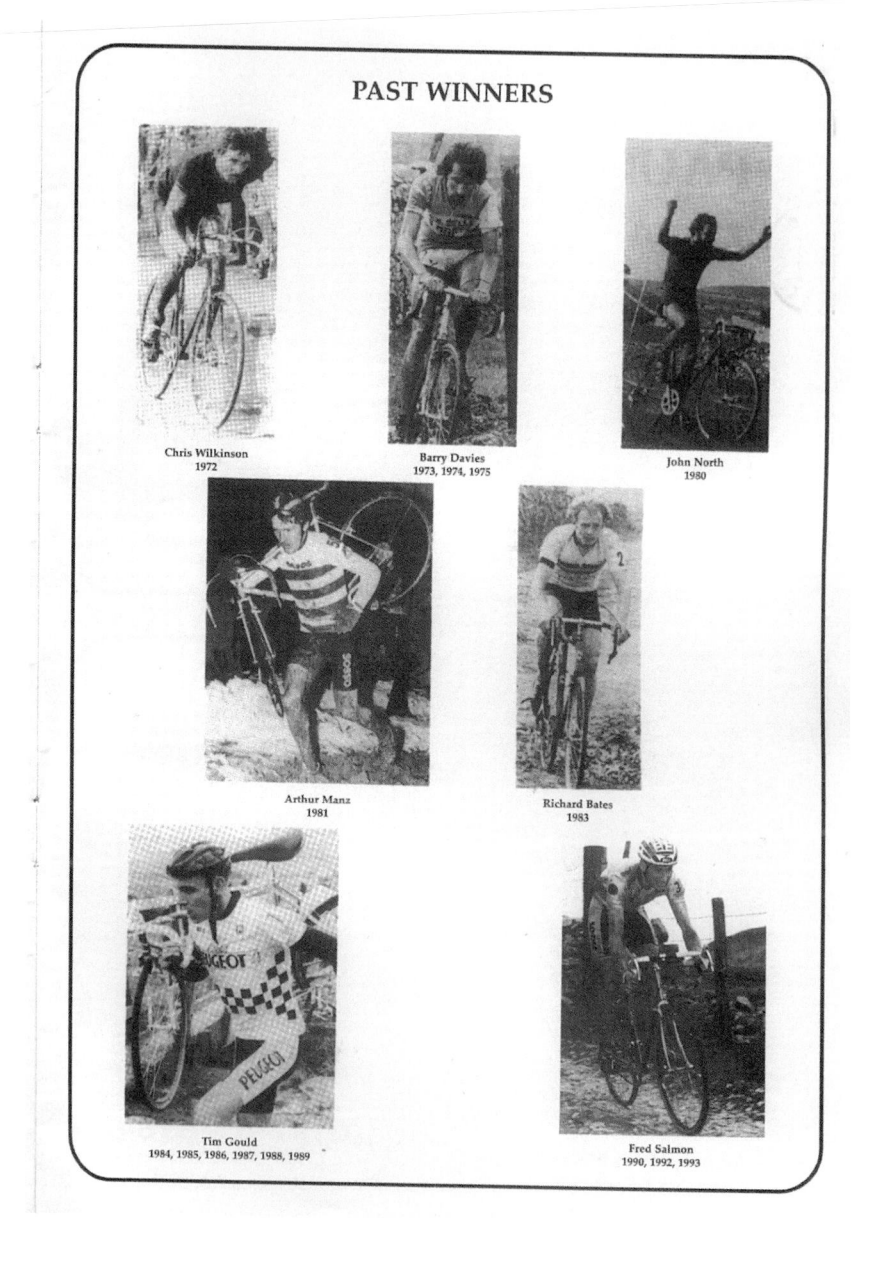

Chris Wilkinson
1972

Barry Davies
1973, 1974, 1975

John North
1980

Arthur Manz
1981

Richard Bates
1983

Tim Gould
1984, 1985, 1986, 1987, 1988, 1989

Fred Salmon
1990, 1992, 1993

11

Morris continues as top Amateur

Season 1974/75

This season started on 1st September with the 'Mablethorpe Carnival Cyclo-Cross', and was followed a week later by an event called the 'Denton Show Committee' at Haughton Green. In London the racing started with an International event listed as 'Invitation Only' and took place in the City of Westminster at the famous Paddington Track.

The price of the handbook this year was raised to 20p and the colour of the cover had changed to white, with a grainy photo of a rider. The size stayed the same with the meagre number of pages creeping up to 44 but otherwise the tried and trusted format remained. A sign of more participation by young females and a look to the future was that several events are listed as 'Boys/Girls'. Flipping through this handbook, an advert for the Norwich Amateur B.C./Target event catches the eye, for it proclaims itself, "The Best Course in East Anglia." Perhaps it also had the most educated riders too, because the course was laid out on the University of East Anglia Campus.

Roger Page (Hereford Rebores) was down to defend his National Veteran Championship jersey, together with 35 other riders, which included A. Summerfield (Elizabethan C.C.) the 1970 champion and A. Winters (Solihull C.C.) the 1971 champion. Defend it he did, winning from Mick Ives (Coventry Olympic) with Harry Bond (Bradford R.C.C) gaining the bronze medal. One official who was kept busy was Jim Court, because not only did he organise all the events but he was also a race commentator and a judge too!

The South Manchester Racing C. C. in conjunction with the Stockport Express and Discount Cycles of Cheadle, promoted an event on Sunday 3rd November at Woodbank Park, Stockport, Cheshire, where there would also be an Inter-Troop Scout Race.

The Boxing Day handicap was promoted by the Coventry R.C. on Kenilworth Common and saw the schoolboys being given four and a half minutes lead on John Atkins (T.I. Carlton) and his co-scratchman Chris Dodd (Coventry Olympic/Viscount). This meant that schoolboys Martin Eadon (Rugby Velo) and Danny McDermott (Wolverhampton Wheelers) had their moment of glory, winning many prizes, until the formidable T.I. Carlton rider forged his way to the front, and added to his wine collection, by winning the next six bottles of wine on the trot. Atkins was doubly pleased, as he was marking 20 years of racing on this course, despite having just recently raced in Luxemburg and having a hectic time at his cycle shop with the Christmas rush.

Over the New Year there were races covering every point of the compass, in the north west there was the 'Circuit of the Cemetery' promoted by the Manchester Wheelers, surely a title to put fear into any rider. Although one rider certainly not put off by the event title, was John Lomax (Claydon Velo), while in the process of winning he also became the North Western Champion. This was an excellent ride in the continual deluge of pouring rain. In the East it was Vic Barnett (Liquid Plastic Coatings) who had been doing his "new of style training'" with "two weeks of home decorating." Perhaps he should have continued that new regime because he soon took control of the lead at the Colchester Rovers/ Percy Contracts promotion, from Cefin Mobbs of the promoting club, with Dennis Brocklesby (Newmarket & D.CC) back in third place.

Meanwhile the North of England Schoolboys Championships were taking place in Sheffield, where 13-year-old Kevin Carr, riding for Selby C.C., became the Champion. Although Martin Eadon was the event winner he did not qualify. It was unusual to see the Professional/ Senior event taking a supporting role on the day. The Great Britain squad held a special training weekend in the Green Shield event organised by the Warwickshire R.C. on the very tough Baddesley Common course, resulting in a grand slam win, with the finishing order of Phil Allison, Martin Springer and Lee Wardley

The January 4th edition of Cycling magazine carried the reports of both the Old Portlians Handicap Cross and the Gemini B.C events, with the bold headline: "Barber-Butler men get 1-2-3 twice." In the first, they started as the scratch group with Steve Walter (Coventry Olympic/ Viscount) and this left the pro's ten laps in which to gain back the half lap disadvantage. The Chris Barber/Geoffrey Butler squad set about forging their way to the front with their leader Keith Mernickle heading the charge. The final result being Keith Mernickle with his team mates Ian Jewell second and Keith Hanson third. This success followed on from the previous Friday's event at 'Footscrays', which ended with the same complete domination by the Barber/ Butler boys, their progress described as "yet another steamroller exhibition."

As has been shown over the years, cyclo-cross comes up with many different ideas to make courses either more exciting or engaging the spectators in the action. Few can have had all in one event, as the Kirkby C.C. did this year. They called their event the 'Yellow and Red Madison', after their club colours and it was to be contested by teams of two riders. Barry Davies (Ron Kitching) was teamed up with Rob Clarke of the Liverpool Premier R.C believing the Kirkby Sports Centre to be his lucky course, because this win would be his seventh in seven visits! The teams were picked out of a hat, with the weakest rider having to ride the final lap. Clark was so encouraged by Davies's skill and effort that he did the ride of his life and they won by a scant 3 seconds.

Each of the three counting events for the I.C.S. Trophy series produced a different winner. The 'Smirnoff' held in October at Harlow was won by Jeff Morris (Dinnington Universal) who took the lead in the series. Then it was John Atkins (T.I. Carlton) who won the 'Chris Barber International' at Forty Hall Park in November. The next event was held in Leeds where Keith Mernickle showed his form by winning that event. Four top Belgians Camille Dedeckere, Freddy Naert, Eric Mathys and Hubert De Meulemeister, rode the first two events, although it was frustrating to both the organisers and spectators that they did not show the form that everyone knew they possessed. When they did not appear for the third event, David Saunders showed his annoyance, by writing in a race report in I.C.S. magazine: "They lost a few friends for failing to turn up and the number of times that foreign teams are down to ride events and then do not arrive is becoming increasingly annoying. The British Cyclo-Cross Association must look into this situation before it gets out of hand."

Jeff Morris was regarded as favourite for the Amateur title at the National Championships this season, although he was still suffering from a painful broken bone in his wrist he was still determined to ride despite the bone not being properly healed. Keith Mernickle was the firm favourite for the Professional title, if his nerves did not get in the way. Once more *The Daily Telegraph* was the sponsor of these Championships for the 11th consecutive time. They would be held at Sutton Park in Birmingham, the 21st edition of the Championships, with Ray Richards was once more the organiser. Among the professionals down to ride were some with new sponsor's names emblazoned on their jerseys, such as Dave Russell/ Milremo, Jack Herne Cycles/ TPD Printing and Liquid Plastic Coatings.

One hundred riders lined up to race for the two titles, with 52 clubs represented in the amateur competition. It was 33 year old John Atkins who was to produce that extra something to win the Professional event for an amazing seventh time, bringing this to a grand total of twelve titles, spaced out over 15 years. Run as a combined race with the Amateurs, it was an amateur, Jeff Morris riding for the Dinnington R.C. Universal Contractors team, who passed under the chequered flag first. David Saunders of the sponsoring newspaper described the event in *International Cycle Sport* thus:

It was a wonderful day in Sutton Park, Sutton Coldfield. The 3-kilometre course, which had to be covered eight times, had all the ingredients to make it a hard race. A vast crowd and even a little sunshine at times helped to improve the scene. Indeed many people thought it the best-ever championships and the sponsors, *The Daily Telegraph*, were delighted with everything about the event. Jeff Morris took the amateur title for the second time with an exceptional ride, finishing over one minute ahead of the great champion John Atkins. The Lord Mayor of Birmingham had sent the 100 riders off on their way by firing a pistol. On the first lap Mernickle, Atkins and Morris forged ahead, with Morris 'putting down the hammer' and the rest could only follow. Lap two saw splits occurring and Chris Dodd losing contact, Londoner Morris continued to tow his professional rival along until they led by nearly a minute by the end of lap four. Morris then took off alone to win from Atkins with Mernickle and then Barry Davies riding in as the third professional at 2-26. The second amateur was Chris Dodd and Phil Allison the amateur bronze medallist. The winning Professional team was Chris Barber/Geoffrey Butler, who placed their three counting riders Mernickle, Ian Jewell 5th and Keith Hanson 7th. The Lord Mayor became so involved in the excitement of the race that he was seen climbing the ladder to join David Duffield at the commentary point, giving the organisers palpitations that he would not be back down to present the awards. The familiar sight of Secretary Ray Richards fully involved in the organization was even more impressive as he was in the agony of an arthritic knee.

Mud was the enemy of all the British riders in their two warm-up events for the World's in Switzerland when they rode at Metz in France. Trip organiser Johnny Morris described it as "We never see anything like it at home" although Keith Mernickle was the best of the British at the unusually named 'Prix Metz-Woippy' event. This weekend was an ideal way to stock up on ideas and see the level of fitness and stamina required to compete with the best. The Saturday event's venue was at a Safari Park, with the route around a fort. Barry Davies the Ron Kitching pro gave Andre Wilhelm, the French Professional Champion a good run for his money before crashing heavily, although unhurt, except for his pride. John Atkins finished first of the British in sixth with Lee Wardley 12th and Davies 13th. Next day, rain battered the riders, the event being won by the French Amateur Champion Alex Gerardin with Davies this time, being the best of the British in fifth. The continuing rain and mud took its toll on both Atkins and Mernickle who both retired after being lapped.

Geoff Greenfield, the British Team Manager, was disappointed with their performance. The amount of mud on this course can be gauged by the fact that Jeff Morris when having trouble with a loosening rear wheel had to run almost a whole lap and yet lost only one place! Cycling reported that: "Johnnie Morris was pleased with the way the British team had ridden ... We had a long, hard journey out ... The Hovercraft was two hours late and we did not arrive at Metz until 9p.m." The Amateurs stayed to train with the French National Team until Thursday, while the Pro's returned home before travelling out to Switzerland. Back in England Vic Barnett was trying hard to keep his record of being almost unbeatable on Eastern courses by recording his 13th win. This time in the Alford Wheelers event held at Well Valley in Lincolnshire.

Melchnau in Switzerland was the destination for the competitors in the World Championships on 26th January. The riders faced atrocious conditions but the Belgians just lapped it up. Sid Saltmarsh pointed out in his report in Cycling that cyclo-cross appeared to be an old man's sport for the men at the top were Vermiere (30), Thaler (25), Baele (38), Wolfshohl (36) and even Roger de Vlaminck was 27. Sid quoted Roger as saying: "I'm good for another ten years yet. I reckon I'll be packing it up on the road when I'm 32, but there's no reason why I should not keep going at cyclo-cross until I'm 35 or 37." Of course nowadays these ages would not be thought of as extraordinary at all. If the above comments by Saltmash are true, then the B.C-C.A's policy of bringing forward young riders could be the right idea and would pay off in ten years time.

The professional crossmen had an opportunity this year to test themselves against two Tour de France riders, as both Cyrille Guimard and Mariano Martinez were competing. But they did not appear on the podium this time, as it was the turn of the younger de Vlaeminck brother to take the Rainbow jersey. Roger de Vlaeminck (Bel) took the gold, then Albert Zweifel of Switzerland silver and his team mate Peter Frishneckt the bronze medal. Cycling only recorded John Atkins as finishing ahead of the two famous Tour de France riders but his exact position and those of his compatriots have not been located.

In the Amateur event Britain's young Jeff Morris tried his best to run the Belgians close despite having his left wrist bandaged as a precautionary measure. The photographs in Cycling by Leo Mason capture the conditions perfectly, for they look more like a section of a W.W 1 battlefield, than a race course. It was just mud, mud and even more strength sapping mud, with the pure speed men being neutralised. Bike cleaning was at a premium in the pits, where the mechanics were kept working at full stretch, with the British fans applauded by Cycling reporter Sid Saltmarsh for "Doing sterling work in the pits." The result of the Amateur event was a rerun of the previous year, for first and second, with Robert Vermiere (Belgium) becoming champion once more, and Klaus-Peter Thaler (West Germany) taking the silver medal, with Holland's Gert Scheffer coming in for the bronze.

Saltmarsh's report carried on by saying that the British riders had: "Hopes for the future-but what consolation, if any, for the immediate disappointment at our teams' showing? ....Britain must look well ahead, continuing to blood the youngsters like Lee Wardley and Martin Springer, who had nothing to be ashamed of in their first taste of the world scene." Once more the report in Cycling does not list the finishing positions of the British riders. But Chris Dodd, Martin Springer and Lee Wardley did ride and finish.

John Rawnsley took up the defence of the British riders performances at the Worlds, with a long letter in Cycling:

> Once again our cyclo-cross riders outclassed and humiliated in the world championships. ...For far to long the emphasis in this country has been on fast rideable courses with the minimum of running and mud. ...We must help prepare our riders for the world championship type courses with 15-20 per cent of running, and we would no longer hear such pathetic remarks as 'On the road after so

much running my legs were so dead I could not get going'. Let us make these changes or before long the Americans and Canadians will be finishing in front of us!

These were strong words from an experienced event organiser, and it produced several extra letters all with differing remedies. Such as more money, low standard of riders, poor coaching and bringing forward the youngsters etc.

The A.G.M was held at Newton Village Hall, Silver Street, Newton, Warwickshire, on the 4th. March at 12 noon. The nine associations present were London C.C.A, Midland C.C.L, Eastern C.C.L, Yorkshire C.C.A, North Western C.C.A, Wessex C.C.A, South Western C.C.A, North Eastern C.C.A, and South Wales.

It is not clear how healthy the Association's finances were during this period, whether they were in profit, just in balance or not balancing at all. As if to agree with this, during the meeting, Joe Dickenson the Chairman, gave out a warning for the year ahead, "The administrative side of the Association has not been without its difficulties this year and if our administration is to keep pace with the rapid growth of the sport a serious overhaul of our procedures must be a priority of the new Executive Committee."

Season 1975/76

The Association handbook remained much the same as the previous year, except for yet another price rise, this time to 30p. S.Rooker took over from R. Bull as Treasurer, and G. Greenfield is now listed as National Coach/Team Manager. The event entry fees continued to show a wide variation of charges from 35p, 40p and even 45p for seniors/juniors, although schoolboys were still normally only required to pay 20p.

September headlines in Cycling were: "First blood to Dodd in cross opener at the expense of the Cashmen" (note the jibe) which covered the first clashes of the new season. A new venture held in conjunction with the World Water Ski Championships caught the imagination, and it attracted most of the top names. It had a new format with 3 heats, each of 5 laps. After fast and furious racing Chris Dodd (Coventry Olympic/Viscount) proved the winner overall, with John Atkins (Viscount/Shimano) second and Keith Mernickle coming in third.

With the season well under way Mick Ives, the Manager of the Coventry/Olympic team, was cock-a-hoop at the performance of his riders in the 'Mister Shandy Scramble' at Halesowen, during October. Chris Dodd winning once more from John Atkins, with Dodd's team mates Richard Travis in third and Paul Dury sixth taking the team prize, with a good-sized crowd enjoying the battle between the leading two. Drink was very much to the fore on the day with 'Mister Cola Cross' being the name of the second event, with the Schoolboys event also having a drinks connection, being the 'Britvic Babycham Cross'.

The following week saw the headline "It's Page Four" as Cycling joked about Roger Page (Hereford Rebores) winning the Over 35 years Veteran Championship for a stunning consecutive fourth time. He delighted his sponsor, who was present to see his triumph. Reporter Dennis Donovan waxed lyrical at the weather that day: "One last reminder of a brilliant summer just gone and the falling leaves in a multitude of colours providing a lovely backcloth to an excellent day's racing." Page was followed home by another tough rider Harry Bond (Bradford R.C.C.) and in third place came Mick Ives to collect the bronze medal. This Gannett C.C. promotion provided an excellent event with plenty of food and drink on offer for all.

The 'Forty Hall Scramble' held at Enfield, Middlesex was the happy hunting ground for the former World Amateur Champion Norbert Dedeckere. The Belgian had already shown the best of the British his heels at the 'Smirnoff Scramble' a month earlier, and he completed the same trick again in this event, where he appeared to pick his own moment to commit the 'Coup de grace'. Meanwhile, over at Trebanog in Wales, Andy Bohin (Bristol R.C.) was clocking up his fifth consecutive victory in the Acme Wheelers (Rhondda) cyclo-cross, although it was punctures that were the talking point of the day. Dave Holliday (Gordano Valley) also had a day he wouldn't forget in a long time, which Bill Brown of Cycling described this way: "He was riding well until he punctured in the second lap, got a quick change of wheel and then had his tub roll off half way round the third lap, when he flew right over the bars, but luckily was not injured."

Fifty-five riders lined up in the Wreake Valley event, with Vic Barnett (Liquid Plastic Coatings) pressing on early before catching the two lady riders who added the glamour to this otherwise male event. Barnett won from his old rival Roger Page (Hereford Rebores) with Tony Wilkins (Coventry/Olympic Viscount) taking the third spot.

It is very noticeable how much press coverage the sport of cyclo-cross was having during this period, with Cycling carrying up to four pages of reports and photographs from its own reporters and local correspondents, who covered every area of the country, including many smaller events which are the lifeblood of the sport. Just a few snippets from the November and December reports include the North of England Champion Barry Davies (Ron Kitching), who punctured on the first lap of one race, and then running to catch up, his wheel caught on a wall, ripping the sidewall of his tyre, so he then had to retire. In the Yorkshire C.C.A. Handicap race, the fourth in the series, a top grass track rider John Middleton (Yorkshire Clarion) won his first cyclo-cross race. Over in the east, the grounds of the University of East Anglia, was the site of another battle between team-mates, this time from the Colchester Rovers/Percy team. Neil Higgs pulling away from Colin Cracknell, with their team mate Neil Pears, being urged on with shouts of "Come on Dad!" Yet, despite organiser Vaughan Read of the East Anglian C.C devising a 'glue-pot of mud in a ditch' where two shoes were lost without trace, Higgs went on to win from Cracknell.

Naturally not all events ran smoothly from the start, as this next excerpt shows. In fact chaos was the best way to describe the start of the Velo Club Clwyd event, at the Buckley Sports Centre in North Wales, where Hugh Porter (Bantel) recorded his second win of the season. Ken Matthews the scribe for Cycling for this event wrote: "There was some aggro at the start and the Pros threatened to strike when the organisers announced they were to be handicapped. Porter, Dave Linehan (Gibbsport/Wilkings) and Graham Bufton (Lutz), made strong protests, saying the event should have been advertised as a handicap. Midst the confusion the flag dropped and away they went. Porter was facing the wrong way and not even on his bike!" But it was not long before he and the other two professionals were soon cutting their way through the field, so that by the end of the third of the 20 laps they were in the lead. Porter then made his move with five laps to go, showing a muddy pair of heels to the other two, long before the finish.

In the Midlands the Leicester Forest C.C's event was managing to cover almost every inch of the Saffron Lane Sports Centre, except for the track itself. The Midlands Champion Chris Dodd of the sponsored club Coventry/Viscount, notched up yet another win, this time from local professional Vic Barnett (Liquid Plastic Coatings) and in doing so showed a high degree of bike handling to triumph.

The cover of Cycling magazine of 6th December featured two young schoolboys running with their bikes battling against the terrain in the

National Schoolboys title race. Ken Whitmarsh described how southerner Andy Sawyer "Wrenched the title from the Midlands and North for the first time", although the South had won a silver and five bronzes in previous title races. This event brought Kevin Carr's run of 16 wins in a row to an end, for despite his obvious talent he could only come fourth. Sawyer almost had a disastrous preparation for the race, having ruined all his best tubulars during the week before while training, had to ride on road tyres that slipped and spun on the wet grass but by the second time down the steps he was away, winning from Steve Davies (Finham Park, Coventry) and Chris Boyce (Whitley Abbey). The new champion came from Poole Grammar School and received the new 'Halfords' Trophy and other prizes from the Lady Mayor of Southampton. Only a few weeks later, Sawyer was in the headlines once more, by winning the schoolboy race at the North Hampshire R.C. event. Then with only five minutes to recover, he started the senior event! The race starting with a 50 yard run for the competitors to collect their machines before the real racing began. Martin Springer (Crabwood C.C.) proved an easy winner, with the young Sawyer not far behind in ninth, completing two good rides in one day.

Cycling devoted almost five full pages to recording the previous weekend trip by British riders in both Luxembourg and France. On the Saturday, Jeff Morris was second behind Andre Wilhelm (Fra) beating in the process the former World Champion Albert Van Damme in the final sprint. John Atkins was fourth, with Mernickle fifth, Dodd sixth and Davies in eighth, demonstrating very tight packing by the British contingent. The Sunday's racing took place at Charleville-Mezieres, the event being the 'Priz d'Aiglemont Madison'. Jeff Morris teamed with Rene Bleuze (Fra) proved to be the winners, with John Atkins and Letellier second, Chris Dodd teamed with Londoner Bill Horne took fourth, then came Mernickle in fifth, teamed with Munch. All of them managed to beat the Tour de France ace Luis Ocana and his team mate, so all in all this was a very good venture abroad.

Ron Kitching the cycling components importer, was at this time producing full page adverts for specialist cyclo-cross equipment, such as 'T.A. cyclo-cross shoe plates' (bolted underneath shoes), 'T.A. and Zeus cyclo-cross chainwheels', plus 'Wolber, Vittoria and Milremo cross tubulars'. This showed that many manufacturers were looking to produce equipment exclusively for cyclo-cross. Geoffrey Butler Cycles were also advertising Lyotard 'double-sided' pedals at £1.95 and Reg Barnett was selling Wolber 'super-cross tub's at £4.50.

Simon Hawkes (Bristol R.C.) was crowned the new Junior Champion despite his moustachiod look that gave him a much older appearance than his 17years. The Championship was organised by the Norwich A.B.C, one of the oldest cycle racing clubs in the country. Their sponsors were Target Windows and the event was smoothly organised by Ivan Jeckell. Of the 55 entries none was more fancied to win than Chris Wreghitt (Coalville Whls.) but this was not a day for fancied riders as Mervyn Cartwright found when his gear entered his rear wheel. Hawkes made his move attacking Wreghitt at the bell, winning by just seven seconds. He then coolly dismounted and began chatting on the microphone within the sight of Wreghitt who collapsed exhausted on the grass nearby. Hawkes then disclosed that two of his ambitions had been realised on one day, the first was to win the race and the second was the news that Geoff Greenfield had told him that he was going to Poland for the World Championships.

A headline late in December declared: "Dodd Pro For Bantel." Bantel was a company wanting a bigger presence in cyclo-cross, having already sponsored a successful road racing team. Cycling noted: "It was undoubtedly (Hugh) Porter's current flirtation with cyclo-cross which has led to this departure for Bantel." Being in top form as an amateur and not being picked for the World Championships squad this season it was an obvious choice for Dodd.

The British riders took to the Continent once more in an endeavour to hone their fitness for the coming World Championships. They travelled to Kluisbergen to ride a Madison, which involved a 'Mudman' to be teamed up with a 'Roadman' making for very exciting racing, the roadmen depending on the crossmen's skill to win. "It was very dangerous," said Barry Davies "Lots of sheet ice- we all fell off." The course was laid through a caravan park, forest tracks and a cobbled climb, which was the cyclo-cross's fearful answer to the famous Mur de Grammont, which was just a short distance away. Jeff Morris was teamed with the Belgium Amateur Champion, and a Paris-Roubaix winner Pol Verschuere, but they could only finish fourth behind the almost unbeatable team of Norbert Dedeckere and the road star Michel Pollentier. The other teams including British riders finished, Mernickle sixth and Davies seventh, both having been teamed with Belgian roadmen. The Sunday venue was Luxemburg, where Dedeckere would win again, this time as a solo rider. The speed being more like that of a road race, Dodd was fifth, Davies ninth, although Mernickle finished with a badly swollen knee.

Christmas week saw National Coach Geoff Greenfield take a group of juniors and seniors over to Belgium, including Tony Lyne and Phil Allison. On the Saturday with only 1½ hours to spare after the Channel crossing, (we do seem to have heard this before) it was a rush to arrive in time for the start at Vladslo. The Belgian Junior champion Messelis was the race winner, with Wreghitt, Springer, Steve White, Martin Eadon, Bob Foskett and Andrew MacDonald all riding well. On the Sunday Messelis was again outstanding, with the British closely packed behind Wreghitt who was placed third this time. The idea of the weekend was to give everybody valuable experience against Continental opposition and in that way it was a success.

"Slaughter At The Palace" screamed the headline for the fourth of the I.C.S Trophy races. The balmy weather that riders had experienced during the early season events came to a sudden end with the New Year. In the event, held at Alexandra Palace, London, Jeff Morris (Diddington R.C.) returned to top form and was determined to show the professionals the back of his heels which he did in fine style. Cycling reporter John Coulson described the conditions thus: "The tricky going and the pressure at the front had the field strung out all round the circuit in no time, slipping, sliding, tumbling, and swearing as frozen fingers fumbled with gear levers. Morris, though, ignored the difficulties and looked indisputably in command from the third lap onwards, mud-splattered but supreme." The result was Morris first with John Atkins (Viscount/Shimano) second and Keith Mernickle (Chris Barber/Geofffrey Butler) third.

Young riders Chris Wreghitt (Coalville Wheelers) and Lee Wardley (Wolsey R. C.) were the early threats to National Professional Champion John Atkins in the 'Dusty's of Dudley' Cyclo-Cross at Aldersley Stadium, Wolverhampton. However it was Chris Dodd (Bantel) who made a determined effort to push Wardley down to third, after first disentangling a branch from his wheel! Winner John Atkins must have had a wry smile on his face after finishing, because both he and all the other riders had to pay a 20p entry fee to the stadium, (not cheap then) before putting on an exhibition of how to ride and win on a difficult course. Dusty's may have been the name of the event sponsor, but wet and cold was the order of the day.

Sutton Park at Birmingham was again the venue for the joint promotion of the Professional and Amateur Championships. The date for these races was the 11th of January with an afternoon start. The Championship programme had the look of a professional design, including this year a photograph of Atkins and Mernickle duelling during a race. Of the 100 riders, 14 were Professional with many of them riding their first championship for new sponsors. It is interesting to note how the prizes had increased over the years for the Amateur victor the Richmond trophy, championship jersey, a sash, a medallion and a salver, plus £25. The Professional winner received *The Daily Telegraph* Trophy, a sash, national jersey, a medallion, a silver salver and a £50 cheque. Keith Edwards, together with his experienced helpers from the Royal Sutton C.C, put together another excellent event. Noel Henderson's report of the championships in an I.C.S. magazine described a side of the event very few knew of on the day. "And successful it certainly was – even before the racing had started. Those people who had been fortunate enough to be invited to *The Daily Telegraph* reception in Sutton Town Hall may have had a little difficulty in reaching the park, copiously washed down by aperitifs and table wines. Fortunately, the distance between the two venues was very short!"

The estimate given of the number of spectators was 15,000, many standing six deep in the finishing straight. The course this year was over a tough (some called it a brute!) of 2.7 kilometres, with a snake through the park and two crossings of the brook, each involving the choice of deep water or trusting the stepping-stones. There were also footpaths and then a series of climbs and descents, before arriving at the end of a lap. Barry Davies (Ron Kitching) was the first to show his hand, followed by Keith Mernickle (Chris Barber/Geoffrey Butler), then Chris Dodd, riding in the colours of his new sponsor Bantel, soon joined him and the pattern was set for the day's racing. Was this to be Mernickle's day, he certainly thought so, for he then powered out alone. Meanwhile chaos was breaking out behind him, with Atkins unshipping his chain, Dodd fell off twice, and Morris had to change bikes. It did not stop there, for even Mernickle began to have problems with his cycle as he pressed on towards to his first title since the 1966/67 season. As he rode triumphantly down the finishing straight for the last time, he saw he had another famous champion in his sights, Hugh Porter, but he was unable to lap Porter before crossing under the finish banner alone. Jeff Morris (Dinnington R.C.) then came in at 56 seconds to take the Amateur title, with Atkins as the runner-up professional. Next was Chris Dodd (Bantel) taking third professional medal, with Phil Allison (Dinnington R.C.) taking the silver medal for amateurs and Tony Lyne (Gannet C.C.) the bronze.

"Mernickle Magnificent" declared the headline in Cycling to sum up the powerful ride by Keith Mernickle in winning the championship jersey for the second time. He claimed that there was no pressure on him to win and was so relaxed that the Cycling magazine also reported: "In the early hours of the same morning Mernickle could have been seen leaving an Oxford Street jazz club, having happily drunk five pints and looking forward to sleeping like a log." Many would think this was not the ideal preparation for a tilt at the championship, but perhaps the Chris Barber/ Geoffrey Butler professional had found a new training trick. Also reported were the final gripping stages of the event: "With four laps to go the pace was killing. Riders were falling on the ridges, others being bulked; most were red with effort – including Mernickle. Gone was that calm look he usually offers to spectators and opponents alike, as if he were on a cruise. Here was a different Mernickle sensing victory, he was bent low, looking haggard as he heaved a huge gear along the road section, his mouth hung open showing a streak of blood. 'Through gritting his teeth' said someone, but it was probably a piece of lashing gorse."

This year the World Championships were to be held at Chazay sur d'Azergues near Lyon in France and David Saunders in his article in *International Cycle Sport* described the course and organisation: "Like most world title courses it was set on a hillside but was hardly a thoughtful choice at the village of Chazay sur d'Azergues, some 15 miles north of Lyon. The roads and parking arrangements were poor and in short, the French organisation was as bad as the Swiss had been good at Melchnau a year earlier."

Mud, mud, glorious mud, should have been the theme song for this World Championship, for rain and snow a few days before the big day turned the course into a quagmire, more rain and even more snow meant the run-ups were now extremely slippery.

The result of the Professional race was first Albert Zweifel of Switzerland, second was Peter Frischknecht his Swiss team-mate and Andre Wilhelm (France) took the bronze medal. The G.B riders were well down with Atkins 18th, Mernickle 22nd and Bufton 26th. In the Amateur race Klaus-Peter Thaler (West Germany) took first place with Robert Vermeire (Belgium) in second and Ekkehard Teichreber also of West Germany in third. The British arrived back in the twenties and thirties with Jeff Morris 29th, Springer 30th, Lyne 33rd and Allison at one lap. The winning team was no surprise for it was West Germany.

David Saunders continued his report with hard, but honest words about the British performance:

All those British readers are by now wondering if G.B. had a team at all. We all remember that the selectors named a team for both title races so what happened to them? I'm not sure that I want to tell you. Perhaps I can spare the details a little, sugar the bitterness by saying that a few of them didn't get lapped. The whole thing was a down-right disgrace and they might just as well have saved the money for next year and maybe done it all a bit better. ....It is difficult to find out exactly what people think, what people have done and why they did it when there is such a series of conflicting reports and you cannot even rely on the people you ask to tell the truth! The team hotel was bad, so they were moved. Morale was non-existent and why should it have been high after a bad and a mad rush to get down in a coach, which lost its Perspex window from its roof on the autoroute. And the fact that it was midnight Thursday when they arrived.

He also had some very strong views on both the British Team Manager and the riders he picked for this World Championships:

The team manager, Geoff Greenfield, is a nice man which is perhaps why he shouldn't be the National Coach and why he certainly shouldn't be the Team Manager. Martin Springer is getting softer instead of harder, Jeff Morris wants discipline and Phil Allison, despite a tremendous improvement at home, needs encouragement. Tony Lyne was his usual dogged self but I'm sure the trip didn't do him any good either ... Britain's amateur cyclo-cross riders are as far away now from gaining any kind of medal in world competition as they were 20 years ago.

As you can read he certainly did not mince his words, it was strong stuff, but they were his honestly felt views and he hoped by expressing them, there would be some changes.

John Coulson, also in *International Cycle Sport* gave a good, if slightly amusing description, of a course designed by Johnny Morris at the new Eastway Circuit in East London: "Cyclo-cross has taken over with a rough, tough course designed with customary fiendish ingenuity by Johnnie Morris, uncrowned king of 'cross promoters. A snag arose in an abundance of glass chippings working their way up through the soil from the old rubbish dump which gave rise to a plethora of punctures in the first 'cross event. However, Colin Lewis (the former Pro' rider, now circuit manager) hopes that assiduous sweeping and continuous inspection of the ground will minimise this nuisance."

During March, this same magazine carried an atmospheric photo on the cover of Keith Mernickle in his Championship jersey just ahead of Chris Wreghitt racing over frosty ground emerging out of a cold misty background that gave the distinct image of a cyclo-cross event in winter. The event was the Liverpool edition of the I.C.S. Trophy League, held at Sefton Park and John Atkins proved to be the winner, taking his total of Trophy League wins to five and just to prove his superiority he won them all in a row.

12

The Senior Championships Go Open

Season 1976/77

A 'Sport for All Week' was held in Hyde Park, during September, where the public were entertained to the spectacle of expert cross men teamed with well-known personalities. The thousands watching enjoyed seeing the personalities floundering about. The boxer Henry Cooper was teamed up with Keith Mernickle, Cooper fell at the very first obstacle, a hurdle, and the crowd loved it. Afterwards, despite declaring, "I'm knackered" he said he had enjoyed the experience. Others involved in this demonstration were, Alan Pascoe, the Olympic 400 metres star, who was teamed up with John Atkins. Phil Liggett, the Milk Race director, was introduced as "Doesn't race now but was fit enough to keep up with Pascoe." More amusement was caused when Alan Pascoe flung himself on to his bike, missing the saddle and landed on his stomach. The event over, they all joined in with a tug-o-war with other celebrities such as Alan Ball, World Cup winner of 1966. Whether this idea would go down with the millionaire superstars of today is doubtful.

When Cycling interviewed Keith Mernickle about the coming season, he gave some interesting insights into his thoughts on the sport in very plain language.

I've seen a vast number of changes since I first rode in the mud back in 1957, the main one being on the commercial side. When I turned Independent in 1963, people said I was mad to turn purely on my 'cross ability, but nowadays every race boasts its complements of pro's, many of whom could not afford to race without sponsorship. I've also seen many team managers come and go. Probably our best managers ever, were in the mid-Sixties when Paddy Hoban and Ralph Jordan were in charge, but in the last two years we've had an all-time low … Men like John Morris, Ralph Jordan, Paddy

Hoban, Mick Ives and also Keith Edwards in his day could all get on their bikes and go out with their teams, and if you're not on form they'll tear the legs off you ... I think that in cyclo-cross having no coach at all is better than having a bad one, because riders pick up lots of bad habits that are hard to break ... I may be old-fashioned, but I think the only way to ride a bike fast over any kind of terrain is to train on a bike and not off it ... Every year £1,500 is spent on our amateur squad and the money would be better spent getting our riders across the Channel more often ... I think the system introduced last year to categorise races according to the prize value can do nothing but good.

His opinion of the National Coach, Geoff Greenfield, was also very forceful.

Last season, when our world pro and amateur teams were offered a very lucrative contract in France (the host nation for the World's) with food and accommodation for a whole week if required, on top of this transport to the venue if needed, the pros of course snapped up the offer, but the B.C-C.A Manager decided that a training and racing weekend in Southampton was more suitable. The French couldn't believe that they'd turned down such an offer, and judging by the old bus that they travelled to Lyons in, I think the transport alone would have been worth going for. ...I think Jeff Morris is probably the best prospect we've had in many years, but because he has arthritis in his joints I don't think we'll be seeing much of him this season. There are not any short-cuts to the top, it's a long, hard slog.

Mernickle also mentioned that Colin Mott of the South Eastern R.C. was the new coach in the London Area, and hoped he would do as good a job there, as he had done with the riders of his own club.

Once more the cover of the handbook was changed, this time a black background with a bold B.C-C.A badge in red on a white centre. There was a big shake-up among the officials this time, with the President now P.Fretwell, Ivan Dodd the Chairman, with S.Rooker taking the job of Treasurer and the post of Press/P.R.O. now in the hands of Life Member Joan Edwards. The number of pages in this edition had climbed to 56, with the number of listed events rising to over 150 for the first time. The reason for continuing to quote handbooks is that, within the pages of these small thin books is a large fund of information, even the layout and type styles show different periods. This handbook prompted a comment from Cycling: "Growing interest in this arduous winter aspect of cycle racing is reflected in the 310 races listed, comparable to the 250 last year."

The Three Peaks this year boasted six previous winners including the three Johns, Rawnsley, Atkins, and Bell plus the course record holder Eric Stone. The Police co-operation was described as 'superb' and the Yorkshire Television cameras were there, as were the B.B.C with John Noakes of the 'Blue Peter' team, all ready to record the race. John Atkins (Viscount/ Shimano) won the £5 prize for topping Ribblehead. On Ingleborough the helpers were awaiting the leaders with spare bikes and wheels, none of which were needed by the new leader Eric Stone who was about to be caught by Atkins and Wilkinson. Over Pen-y-Ghent, Atkins had opened an impressive two minute gap and was heading as fast as he could for the finishing straight in Horton, arriving to the cheers of the largest crowd ever seen at the event. Stone and Wilkinson sprinted for second place, with Stone winning the battle when Wilkinson's chain jammed at a vital moment. Tom McDonald (Bronte Wheelers) finished as first veteran, and Martin Eadon (Rugby Velo) the 1974 schoolboy champion, was the first junior.

The 2nd of October edition of Cycling had five large adverts for cyclo-crosses, showing a wide spread of events. North Bucks had the 'North Bucks M.K.V.' event, Greenwich the 'Harry Perry' organised by the V.C. Elan club, then there was the 'Barnswood Camp' promoted by the Newbury R.C. in Berkshire, and up in Lincolnshire, the 10th 'Annual Luda Valley Championship' sponsored by Falcon Cycles, which had a prize list of over £200. This prize list must have been very desirable, for the average wage was probably about £35 a week and organisers of most small, unsponsored events, did not even plan what the prize list would be until they had all the entry fees gathered in.

Graham Bufton (Falcon Cycles) gained his second win in two weeks, giving an indication that he was on his top form this early in the season. Schoolboy Kevin Carr was another rider with two wins under his belt. There were no Belgian riders this year at the 'Forty Hall Scramble' and so Keith Mernickle (Chris Barber/Geoffrey Butler) out-performed everyone to win. Mernickle just cruised home in this Wembley R.C. promotion, after an early tussle with the other main contenders Chris Dodd (Bantel), Springer (Crabwood), Hanson (Mills/Pearson) and Wardley, now with the Diss & District/Huret team. These events in early October always take part at a time of year when various cycling disciplines merge, road races and time trials tapering off, the hill climb specialists are in the midst of their season, and the cyclo-cross riders are only just getting into their swing.

A good example of all this merging of disciplines and the trials of being an organiser can be understood when Jack Brace of the Stevenage C.C./Scotplas team organised a road race one week followed the next week by a cyclo-cross event. It was to be no easy race to start, as the riders had to wait for a Motor Club event held on the same circuit to finish first. National champion Keith Mernickle, having won earlier in the day in South London, could have benefited from the delay but not this time, because the riders had to await the start in cold driving rain, and were becoming very impatient. Finally after being delayed for an hour and a half, the race got underway in incessant rain, with the riders now very rebellious indeed. But Chris Dodd (Bantel) adapted best to the delays by winning by 30 seconds from John Atkins.

The end of November saw the competition for the Area titles. Two of the new champions were Tim Butler (Diss & District/Huret), who triumphed in the Eastern Area, he held off a surge of four local rivals, Cefin Mobbs, Colin Cracknell, junior Duncan Chenery and veteran Neil Pears all from the Colchester Rovers/Percy club where continuous rain fell both before and during the event. In Wessex, Paul Kissane (Rufus Whls.) was to take his second championship win in two years in an event called the 'Sotonia Autumn Scramble'. Paul, who was often troubled with mechanical problems, watched Ian McDonald (Coventry Olympic/Viscount) being the victim this time, first having to change to his brother's bike, followed by two falls, but at the end still remained ahead of junior Mike Teague of the Crabwood C.C. who took third.

In the fight for the Schoolboys title, it was the very talented Kevin Carr (Sherbourn High School) in his distinctive yellow jersey who proved the winner from Dave Miller (Grove Comp.). On a bright cold afternoon 90 of the 120 entries lined up along side a football pitch, ready for the mass charge. Ken Matthews and the National Road Race Champion Doug Dailey had devised the course, making the most of the area around the Kirkby Stadium, with the Kirkby C.C. as promoters. Mike Bell, the London Schools Champion, took third place and the team award went to the Sheffield's Rowlinson School with R. Freeman, C. Ledger and D. Broomhead. Kevin Carr not only excelled at cyclo-cross but also had several wins in road races, although he was said to still prefer the winter sport.

The next of the titles to change hands was the Junior Title, which was fought out between two Davies, the winner Steve Davies coming from the club that had produced so many champions in this sport, the Coventry R.C. He proved to be the stronger, winning from Mick Davies (Wreake Valley C.C). Cycling's Ken Whitmarsh described the winner's ride as "None could match the bustling style of the eight stone pocket Hercules who failed to make the grade in the early season selection events."

Just before Xmas John Atkins would add another landmark to his already illustrious career when he became the first rider to pocket £100 in a home cyclo-cross event. The 'Dusty's of Dudley' event was organised by the Wolverhampton Wheelers at the newly named Wolverhampton Stadium. Punctures were very much a talking point that day, with Dodd, Atkins and Jewell all collecting a trio each! Other comments were about the large difference between the first and second prizes, which was £50, and the absence of the National Amateur Squad. Most of the experienced riders agreeing that hard racing would have been better for them than two hours training followed by gym work. One amateur competitor who proved to be a tough racer on the day was Lee Wardley (Diss & District/ Huret), who finished the race sandwiched between six professionals, three ahead of him and three more behind.

The New Year started well for Keith Hanson's sponsors Mills-Pearson, who must have been delighted with his clear win in the event that they were sponsoring in Morden Park, Surrey. Hanson was sometimes known at this time as, "The Eternal Second", but this event proved the image to be wrong. The Redmon C.C arranged for the Union Jack to be dropped by the British Cycling Federation President, Eileen Gray, as a gesture towards harmony between cycling disciplines. Cycling said, "Hanson who normally gets by with no training except his ride to work (on 86" fixed) each day, had put himself out and trained for this one during the holiday."

The final event of the I.C.S. Trophy series was to see John Atkins (Viscount/Shimano) win from his perennial rival Keith Mernickle of the Chris Barber/ Geoffrey Butler team and therefore place his hands on the trophy for a moral boosting sixth time. Professionals took the first four places, Atkins, Mernickle, Dodd, and Jewell followed by Wardley as first amateur. Looking at photographs of this event, it is evident that head protection was still not a high priority with most riders. Wardley in the top finishers competing in leather 'crash-hat' was perhaps the exception, was it just bravado, or did they see no danger in their chosen sport?

Keith Mernickle, as the reigning champion, was featured on the cover of the first 'Open' Championship programme. An 'Open' championship meant that the previous Professional and Amateur Championships would now be merged into one race, with the winner being the first rider to finish, whatever their category. The venue now seemingly settled at Sutton Park, Birmingham. Ten reserves were listed for the first time for this event, with 50 clubs having representatives. The course had a different layout from the previous years, with only 8 laps being required. The notion that the number 13 was unlucky probably didn't occur to John Atkins as he crossed the line alone to the applause of a massive crowd, estimated at 20,000, to win making it his 13th National Title. It was also the same number of times that *The Daily Telegraph* had been the sponsor of the National Championships, mainly because of the continuing support of their chief Sports Reporter, David Saunders.

Keith Mernickle in second place commentated to Cycling: "Atkins on his day is a hard man to beat. I don't think it was a disgrace to finish second to him." The course proved to be a truly tough one, and tested all the riders to the limit, during the 16 miles of racing, Atkins and Mernickle rode as if a strip of elastic was joining them together, with first Atkins drawing ahead, then Mernickle fighting back. Meanwhile the amateurs were battling further down the field, among them the four that were picked afterwards to ride the World Championships. The four chosen were Martin Springer, Chris Wreghitt, Phil Allison and Lee Wardley. David Saunders described Wardley's ride: "Wardley rode well, in view of losing his roof rack from his car when travelling to the event. He rode a borrowed machine, pulled a wheel over, fell and had other problems and still finished seventh." Cycling also covered this incident, by reporting that the Motorway Police were soon on the spot, having had a report "that someone was mending a puncture on a pushbike." Mernickle suffered a puncture, but never gave up, and closed within just 17 seconds at the finish line. Ian Jewell, Mernickle's team-mate finished third. Cycling headlining Atkins's win as "John Atkins Crowned Cross King Again" over their report of the Championships. Chris Dodd the Bantel sponsored rider was unfortunately forced to withdraw from the World's team as his wife was expecting their first child; Keith Hanson would take his place.

On Wednesday the Thames T.V programme 'Sports Scene' featured Keith Mernickle before he flew out to the World Championships on the Friday with the rest of the team. Cycling reported his comments: "It's a preview of the weekend's sport, I've got a four minute spot out of the

15 minute programme. They've really done us proud this season with coverage of the I.C.S. events."

Albert Zweifel (Switzerland) had had his critics before the World Championships held in Niedersachsen Stadion, Hanover, West Germany. He silenced those critics in the most decisive way by winning the World crown for the second time. However, the British riders, particularly the professionals, continued to take a lot of flak from the critics back home, for what some considered their aim 'was just to finish', rather than make an impression on the race.

David Saunders in his report in *International Cycle Sport* wrote: "Atkins is a distinguished veteran and it was wrong to pin hopes on his doing well. It may have been wrong to even select him but, with his record and looking at what was left, there was no one else to send. Let's face it. John Atkins really chose himself but it was all a bit of a waste of money. I asked him before the start if he thought he could make the first ten and he told me, 'I shall be delighted if I make the first 15. Believe me, if I do, we'll all have a booze-up tonight to celebrate'." Was Atkins just being realistic by stating the above, rather than demoralised before racing. It must be remembered that John Atkins was returning to Hanover after a gap of 16 years and a long and distinguished career. Winner Zweifel, was followed home by his team-mate Peter Frishneckt, who was also the silver medallist for the second year running. Amazing multi-champion Eric de Vlaeminck, now near the end of his career, had to settle for the bronze. The British riders came in much lower down, with Atkins in 20th at one lap, I.Jewell 23rd, K.Mernickle 25th and K.Hanson 29th. Adding to their woes the G.B. team were placed eighth, with only Luxemburg counting lower.

Meanwhile the G.B amateurs, although not making an impression on their race, escaped the harsher criticism; some commented on the fact, that the British riders had not spent enough time racing on the continent or on courses against the top riders. The injured Jeff Morris was the exception from any of these remarks, having regularly beaten both Jean-Yves Plaisance and Alex Gerardin who finished sixth and seventh in the Championships. Belgium again produced the Champion, with Robert Vermeire, who took his fifth Rainbow Jersey since 1970. Ekkehard Teichreber of West Germany was in the silver medal position, having improved one place since 1976 with the Czechoslovakian Voitek Cervinek as the bronze medallist. The British amateur placings were C. Wreghitt 28th, P.Allison 36th, M.Springer 39th and L.Wardley 44th. This was also disappointing, as the Great Britain team finished ninth only just ahead of Denmark, Spain and the U.S.A.

Cycling's Editorial the next week was scathing about the G.B. team's performance:

> British Cyclo-cross officials must have an endless supply of drawing boards to go back to. Once again our Amateurs took a thrashing, which wasn't quite what we expected. Among those who beat all but one of our riders was a U.S.A. rider Laurence Malone, who realised home competition wasn't enough, so went to live in France. In the nearly-past season Britain's international hopefuls haven't been abroad as much as before, and they have suffered as a result.

The Ogmore Valley Wheelers event in South Wales found riders trying to cope with deep snow. One of the climbs was aptly named 'Everest' and on a day of severe winter weather, this climb lived up to its name in the eyes of the riders. Austin Heath (Bynea C.C.) overcame the conditions best to win, but it was the young schoolboys who showed real gritted teeth on such a day in their event, with Andrew Price (Gannet C.C.) taking the victory.

13

Wreghitt wins the first of his five-in-a-row

Season 1977/78
As we move towards the last few years of this decade, an interview with
Lee Wardley, during the autumn of 2007, gives an insight into this period.
British riders were still racing on a shoestring budget, not having moved
on very far since the fifties and sixties.

I rode with straight handlebars until well into the time I was riding
with the G.B. Squad, because I always felt I had better control. I
had to change as courses became faster and faster, this was long
before I had seen a Mountain bike. I had the nickname of "Carrotcruncher" which I believe was because I came from Suffolk.

...We got a big shock when we raced abroad, for instance we
travelled to the World Championships with only one bike and spare
wheels and we had to de-clog our own bikes as we went, while the
Continentals exchanged their machines for clean ones as often as
required. We were only supplied with stirrup pumps, with a bucket
and brush, while they had all the best cleaning equipment

...Travelling arrangements were very basic too, on one occasion,
we were to travel abroad in two cars, but when we got to London
one was not up to the trip, so we all piled into Johnny Morris's
American estate car. I and another rider squeezed into the rear part
to travel across France, not the best way to prepare for an important
event.

...On another trip we arrived at the French Customs, only to
realise that all our passports were in our luggage in the other car,
there where no mobile phones then, so we could not contact the
other car. Morris told us to 'just keep quiet', so with him speaking
French and lots of charm we crossed over the borders of France,
Belgium, and Germany and on into Switzerland. I don't know what
he said, but I bet it had lots about us being Cycling Champions in

a hurry. ... Morris was a 'riders rider' he understood what a rider needed and always kept our spirits up, he was a man to get things done, including finding funding to help us. On one occasion we stopped at his boat on the Thames and had a ride in his E-Type Jag. Geoff Greenfield was a different person, a quiet, nice man but didn't inspire.

There were other things we were surprised at in Belgian races and not just the awful 'Flanders mud', but at one event I was standing ready to start when the Belgian next to me just pushed me over onto the grass, by the time I got up the others were off and 100 yards ahead. Another tactic which caught us out, was that because there were no rules on where a bike should be exchanged, they had their clean bikes at the top of a greasy slope and would throw their muddy ones down at the slope bottom, running up without them! As we only had one machine we were at a big disadvantage, as we had to keep ours with us, this type of thing was not always shown in reports in the home press.

Many funny things did happen though, I remember once in Switzerland, I was told to ride in ladies tights because of the severe cold, when I finished they were torn to shreds ending as more ladders than tights!

...My training was about 200 miles a week, which was nearly all on dark winter nights. One night I well remember, was while training hard and fast, I shot into the air because I hadn't seen that the road turned right! I ended up on the grass between two telegraph poles. The night training meant I needed good lights, so one day I went to my local cycle shop and asked to have a dyno-hub put into a sprint rim, believe me, he gave me a very odd look.

On the equipment side, we had to do lots of things ourselves. I remember once cutting off all the teeth on two 52-tooth chainrings, and then bolting one each side of my chainring. I did this so that the chain would not de-rail, I don't think they would be expected to do that these days. The fashion when I started was for 5 speeds, but by the time I finished 10 speeds were the thing. We were also still wearing those woolly shorts and tops that went all saggy and loose when wet, as Lycra had not yet come in for us. I was very lucky not to break any bones but I did finish one event where when I took my helmet off (a foam Bell type) it had a deep gash where I had hit a tree!

Another new season, and riders with more mud than blood in their veins were looking forward to sunny frosty mornings, icy starts, biting winds, water splashes and even snow on occasions, all these elements doing their best to make the courses even more difficult for their adversaries. Whether they raced in front of big cheering crowds or just a few spectators and a dog, all the riders were willing to give of their best in their winter sport.

There was little in this year's handbook that differed from previous years although remarkably, every one of the National Officers and local officers running the Areas remained in their posts, therefore making for a very stable B.C-C.A.

'The World's Toughest Cyclo-Cross Race' otherwise known as the Three Peaks was run for the seventeenth year on 25th of September. The true picture of how awesome this really is, can be judged by the fact that very few sporting events have details in their programme of 'Where to see the Riders' with the main ones listed as Ribblehead at 1,000 ft, and the summits of Whernside 2,414ft, Ingleborough 2,373 ft, and Pen-Y-Ghent 2,273ft. Event organiser John Rawnsley had two proud points in his programme notes: "This year there is a 50% increase in the number of competitors making a total of 146, a record for cyclo-cross in Britain ... I am especially pleased to welcome back last year's winner and current National Cyclo-Cross Champion John Atkins, one of the few professionals who have the courage to ride the 3 Peaks."

In the end, after two hours and forty minutes of hard endeavour, it was Eric Stone (Bradford R.C.C) who was triumphant. The final 130 riders had first to tackle five-and-a-half miles of tarmac before the off road riding began. Steady rain descended throughout. Cycling wrote: "This was the most electrifying start of a Peaks." Three men went away, former winner John Bell (Bronte Wheelers/MacManus) Alan Mellor (Tame Valley) and Bob Swailes (Kent Valley) but it was the big names that finally came in to take the applause of the waiting crowd. Last year's winner John Atkins (Viscount/Shimano) came in second at nearly eleven minutes and Colin Wilkinson (BronteWheelers/ MacManus) a further 12 seconds back, who also led home the winning team.

A memorable victory for Chris Wreghitt (G.S.Strada) came in the Bearwood 'cross in October, when he triumphed over National Champion Atkins, at the Manor Abbey Stadium, Halesowen. Wreghitt had surged ahead to take the scalp of 'King John' by 26 seconds.

Illness was the topic among riders and spectators during the middle of the month, with Vic Barnett (Liquid Plastic Coatings) arising from his sickbed, to once more win the Luda Valley Senior Cyclo-Cross Championship. He was not the only one, for Mick Daley (Rothwell C.R.T/Cherry Valley) the previous winner, was suffering with a heavy cold and could only finish eighth.

The first I.C.S. Trophy event was blessed with a glorious Indian summer afternoon, with Cycling's reporter John Coulson entitling his report 'Battle of the Giants'. The 'giant' was once more John Atkins (Viscount/ Shimano) who was now classed firmly as a veteran. His only rival, Keith Mernickle, was dropped with just two laps to go at the chequered flag, with Hanson taking third spot. Another event billed as "The Mud in the Meadows" held at Footscray on the first Saturday in October, was a dry and 'hard as a bone' affair. Keith Mernickle was noted to be in a state of advanced fitness for this time of the season, displaying it to the full by winning the event by over 2 minutes. The revelation of the event though, was Steve White (De Laune C.C.) who came second on this course, which had a new up hill start to sort out the massed field of riders.

A well-known face from the past was present at the T.D.C.Cross event promoted by the Royal Sutton C.C. The face belonged to the former triple National Champion Mick Stallard, who was to surprise many by remaining in contention for most of the race, finally finishing a creditable sixth. But it was John Atkins who was the most delighted, by returning to his winning ways.

Graham Bufton (Harry Quinn Cycles) retained his Veteran title in the Midland Bank sponsored championships at Loughborough. It was held over a tough course that caused many problems for all competitors. Mick Ives (Coventry/Viscount) took the silver medal for the second successive year, and then came Tom McDonald of Bronte Wheelers-McManus-Poole, (surely one of the longest club names at this time). Three stream crossings were the main problem spots for both the top and less experienced riders. Ives, in particular, being unhappy each time he approached the third crossing, for the rocks placed as stepping stones tended to move under the rider's feet. Competitors would have to skip across or find they were sinking a foot into the oozing mud.

The Belgians were back in Britain during early November for the 'Smirnoff Scramble'. The Flanderian, Freddy Deschacht demonstrated how to ride both fast and true, to win by 25 seconds. After the ploughed fields he was used to back home, Deschacht had little difficulty with the mud on this course; young though he was, he put on a master class in how to pick the right route through the cloying clay, with a light footed disdain. The sprint between the following English riders for second place resulted in John Atkins heading Keith Hanson (Mills/Pearson) who had to settle for third after taking the wrong line in the finishing straight.

A sorry tale of more oozy mud and a small branch spoilt Chris Dodd's 26th birthday, resulting in no gift of a win in his father Bill's promotion, at Baginton for the Coventry-Olympic-Viscount club. The site of his mishap was near the finish on the very last lap, Atkins and Dodd both running with bikes on shoulders, then Dodd's bike caught in a overhanging branch allowing Atkins to go on to win. But the black and white clad Bantel rider was left less unhappy when he heard that he had led home the winning team.

The Daily Telegraph brought over three world-class continental riders for their sponsored International Cyclo-cross and the B.B.C. T.V. cameras were there once more to record their presence. But Dennis Donovan of Cycling posed this question in his column, "Where were the crowds?" and summed up the reason as "One can only assume that the dearth of spectators was due to them remaining indoors to watch, instead of providing a show of strength to the watching millions." The extra class of the continentals can only be gauged by the fact that Keith Hanson (Mills-Pearson) was our best rider in fifth at over 2 minutes.

But the race was always between the glittering array of Europeans, Willi Lienhard of Switzerland, Robert Vermeire, the Belgian Amateur World Champion, Klaus-Peter Thaler the former World Champion and his countryman Uebing. Gertie Wildeboer the Dutch champion and not least, Michel Pollentier the winner of both the Tour of Italy and Switzerland. Seeing these stars must have been a delight to those who took the effort to turn up. Before arriving at the Peoples Park, Luton, the two West German riders flew in just in time, after surviving a car crash on an Autobahn and Wildeboer who had decided to travel by boat, spent five hours being seasick. Originally the plan had been for 14 laps but this was cut to nine to accommodate the T.V. programmers.

As the season neared its half way mark, Eric Stone (Ron Kitching Cycles) was in commanding form in the north, winning at both 'Thieves Wood' organised by the Mansfield Aces and the Calder Clarion event at Thornes Park, Wakefield. The club had permission for the first event from the Forestry Commission only 14 days beforehand. Stone made light work of all the obstacles, to win from Paul Gilbert of the Dinnington R.C/ Universal Contractors club. His second successive win was also clear, this time from Phil Allison (Altrincham R.C/Rotalac) a winner himself the previous week.

A Cycling headline during December implored jokingly: "Can no one stop Atkins?" which must have echoed the thoughts of many riders and organisers over his long and illustrious career. Although many might believe that he was destined to be a cycle sport champion as his mother had held so many place-to-place records including the famous End-to-End and his father had been a fine racer and founder B.C-C.A official, promoting many cyclo-cross events. The Cycling headline though, was commentating on his display in the third round of the *International Cycle Sport* Trophy Series held over a one-mile circuit at Timperley, Cheshire. This win ahead of Keith Hanson left him at the top of the Trophy table with 89 points, Hanson with 85 points and Mernickle in third with 78.

Chris Wreghitt had a busy time during the Christmas holidays trying to prove that British riders could be competitive abroad and with style. He achieved a second placing on Christmas Day in the Wambrechies Madison at Polle in France, being partnered by the Belgian P.Pauwels, they finished behind Hennie Kuiper and Rene Bleuze, but ahead of Tour-de-France riders Joop Zoetemelk and Roger Alban. The day before, he had finished a fine tenth, and then on Boxing Day he was seventh in another Belgian event. He finished third at the New Year in Luxembourg to the Dutchman C.Van der Wereld and finally took a fourth placing at Grevenmacher also in Luxembourg, so completing an altogether very rewarding and successful expedition.

The arrival of 1978 marked a double centenary year. The Cyclists' Touring Club formed as the Bicycle Touring Club in 1878 and The Bicycle Union in the same year. The B.C.U metamorphosed first into the National Cyclists' Union, which then became the British Cycling Federation and finally is now British Cycling. Although strangely enough it was C.T.C members, who as described earlier, were at the forefront of 'rough-stuff' and cross-country races.

The second edition of the Redmon C.C. Mills/Pearson promotion sounds a very innovative event. It was held on January 2nd and included extra to the main Grand Prix and Schoolboy/ Junior/Ladies races, a Penny Farthing Match race, a Toddler's race and even the 'Merton Bed Race', whatever that might entail, it all sounds like a good day out full of crowd pleasing fun.

John Atkins won the final event in the *International Cycle Sport* Trophy Series at Wolverhampton, for an amazing seventh time. In recognition of this feat, Peter Fretwell the proprietor of I.C.S magazine presented John with a bonus of £100. The final I.C.S. overall table finished with John Atkins top with 119 points, followed by Keith Hanson 110 and K.Mernickle with 105.

In Devon, Roger Dean (Exeter Wheelers.) led all the way after the first 200 yards to win in his own club's promotion. He was so far ahead near the end, that he had lapped every other competitor, knocking up two wins from the three races in the series.

Sunday 15th January 1978 was a big day for Birmingham, the venue for the British Cyclo-Cross Championship. Once more the riders had to contend with a selection of road, grassland, paths, hard tracks and hurdles, all of which would test the competitors to the utmost. The B.C-C.A expressed their gratitude to *The Daily Telegraph* for their support of this event once again. John Atkins (Viscount/Shimano) at the age of 35 could qualify for the Veterans Championship although he was still a man to respect even in this race.

David Saunders in pre-race predictions in his Daily Telegraph column went out on a limb by predicting Chris Wreghitt (G.S.Strada-Lutz) as the new champion. His prediction would prove to be right but only by the closest of margins. Whether he would have still had his money on Wreghitt with 100 yards to go, only he could say, for the defending champion John Atkins, was only out sprinted by Wreghitt in the last few lunges to the line. Dennis Donovan in Cycling describes the battle thus: "This Daily Telegraph sponsored event was a real cracker, no quarter given and none asked, with an enormous crowd watching one of the closest finishes yet, and a battle that will be talked about far into the more conventional racing season."

Chris Dodd (Harry Quinn) in his red jersey was the first to emerge from the grip of the 100 riders spread out over the starting meadow. Next in line were Stone, Wreghitt, Atkins and Allison, followed at a gap by Andy Jones (Toutourien/Tower) and Vic Barnett (L.P.C.). With two laps over, it was Wreghitt in the lead with Atkins close on his tail, showing all his years of experience with his smooth pedalling style. At half way it was still Wreghitt and Atkins in the lead and riding in tandem. Keith Mernickle could be heard approaching, his breathing sounded like a rasp saw as he attacked Stone and Dodd. Donovan's report of the final moments continued: "It was elbow to elbow, Wreghitt not afraid to show some aggression, but as the vast crowd craned their necks to see who would get there first, Atkins got ahead. He looked as if he was to make it first, but then Wreghitt came again, jumping like a track sprinter, and Atkins, who has seen only two men go past him before in a championship, saw the third slip by and his hopes with him."

The organiser Reg Ward must have been delighted with his promotion for he had followed on from Ray Richards, who had laid down such a high standard. Hence a new champion had been crowned, with the old champion, Atkins, in silver at just one second and Stone (Ron Kitching) in the bronze placing. The cycling reporters during this period of minimal colour printing and hardly any T.V. coverage, had to conjure up the colourful and exciting racing before them into pages of script, for the many fans awaiting the thump of their favourite weekly or monthly cycling magazine.

Four Professional and three Amateurs were selected to represent Great Britain at this year's World Championships, to be held in Spain on January 22nd. Chris Dodd (Harry Quinn Cycles), Eric Stone (Ron Kitching) who was making a comeback to International scene, Keith Hanson (Mills/Pearson) and the rider who always put in a good performance in a G.B. jersey, John Atkins (Viscount/Shimano). The amateur riders selected were Martin Springer, Chris Wreghitt and Phil Allison, with a fourth to be picked later. The team was to be backed up by Bob Thom as Manager, Steve Snowling as Mechanic and Frank Westell the Masseur.

The first edition of Cycling magazine after the World Championships carried the front page headline: "Britons Slump in World 'Cross" followed by "Britain's Pro and Amateur teams slumped yet again in the World Championship cyclo-cross events near Bilbao in Spain at the weekend, with the cruelly muddy conditions putting paid even to the hopes of new National Champion Chris Wreghitt, who pulled out, for the rarest of reasons." All these words were printed in a white out of a black panel, as if the magazine was in mourning for British cyclo-cross aspirations.

The Championships this year were indeed only for the toughest of the tough, because the course would dictate that only the hard, fit men would stand on the podium. The week before had seen rain and snow fall on the course and an overnight storm turned the Amorebieta course into a quagmire. Professional Albert Zweifel of Switzerland proved to be the outstanding rider for the third year running, winning by over a minute from his countryman Peter Frischknecht. The result proved to be to the delight of Zweifel's 400 fans who had chartered four planes especially to see their hero. The fans watching the finish saw their men almost unrecognisable as human beings, for they were covered from head to toe in mud. Klaus-Peter Thaler came in for the bronze at over 2½ minutes down. Eric Stone was the first Briton home in 17th place and the only one to avoid being lapped, next was Atkins in 21st and then came Dodd in 22nd and Hanson 24th. Atkins arrived showing evidence of a tumble and was now a complete sheet of mud with only the whites of his eyes showing, to the delight of the Belgian journalists who asked if this "camouflage was a new British tactic."

Six laps faced the 44 amateur riders in their Championship, with 33 year old Vermeire (Belg.) hoping to gain himself and his fans a sixth World Championship, but after the first lap he was down in seventh spot. The orange jersey of Dutch rider Johnnus Stamsnijder led after the first circuit, but the British riders were already trailing. Dennis Donovan, once more writing in Cycling: "Liboton (Belg.) led on the second lap and a woman near the grandstand started to cry. It was his mother, who was unable to keep back the tears as she watched her son pound into a small lead on Gilles Blaser, Switzerland. ...As 20-year-old Liboton took the bell his mother wept again as she was led towards the winner's rostrum. There were tears too from Wreghitt who turned round in the road and went back down the course, unable to see through the thick mud plastered on his face, and in agony with his contact lenses, he retired weeping." Liboton crossed the line alone with only the white teeth of his smile showing out of the muddy figure, hands held high.

"I was sick for the first three laps," said Springer after finishing 34$^{th.}$ Brookes came in at 38th and Allison 39th all still in the same lap as the winner. So it was a Belgian winner once more, followed by two Swiss, Blaser and his team mate Karl-Heinz Hebling, Switzerland therefore taking home four of the six individual medals. Donovan's final comments were: "It would be quiet night for the British for although they had tried their best it was still not good enough. Both they and I would still like to know the answer."

The season always begins to tail off after the World Championships, so the final event of the Welsh cyclo-cross calendar organised by the Wales Cross League in the Lower Swansea Valley, tended to be low key. Winner was the veteran John Griffin finishing just over half a minute clear of C. Glithero (Newport Phoenix.) with P. Prothero (Gannet C.C.) in third. In East Anglia, Neil Pears the Hon. Secretary of the Eastern Area for more years that he would care to remember was the organiser of the Colchester Rovers/Percy Contracts event at Layer-de-la-Haye, Essex. Lee Wardley dominated from the start to finish, winning from R.Smith (Festival R.C.)

and the promoting club's rider C.Mobbs. Tim Butler the previous year's winner had to retire. Further north there was an event advertised with a title to strike fear into the hearts of any rider, 'The Carnegie Kamikaze Cross.' Perhaps its title scared some off, as there were only 17 starters. The senior event had a real end-of-season feel with Eric Stone (Ron Kitching Cycles) winning from P. Stevenson (Hambleton R.C) a junior who had hoped to be picked for the Junior World Championships. But when asked by a Cycling reporter, what were his thoughts were on not being selected, "Disappointed" was the only reply the reporter was prepared to quote.

The very last event listed in the handbook this year was the B.C.F Centenary Cross, which was yet another promotion by that prolific organiser Ray Richards and described as being in the Warwick area, with details to be announced.

Season 1978/79

National Champion Chris Wreghitt couldn't have dominated the first event of this season's I.C.S. Trophy series more than he did in the Cleveland C.C. event at Middlesborough's Clairville Stadium. Although it did not begin that way as he pulled his wheel over just after the start, and then had to run 150 yards for a spare machine. Keith Hanson (Mills/Pearson) had to execute a track finish on John Atkins (Harry Quinn) taking him up a bank and then descending to the finish, which decided second and third places.

The price of the Handbook this season remained the same at 35p and most of the officials continued to fill the same posts. National Coach moved into the hands of F. Westell, with R. Thom as National Team Manager. John Atkins was elevated to the honour of becoming a Life Member.

By mid October, Eric Stone (Ron Kitching) was still unbeaten at this time in the season with seven wins out of seven rides, the last being at the Ravensthorpe C.C. 'Eagles Nest' event. He put in an impressive performance, which even Open Champion Chris Wreghitt (G.S.Strada/ Lutz) could not match. The event took its name from the fact that the course circuited the 'Eagles Nest' Public house, which stands on the slopes of Standedge on the Pennines between Yorkshire and Lancashire. Ron Kitching's other professional, Ian Jewell was also in dominating form but this time down south at Footscray Meadows. The course proved both fast and dry, with Jewell riding away alone to win from K.Hanson (Mills/Pearson) and Gemini B. C's S.White.

Chris Dodd, now riding for his new sponsor Harry Quinn/Galli led a team one-two with his new team mate and old rival John Atkins in the Halesowen C.C. event. If the senior event was straight forward, then the junior event was certainly not, for Ralph Digges had devised a course with a five foot mound and it was here that National Junior Champion Chris Worton (Halesowen) snapped his forks, therefore losing all hope of winning his club's own event. Mike Bell (Orpington) went on to win from Paul Watson (Coventry Olympic/Viscount) who was riding with ten stitches in his head!

The Viking Air Freight Scramble in Surrey was expected to be an all out battle between Northern and Southern riders, however Keith Mernickle (Chris Barber/Geoffrey Butler) had different ideas and went off for a runaway win. Chris Wreghitt (G.S.Strada/Lutz) came second and then travelled to Poland straight after the event. He followed that with 3 weeks in Switzerland over the Christmas period. The heroic ride of the day was by Andy Palmer (Haverhill Wheelers), who would just not give up despite a list of misfortunes; first his chain came off, so he changed his machine, then he crashed writing off his frame (both top tube and down tube) he was then lent a bike but it was too big, however none of this stopped him from finishing top junior and winning £3 and a medal for his endeavours.

Chris Wreghitt found that many of the disadvantages encountered by British riders venturing to race on the continent had changed very little. This was displayed during a full dress rehearsal for the World Championships held on the same course in Italy. He had to stop and clean the mud from his bike, while such as Klaus-Peter Thaler just exchanged a muddy one for a clean one. Three Germans filled the top three spots, Wreghitt led the field after the first lap, but then his troubles began as he stopped to clear his machine, finally finishing fifth, although this did give him some hope for the real event. He had only taken one bike with him because he was travelling by train and the trip took 18 hrs, only arriving in Padova three hours before the event start. After the finish he had to look forward to yet another long journey without a sleeping compartment.

These difficulties that British riders had to contend with were often hidden, so that their achievements were not always recognised by the press at the year's end, seeing only the bare results. He recorded a ninth place at Lille in France only two days after his ride in Italy and another good result in Holland. Chris Whorton the Junior Champion also travelled to this venue and recorded a fifth place in the junior event. As he was searching for experience and tougher opposition, a Sports Council Grant paid for this trip, which helped his pocket.

The weekend before Christmas showed a lull in the top rated events, although one B and nine D category events still went ahead. The B event was the Mid Shropshire Wheelers, which had a handsome £100 prize list. On the same weekend in Luxembourg, Keith Hanson (Mills/Pearson) was the hero of the day, although he did not gain a podium place. He attacked the Germans, Swiss, Dutch and Belgians, gaining much praise from Johnny Morris: "He did all the work but had no reward."

A race long battle between Martin Springer (Antelope R.C.) Keith Hanson (Mills/Pearson) and Peter Brookes was described by Ken Whitmarsh of Cycling: "Any spirit of Christmas which might have existed between the three leading riders in the 'Royal Navy Earwaker Memorial Cross' after they had shared five tough circuits of the shore-based establishment of H.M.S. Dryad, was sharply dispelled when the chequered flag finally hove in sight."

John Atkins, otherwise known as the "King of Kenilworth," had to start alone on the scratch mark in the T.S.B Grand Prix event, due to none of the other scratch men appearing. Starting at a one-minute deficit, he alone had to catch all the four groups ahead of him, with a fine display of class riding before going on to win. On Boxing Day his great rival Keith Mernickle was also in winning form, but had a much more eventful race at the Paramount Grand Prix, promoted by the Crabwood C.C. On the fifth lap, he swooped down a steep drop, planted his front wheel into the ditch and as a result he wrote off his favourite frame. However, both Brookes and Springer had similar crashes at the same spot and Mernickle had time to recover and draw away to take the chequered flag.

January saw a win by Eric Stone in the Smirnoff Scramble. The expected challenge from three Belgians did not materialise, although two did arrive when the event was half way through. It was to be Stone's day this time and after winning by 2 seconds from Atkins he said, "This was a strong mans course and when I'm feeling strong then I'm the strongest in the field. I had a terrible start but got knocked off. Atkins is a crafty so-and-so but halfway round I would have marked Hanson down as the winner." After the finish the B.C-C.A selectors laid out their short lists for the World's in Italy at the end of the month and the Junior Championships in Spain due to take place in February. The Professional and Senior Amateur squads were full of well-known riders, but the juniors listed were less known and came from a wide spread of clubs. Chris Whorton

(Halesowen A.C.C.), Mike Bell (C.C.Orpington/Saba), Chris Ledger (Norton Wheelers.), Craig Stevens (Becontree Wheelers.), Paul Watson (Coventry Olympic-MidLet), Kevin Carr (Selby C.C.) Robert De Bie (Brereton) and Niki Davis (Lindsey R.C.C.)

More and more clubs were gaining sponsors at this time and jerseys were becoming emblazoned with the names of local, national and even international companies. It was therefore becoming more difficult for the casual spectator to distinguish between the Professional and Amateur riders.

Frank Westell the National Coach declared before going to the World's at Saccolongo in Italy: "I feel our programme has got to be on a five-year basis. But I like the way the juniors have developed that little bit of confidence this season. We want to see them nudging the seniors soon, with the seniors pushing the Pros."

The Saturday of the World Championship weekend saw an amateur Italian railway worker Vito di Tano turn the 'Tifosi' (Italian supporters) into a "Delirium of delight" (Cycling). The event was run in pouring rain, but he turned on the class to head Hennie Stamsnijder (Hol.) by 41 seconds at the finish, with Üli Müller (Switz.) back at just over one minute. Only two weeks previously the Swiss National Coach had described the course as "Like a criterium circuit" as it was packed snow which was rideable for almost an entire lap. The organisers therefore decided that the local fire brigade should be called out to spray hot water on the course to make it muddier.   Then came the thaw and to add to the dismay of the riders, heavy rain fell throughout the day before, meaning that once again the World Championships were to be played out in quagmire conditions.

The British riders could only record a tail of woe, having a torrid time at the rear of the field. Chris Wreghitt was among the first twenty on the first lap, but finished as the top G.B rider in 30th place. Phil Allison lasted only one lap after going off course on an unrideable section, Phil Brookes was 34th and M. Eadon 43rd. Johnny Morris would comment: "As a comedy for children's T.V. it would have been great" and Dennis Donovan wrote in Cycling what many observers probably already thought: "It seems that British sport took a wrong turning a long while ago, for we are still amateurs in our outlook and presumably enjoying it. The rest of the World are wrong and hating it. Or are they?"

On the Sunday it was time for the Professionals to battle it out for their Rainbow Jersey with the Swiss team continuing to try and make a clean sweep at the Championships. Albert Zweifel put on another class act to win by a massive 4 minutes 3 seconds from Gilles Blaser his teammate, and Robert Vermeire of Belgium. The last lap saw Zweifel attack with such a magnificent effort that his teammate Frishknecht was left gasping and was then helped into an ambulance with an achilles tendon problem, at the very moment his colleague was crossing the line to a cacophony of cowbells. Of the British riders Stone ended up a worthy 10th having tried to the very last inch and Dennis Donovan recalled his effort: "Stone fell off his bike as he finished, his legs rubbery after eight punishing laps of effort, and photographers fought one another in their haste to take his photograph. Manager Bob Thom was there to catch him, the B.C-C.A.'s Reg Ward too, and B.C.F President Eileen Grey rushed over, concerned at his condition. But seconds later he was joking again, though his comments were not for printing." The next G.B rider home was Keith Hanson in 17th then John Atkins at 19th followed by Keith Mernickle at two laps. Switzerland won the team race with only 8 points, the G.B team coming in fourth with 46 points.

Two landmarks were reached with the third British Open Championship, on 18th of February. For the fifteenth year running the B.C-C.A had been delighted to have the generous sponsorship of *The Daily Telegraph* and this was the twenty-fifth year of this Championship. We can only guess at the satisfaction enjoyed by those early torchbearers for cyclo-cross way back in 1954 who were still heavily involved in the sport and able to enjoy seeing their baby reach its twenty-fifth edition. A note in the programme outlined the difference between the riders. "To conform to Amateur Rules. Any awards totalling more than £10 claimed by an amateur will be given in the form of a prize voucher."

General Secretary, Ray Richards, used his page in the programme to include a tribute to *The Daily Telegraph* reporter, David Saunders, which alluded to the sudden death of this great supporter of cyclo-cross:

Sadly, David Saunders, who did so much to make this championship what it is today, will not be with us but his contribution will never be forgotten.

The Royal Sutton Cycling Club/T.D.C. had a page in the programme, which outlined their job as planners, marking out and also marshalling the course. The article recorded the enormous amount it had done in organising National Cyclo-Crosses for the B.C-C.A. "The present Club was formed in 1968, organised the Schoolboy National Cyclo-Cross in 1971, and the Junior National in 1973. We have fulfilled our present duties for the 1973, 1976, '77 and '78 Senior Title Races, and in addition have promoted English Schools C.A. Championships at area and national level." All-in-all a very impressive list of people giving up their own time for the sport they love and without which no events, whether large or small, could exist.

Cycling carried a full-page photograph of Chris Wreghitt on its cover for the 24th of February edition to mark his second win in the Senior Open National Championship. Inside, the event was covered with almost two full pages of type and pictures illustrating the high coverage of cyclo-cross results during this period of the late 1970's. The report by Martin Ayres started: "Any hopes his challengers may have had of lifting the National crown were dashed on Sunday as the 21 year old student from Loughborough proved he was the complete master of snow-bound Sutton Park."

Wreghitt had attacked with seven laps to go and took the lead, remaining there to win by 40 seconds. The 100 strong field faced a freezing wind and snowy conditions, with the start a shambles as the usual creeping forward by the front riders started. The Chief Judge had already foreseen this happening so had given written instructions to the effect that this would not be allowed, with any who continued, being withdrawn from the race. However, before the Lord Mayor of Birmingham could drop the flag to start the race, 80% of the field were away, including all the top men. The Chief Judge decided he would recall everyone, for many were by now almost halfway round the first lap! After a restart the disgruntled riders were then on their way once more.

In contrast to the recent World's there were only two points where running was necessary, most of the surface was areas of slush caused by the wheels of the racers. The riders, including Wreghitt, recorded tumbles and delays with snow-clogged wheels. Among those riding was Glen Longland, the current 12 hour Champion, trying the off-road side of cycle sport. It was to be Phil Allison (Altringham R.C./Rolalac Plastics) who emerged as the second placed rider, with Eric Stone (Ron Kitching) in third.

The last week in February saw the great British multi-cyclo-cross champion racing for the very last time, but even then John Atkins (Harry Quinn-Galli) competed well and gained the third spot on the podium behind Chris Wreghitt and 18-year-old Steve Davis the Coventry Olympic- Mid Let rider. So it was that the 13 times champion bowed out, still a threat to anyone, with the words: "You may see me riding again when I'm a vet, it depends what I'm doing in four or five years time." This closed a very illustrious career, that will remain for many years as a record for top 'cross riders in this country to aim for.

14

A new decade saw little progress
on the world scene

Season 1979/80

During September this year there was a notice in Cycling, advertising what would prove to be the popular Eastway Series of children's cross races. They were to be held on the first Sunday in every month, with distances to suit every age group, and would be ideal for the novice rider.

The Association celebrated 25 years this season, and the handbook marked the occasion with a large blue '25' on the white cover. Stability was once more the name of the game with all the National Officers remaining in the same seats.

Once more the world's toughest cyclo-cross, The Three Peaks, saw Eric Stone (Ron Kitching-SunTour) as the winner. This edition provided several notable records, with Brenda Atkinson (Stoke A.C.-Draka Foam) becoming a role model as the first woman to finish this gruelling event. The Junior record was smashed by Phil Webster (Bronte Whls.McManus & Poole) who took an amazing 18 minutes 4 seconds off the previous record. It also marked the first foray by Belgian riders ready to tackle this monster of a race. Former World Champion Norbert Dedeckere and his brother Kamiel, turned up with Luc Pauwels, all of whom trained on the course for three days before the event. Colin Willcock of Cycling described the race as "organised probably better than ever before by John Rawnsley and his men from the Bradford R.C.C.".

As to the race itself, 15 riders were clear by the first prime at Ribble Head, where Dedeckere took the prize. Stone then took off and by Ingleborough was 2 minutes clear, with John North (Bronte Whls/Draka Foam) and Barry Davies (G.S.San Marco) leading the chasers. Dedeckere was by now out of the race, as negotiating a wooden fence he jammed the spike of one of his shoe plates into the wood, causing him to sprain his ankle. He then managed to crunch the other plate into another piece of wood spraining his other foot, so disappointedly had to retire. Stone won in 2 hours 40 minutes followed by North in just over another minute, and then came Davies back at almost eight minutes. In fourth spot came R. Bates of the Bradford R.C.C. who improved his previous time by an amazing 50 minutes! The day was cool which helped many to improve on their best times; even so Colin Willcock emphasised the dangers: "Stringent safety precautions were enforced. Each rider carried a compact plastic survival bag and whistle, and for the first time there were time limits that could lead to riders being pulled out."

Across England the weather varied widely during October, with unusually dry weather being experienced at the Senghenydd Mountain Cross in South Wales, where Barry Davies (G.S.San Marco) led almost all the way, the firm surface helping him to record a new course record. In County Durham the very opposite conditions prevailed, constant rain the day before and overnight, meant mud was the name on everyone's lips. Consett Wheelers were the promoters and an exciting race ensued. When Hilton McMurdo an early leader, slipped on a muddy track, it allowed John Fenwick of the promoting club to take the win, then much to the delight of his supporters, McMurdo recovered to claim second spot ahead of D. Johnson (Newcastle Cheviot).

Barry Davies, now unsponsored, had very good form on the North Downs escarpment in the 'Circuit of Little Switzerland' held near Woldingham promoted by the Croydon R.C.Davies was later quoted in Cycling: "Next to the Three Peaks, that's got to be one of the best courses I've ridden. We need more of this kind of stuff, because sooner or later you'll come up against it abroad." As an ex-runner this bearded Manchester man had used all his old skills to win from Keith Mernickle (Geoffrey Butler-Nico Sport).

"Seeking fitness" was a report in Cycling during October this year that continued with: "Concern over the standard of fitness among current cyclo-cross riders – especially those aiming to ride the world championships – has meant that the British Cyclo-Cross Association coaching committee of John Morris, Barry Moss, Ralph Digges, Mick Shakespeare and Keith Edwards have named only C.Wreghitt for their proposed senior squad. ...In a bid to seek fitness Ralph Digges is to take riders over to Belgium during December for races in the Ostend area, plus coaching and training sessions with Norbert Dedeckere."

During early November Roger Page took the National Veterans title riding for his new sponsor Elswick-Falcon. The event proved to be a successful promotion by the Bradford R.C.C with generous sponsorship from Horsman Cycles of Keighley. The weather at Myrtle Park, Bingley, Yorkshire consisted of bone chilling showers brought in on a strong westerly wind to drench the riders. Early on, a sort-out saw Harry Bond from the promoting club leap away from Page and Rawnsley but Page closed this gap and attacked, finally winning the gold from Stone, with Alan Winters (Coventry C.C.) coming in for the bronze. Afterwards Mick Ives caused a smile among the reporters, when he said that while in third spot, he got up to sprint and thought he had snapped his braces, only to find it was a muscle in his back not the elastic in his braces, although the injury did cause him to retire.

The Smirnoff Scramble this year, saw the in-form rider Freddy De Schacht as the winner, his second win in three rides in this prestigious event. The course had been well and truly worn by the earlier races, one of which had been won by Chris Ledger of the Brook C.C. The main event saw a false start with the first big sort out at the water-splash. On the sixth lap the Belgian made the move that mattered and Chris Wreghitt had no answer to his pace. The last part of the race was described by Dennis Donovan in Cycling: "The large crowd, who had been enjoying the late autumn sunshine and laughing at the less fortunate at the water-splash, began to drift towards the finish area and Phil Liggett's commentary, for organizer Willi Tarran had seized hold of a large bell and was about to ring for the last lap. ...De Schacht crossed the line to generous applause and grinned a thank you to the crowd." Third man in Peter Brookes cheerfully summed up many a 'cross man's comment on a day full of incidents: "I fell off at the end of the third lap when Richard Bates fell on me. I also clobbered my knee on a post."

Another November edition of Cycling, included a two page feature on "A Bike for Cyclo-Cross." A serious rider these days, would find this latest edition of the Ron Kitching machine, which was featured, as an antique! Perhaps some of the most noticeable features were the long brake cables, looping high above the handlebars, the bar end gear levers and the shallow rims. Small diameter frame tubes, the openness of the frame itself and the double toe clips and the leather straps that today would seem very strange. This machine was also headlined as having: "The seasons innovation, the Sun-Tour Ultra seven-speed block."

November was also the month of the Halfords International, which was won by the West German Dieter Uebing just one minute one second clear of Chris Wreghitt for G.B. and H. Steeckers of Holland in third. The event also had other international riders from France and Switzerland. Once more the B.B.C T.V cameras were there filming for viewing later, with top commentator Barry Davies, this with a large crowd made for an excellent event.

Over the Christmas period, riders had to face consistently muddy conditions although the hard men still came out on top, including Eric Stone (Ron Kitching) at the Stockton Wheelers event and Barry Davies (Trumann Steel –KFP) in the Horwich C.C/Leverhulme Cross which was sponsored by the Warburton's Bakery. Meanwhile over in the east, Duncan Chenery (Colchester Rovers) strolled away with the Yarmouth and Gorleston Wheelers event, sponsored by the local Ladbrooke Holiday Village. Martin Springer gave his club a very Happy Christmas by winning the Bournemouth Arrow- Fircroft Hotel event held in the New Forest.

The new decade started impressively for 16-year-old Steve Douce, who took the scalps of many top riders in two Christmas holiday events. The first was the V.C. Elan/Harry Perry event promoted at Footscray Meadows. Riding for the promoting club young Douce was only beaten to the line by in-form Ian Jewell (Emperor Sport-Ray English). The three log jumps provided the spot where the sorting out took place, as Jewell drew away, lap by lap from Douce and Chris Dodd (Ron Kitching-Sun Tour) to finish almost two minutes clear, with young Douce finishing as the 'meat in the professional sandwich.' On Boxing Day Douce was second again, this time to Peter Brookes of Altrincham R.C. Rotalac at the Crabwood C.C. promotion.

The battle for this year's Junior Championship appeared to be between Paul Watson, Craig Stevens, John Wainwright and Steve Douce, because these were the four outstanding contenders out of the near 60 strong field. Paul Watson triumphed to become the new champion, but it was Chris Ledger of the Brook C.C. who the press named as the hero of the event. Held at the Eastway Cycle Racing Circuit, poor Ledger finished in tears after attacking early on and gaining seconds on every lap, until with two laps to go and with a lead of 31seconds disaster struck, not once, but five times when he had to change bikes. The race then developed in dramatic style with the chasers catching him and then attacking each other right up to the line, with Watson gaining the edge. Young Steve Douce came in second, with the dejected Ledger having to settle for the bronze medal and the Brook C.C. taking the team award.

Keith Hanson (Mills-Pearson) was a very unhappy and disappointed man, when he found out he was not selected for the coming World Championships, expressing himself in very strong terms when speaking to Cycling: "Barry Moss told me that I was not going because I hadn't been selected. I'm the leading pro' in the National Trophy League ... I can understand both Barry and Eric going because they are both runners, but I can't understand why I wasn't selected."

Those going to the World Championships this year were being helped by manufacturers such as Been Bag who offered a dozen pairs of training bottoms and skin shorts. The British Shoe Corporation supplied racing socks and Alisian provided 30 G.B hats plus jars of chamois cream and G.B crash hats. Lutz also helped by supplying tracksuits and Gibbsport gave jerseys. The riders would also benefit from £120 that had been donated to help the G.B riders.

The Redmon C.C. promotion, the Mills-Pearson Grand Prix, run at Mordon Park, Surrey, saw the farewell performance of Keith Mernickle. But Chris Wreghitt (G.S. Strada-Lutz) was the star of the day, proving by winning, that he could not be beaten in this season's National League. Mernickle was riding his very last race on his 36th birthday, although he put on the usual gritty performance that had delighted spectators up and down the country over many years. No one was going to give him the birthday gift of a win and he finished in fourth spot. Chris Wreghitt gave an insight into his win afterwards, by saying, "I'm very pleased with my form so far, my injured foot is still a bit sore, but it is better than I thought it would be." Mernickle's surprise reaction afterwards was to put his bike up for sale for £150, and declare: "Perhaps now I can lead a normal life." So ended the career of one of the big personalities of British cyclo-cross, marking the end on an era, with John Atkins retirement earlier in the year.

Youth, in the form of Paul Watson, took the scalps of both the seniors and professionals at the Greater London Championships. In the final selection it was Watson who surged forward to win by a few seconds from the in-form Keith Hanson. Hanson finished displaying two fingers covered in blood, where he had tried to remove a twig from his spokes. Another young hopeful Chris Worton (Halesowen A.C.C) also rode well crossing the line in third. Watson was very pleased to take home the first prize of £50 for just 15 miles of effort. Lots of the spectators spent their time looking out for continental roadman, Paul Sherwin, who was resplendent in his new La Redoute-Motobecane colours, he did not disappoint, putting on a good show to finish a creditable fifteenth.

Wetzikon in Switzerland was the location for this year's World Championships and it produced a wealth of stories. There were three titles on offer over the two days of the weekend.30,000 spectators paid £7 a head to see this sporting spectacular. On the Saturday the Swiss Fritz Saladin won the Amateur Rainbow Jersey after a dream ride. The massive home crowd cheered their countryman and rang their monster cowbells to encourage him, from the 45 riders who started under steel grey skies. The course was a real test with an awesome descent, roller coaster hills and adverse downhill cambers, in addition to the icy surfaces and glutinous mud.

Cycling described the winning move: "He closed in on Messelis like an income tax inspector homing in on a tax evader." The three medal places went to Saladin the gold, Polish riders Andrej Makowski the silver and Gregorsz Jaroszewski the bronze.

So where did the British riders finish? Chris Wreghitt finished with tears of frustration down in 22nd place, claiming when interviewed, that last year's World Champion, the Italian Vito di Tano had leant over and pushed his gear lever at the start, so that he was left stuck in his highest gear. The other three G.B riders had no complaints, having been left trailing by stronger, fitter men. Peter Brookes coming in at almost 8 minutes in 35th place, then Richard Bates placed 39th and Chris Whorton 41st.

The Sunday morning saw the junior laurels being shared between Czechoslovakia, Spain and Switzerland. 40 riders started the race representing 12 nations, with the snowy, icy dips and climbs mentioned above, ready to sort out the strong from the weak. Radomir Simonek showed his good form right from the start. A Great Britain jersey was seen near the front early on, that of Paul Watson, but he slowly slid back to be eventually overtaken and dropped by both the other British riders Douce and Ledger, resulting in Ledger 24th, Watson 33rd and Noble 37th.

Afterwards Ledger's only comment was to say: "Please no 'well done' for me." Steve Douce after fighting back from a collapsed rear wheel was shocked when he was disqualified for missing a random dope control. Such a thing should never have happened to this young rider and the B.C-C.A officials were firmly blamed in Cycling: "A monumental blunder" and emphasised: "The blame must lie at the feet of manager

Barry Moss, for slipping up on an elementary part of World Championship requirements."

The afternoon saw the Professionals lining up to find their first champion of the 1980's. Belgian Roland Liboton took the Rainbow Jersey, breaking the four-year reign of Albert Zweifel. The race was full of action right from the drop of the flag, last year's Dutch amateur silver medallist Stamsnijder took the lead and the pace just increased lap after lap, with Vermeire, Thaler, Zweifel, Frischknecht and, of course, Liboton shelling out all the other riders. By the seventh lap Liboton was alone in the lead and recording the fastest lap so far. At the finish banner he was still clear of the tandem of Thaler and Stamsnijder who sprinted in with the former Tour-de-France stage winner Thaler taking the silver medal.

From the British point of view it was a question of once again making no impact on the world stage, with Davies finishing 26th and Stone 27[th.] It was not through any lack of endeavour or courage on their part. At the finish Stone was unable to speak, so hard had he tried, and Davies said to Cycling: "I've never ridden so hard to come last but one. …We started fast, then they accelerated five miles an hour on a patch of rough-stuff, then accelerated even more, the sheer speed just got to me."

The next Wednesday's cover of Cycling carried the bold yellow words "The Sad Story of the 'Cross World's'" and inside Dennis Donovan lambasted the B.C-C.A and the current riders with the headlines" "Are we playing at racing?" and "It's no laughing matter." He then outlined his case with:

> Every year a jolly party of very nice British lads go abroad to ride the world cyclo-cross championships, and every year a very nice bunch of British lads get hammered by all and sundry. It's a familiar story to all by now; of courses that don't suit our riders, of mechanical mishaps, grotty hotels and just about every excuse under the sun … Our manager was Barry Moss, national amateur champion in 1969, our soigneur Bill Shillibeer, our mechanic Dick Broderick. All men with experience of the international scene … It's a sad fact too that the B.C-C.A handbook only carries the names of our national champions. Or perhaps I've got it all wrong, and we don't really want world champions and good international performances, but plenty of rides for the lads and everyone having a good time and playing at bike racing… I don't know what the answer is, I feel sorry for a nice bunch of lads who take some stick

from me and my peers each year, and I feel angry when I return to the Press room to file my story and those smug Continentals are laughing at the British again.

All the above sounds hard, but perhaps it had to be said by someone who obviously did love the sport.

Sutton Coldfield was to see Chris Wreghitt (G.S Strada-Manulife) win *the Daily Telegraph* sponsored Open National Championship for the third time after he had fended of an early challenge from Paul Watson (Coventry Olympic-Mid Let). Wreghitt was not to be headed again apart from a momentary lapse before midway, gaining more and more space between him and his challengers. At half way he was clear by 50 seconds on the next four chasers, none of whom would see him until after the finish. Thirty-four year old Stone (Ron Kitching/Sun Tour) finally rode clear of the pack to finish at1 minutes 26 seconds for the silver position, then came Peter Brookes (Altrincham R.C.Rotalac) for the third spot on the podium out of the 53 finishers. Ron Kitching/Sun Tour were the winning team.

The Annual General Meeting was held at 12 noon on March 2nd at Bagington Village Hall. Some of the proposals on this year's agenda were rather controversial, but chairman Ivan Dodd made sure that the meeting proceeded fairly rapidly. No challenges were made to the team manager or the coaching committee despite the performances at the last world championships fresh in everybody's minds. The very respected team manager Bob Thom, was proposed by Wessex C.C.A and voted in as the new President, but Barry Moss only narrowly defeated Bill Beagley as Team Manager. Next season would see a separate Vets section in National Trophy events. The reintroduction of private members was agreed with the fee being £4. The decisions made at this A.G.M would stretch out into the new decade. How would the B.C-C.A to react to the recent criticism in the press? Perhaps all will be revealed as we travel along in this story.

Season 1980/81

A photo of Chris Wreghitt running through a knee-deep stream, bike on shoulder, appears on the cover of the new handbook. A green border outlines the picture and the purchase price is 60p. Most of the official posts remain in trusted hands, although the Chairman of the Coaching Committee is now shown as R.Digges and Barry Moss is listed as National Team Manager.

At his fifth attempt John North, riding in his Great Britain jersey, won the Three Peaks. This was the first time that a full international team from Switzerland had taken part. Their decision to take up the invitation proved very worthwhile, as they took home the team prize. An astonishing 224 riders entered, although only 168 actually came to the start line, with three previous winners lining up. Former Junior Road Race Champion Ian Leckenby (V.C York-Denison) was off like a hare to win the prime at Ribblehead, but soon slipped back allowing the main contenders to forge ahead. The conditions were described as the best for two years. On Inglebough two riders were side-by-side, Richard Bates and North both riding for G.B. were followed by Steiner of Switzerland. After this prime, Hagi (Switz) punctured and snapped his back brake, not that either deterred him, he just pulled off the tubular and continued to charge down to Selside on a rim, on one brake and lots of good luck. By Pen-Y-Ghent North was away, finally arriving at Horton-in-Ribblesdale with 3min.11secs over Bates, with acrobatic Hagi in third punching the air as though he had won. The British team's bid for victory hadn't started too well, when Barry Davies declared he didn't need to wear a G.B. jersey, having arrived dressed in a skinsuit. Strong words were exchanged and he was replaced by Peter Stevenson (Humbleton R.C.) Tim Gould finished 1st Junior and as a footnote, bearded John Rawnsley and Neil Orrell each both completed the event for a 20th time.

The Halfords Company declared they would sponsor the National Trophy events this season plus five extra events, with a G.B. team to compete in all. All the organisers agreed to help the G.B. riders with expenses; in exchange the G.B. riders would don their National jerseys.

The first of this new sponsorship was the Cleveland C.C. event that was held at Middlesborough and was dominated by Chris Wreghitt (G.S Strada Manulife), who showed his class as a National Champion. He told Cycling: "I was trying to keep my record of winning events by two minutes", although he failed but his consolation was to take home the £120 first prize, out of the generous £650 prize list.

A wide range of riders were winning the races during the months of October and November. Chris Wreghitt supreme in the mud, on a misty dank day at Halesowen, where the thick mud clung to the riders' body numbers creating confusion when the judges declared the result, with disputes among the riders as to who finished when and where. Although there was no dispute as to Wreghitt winning from Chris Dodd, now riding for Roger Page Cycles.

Barry Davies (Trumanns Steel-Been Bag) was another winner, this time at the Kirkby C.C. event, having led throughout. Meanwhile, Eric Stone took the Brook C.C. event at Richmond College, Sheffield, this win being in the colours of his new sponsor Benotto-Pnuedan-ICS. Stone, was now 34 years old and had been riding 'cross since 1969, turning professional for the first time in 1972.

In the Saddleworth Scramble at Diggle near Manchester it was another professional, Graham Bufton (Harry Quinn-Galli) who finished 20 seconds clear of the chasers. A glance at the schoolboy winner on the same programme, shows a certain David Baker, a name that will occur many times later in this story.

As November came to a close, a three-man G.B. team was picked to ride events at Fay-Billot in France and in Luxemburg. The three selected were Richard Bates, Chris Ledger and the senior professional, Eric Stone. New area champions were also hailed this month. Paul Watson (Magnasport) who at only 18 was the South of England victor. At Bolton it was Chris Ledger (Altrincham R.C-Rotalac) who triumphed in the North of England event, The Midland title was held this year not far from Shrewsbury and was won, as predicted, by Chris Wreghitt.

At the end of month the Halfords International was sprinkled with world-class riders and was won by former World Champion, Albert Zweifel (Switzerland) showing all the class and skill expected of such a champion. Thousands of spectators were treated to the sight of the British riders, who put up a stiff challenge but failed to outride the top the Continentals. The result showed this plainly, as Zweifel was followed home by Wreghitt (G.B.) then by Stone (G.B.) in third.

The headlines during December seemed to feature mostly the successful exploits of Chris Wreghitt. Early in the month he was winning in France, gaining victory at Lesneven in Brittany where his manager Johnny Morris said, "He knew it was on from the start, and he absolutely destroyed the field." The three other British racers were not so lucky, while travelling to a race near Dijon, Steve Walter, Richard Bates and Steve Douce, had all their five bikes written off when their car descended down a 20 foot ditch. Much to their credit they were not deterred, borrowing bikes and finishing the event with Bates in sixth, Douce 15th, and Waters close behind in 16th.

Despite the handicap of two punctures and a fall, no one had an answer to the flying Wreghitt, who allowed nothing to slow him in his progress to the top spot on the podium at the Milton Keynes Velo Sport International. Frenchman Patrick Robin finished second at over 4 minutes. There were top class riders from all over France, Holland and Belgium and the cream of the British riders were there too. The next week at the Halfords National Trophy event at Southampton, the rain was so hard after the fourth lap that Cycling reporter Robert Garbutt commented that he was unable to write his notes, due to the continuing downpour. The sun did come out in time to greet Wreghitt just as he crossed the finish line, arms aloft, to the applause of the crowd.

During late December Wreghitt was racing more and more across the Channel and his main comments to Cycling were: "The cold is taking some getting used to. It's seven or eight degrees colder than England. ... It's such tough opposition over here all the time." While Wreghitt and Barry Davies were away, Eric Stone (Benotto) was busy clocking up the wins in England, the first in the Boxing Day T.S.B. Grand Prix at Kenilworth, winning from Steve Davies (Coventry Olympic- MidLet). Then again in the Manchester R.C.C. event he led the field from the young Martin Eadon (Altrincham R.C.)

Boxing Day produced three races of entirely different styles and results. John North clung to overall victory in the Yorkshire C.C.A. Handicap Series, which were held at Myrtle Park, Bingley, despite a broken hand he had suffered 10 days previously while out climbing. The Crabwood C.C. Wadham Stringer Grand Prix, developed into a Xmas Panto-cum-Farce, when an unusual number of riders were hit by punctures and damaged wheels. 17year old Steve Douce (V.C. Elan-Harry Perry) glided on, showing all his class, as chaos ensued behind him. He romped home ahead of Steve Walter (Emperor Sport-Ray English).Peter Brookes received his first Xmas gift of a puncture, followed by Walter with wheel problems, then he and Armitage punctured and both had to replace wheels. The unkind comedy continued with Brookes having another flat tyre, leaving all except Douce looking for better luck in the New Year.

The organisers of the Barton Wheelers event received a New Year bonus when the Yorkshire Area event was cancelled, leaving no races that day for a radius of 150 miles. Therefore a big entry of over 80 riders lined up for the Barton event. The local Lincolnshire riders were not happy when the top three places went to the Yorkshire invaders, Mick Stenton (Norton Wheelers.) S. Burton (Calder Clarion) and R. Blackburn (Norton Wheelers).

The National Junior Cyclo-Cross Championships saw Steve Douce (V.C.Elan-Harry Perry) in excellent form at Northallerton, winning from Mark Noble (Halesowen C.A.C) by just over a minute, a story of young bloods battling it out for the spoils. The circuit had changed from bone hard during the week to churned up ankle deep mud after overnight snow. The event started in Northallerton main street which was closed to traffic for the promoting club, Hambleton Road Club. A strong fast group forged ahead early on, including Douce and Noble plus Chris Young (Bradford R.C.C.) and Dean Hemming (Coventry Olympic/Mid Let). Douce soon rode clear having been training hard behind a motorbike in preparation for this event. It had been a good idea because his challengers just could not match him for speed. After the finish North was philosophic about the result but Young just smiled, as he knew that next year he would be back for another chance. Steve Douce had brought the Championship trophy (the Adrian Longland Memorial Trophy) to the event, only to proudly take it home again to Caterham.

By mid January, National Champion Chris Wreghitt riding for G.S. Strada- Manulife continued to sweep all before him, not only winning the fourth of the Halfords Trophy Series but also scoring the overall win. Afterwards David Duffield announced that Halfords had pencilled in the series for their next year's budget.

Long-term top rider Chris Dodd announced his retirement was to be at an event in France, but he would ride the British National Championships the week before. He had been riding cyclo-cross for 15 years and at 29 yrs old, he told Cycling: "I would like to coach at National level, particularly juniors. I don't want to disappear from the sport like so many others, especially when I feel I have something to pass on."

The well designed course at Sutton Park, Birmingham, was the venue for Chris Wreghitt's latest triumph in the National Championships. He was described in a Cycling report as "the white tornado" as he zoomed onwards towards winning the title. He was just unstoppable as he descended fearlessly down the steepest descents. Keith Bingham also reported him as saying: "The only time I was worried was when I punctured (on the third lap) I changed bikes but the chain jammed, so I had to run to the next pits. Fortunately they were only 200 yards away." The silver medal winner was the 18 year old Chris Ledger (Altrincham R.C- Rotalac Plastics) who finished back at 41seconds. The bronze medal ride was won by near veteran Eric Stone (Benotto) who at 34 years was almost twice as old as Ledger but was still riding as powerfully as ever. Once more the B.C-C.A were delighted to have *The Daily Telegraph* as the main sponsor. Chris Dodd was saying farewell by giving a fine final performance in England, to finish a very creditable tenth.

Despite the big build up in the British press, that Chris Wreghitt was destined to gain a high placing in this year's Amateur World Championships at Tolosa, near San Sebastian in Spain, it was the juniors who made all the headlines after the championships were over.

Grabbing the headlines were Steve Douce in 11th followed by Chris Young 13th and Steve Barnes 15th, the last two riding these Championships for the first time. The juniors raced on the Sunday morning in bitter cold pouring rain, the mud once more was a big feature, with every rider soon taking on a covering of brown gooey mud. West German Rigobert Matt was the outstanding junior, deservedly the winner of the gold medal, followed home by Miroslav Kvasnicka of Czechoslovakia, and Konrad Morf (Switz).

Steve Douce was pleased to have wiped away the memories of last year and the good placing of Young and Barnes meant they were third in the team race. Mark North had tried so hard for his 26th placing that at the finish he was shaking and his eyes were glazed over with the effort and cold.

Czechoslovakian rider Milos Fisera won the Amateur Rainbow jersey by sprinting away from his two rivals G. Jaroszewski of Poland (who was third last year), and R. De Brauwer of Belgium. So close was the sprint that he was recorded as winning in the same time as his two rivals. Although Wreghitt got off to an excellent start, he ran out of steam after just three laps and he finished 29th at over three minutes, with the other British riders finishing way down the field with Paul Watson 41st, Chris Ledger 43rd and Steve Davies in 46th place after being lapped. Wreghitt was in tears at the finish saying: "I just blew, I just felt lifeless, I didn't feel I was going well."

In the Professional title race, Dutch supporters were delighted when their countryman Hennie Stamsnijder powered home to win by 32 seconds from last year's winner, Roland Liboton of Belgium. Albert Zweifel (Switz.) the champion for the last four years finished in third place, after a hectic sprint over the shale track. The 26-year-old Dutchman, a farmer by occupation, became Holland's first winner of the gold medal and Rainbow Jersey in this event. Twenty-seven professionals had lined up with Stamsnijder's prayers having been answered, for the heavy rain meant it would make the sticky, muddy conditions ideal for his kind of racing style. The class of riders in the field meant the pace was bound to be a lung bursting effort from the start. Great Britain's Eric Stone declared he was "quite pleased" with his performance of 19th, as it was his 35th birthday. But his younger team-mate Steve Walter was very disappointed to be both lapped and last man home.

15

British Junior Team wins Gold at World Championships

Season 1981/82

Our regular look at the new season handbook reveals that Bob Thom has now become President and all the other main posts remain in tried and trusted hands. The Coaching Committee is listed as B.Watson and John Morris, with Morris having a second job as the National Team Manager. One more Life Member was added to the impressive list of names that of R.P.Ward. The cover of this edition has riders running up a steep bank with bikes over their shoulders and the price to members, now 75p. A new section included a 'Personal Event Diary' where riders could record their own race details.

Looking at the list of Areas, most now have their own racing colours, with London being Red & White, Midland Gold & Black, North Western Pink, North Eastern Orange & White, South Wales Red, Wessex Blue & Maroon, Yorkshire Royal Blue & White, and Eastern Dark Blue. South Western was listed as "to be decided" and Lincolnshire's colour is just left as a blank. More Veteran riders were racing and this showed up in the handbook, with extra events being listed as Pro/Sen/Jun/ and Veteran.

Chris Wreghitt having finished his studies at Birmingham University, declared that the main difference between British and Continental riders was that the latter trained so much more, so in preparation for the coming season, he had been doing lots of running and weight-lifting since July. He was also fortunate to once again receive a grant from the Sports Aid Foundation and had been able to have a week training in the Alps. The sum he received had been increased because the cost of living in Switzerland was so high. With the aim of a high placing in the next World Championships, he was riding full time, while living with a family in Zurich.

Looking at the adverts in the cycling press for cyclo-cross equipment, it appeared that things had moved forward very little over the last twenty years, The adverts were still for 6 speed blocks, special cyclo-cross double toe clips and straps. Shoes fitted with alloy plates, one at the front with wide slots and one with "two sturdy studs" for the heels, the shoes were also advertised as being light with waterproof nylon uppers. The 'ideal' frames were shown as having 73° head and seat angles, with prices at £185, with shoes at £23 and £6.58p for "rat-trap" type pedals, also remember, all brake and gear cables were still exposed.

Late September saw Eric Stone (Benotto) in good early season form, winning what most people regarded as a fine warm-up for the Three Peaks race, the 'Withins Moor' event at Haworth, a Bronte Wheelers-McManus & Poole promotion. Even catching his ankle on his pedal, causing a very nasty gash, could not prevent him from winning this event for the fifth successive year.

The Three Peaks this year took the name 'Andrews B.M.W. International' and was dominated by Swiss riders. The Continental invaders Arthur Manz, K.H. Haslebacher and Arthur Zeigler took first, second, and fourth places, with bearded John North, last year's winner, squeezed into third spot. North's was the most courageous ride that day, because he rode with his left arm in a plaster cast, having broken his arm in a road race, and was riding against his doctor's orders. Low cloud hid the riders from those watching as they crested Whernside, the highest of the three peaks, Manz made his race winning move on the slopes of Ingleborough, as a former national champion cross-country runner the climbs were just up his street. He made no mistakes in his progress, although near disaster struck with just 400yds to go, when he collided with a young cyclist, he got up and crossed the line to the applause of the watching crowd. Stewart Towers was having quite a day, for at one point he led the race by two minutes, then looking down saw his frame breaking beneath him and his race was done. One rider, Dave Phillips, was delighted with his 25th place, for he had read about the race and travelled all the way from his job as a bike builder in Toronto, Canada.

The first of the Halfords National Trophy events was held in Woodbank Park, Stockport during early October. The two Chris's Wreghitt and Ledger overcoming the power of the Continental riders D.Uebing (W.Ger.) and the two Belgians E.Vervaete and F.Van Paris. One of the rides of the day was by junior Steve Douce (C.C.Basingstoke), who elected not to ride the earlier junior event in favour of riding the main event and in doing so rode to a very creditable sixth spot.

Paul Watson (Anglia Sport-Huret) recorded his second win of the new season at Enfield, North London in the Wembley R.C. Sports Aid Foundation event. He rode strongly to keep Steve Douce and Martin Springer (Bournmouth Arrow/Fircroft) in second and third places. Meanwhile at Standedge, near Huddersfield Steve Barnes (Seacroft Wheelers.) was battling in what Cycling described as "The worst weather conditions ever known for the Eagles Nest cycle-cross." The thick mud, strong winds and driving rain caused the organisers to cut the race time from one hour to 45minutes, so as not to cause the riders even more punishment.

Headlines such as "Wreghitt wins Zurich 'cross", highlighted his outstanding win over such great names as the 1980 world professional champion Roland Liboton and four times champion Albert Zwiefel who were placed second and third behind him. Other riders left in his wheel marks were the current world champion Hennie Stamanijder in sixth, Fritz Saladin 11th and Klaus Peter-Thaler in 12th. His ride was not without incident for he fell on the very first lap, but having got up to the leaders once more he attacked through the woods and then descended bravely to win by four seconds. This was clearly his best ever success but had he peaked too early? The World Championships were not until February.

The Smirnoff Scramble this year saw Freddy Deschacht (Belg) win for the fourth time An easy win from Dolfsma (Holland) who was left almost a minute adrift, with the British riders Paul Watson (G.B.) and Eric Stone (Andrews-Bradford BMX) both recording the same time as they finished third and fourth.

The November prizelists were spread across many riders with the Copystatic Super Cross won by Paul Watson, Mike Teague (Crabwood C.C. Wadham Stringer) was the easy winner of the Southern Velo event held at Ranmore Common, Surrey. Steve Douce (C.C. Basingstoke) was in rampant form in the Tooting Bec's. 'Circuit of the Sods' now on a new course at Shirley Hills near Croydon. Two team mates dominated the Gannet C.C. 'Dinedor Scramble' held at Hereford, which also incorporated the South Wales Championships. Phil Prothero of the promoting club took the title but it was Lance Ravenhill who outpaced Mick Ives by 32 seconds, both of Coventry Olympic MidLet. It seems apparent that more sponsors were lining up to have their names associated with the sport of cyclo-cross, and club names were getting longer and longer, which was fine for the clubs but hard work for reporters and officials.

There was an announcement from Czechoslovakia during December that the World Cyclo-Cross Championships had been awarded to Great Britain and would take place in Sutton Park, Sutton Coldfield in 1983. Phil Liggett reported in Cycling that a stalemate situation had developed after the professional body, the F.I.C.P., voted their title races to Britain, but the amateur F.I.A.C. gave them to Italy. It all ended amicably as Italy were applauded when their delegate said: "I stand only to say we withdraw in favour of Britain." Eileen Gray, the B.C.F. President, thanked the Italians and flew back to England, where she informed the B.C-C.A. just in time for the riders at the Halfords International to be told that Britain had just succeeded in their desire to bring the Championships back to Britain.

There was no rest on Christmas Day for the British riders abroad such as Wreghitt, Douce, Watson, Springer and Nigel Hay. The event they were all riding was at Semmersaker near Ghent, the 25-kilometre course included two descents, which were enough to frighten all but the bravest with the rutted bone-hard frozen conditions. De Brauwer won from Wreghitt with Douce 10th, Watson 14th, Springer 18th, and Hay 29th. Two days later, Wreghitt once more had to settle for second place, this time it was at Oss in Holland, where Rein Groenendaal, another acknowledged class rider, beat him. He returned home with the knowledge that only the very best riders had beaten him.

Back in England the McDonald brothers, Andrew and Ian, were racing into first and second places in Wessex for the third time this season. Both were riding for G.S.Europa and the brothers fought each other until the younger, Andrew, drew away to win. In the Barton Wheelers event, the Norton Wheelers-Hoya team almost made the race their own, for they placed their men in every spot, from first with Russell Beresford down to P. Sleaford in sixth, with only the tough veteran Ian Small splitting them in fifth. On the far edge of the Norfolk coast, Colin Cracknell (V.C.Olympic Sport/Vinskins) was gaining victory from Mark Farrow (Norfolk Olympic/Tuckswood) in a Great Yarmouth event on a course, which included a tricky 45° concrete wall that ran close to the choppy white waves of the North Sea. Two riders had contrasting styles, Neil Pears the E.C.C.A Secretary spun his hub gear smoothly into third spot but Norwich Amateur rider John Vincent hurled his machine over the gate and then appeared to re-assemble it again on the other side!

By mid January, most of Britain was under several inches of snow but it did not stop Colin Cracknell from recording his fifth win of the season, in the Wolsey R.C event over Blaxhall Heath in East Suffolk, the snow not being deep enough to stop the days racing. Previous winner Robin Everson (R.A.F. C.C.) defied the elements to ride the 25 miles from his station, only to be forced to retire early due to injury. Afterwards winner Cracknell told the secrets of his fitness. He had little work during winter as a house painter, so more time to train.

A rider in top form at this time was Eric Stone, recording his 12th win of the season, despite sometimes working up to 90 hours a week in his job as a factory manager. He was still hoping for a medal at the National's declaring that his wife Susan had to keep "Pushing me out at night when I don't feel like going out."

Deep snow that halted the Junior Championships was big news among many B.C-C.A officials, with Bill Bolton telling Cycling: "After I struggled home from work in the thick snow of Friday night I phoned round the club officials and to Bob Thom ... We decided to cancel, as so many riders would not be able to make it. The snow was particularly bad in Wolverhampton and the Stadium area ... The championship will be rescheduled within the next couple of weeks."

It was not the only event to be cancelled, with organiser Keith Bohin of Bristol R.C declaring: "There's 18 inches of snow around here and it's even deeper in the drifts."

National Championship win number five for Chris Wreghitt was again at Sutton Park, Birmingham and his winning gap at the finish of 1min.45secs proved that the class of this multi-champion was not diminishing. He rode away from the best of the field before a crowd estimated by the Police as not less than 15,000. The group chasing the flying leader consisted of Watson, Barnes, Douce, Springer and Noble. Paul Watson managed to hold off the chasers to win the silver medal with Martin Springer claiming the bronze. Chris Wreghitt gave his opinion afterwards, that a race distance of 14 miles was too long for amateurs. His feeling of triumph turned to shock, when he found his two special Team Raleigh bikes had been stolen from his roof rack.

The first professional home was Eric Stone (Andrews BMW), followed by J. Wightman (Galli/Fibrax).

Success at last, must have been the reaction of the hardworking B.C-C.A officials when they heard that Chris Young in fourth, Tim Gould seventh and Steve Barnes 12th, were the winning team at the Junior World

Championships. It was the breakthrough that the Association had been awaiting for a long time. Young had done an outstanding ride and had been well backed up by his team mates. Switzerland's own junior champion Beat Schumacher was to add a Rainbow Jersey to his collection in the pouring rain and squelching mud. The event took place at Lanarvily in Brittany, where the silver medallist was Holland's Erwin Nijboer and the bronze went to the Czechoslovakian rider Radovan Fort. Close behind was Young at a mere 6 seconds, the nearest a British cyclist had got to a cyclo cross medal in 32 years. British Junior Champion Mick Hammond was the victim of a crash but came back from the disaster to gain 15th place. There were many other hard luck stories including a pile-up when a Spanish competitor skidded, bringing down both Gould and Hammond. Gould recovered quickly and recorded the fastest lap to regain the leaders, but Hammond was left with a wrecked wheel and had to run with his bike to the nearest pits. Interviewed after the race Young told Denis Donovan of Cycling: "I knew I was in with a chance until the Swiss went. The conditions suited me, it was just great." Gould was pleased too: "I was O.K once I got going but I thought it was all over when I crashed."

In contrast Chris Wreghitt was in a very angry mood after finishing 11th in the Amateur event, claiming, "I was pushed off." Milos Fisera of Czechoslovakia rode into the record books by retaining his title although he would have to sprint like a rocket to win from his teammate Radomir Simunek with both punching the air in delight at their success. Ueli Muller of Switzerland making the third place on the podium. Wreghitt was devastated, having lived, trained and raced in Switzerland with the sole point of gaining a world medal at these championships. The medal looked a good prospect as the riders entered the seventh and last lap, then disaster struck as he was brought down, all hopes of the medal lost in seconds. Cycling reported the scene at the finish: "Wreghitt rode straight past the finish line and the whole British team retired to their team caravan." Paul Watson also had a nightmare ride when his block fell into pieces all over the road shortly after the start.

The Professional race ended with success for youth against age. Roland Liboton edging out the great Swiss rider Albert Zweifel and winning his second world crown. Last year's winner Hennie Stamsnijder of Holland could not hold the pace of the flying duo but still remained clear of the chasers.

On returning to England Young discovered that he had won the 'Ofmega Personality of the Month', receiving an Ofmega chainset as his award. In Cycling there were two full pages of photographs from the championships, which mostly showed Wreghitt looking dispirited and Hammond with his disabled machine. The main project for the B.C-C.A would be to build on this success by the juniors in the next year.

Season 1982/83
Why the price of the new handbook rose by an inflation breaking 25% to £1.00 is not clear. Whether it was because the price had lagged behind and should have been increased in previous years or had there been an increase in printing costs. Only one colour was used on the cover but it was used to good effect, royal blue with the wording and badges in white. The words "Championnats du Monde Cyclo-Cross 1983" reminded the readers that the World Championships were returning to Britain in only a few months time. Some of the items from the Publicity Department (sounds like a Government Dept.) were B.C-C.A. ballpoint pens at 25p, racing caps (80p) ties (£2.50), brooches (50p), and car stickers at 35p. Over the years the Association had tried to sell various items to raise funds, such as coffee beakers, diaries, key rings and even a Penny Farthing picture.

September saw a delighted Eric Stone take a record breaking fifth win in the Three Peaks event, it also coincided with his sponsors, B.M.W Andrews, fifth year of sponsoring the event, although during this race he was actually riding for Great Britain. He did not have an armchair ride because the top two Swiss riders were always chasing with the 138 other riders who had charged away from the flag. At the finish Stone told Colin Willcock: "That was hard, with those two Swiss lads pushing me all the way there was no chance to relax." All the finishers were regarded as heroes by their supporters, among them Alan Evans in 12th spot took the award as first Veteran just pipping 47 year old Derek Lawson (Keighley Velo) and yet again the awesome duo of John Rawnsley and Neil Orrell, who each completed the event for the 22nd time. Rawnsley was also riding well enough to be third counter in the winning team of the Bradford R.C.C.

Tim Gould won the opening event of the National Trophy Series riding for Chesterfield Coureurs/Ness, where he put on an impressive display. With Cycling describing him as "Lightweight youngster from Matlock" he was headed from the start by Eric Stone, a man who was "seriously considering retiring", but Gould soon took over the lead. The race held at Graves Park, Sheffield caused the reporter to declare it "An epic race that set a high standard for the rest of the season." Gould was followed home by teammate Chris Ledger with Steve Douce (Bedouin C.C.) in third place.

When you lap everyone in a field of 54 except 17, you are in an exclusive class, which is what Hennie Stamsnijder (Daf Trucks) did in the Cleveland International. The rain descended early on and he left behind former Amateur Champion Norbert Dedeckere and his countryman Eric Vervaet. There was a very novel prize on offer for the British riders, with the first British finisher earning an extra £10 for every foreign rider he finished ahead of, making it possible to take home an extra £60 bonus. The Flying Dutchman made light work of the churned up mud to win by over a minute ahead of Vervaet, with Steve Douce in third. The winner of the schoolboy race was Mark Cottrell of the Houghton C.C. who triumphed at last, having ridden the race 5 times before, despite being still only 15 years old.

Across the country other names were taking victories, Keith Hanson (Pedersen Cycles) taking the Caldicot Castle Cross promoted by the Wyvern C.C. from Andy Auburn of V.C. Bristol. At Shirley Hills near Croydon, Steve Douce lapped every rider except Colin Cracknell (V.C.Olympia Sport). Douce was so dominant on the day that he won by a massive 6 minutes 30 seconds. The crowd took special note of the rider running over the line in ninth place, Peugeot professional Sean Yates, who had to cover the last few hundred yards with a wrecked wheel.

Over the Channel, a three man G.B. team of juniors was riding well but with mixed luck, at Lieden in Holland. Chris Young was top in fifth place, with Steve Barnes sixth and David Baker eighth which was a very good showing, after the G.B. team had been placed in the fifth line on the starting grid. The next day at Tilburg, Barnes improved to fourth with Young fifth and Baker again eighth.

Retaining a championship is said to be harder than winning the first time because you are then the marked man. Mick Ives (Coventry Olympic) didn't let that stop him defending his Veteran's title at Conyngham Hall Knaresborough. It takes a brave club to make their first promotion of a cyclo-cross event a National Championship, but that is just what the Knaresborough C.C. did. Forty-three riders lined up to take the start and Ives was soon into his stride, joined by Graham Bufton (Telford C.C.) and followed by Ian Small (Zodiac C.R.C.). Ives then put his head down to win the title by over half a minute, with Bufton in silver and S.Burton (Calder Clarion) in the bronze position. In fourth position came Ian Small to claim the Senior National title and Don Hoare (Yorkshire Century) became the Grand Veteran in the over 50s class. The Championship was sponsored by Ron Kitching, as was the supporting event, 'The Ron Kitching Grand Prix', with the likes of Eric Vervaet of Belgium being involved. The first three finishers all knew they had 'been in a race' with the slippery surface causing riders to be very unsettled, but the class of Vervaet was too much for the second and third finishers, Ledger and Stone.

All the Area Championships were held during December and resulted in the North going to Chris North, Midlands's title to Mark Noble and an Englishman, Darren Lyne, won the South Wales's championship. Steve Barron won the East title and the South went to Steve Douce. The weather that weekend was simply atrocious with many tales of heavy rain, wind and floods with the gloom cutting one event by several laps.

Once more the British travelled over the Channel at Christmas with Christmas Day bringing a well-earned present to Chris Wreghitt, with a fourth placing behind the World Champion Roland Liboton near Ghent. This was a sign showing his good progress back from injury, he had been training behind a motorcycle at the Zurich track to find more speed and it meant he could still return to fitness, while deep snow was prevented training on the roads. Chris Ledger had the best result out of the raiding party on Boxing Day when he finished in seventh place at Kernlis in France. Barnes was tenth, Mark Noble followed in 11th, Hammond in 14th and Nick Noble 16th. The destination of other British riders on New Years Day was Rillaar in Belgium but it turned out to be a disaster, although Chris Wreghitt was placed 18th, Young, Hammond, Gould and Barnes were all prevented from starting because of a new rule which had come into force on January 1st. It stated that riders under 19 years were now barred from riding in senior races, this new rule had slipped past the B.C-C.A. officials, who should have checked before sending these young riders abroad.

Back in England over the Christmas period, Yorkshireman Eric Stone was busy winning on Boxing Day at the Zodiac C.R.C. event at Woodbank Park, near Stockport, and in the Witham Wheelers event. Another traditional Boxing Day event was on Kenilworth Common promoted by the Coventry R.C, where Martin Eadon (Archer R.C./Saba) took his fifth win of the season. Second placed Chris Dodds (Roger Page/Garriane) had problems when a twig caught him in the eye leaving him to race on with vision in only one eye. Bright winter sunshine caught the colours of a group of well-known roadmen trying the sport of cyclo-cross for winter training. Among them were John Herety, Ian Binder, Mike Williams and Pete Longbottom but it was still the sports specialists such as Eric Stone who led the way.

Colin Willcock started his report on the Bradford C.R.C event in Cycling: "To quote an old saying – there was Trouble at t'mill." Riders started to complain that Eric Stone was cutting a corner on the course, so organiser John Rawnsley went to have a look; an angry confrontation ensued and Rawnsley was left holding a suspected broken nose. Stone then retired, leaving the win to go to Tim Gould with Chris Young second.

The big surprise in the National Junior Championships at Myrtle Park, Bingley, was not that in-form David Baker won by over two minutes but that the bronze medal spot was taken by 15 year old Stuart Marshall. National Schoolboy Champion, Marshall, riding for the V.C. Lincoln/ Metheringham club, was not old enough to be picked for the Junior World Championships. The silver medal went to Matthew Rigby of the Brook C.C. who also led home the winning team with R. Dane and S. Shaw.

Some names of the future were also winners in the English Schools Cycling Association's Championship during January of this year. Stuart Marshall (Yarbrough High School) won the Over 15's and Nick Craig (New Mills Comprehensive, Stockport) the Under 15's. This was Marshall's twelfth win of the season and his third National Championship. Proving E.S.C.A events were a great breeding ground for bringing forward many good riders to cyclo-cross.

About this time there were some splendid adverts appearing in the cycling press for the forthcoming World Championships. They showed a rainbow with three stylised cyclists in gold riding the rainbow. The poster also covered all the main details with logos of both the U.C.I. and B.C.F (note no B.C-C.A!), and Halfords appeared as the main sponsor. Then all the races were listed; Saturday 19th February Amateurs at 1.30p.m, Sunday 20th Juniors 12 noon and Professionals at 2 p.m. Altogether a splendid advert for what everyone hoped would be an exciting event.

Joan Edwards in her column in Cycling wrote, "To encourage our friends and club mates, and make up small and large parties, and make the weekend of Feb19-20, 1983, one to be remembered and savoured for years to come." Cyclist Monthly's February edition did its best to encourage fans to travel to the forthcoming World Championships, by producing five full pages of photographs and text showing 15 descriptions of the course that was to be used on the big weekend. *The Daily Telegraph* also did its bit to publicise the event by producing a quantity of double-crown (30"x 20") sized posters, some of which are still in the B.C-C.A archives. They are in the style of newspaper flysheets that could be placed on show outside newspaper shops as pre-event publicity.

Also in the archives is one of the menus produced for the Banquet on the Saturday evening of the Championships, at the Grand Hotel, Birmingham. It is printed on card in gold, with the championship logo in full colour. The toasts were, 'Her Majesty the Queen', proposed by Mrs. Eileen Gray O.B.E (the B.C.F President), who also proposed another toast to, 'Union Cycliste Internationale'. The response was by Louis Puig (President of the U.C.I). The next toast was, 'The City of Birmingham' by Ivan Dodd (Chairman of the B.C-C.A), with the response being made by The Deputy Mayor of Birmingham. The B.C-C.A President, Bob Thom, welcomed 'Our Sponsors', with M.M. Rushmere the Chief Executive of Halfords Ltd. replying. One black mark of the weekend was that the 'comedy' routines presented as entertainment to the U.C.I and Civic Dignitaries at the Banquet went down like a lead balloon. To put it simply, it was tasteless, being based on jokes about how funny 'jolly foreigner' was. The performance was greeted with a stony silence and was brought to an end early.

The whole cover of Cycling the week after the Championships was a reproduction of the colourful World Cyclo Cross Championships poster described earlier. Unfortunately the headlines inside said it all: "Sutton Success but British Fail" followed by six full pages of reports on the events at Birmingham. The conditions were almost perfect for racing, cold but dry, producing some very fast events. It seems that the Continentals not only outrode the British but also out sang them too, for they made far more noise with their air-horns, cow bells and even a Belgian bagpiper to top up the volume. Czechoslovakia took the lion's share of the medals with two gold, two silvers and two sets of team wins.

Professional Roland Liboton described his third win at this grade as "I didn't fear anyone", and that in a nutshell is just what the great Belgian showed. Behind him Albert Zweifel (Switz) held off Klaus-Peter Thaler by just one lone second for the silver medal, unlike Liboton who just freewheeled to the line. The British fans had very little to cheer, for Eric Stone came in 25th at just over six minutes and Chris Dodd was a disappointing last at 1 lap. They tried their utmost but they were just outclassed, the Belgians also took the team prize.

As related earlier, Czechoslovakia had a wonderful championship, starting with Radomir Simunek taking the Amateur race to win the

Rainbow Jersey from Belgian Werner Van Der Fraenen, the gold and silver only being decided by a shoulder-to-shoulder sprint. In bronze was Simunek's compatriot Petr Kloucek a mere 2 seconds further back. Simunek's cousin, Milos Fisera, had been champion for the past two years, so he had kept the Rainbow Jersey in the family. The British riders were unfortunately well down the finishing list. Wreghitt coming in 23rd. and Douce a little further back in 27th then came the first timers, Young 34th and Barnes 38th both with time on their side to return next year.

The Junior Gold went to another Czechoslovakian Roman Kreuziger, who won by just 6 seconds from Dutchman Martin Hendricks with yet another of this year's all-conquering Czechs Petr Hric in third. Any hopes of a top 20 spot for the British was dashed when David Baker crashed and finally came in 24th, Robert Dane rode well for 31st as he still has one more go at this age title, Noble was 42nd with last man Rigby in 46th.

Nine Professionals were fined 50 Swiss francs each, for not wearing crash helmets, four French, one German, two Dutch and two British riders just to add to their woes. Did they not know the rules, or did they just choose to ignore them?

It became clear afterwards that the B.C-C.A officials were put in an awkward position just before the start of the event because B.B.C. T.V. found that the horse racing they were hoping to cover was off. So they offered to screen the Championship races live if the race could be put forward by 30 minutes, but the officials decided to keep faith with the fans, many would have arrived for the start time, only to find that the amateur event was already underway.

The next week Dennis Donovan in Cycling lambasted the fans who did not turn up, quoting Ray Richards as saying: "The Saturday attendance was diabolical in my opinion". The B.C-C.A had expected to make at least £30,000 profit but Richards admitted "I was very disappointed with the size of the crowd, even for Sunday. It was below our expectations." Total ticket sales were not expected to be over £25,000, however it was pointed out that Halfords had guaranteed that the profit was to be at least £5,000. On Saturday about 3,000 spectators turned up to pass through the gates and paid about £4,200, with no more than 5,000 paying to watch on Sunday. Richards was quoted as saying: "Half the crowd came from Europe … and some said that ticket prices were too high, but nobody wrote to us beforehand to say so."

Donovan also put forward the argument that the British were just not ready to pay to watch cycle racing: "Would 20,000 Belgians pack Brussels for instance to watch a Cricket match?" However Donovan did end his report with "Congratulations to B.C.F, B.C-C.A. and Halfords for making it possible." John Wilcockson writing in Cyclist Monthly put forward one reason why the Czechs had done so well, "With State money behind them (Simunek, a 'Technician' in the army), the Czechoslovakians have brought cyclo-cross firmly into the 1980s and that one of their secrets is racing them over courses that are much longer and harder than those used for the World Champs." He also quoted Dr.Vladimir Kudlicka their Doctor and Dietician as saying: "We sometimes have them out in temperatures of 15 degrees below zero intentionally." One wonders how the British Amateurs would react to such a regime and whether the Association had thought of appointing a Dietician?

The Association's A.G.M. was held at Warwick, Globe Hotel., on Sunday 5th March with a Prize Presentation Buffet following in the evening. The meeting voted to extend the junior age limit to 19 years and in doing so hoped to change the rules of both the B.C.F. and the U.C.I. Brian Watson, the coaching committee chairman, declared: "Some parents of squad members were finding it a bit tight having to pay their lads expenses. We must give them assistance so they can ride together." Although *The Daily Telegraph* had sponsored the Championships for 10 years at Sutton Park and might increase their commitment, Keith Gibson indicated, "The London C.C.A. would make a bid to bring the championships down south."

Auditor Mike Radford stood up to say that the Accounts were not being "satisfactorily presented" and the income from grants, which accounted for 60% of the B.C-C.A income, had a deadline for grants at the end of March.

16

At last an individual British World Championship medal

Season 1983/84

Delving into the new season's handbook, two adverts catch the eye one for the Cleveland Grand Prix, which appeared to be organised by the B.C.F. because there was no listing within the handbook and details could only be obtained from the B.C.F. The prize list was an amazing £1,600. Were the B.C.F. trying to muscle in on the B.C-C.A.?

The other advert was for the Peak Cycle Centre advertising: "Large stocks of all specialised 'cross equipment, including Alan Framesets, 'Cross Hubs, Shoes, Chainsets, Superb Cross Wheels, & Framesets built." The cost of entry fees was Boys/Girls 25p-30p, Pro/Sen/Jun/Vet at anything from £1.00 to £1.30p with Cat A at £1.50p.

The Association took a full page of the handbook to thank the companies who had supported them by donations of racing equipment to the squad. They were: T.I. Reynolds – twenty 531 tubesets and twenty tracksuit tops; Clarkes Cables – 500 brake cables and 500 gear cables (inners & outers): Advance Tapes – 150 rolls of tub tape & cloth; Gibbsport – World championship skinsuits, tracksuit tops & hats; Alisian – Twelve team bags. Almost 200 events were being promoted this year with most events having up to three races for different categories. So a very busy year of racing was in store.

Joan Edwards, the Association Press and P.R.O. Secretary was given a whole page in Cycling to outline her views on the season ahead, with a calendar of all the main events showing the magazine's backing for the sport during this period. She started by looking back to the past season by saying : "The glow from the successful promotion of the latter event (World Championships) still lingers, as does the determination to improve and expand the sport … A number of riders have been nominated as national squad 'possibles'; Coaching Committee Chairman Brian Watson held the first get-together last week-end at Hanslope, near Milton Keynes. Various area-coaching sessions have been, or will be held. Steve Douce's father Phillip, is organising a training day on Saturday September 24th. Chris Dodd has a Midland area session arranged for October 9th … One of the resolutions passed at the A.G.M. last March was a request that organisers should include in their promotions an event on a simplified course for the youngsters of under 12 years of age. Entry is free, and any type of cycle can be used, be it B.M.X., Chopper type or whatever!" From this resolution, which recognised a ground swell of desire, developed all the age groups now in place.

The biggest early season event, The Three Peaks was reported in Cycling: "After being out of cycling for more than two years former international Richard Bates (Bradford R.C.C) made a triumphant return on Sunday to achieve his ambition of winning the Three Peaks Cyclo-cross, then promptly announced that it would be his last race of the season and possibly his last ever. His record in the current 'cross season is two rides, two wins, packed up." The event this year was longer than ever at 56 kilometres, with less running and more riding, with the peaks being attacked in a new order, first Ingleborough then Whernside and finally Pen-Y-Ghent. Young Tim Gould led over the first peak but then Bates took over, never to see a rear wheel again until he crossed the finish line. Bates was delighted at the finish saying: "I seem to have trained half my life for this." Gould retained his second place, holding off the leader of a strong Swiss team Arthur Manz, who had been first, second and now third in the last three years. Bates's day was made complete by leading in the winning team with B.Pearce and S.Towers.

During November Chris Young and Steve Barnes were embroiled in tough battles each weekend. The first weekend seeing Barnes (Seacroft Whls) win in the Copystatic 'Super' 'cross, held on a testing course in Bramcote Park, near Nottingham. Next day the positions were reversed in the Ravenshorpe C.C. event at Coalville, with this time Young (Burnley C.R.T) turning the tables on Barnes by taking the honours. Barnes was not content with second placing, for the very next weekend he dominated the famous Smirnoff Scramble at Harlow. In winning this 24th edition of the Scramble he beat the Belgian Freddy Deschacht, who had already won five editions and was eager to make it six. This also took Barnes to two National Trophy wins out of two rides.

The Area Championship winners this year also included the on form Steve Barnes who won the North of England title held at Wakefield. The Midland title saw race favourite Chris Ledger (Bolsover Wheelers) fade in the last two laps, when the 6ft.4 ins frame of Simon Burney (Bridgegate B.M.W.) took full advantage to win. The South of England men fought it out in the mud and wet of the New Forest, Paul Bennett (Ross Wheelers) being the winner from Martin Springer (Crabwood C.C.) with the Pederson Cycles professional Keith Hanson next. An R.A.F C.C. rider Robin Everson took the South Wales title, having lapped every rider except Darren Lyne (Gannet C.C.) who was almost 4 minutes back, the third spot going to M. Hughes (Port Talbot Wheelers). The last of the titles was the East Championship won by Mike Daley (Cherry Valley R.C) on a course at Bowthorpe on the edge of Norwich City which was mostly rideable, allowing him to show his talents as a first category roadman and grass track champion. Lincoln riders came in second and third with D. Booth (V.C. Lincoln) and S. Barber of Lincoln Wheelers.

Preventing injuries to the World's squad was on the mind of Chris Dodd, when he said in Cycling: " With just weeks after the Nationals, we don't need injuries to any of the World's teams." The Midland officials therefore asked National Championship organiser Reg Ward to cut out the ford on the famous Sutton Park course. He decided to discuss the request with course director Keith Edwards. Dodd continued: "Riders warm up before the start then it seems after the race begins they have to ride through freezing water that can temporary paralyse muscles." Edwards though, was sceptical of this change saying: "The water splash was an attraction for spectators. It is supposed to be a cross-country race. Now cyclo-cross is becoming more like a miniature Paris-Roubaix. The day they took hurdles out of cyclo-cross was a detrimental step." From this statement it was clear where Keith Edwards' thoughts lay.

Paul Dixon was in fine form during the Christmas/New Year period with a win on New Year's day. Relentless heavy rain meant that the lap scorers had to check not only the colours of riders' jerseys but checking their faces too. Junior, Dixon, riding for the Mirfield C.C. also won the Brook C.C. event at Sheffield from the promoting club's Robert Dane and M. Rigby of South York Road Club. Lashing rain and winds also dominated the Macclesfield Wheelers event, where Chris Young took the lead from Mike Daley (Cherry Valley R.T.) having battled with Dixon, Dodds and Burnley early on.

Christmas brought the wrong kind of present to Chris Wreghitt, who after returning from Switzerland received the news that he had a stress fracture of the femur. The Bianchi professional told Cycling "It could mean the end of my cyclo-cross ... I think it was probably road running that caused the injury." This of course was a great blow, not only to Wreghitt, but also to the hopes of British cyclo-cross, as he would probably be riding the coming World's at the very least.

The Yorkshire 'A' squad retained the Inter-Regional Team Championships title winning by just 4 points from Midland 'A' squad. The third placed team was Lincolnshire 'B' with altogether 13 teams taking part. Steve Douce of London 'A' was the individual winner, keeping his form for the Nationals by making this his seventh win in twelve days.

In-form Chris Young (Burnley C.R.T -Kiblaze) won the Senior National Title at Sutton Park. He left defending champion Steve Douce struggling at 50 seconds, on a course that had been criticised by some as 'Mickey Mouse' although the riders produced racing that was anything but. Twenty-year-old Young was among many delayed at the start as riders fell, causing chaos, but Young's skill soon saw him at the front, having passed 40 riders in the process. Young rode in alone to the applause of the large crowd to take the Gold medal and the Champion's jersey, and in fact he really needed a small van to take away his prizes, which also included; a cheque for £120, a sash, a silver salver and a trophy. He was followed home by Steve Douce for the silver medal and Steve Barnes for the bronze. With the Norton Wheelers-Harrison team of Beresford, Baker and Stenton taking the top team medals and £10 each as their prizes. David Baker was also delayed in the pile-up and came in to finish eighth, although he still had another year to ride as a junior, with a birthday just before the coming World's. *The Daily Telegraph* was sponsoring the Championships for the very creditable 20th time, an amazing record of backing for a minor sport and they also presented Baker with a special prize for his "Gutsy ride".

Paul Dixon became a cycling champion in two disciplines when he triumphed in the Junior Championships, having already won the West Yorkshire Road Race Championships the previous season. Seventeen-year-old Dixon while riding for the Mirfield C.C. led from the start, with Steve Noble (Seacroft Wheelers.) putting up early resistance, only to drop back for Michael Bradley (Solihull C.C.) to take up the challenge. Bradley was left rueing a collision with a tree root on the last section, leaving room for Robert Dane (Brook C.C.) to sprint forward and take the silver. Stuart Marshall led the winning team from V.C. Lincoln.

Looking through the programme, it shows many familiar names putting in more sterling work as officials, to add to all the other work they were still doing for the B.C-C.A. R. Richards was Chief Commissaire, R. P. Ward the Organiser, K. Edwards Course Director J.Court Chief Recorder and Joan Edwards and G. Ward as the recorders.

At last! Must have the reaction of both B.C-C.A. officials and supporters alike, when they heard the news that Robert Dane was to bring home a silver medal from the Junior World Championships in Oss, Holland. Being the first individual Great Britain cyclo-cross rider to win a world medal of any colour after 34 years of trying. The man who prevented him taking the gold was Ondrej Glajza of Czechoslovakia. The large crowd cheered Dane on after he crashed and lost his grip on that elusive Rainbow Jersey. None of the other G.B. riders could get better than Dixon at 23rd followed the third lap and when he fought back, from what British Manager Johnny Morris estimated as 30 seconds lost.

Dennis Donovan takes up the story in Cycling with: "Dane led through the finishing straight to start the second lap, followed by Glajza, Johnny Blomme (Belgium) eventual third placed Richard Koberna (Czech) and Dieter Runkel (Swiss) ... Glajza led through on the next time round with Barnes right on the 18 year old Czech's wheel." Afterwards Dane described his disaster thus: "My front wheel slipped on a descent and I hit a pole." As he crashed, so did all hope of Britain's Marshall 27th and Bradley in 38th from 43 finishers. Czechoslovakia won the team gold medals with just 8 points with G.B. in a respectable fifth with 52 points. It seems a pity that on the very edition that Cycling reported the success of Robert Dane gaining that first individual medal, he did not feature on the front cover. Although the magazine could hardly be faulted in the way it covered cyclo-cross in such depth during this decade.

The Amateur Championship was always in the control of Radomir Simonek of Czechoslovakia as he retained his title. Finally winning from his compatriot Milos Kvasnicka, with Dutchman Frank Van Bakel in the bronze spot. The course was littered with rutted ice patches causing many to fall heavily. The super-fast start caught out the British riders once more and they were never in contention for a high placing, finishing with Steve Douce the best in 20th Young in 30th Barnes 35th and Baker finished as perhaps the youngest rider in the race.

The North Western C.C.A held their Buffet Dance at the Civil Service Club, Timperley on Saturday 25th February, with dancing starting at 8pm. The tickets were £4.00. The Association's A.G.M was to take place at the Globe Hotel on Saturday March 3rd. at noon followed by the National Prize Presentation Buffet & Dance, with the tickets available from Ray Richards, yet another 'hat' to add to his collection.

Season 1984/85

During September, Joan Edwards writing in her regular column in Cycling gave her views on various subjects such as, "One of the riders I would really like to see in the 'cross scene, although I fully realise that his ambitions lie elsewhere at present, is new National Road Champion Neil Martin. As a schoolboy he used to ride 'cross occasionally on single freewheel, and was always in the first three ... We all wish Chris Wreghitt every success in whatever new career opens up for him ... This year there was another recruit to the Pro' ranks 29 year old Tony Wilkins, who will be riding for Car Identity of Milton Keynes. He was a National Squad rider 10 years ago and is an able roadman." She also mentioned "Crash hats are now compulsory wear for all competitors over 12 years of age." Coaching Committee Chairman Brian Watson had once more organised a successful National Squad weekend near Milton Keynes. Described as "deep in the outback" and the riders endeavour and behaviour had pleased Watson and also impressed the local farmers who provided the accommodation well as training areas.

The cost of the annual handbook was now £1.25p. Lincolnshire Area was now listed as Lincolnshire & South Humberside C.C.A. and readers would find that Mrs.G.Wreghitt was now the National Treasurer but the rest of the Officers remained in their posts. It would be interesting to see how organisers would react to a new rule that asked them, 'not to direct courses through water, where they could find an alternative route'. This was to be a big change for many organisers, who had delighted over the years in selecting devilish wide or deep streams for their races to cross.

Tim Gould (Chesterfield Coureurs/Ness) dominated the twenty-fifth running of the Three Peaks race, which was still being described as "the world's toughest cross." Conditions were very difficult with heavy rain making the going very soft, and the gale force winds battered the riders continually. Gould won from Barry Peace (Bradford R.C.C.) with Mike Johnson (Coalville Wheelers) in third. Afterwards Gould's father Harry indicated that his son found it hard to concentrate, finally keeping his mind focused in a novel way by reading the words on the wrappers on his energy bars! The very next week Douce was repeating his good form by attacking straight from the start in the Addiscombe C.C. event at Shirley

Hills. Only his brother Graham could match his pace, before fading to third spot behind, Barry Coomber (V.C.Etoile) who came through to take second. Not allowing his form to slip, Douce made it a hat trick by winning in Yorkshire in the Norton Wheelers Trophy race. The former Champion powering away over the Graves Park course in Sheffield.

A superb full colour action shot of Chris Young running with his bike on his shoulder, leaping down a banking appeared on a cover of Cycling during December. However, he took a back seat in the Halfords Nations Cup behind Steve Douce, who despite the effects of 'flu was winner one more. His win giving George Shaw a boost in his new job as National Team Manager, for in the team race G.B. came top. In second overall was the impressive lone Italian Vito Di Tano with Chris Young back in third. A name of note was Peugeot professional Sean Yates who raced well enough to finish in 15th.

This Cycling also carried a report that the B.C-C.A. had increased the size of the Coaching Committee for the season, despite both John Morris and Brian Watson both resigning their posts. A vote of appreciation was passed thanking them for their work for the B.C-C.A. Their replacements were George Shaw and Brian Cossavella. John Rawnsley would become the Coaching Committee Chairman; Geoff Greenfield was added to Chris Dodd and Andy Jones on the Committee. The Executive Committee agreed with the decision by Ray Richard, General Secretary, to reinstate Chris Young, who had been suspended by the previous committee from the G.B. squad. Johnny Morris added this comment on the event to Cycling, saying: "I put everything to do with cyclo-cross, all my books, in a big black sack and gave it to the dustman on Thursday. I'm going sailing." It seems a great pity that he destroyed all that useful data and experience on running an international racing team, which could have helped future managers.

The Regional titles this year went to the top men of the moment, Chris Young (Paragon R.T. Gazelle) became the North of England Champion, Chris Douce (Wembley R.C.-Nico Sport) the Southern title winner, with Simon Burney (B.M.W.- Bridgegate) taking the Midland Championships. In the West, R.A.F.C.C man Robin Everson, took the South Wales title, and in the East, Steve Barron (Lincoln Wheelers/Linpave) made it a hat-trick of wins.

Joan Edwards in her 'Crosstalk' column noted that the B.C-C.A. had a long way to go, for despite a rule, now 2 years old, that promoters run under 12s events, "One (promoter) I contacted didn't even have a handbook. So no wonder the kids do not come back for more."

Chris Wreghitt having been forced to retire due to injury was enlisted to write a series called "Coaching with Chris" for Cycling, described as a 'Cyclo-cross Masterclass.' In part one entitled 'Cross is fun' he disclosed that his own introduction to the sport was through the English Schools Cycling Association. In part two he wrote, "For several years I received much valuable advice from Mike Dawn, who is an athletics coach, but he was able to understand the physical and mental strain of competing at a high level ... You see the days are over when cycling was regarded as the best form of training for cycle racing." In the fourth episode he gave an insight into his outlook on equipment, with him advocating: "Don't be an equipment freak ... My only concern has been to use equipment, which is robust and reliable. In 'cross there is a danger that, in trying reduce weight because you have to carry the bikes at times, you will fit equipment which is too fragile ... I never had a chainstay bridge to reduce the likelihood of mud clogging up that part of the frame. I raced with a single 44-tooth chainring and a six-block, 12 to 26. That suited me 80% of the events. I experimented with various brake blocks – Fibrax have been doing interesting things with materials." Also in this part, he disclosed some of his other thoughts: "Originally, there was a preference for frames with a high bracket and short cranks. The theory was you rode over obstacles more easily. Now, brackets are lower and I used to ride 175mm cranks for 'cross and 172.5 mm for road ... With a handlebar changer it was easy to have a concealed cable, which went inside the top tube and then down inside one rear stay, to the changer. It also created a clean 'working area' – that part of the frame which you are continually grasping, carrying and lifting." All the above provided an insight into the mind of a multi-champion cyclo-cross rider.

During December it was revealed that Chris Dodd had developed "The first cyclo-cross training course in the country", with Butts Stadium as the venue: "We have a safe place to train, off the road, and it is only a matter of time before this type of training becomes the norm ... Riders are beginning to realise that cyclo-cross is more than just riding a bike."

Over the Festive Season, Daryl Webster the '25' Mile T.T, Track Pursuit and Hill-climb Champion also tried his hand at 'cross. Riding well enough to finish high up in the East Midlands event at Western Park, Leicester, although Steve Lawton (Beeston R.C.) won easily, leading from the start to finish banner.

When Steve Douce finished fifth to former world champion Hennie Stamsnijder in a race over the New Year period, it was described in

Cycling as "his best ever ride". However it may not have turned out that way, as due to lack of funds the British squad arrived with only 45 minutes to go before the race start. The team consisted of Douce, Young, Barnes, Gould, Burney and Steve's brother Graham. As they wanted to save on an overnight stay they had started from England at 5 a.m. on the morning of the event, and then had to drive 310 km. to Rigkervesall, Belgium, near the Dutch border. None of this seemed to affect Douce as he only lost out in a three-man sprint for third spot to the Amateur World Champion Radomir Simonek.

Despite encountering arctic weather, Mick Ives riding for the Coventry Olympic team, took home three of the four medals on offer in the National Veterans Championships for this year, sponsored by 'Golden Eggs Limited', held at Coalville, Leicestershire. He won the championship medal, the over 45 years medal and a team winner's medal with Lance Ravenhill and Graham Clements. The course was described as "made for downhill skiers" and the racers had to ride in blizzard conditions, which was apt, because Ives was wearing his ski thermal skinsuit beneath his tights and this proved a good choice in the Siberian weather. After 45 minutes of battling through snow and bitter cold winds Ives emerged as the winner from Ravenhill and Ian Jewell (Southern Velo). Picking up these medals today topped up Ives national medal tally to 26, and he showed no signs of easing up.

Keith Bingham headlined his report in Cycling on the National Championships this year, which were won by Steve Douce as: "Their thrilling battle over this very fast course was matched by the scrap for third place." this was how he described the race long tussle between Douce and Chris Young. Once more it was held at Sutton Park, with *The Daily Telegraph* supporting the event with impressive sponsorship. In the end it was a "brilliant Victory" by Douce who was riding for the Wembley Road Club/Nico Sport team, with Chris Young of the Paragon R.T. second and just over a minute back in third was Steve Barnes (Brook C.C.). Douce told Bingham afterwards "I got myself comfortable, got to the front and didn't have any problems." Young's thoughts were more on what might have been, "I had been given 76th place in the draw but they didn't shout out any numbers and I thought, I am not going to hang about and wait to be called. I got away behind Steve." Afterwards, the B.C-C.A decided not to select any professionals to go to the World's this year, so G.B. would only be represented by Amateurs and Juniors in Munich.

On the Saturday of the World Championships, the Amateurs raced in front of seven thousand spectators cheering them on, while fans at home in Britain were able to watch on B.B.C Grandstand, due to all the other sport expected to be covered by the B.B.C cameras being abandoned due to the 'big freeze'. A late night call on Friday to Hugh Porter, meant he had to do some urgent extra homework, ready for the Saturday screening. It was another West German victory, in the form of Mike Kluge a 22-year-old dental mechanic, who left Beat Schumacher (Switzerland) behind to win with Bruno D'Arsie his Swiss teammate taking the bronze medal. All the riders found the snow filled circuit tricky with the British squad having to find their own standard of racing, Douce finishing 21st, Baker 24th, Barnes 31st and Young 42nd. George Shaw, the British team manager, commented to Cycling, afterwards: "It was like the start of a five-mile race on the track, all our riders were involved in the pile-up just outside the stadium. Twelve men went clear and that was the end of the race." Asked why the British were among the few who chose to go barelegged, he replied: "It was their own choice, we impressed upon them before the start the importance of covering their legs or not."

Britain's hope of continued success in the junior event, was unfortunately not to be, for although at one point Stuart Marshall was riding in third place and looking good for a medal placing, a crash and a loss of power with two laps to go meant it was not to be his day. The Swiss cowbells were ringing loudly as Beat Wäbel came into view to win the title clear of Jürgen Sprich of West Germany, and then at over half a minute came Willem DeVos of Holland. The British riders crossing the finish line were Marshall in 15th, Steve Noble 33rd, Dean Booth 35th, and Michael Young in 38th. Cycling summed up the juniors' performances, as: "Marshall was incapable of uttering a word. He had given his all and hadn't let anyone down, and for that matter neither had the rest of the junior team. They had done their best and you can't ask more than that." The extreme cold and icy conditions were described by Dennis Donovan in Cycling: "It was something they had been warned about some months before, when John Morris had made a course inspection, - the former team manager, had advised, thick gloves and covering the legs." Then when given the choice by manager, George Shaw, they rode without, which was probably one of the reasons why David Baker was put into an ambulance afterwards suffering from the effects of the cold weather.

Klaus-Peter Thaler of West Germany at 35 years old was both a stage winner and a yellow jersey holder in the Tour de France back in 1978 and showed his undoubted class by claiming the Professional Rainbow Jersey from Dutchman Adrie Van Der Poel. With Claude Michely of Luxembourg taking the bronze. Thaler winning this first Professional Championship in front of 11,000 enthusiastic fans over a course at the Munich Olympic Stadium. Cycling described it as the "Duel in the sun." One highlight for the British fans was that the professional event was shown on T.V. back home the following Saturday afternoon.

A Ron Kitching advert for cyclo-cross equipment described the sealed bottom brackets as "The growing tendency towards the fitting of sealed annular-bearings unit is bound to be accelerated." With the prices of the top flight ones being £32 and the basic sealed bottom brackets being just a mere £8.00.

Jim Court writing in the North Western C-C.A Annual for this year outlined the vast amount work many officials did, with many riders not realising how much, just so that they could enjoy their sport: "Every sport needs its officials, often retired participants, to carry out those things necessary to ensure efficient administration and fair competition in the sport ... The affairs and the development of the Area (North Western) are controlled by the Committee who meet around four times a year to select teams, appoint commissaires and generally make decisions on behalf of the Area." He then went on to describe the duties of the various officials: "Every race must have an appointed commissaire. But, as our racing normally takes place off-road, we do not have the same outside pressures put upon us as road race commissaires." He continued by outlining all the many duties of a commissaire on the day, to achieve a fair start, adjudicate on complaints and irregularities such as 'short cutting', which probably causes more arguments than any other item ... Equally as important are the judges or lap scorers. Unlike the one-off decision of the road race judge, the lap scorers must stay alert throughout the race and try not to be distracted. They must record every rider on every lap, not an easy job when numbers become obscured, muddy or even lost."

Hundreds of lap scorers over the years will empathise with these last comments and give a wry smile at the memories. Jim also took space to remember a schoolboy's event where 140 riders finished, all within four laps; a schoolmaster then asked the judges virtually as the last person finished, "who was the third team?" Jim continued: "We are fortunate in the North West as we have an international class team of recorders in myself, and Reg and Gillian Ward whilst Alison Court, as well as being a new member of the team, has judged many of the Schoolboy and Under 12 races on her own."

17

Stuart Marshall becomes
World Champion

Season 1985/86
In compiling this book, it has been difficult to discover details of the early Treasurer's records or Annual Accounts, because very few of these appear in the Archives. However, Harry Gould has been kind enough to give an insight into how financial matters were conducted during the 1980's by saying: "I cannot comment upon events prior to the 1980s but I have a confidential letter dated 12th August 1985 to myself, entrusting me with the B.C-C.A Accounts and stating that and I quote: 'The figures are confidential to the National Officers of the Association.' It goes on to say the reason for non divulgence is that to divulge the complete figures to members would hinder progress."

What we are meant to make of that statement is not clear although it all sounds rather interesting. Harry goes on to explain: "Brief facts on Income and Expenditure – With the success of the British Junior Team in winning the 1982 Cyclo-Cross World Championships in Lanarvily, cyclo cross expanded and by the Financial Year commencing July 1st 1985, a Four Year Development Plan had to be agreed with the Sports Council to take the B.C-C.A's activities forward. There is no doubt in my mind that the professional approach of the B.C-C.A to these 'Sports Council Business Plans' and their subsequent delivery contributed to the B.C-C.A's acceptance in the upper echelons of Great Britain's Sport Administration as one of the best managed and reliable National Governing Bodies."

Harry continues, by outlining that the B.C-C.A was funded for development, and as he was a businessman, he was seconded from the B.C-C.A Executive with other National Officers to set up plans to oversee their execution.

1985/86 was to be Year 1 of the first 4 Year Plan reproduced below:

Income	£	Expenditure	£
Members Services	7,460	Members Services	7,660
National Programme	1,130	National Programme	16,350
International Programme	1,000	Internat. Programme	19,898
Coaching Dev. Ssceme	1,200	Coaching Dev. Scheme	4,792
Development	-	Development	9,750
	£10,790		£58,450

As can be seen, there is a shortfall of £47,660 which Harry Gould goes on to explain, "The submission yielded the B.C-C.A a grant of £26,600 rising to £26,800 plus addition for inflation for the next 3 years and we had to report progress in full each year thereafter, which we did, in full, always on time. The Sports Council was impressed with our honesty, speed of delivery and progress."

Steve Douce was seen smiling on the cover of this season's handbook resplendent in his 1985 Championship jersey, holding the Championship cup. The handbook shows those now running the Association listed under two columns. 'National Officers' with the only change B.Cossavella to International Racing Secretary. The second list was 'National Officials' and showed the Coaching Development Officer as K. Edwards, National Team Manager, G. Shaw and Clerical Officer that amazing stalwart, Mrs Joan Edwards, who was taking on yet another job. R.P.Ward and R.Digges were added to the Life Members list.

The prizes for events planned for the new season were categorised as follows:

Cat A- Minimum prizes £150 spread over at least the first 20 places. First prize not to be more than 25% of the total prize value.

Cat B - Minimum prizes £75.00 spread over at least the first 15 places. First prize not to be more than 25% of the total prize value.

Cat C - 15 prizes any value.

Cat D - Unspecified prize values.

Organisers shall provide a minimum prize list.

Cyclo-Cross racing has always come up with odd or funny names for events and this year was no exception. In September you could either ride the Godric C.C. 'Hog Fair' event in Suffolk or the G.S. Europa 'Regent Scramble'; during October there was the opportunity to ride the Alton 'North West Meat Scramble' or the Cherry Valley 'Duckling Cyclo-Cross; in December you might like to compete in the Oxonian 'Christmas Scramble.' By the end of the year you might fancy your chances in the Port Talbot 'Sandunes'or even the Alford 'Butterbump' Cross. Then if you had some energy left why not try the Wessex Triathlon at Portsmouth, consisting of a Swim, Run and then Cyclo-Cross.

On a more serious note, looking back at the coverage of Drugs and Stimulants there was a warning, of only three lines long, in the 1980 handbook. Now only five years later, it had grown to two and a half pages and a listed sixty-one banned substances most of which are almost unpronounceable and cover six types including everything from 'Anabolic steroids' to 'Narcotic analgesics'.

During early October, National Champion Steve Douce won his debut race as a professional at Milton Keynes. His sponsor T-Shirt Sales-Leisure-Dauphin Sport must have been pleased with his performance, as within half a lap he had taken command. He ended up lapping all but 14 riders and was followed home by Steve Barnes (Brook C.C.) and David Baker (Paragon R.T.)   Douce continued his fine start to the season by winning the Copystatic Supercross at Nottingham and the next day he tackled the South Western Road Club's ' Holdsworth Cycles' event on the Shirley Hills, near Croydon, where he won from D. McMullen (Wembly R.C.) and fellow professional P. Sanders riding for Polar Pools. He then added to this good start when he led the National Trophy League after the second event at Heaton Park, Manchester with two wins. The top junior was Stuart Marshall, with the leading Veteran Lance Ravenhill (Coventry Olympic), making it a trio of leaders all on 80 points.

The Area Championships this season ended with a wide variety of new champions. The North of England title went to Chris Young who retained his title and the Midland was won by National Squad rider Mike Bradley (Solihull C.C.) after a ding-dong fight with Glen Coltman (De Montfort B.C.) and defending champion Simon Burney (Alan Romarsport), Paul Bennett (Ross Wheelers) proved the winner in the South of England championships, held at the Royal Navy's Establishment at Southwick, Hampshire where he won from professional Pete Sanders riding for the Bilton-Condor team.

The Sports Council increased the grant to the B.C-C.A. this year, enabling the Association to talk about establishing a National Centre for Cyclo-Cross at the National Water Sports Centre, Holme Pierrepont, Nottingham. The National Committee greeted this with great enthusiasm because this meant that the riders would be able to train both indoors, and out within the complex. The centre could now be used for the National Squad training, in sessions supervised by expert B.C-C.A coaches and the floodlit areas would enable local riders to train safely on dark nights. The Great Britain team picked for the next World Championships at Lembeek in Belgium held a training camp at the centre during January and the Coaching Committee planned a coaching seminar there for March. There were high hopes that this first man-made cyclo-cross course of world championship standard could at last be created, and it would provide high quality accommodation to complete the complex.

A splendid colour photograph of Steve Douce leaping over an obstacle appeared in the New Year edition of Cycling. He was also featured inside over two pages, with several close-ups of his racing machine. One of the photographs shows his brake and gear cables running along the top tube and another his gear cable down the inside the seat stay. He explained the reason was that he did not interfere with them when lifting the cycle. Another shot shows his "expensive Lyotard 460 double-sided pedals." The article then goes on to say that his toe clips are split into two so that they do not collect mud, the chainwheels were 48 & 42 toothed and ran on a 5 speed block of 14 to 25 teeth. The whole bike weighed in at 19lbs and had 28 spoke wheels. This proved an interesting insight into a top professional's machine of the period.

The European Trophy Challenge for amateurs was fought out at Leonhout in Belgium, with the first snow of their winter falling during the night before. After the second round, the British team were equal with Holland, each having 63 points. In this third event it was Peter Kant of Holland who won, with Chris Young in third, followed by Robert Dane sixth and Barnes 13th. The final overall result was a win for Holland with 113 points, G.B. second with 91, and France in third with 88.

On the day of the Veteran Championships, the course was described as "conditions more suited to mud wrestling than bike riders." Tough man Mick Ives (Coventry Olympic-Wimet) retained his title by crossing the line more than a minute clear of Ian Jewell (Southern Velo) with third man Lance Ravenhill also of the Coventry Olympic club, who with the addition of team mate Clements, won the team prize. Torrential rain soaked the 40 riders who finished as they also had to battle with what Graham Snowdon in Cycling described as "near gale force winds and spindle-deep mud." The event was promoted by the Rutland C.C. on a 1½ mile circuit in Sheffield, the £750 prize list was put up by the South Yorkshire County Council..

The first reaction of the British cyclo-cross fan was delight when they read the headlines "Magnificent Marshall's Golden Ride". For these were the words used by Cycling to sum up Stuart Marshall's win at the Junior Cyclo-Cross World Championships at Lembeek, Belgium. These words were accompanied by a photograph of him wearing the Rainbow 'V' Jersey with the gold medal hanging round his neck. Dennis Donovan wrote of the emotional scenes that greeted the young Briton: "At Lembeek in Belgium on Sunday we saw the Union Jack raised, sang God Save the Queen, and unashamedly wept at this magnificent performance." Marshall did not have to wait for the sprint finish, for he just rode away from the opposition with a lap to go, to win by 30 seconds. It might not have ended so happily because he nearly fell foul of the U.C.I rules being interpreted incorrectly, but he was allowed to ride as his birthday was February 6th, when he would be nineteen. The closing date was January 31st, however the regulations state that a junior riding the year before can ride after that date.

The British Cycling Federation President Ian Emmerson was doubly delighted, not only because it was he who discovered the correct rule but because Marshall belonged to the same club as himself. Behind Stuart Marshall came Beat Berchbühl of Switzerland for the silver medal, and Wim de Vos of Holland taking the bronze. Afterwards Marshall was quoted as saying: "I was quite confident before the start, and it hasn't sunk in yet. Once I got past them on the second lap I looked back, saw I had a gap, and kept going." He did however keep his fans on the edge of their seats before they could celebrate, as Dennis Donovan described with feeling: "Suddenly Marshall appeared on his own. There was a stunned silence at first from the British spectators, hardly able to believe their eyes. Memories of Dane at Oss came flooding back. Could he hold on? It seemed an eternity before the riders appeared again. Looking down into the village a group of riders could be seen, but no G.B jersey among them. What had happened to Marshall? It soon became clear. He was hidden in a fold of the hill leading up to the straight and he was still in front of the chasing group." Another photograph appeared on the cover of Cycling the following week with Marshall shown resplendent in his Rainbow jersey, gold medal around his neck, and still holding his winner's bouquet of flowers, looking as if he might be singing the National Anthem.

Included in the riders picked for the World Championships this year was Mike Young, the younger brother of senior amateur Chris Young. Steve Noble was also chosen although no account of their participation has been located.

The new Amateur World Champion, Vito di Tano was hugged and kissed by his supporters after his victory for his second Rainbow Jersey win, the course being just to the liking of this tall Italian. Two Belgians, Yvan Messelis who rode to silver and his teammate Ludo de Rey taking the bronze medal followed him home. The first British rider home was Chris Young in 13th his best ride in a world's, afterwards he commented: "I couldn't get round anyone on the road, I improved steadily throughout and went up to 10th with two laps to go. Then I died a bit, you are bound to." Robert Dane finished in 32nd as he had found riding against senior amateurs a much harder task. "I just cannot run to that extent, I'm not a specialist runner," he said afterwards. Steve Barnes arrived in 20th spot but David Baker unfortunately had to abandon, due his frame braking on the very last lap, after a very good start.

The Professionals also had to battle through thick mud, with Albert Zweifel turning back the clock to 1979, when in similar conditions he had turned in a race-winning ride. Behind him came the 21 year old Swiss, Pascal Richard who led early on, but then faded, with the bronze medal going to the Dutchman Hennie Stamsnijder. Britain's Steve Douce rode very well to finish 13th, a fine ride for someone riding his first World Championships, and riding as the lone G.B representative. Even if Marshall hadn't won a Rainbow jersey, the results of Steve Douce and Chris Young would have been regarded as an improvement over previous achievements.

"Red Hot" was how Keith Bingham described Steve Douce's ride to win the Senior Open Championships for a third time. Douce riding for T Shirt Sales/Leisurewear, made riding on the many frozen surfaces look very easy. Most of those behind him found themselves doing more sliding and skating, rather than riding in a straight line. Two previous champions, Chris Young (Paragon R.T) who had been the 1984 Champion, was beaten into second place, with the 1983 Junior Champion David Baker (Paragon R.T) coming in third. This was Douce's fifteenth win of the season, proving he was now at the very top of his form. His was not a trouble free ride though as his chain came off twice and he also snapped a toe strap. Afterwards he said to Cycling: "I had to slow down over the last two laps, there was ice everywhere." Stuart Marshall was asked to stand on the podium after the race and show off his new gold medal, many fans then mobbed him for his autograph. He was placed thirteenth in the race, a fine ride for someone only just old enough to ride senior events. Brook C.C. won the team prize and a very creditable number of 62 brave riders completed the event despite the dangerous frozen conditions.

The 1986 Cycling Year Book also covered the inspiring win of Stuart Marshall with the headline: "Marshall plucks rainbow jersey out of Lembeek mud." and Joan Edwards reminded everybody: "This was the first Gold Medal at world level won by a junior at any cycling discipline."

Steve Noble riding for Seacroft Wheelers gave himself a welcome 18th birthday present, by winning the Junior Championships. He was not certain to win until late in the race as Nicholas Craig (V.C.Elina) chased him down and at one point even took the lead when Noble lost his chain, but the more powerful Noble went on to win by eleven seconds from Craig, with Martin Maskell (Glendale C.A.C) taking the bronze medal The winning team was V.C.Lincoln/Metheringham Cars.

Joan Edwards wrote in the Cycling Year Book: "To encourage participation, a Juvenile Award Scheme has been established for riders under 16 years. Finishing in a requisite number of races will gain qualification for the lower award, but a number of appropriate placings have to be obtained before the higher awards can be claimed ... Floodlit mid-week training venues are becoming an increasing feature of the 'cross scene. The Midlands led the way with facilities at the Butts Stadium, Coventry, followed by those at the National Water Sports Centre at Holme Pierrepont, virtually beneath 'Spaghetti Junction' is also being used, and Southampton are well advanced with similar plans."

She also argued for cyclo-cross in schools in this piece: "No school could hold even a five-mile time trial in its limits, a few may have a possible circuit, but many could arrange a cyclo-cross course with the help of stakes, tape, a few gym forms, and a little imagination. The rudiments of 'cross can be taught without the need of specialist cycles, particularly if all participants are similarly equipped."

This just shows how far thinking her ideas were at this time, if only schools could have taken up just some of her ideas outlined above, not only cyclo-cross but the health of children would have benefited. Also in this article: "The B.C-C.A has been offered the opportunity to produce an eight-minute video, which will be shown on Channel 4 sometime in the future, in a series that will include some 35 other sports ... Someday soon sponsors are going to realise the T.V. potential for 'cross, and it will then take off dramatically."

What a year it had been, a British World Champion at last and progress on many fronts, with the plans for some very far-sighted schemes being progressed. The B.C-C.A officials had their sights on what was to be done and had the plans; it was now up to the riders to come up with the goods in the last quarter of the 1980's.

Season 1986/87

Anyone receiving the new 1986/87 handbook in the post would be pleased to see the full colour photograph of Stuart Marshall on the cover, they would also notice that it was slightly thicker with 12 extra pages but the price had increased by 25p to £1.50p. One detrimental point though was the choice of the minute size of type now used, a free magnifying glass would have been a useful item supplied with every copy. This edition was also packed with the details of 207 events and six pages of black and white photographs, which included World Champion Marshall, Senior Champion Douce, Veteran Ives, Junior Noble and Juvenile Hempsall. Ray Richards was now in the new post of Life Vice President although he remained General Secretary, Jim Court, the Association Chairman and the Membership Secretary was Reg Ward, with the new style handbook now in the hands of Madeline Beagley.

September saw the Wessex Area produce the first issue of their new magazine Newsletter. It was a small neat production. One of the articles outlined a project called 'Come and try it' and included an 'Introduction with videos' followed up by outdoor training events.

The first major clash of the new season was at Milton Keynes, with Steve Douce outsmarting David Baker at the last moment to win by just 5 seconds. Chris Young (Paragon R.T.) had his usual slow start and then recovered well, to finish third. This was just days before taking himself off to Switzerland, where he was due to ride for Chris Wreghitt's old Swiss club for the rest of the season. Afterwards, Douce described the course: "It was more like a road race, the ground was so hard and fast."

November saw the Frenchman, Bruno Lebras score a run-a-way win in the European Challenge race held on the Crystal Palace course. He rode away unchallenged from the moment he took the lead on the first lap. He was never seen again by the chasing pack until after they had crossed the finish line. The result sheet showed that only three British riders had fought their way into the first fourteen to finish, with Baker in second, Tim Gould fourth and Sean Yates at fourteenth. Apart from Baker and Gould the riding of the French, Belgians, Dutch, Swiss and West Germans was just too classy in the wheel clogging mud. On the same day, the London Championships were held on the same course, with the winner Arno Van Boeijen from Holland, another prize going to a rider from over the Channel.

Over the Christmas period, the G.B. squad were riding events in Holland and Belgium, and then afterwards it was back to Wolverhampton where the final selection for the world championships would be made. During this period cyclo-cross was getting excellent coverage in the newly named and designed *Cycling Weekly*. It included not only cover photographs but many column inches, covering races, and interviews with top riders, plus a column by Joan Edwards called 'Cross Talk', demonstrating one of the advantages that cyclo- cross has of being a mainly winter sport.

A park in Milan, Italy during November was the scene of another fine ride by Steve Douce, where he gained seventh place ahead of the amateur world champion Vito di Tano, with the former world amateur champion Mike Kluge of West Germany taking the win. Meanwhile back in England, David Baker (Paragon R.T-Gazelle) was honing his form for the New Year by winning the Nottingham Council event, holding off the challenge of the fast finishing Eric Vervaet of Belgium.

Joan Edwards in one of her regular columns reported: "A year ago Ralph Digges was the proud recipient of the Torch Trophy presented to him by Princess Alexandra. This year it was Joan Milsom (Calder Clarion) who received her award from the Duke of Gloucester. She has been a stalwart of Yorkshire cyclo-cross for 20 years, carrying out judging, lap scoring and time keeping, hostess to the committee for 10 years and Prize Presentation organiser for 20 years. Cyclo-Cross is a male sport, but it is fortunate to have a few hard-working women officials without whom the sport would not be in its present challenging position." Joan's comments praising hard-working women, also applied to Joan herself, as she too was one of those who gave thousands of hours to the B.C-C.A.

Steve Douce (T Shirt Sales-Dauphin Sports) sealed the National Trophy Series for the third consecutive time in the first week of December by victory in the final round at Sheffield. His runaway win was from amateur G.B. squad member David Baker and professional Mick Hammond, riding for the Advance Reprographics team. Robert Dane received a big blow to his planned season, when he was operated on for acute appendicitis in Eindhoven hospital, in Holland. His aim of living and racing in Holland was now dashed just when he was enjoying good form and he had been earning between £100 and £150 per contract for every race he rode. He had been seeing riders such as Stamsnijder, pick up £1,000 per event, so he expected to make a good living from cyclo-cross rather than road racing. In *Cycling Weekly* he disclosed the standard required by the German Organisers: "In German races, it also required you to turn up with two clean bikes, two clean pairs of wheels and polished shoes. Dare to stand on the start line in dirty shoes and money would be deducted for a poor show."

One of the biggest fields in years assembled for the Southern Championships. Graham Douce the older brother of the national champion Steve, slipped when in the lead, thus allowing his team-mate Dave McMullen of the Wembley R.C/NicoSport to race on to win. The veteran winner was Ian Jewell (Southern Velo) who finished with blood pouring down his face, having forgotten to duck in the woods and so caught his nose on a branch! Another well-known veteran riding this event was Keith Mernickle on the comeback trail. Mernickle always proved a good source of blunt comments, as is shown by this quote from *Cycling Weekly*: "I am not putting much into it these days – so I cannot expect to get much out of it. In the race in Italy recently where Steve Douce finished 23rd, I was third, years ago. He said he was tired after travelling, but we used to travel just the same. John Atkins regularly made the first six in the big Continental races ... The standard is not very good these days, and even on my little training I have managed to get three fourth places this year. I am now doing 50 miles a week, whereas I used to do 50 miles a day. The old magic is gone."

The Eastern Championships had the honour of the World Junior Champion outclassing all the opposition at the Mildenhall C.C./Dairytime event, where the course had a bank that only Marshall could ride. The South Wales winner was Robin Everson (R.A.F.C.C.) who finished an impressive four and a half minutes ahead of M.Stacey of the Port Talbot Wheelers.

What sounds like the comic start of a race, was certainly not for those involved in the A.B.C Centreville event. As the riders leapt away from the start Mick Hammond (Advance Photographic) rode straight into the organiser, they both picked themselves up and Hammond made off after the other competitors, thus being last away. The course was tough, with one section five inches deep in mud, but Hammond was tougher and by lap two was in the lead. At the finish he crossed the line 25 seconds ahead of Michael Young (Bradford Wheelers) with the Raleigh professional Paul Sherwen in seventh spot.

Another rider who mixed cycling disciplines successfully this season, was National Kilometre Track Champion Gary Coltman (something not expected in 21st century track stars). He was an easy winner on Boxing Day on Kenilworth Common, Warwickshire. Coltman, riding for Zenith C.C./Julies Cycles started in the scratch group in this handicap race but hit the front with 15 minutes still to go and continued at full speed for the victory.

The B.C-C.A. selectors picked their teams for the World Championships after the final selection race at Wolverhampton. Their full selection was Steve Douce, our only representative in the professional event, with David Baker, Barrie Clarke (described in *Cycling Weekly* as "The find of the season"), together with Chris Young and Tim Gould for the amateur event, with G.Coltman and S.Barnes as the non-travelling reserves. The juniors picked to go were M. Young, I. Wright, N. Craig and S. Noble, with the non-travelling reserves S.Hempsall and M.Maskell.

Paul Dixon had been the winner on Boxing Day in Yorkshire, just 48 hours after winning the ANC Macclesfield Supercross, but it was very noticeable that many were showing the effects of over indulgence during the Christmas holidays, leaving only the committed to dominate.

During January the Stockport Clarion put on a new venture, a women's only race at Gatley Hill, Cheadle. Eleven riders took part over a course involving two-thirds of the men's course, covering four laps. It resulted in a win for 34-year-old Jill Wilkinson (Coventry R.C.) who held off Anne O'Hare (Weaver Valley) and Helen Clarke (Bolsover Wheelers) for the win, Clarke riding well for third spot at the tender age of only fourteen. Would promoters take note and provide more events for women, we will just have to wait and see?

Once more the aim of those wanting to catch the selector's eye was to ride on the Continent. Baker, Burney, Gould and Salmon had all been resident in Germany for the cyclo-cross season in order to compete every week at European level, only returning to the U.K for the major British races. In Luxembourg David Baker gained a fine second placing and Tim Gould a third but neither could better Claude Michely (Lux.). Michely also led them home in another Luxembourg race, but this time it was Gould third, Baker fourth and Coltman in seventh. The group then moved on to Belgium where Baker gained eighth, but Gould and Coltman could only finish well down on the speedy Dutchman Huuv Kools, although a series of races over Christmas also in Belgium found their results nowhere near as successful.

The 'European Challenge' was also held in Belgium, at Loenhout. It was Hennie Stamsnijder (Hol) who would outpace all challengers to win, with Barrie Clarke taking 17th place, Gould 18th and Baker 24th. The overall winning team was Holland, with 165 points, then Poland, Belgium and West Germany with G.B. in fifth place with 69 points.

This season both the senior World Championships were dominated by West Germans at Mlada Boleslav in Czechoslovakia. Icy cold conditions were to prevail throughout the senior events; it was so cold at one time that a wolf was seen on the course, carefully watching the strange things humans do on bicycles. Steve Douce rode well as the only G.B representative in the Professional race, finishing in the same placing, (13th) as he had in the 1986 championships. Thirty-six year old Klas-Peter Thaler added to his tally of three Rainbow Jerseys with Danny De Bie of Belgium taking the silver, and Christophe Lavinne of France the bronze.

The atmosphere at the Amateur race was described by Dennis Donovan in *Cycling Weekly*: "The crowds and their enthusiasm were tremendous, and the amateur race will live in the memory for a long time, as one of the most exiting 'crosses of the season." Mike Kluge (W.Ger) had been the champion two years before, but this time had to fight all the way to hold off the challenge from the home nation's riders, Franticek Kloucek and Roman Kreuziger both of whom were swept along on a tide of cheering from a massive crowd of 20,000 plus spectators, to take the silver and bronze medals. The G.B. riders were left to dream of what might have been and their coaches to rethink their programmes. David Baker finishing 26th, Chris Young 37th and Tim Gould (after frame problems) 45th. Once more the super fast start caught the British riders out, prompting team manager Bob Thom to declare that he now wants to get his squad riding hard road races as pre-season training after witnessing the riding of the Czech's, who had three riders who had finished the Peace Race in their amateur team.

The same rapid start, as happened in the senior races, left the British juniors gasping and dismayed in their title race. They learnt very quickly the level of speed that they needed to even just keep with the pack at this level, with the sight of Wim De Vos of Holland, turning up with a disc rear wheel doing nothing for their spirits. On lap one Steve Noble passed through in 17th place but faded to finally finish 28th, but still the first G.B rider home. Next was Nick Craig 34th, with M.Young 42nd. The new Junior Rainbow Jersey wearer was Marc Jassens of Belgium, with Ralf Berner of West Germany in the silver medal position, and Tomas Port also of Belgium in bronze.

During February an event at the Parc Cwn Darran in Mid Glamorgan, saw Barrie Clarke (Surrey R.C.) win the event by over 3½ minutes from Martin Maskel (Glendale C.C.) with T. Davies (Abertillery Wheelers) in third place, despite the fact of Clarke puncturing close to the finish. Looking further down the result sheet, the eye catches on the name of the Juvenile winner, the double English Schools C.A. champion, Roger Hammond of the Hounslow & District Club.

Joan Edwards, writing once more in her weekly column 'Cross Talk' told of a change in the U.C.I rules: "National Championships must take place two weeks prior to the World's in future years." She also called for more handicap events, so as to discourage the continuing practice of a small number of riders dominating small local events. Such handicap events would make the top riders work harder for their victories and it would raise the standard of all classes of riders.

Twenty-three year old Steve Douce (T Shirt Sales–Leisure wear) put the opposition to the sword in the British Championships, where he won from David Baker (Paragon R.T.) and Tim Gould (Ace R.T). Seventy-four finished the race and Ace R.T/ Roma Sport were the team winners. *The Daily Telegraph* was once more the main sponsor, giving good coverage of the event in their newspaper. Douce said afterwards: "This must rate as my best win of the season, I came off in the sandpit on the first lap. It took me a while to get back to David (Baker). But I got back to him and straight past. It (the course) was the hardest I have ridden, it was like the Grand National. I fell off a few times, but everyone fell off." This event was to see the end of the wonderful sponsorship of *The Daily Telegraph* who had been the main supporters of these championships since 1965, a long time for a main sponsor of any sporting event.

The Junior title race saw Ian Wright (CVC Lincoln-Metheringham Cars) lead from start to finish, winning from Nick Craig (V.C. Oldham) by 34 seconds. Martin Maskell (Glendale C.A.C) was next in, almost two minutes later for third. Wright expressed his attitude to racing, when speaking to *Cycling Weekly*: "I was determined to get the gold medal today. When I was 14 Nicky beat me in the Schoolboy Championship."

Ian Small was still editing the excellent magazine of the North Western C-C.A, called the Annual, with Jim Court not only typing the copy but also writing articles, such as "Jims Ramblings", which included: "On the official side I tried to combine the National Chairmanship with that of the Area which took me away from the local events more than I would have liked." At National level he explained: "Reg Ward took over from me as Membership Secretary and produced some real space-age computer graphics to support the information."

This year the tickets for the Annual Dinner Dance and Prize Presentation were £10 each, held at the Holme Pierrepont Hotel on Saturday 14th March. For anyone wishing to stay overnight, there was hotel accommodation available at a cost of £12.50 a night. The Wessex magazine, Newsletter, had a reminder for their Prize Presentation to be held at Oakdene Holiday Village, St. Leonards, at the season's end. It certainly sounded a jolly affair, which included a Disco, Games and Chicken & Chips, all for just £3.00. So with these functions the season 1986-87 drew to a close.

Phil O'Connor

Steve Douce,
seven times National Champion.

Barrie Clarke,
twice Senior National Champion

THREE PEAKS

PAST WINNERS

Nick Craig
1991

Andy Peace
1995, 1996

Chris Young
1994, 1997, 1998

Ian Cuthbertson
1999

Phil O'Connor

Tim Gould, twice second and twice third in the National Championships, tackles a water hazard

Programmes 1992

Great Britain Cyclo-Cross Squad 1991/92

Great Britain Cyclo-Cross Team 1992

Great Britain Cyclo-Cross Team 1995/96.

Great Britain Cyclo-Cross Team 1998.

THREE PEAKS
Past Winners

1998 Lady Winner: Sue Thomas
(Photo : Tony Fickes)

1999 Lady Winner: Kali Taylor

Phil O'Connor

Caroline Alexander, five times Women's Champion

Roger Hammond,
World Junior Champion 1992
British Juvenile and Junior Champion
Three times British Senior Champion (B.C.C.A.)

18

Douce dominates

Season 1987/88

This year there was a change to the handbook, which was now bound with a stiff back and Steve Douce had returned to the front cover. Once more the price had crept up by another 25p making it £1.75. It had lots of full-page adverts and a quick look at the changes made to officials, shows R.Brogan was now Chairman, and the Press Officer M. Brown. The Coaching Development Officer post was left unfilled, but the National Team Manager was now R.Thom Jr.

Joan Edwards was still executing the job of Clerical Officer but was also busy in many other ways, including writing her regular column in *Cycling Weekly*, where during September she discussed the subject of how triathletes were interested in keeping in trim by doing cyclo-cross during the winter months: "I have already had several enquires, and local clubs could find some likely talent among the triathletes, who certainly don't mind running and aren't afraid of getting wet."

She also declared that after 12 months hard work by Gill Wreghitt and Keith Edwards, cyclo-cross training was taking place at Gateshead Stadium. This was at the invitation of the North Eastern C.C.A, Gateshead Borough Council and the Northern Region Sports Council, who were all getting together with one aim in mind. This had enabled the purchase of several cyclo-cross machines, which were to be used and stored at the stadium. There were also plans for races between cyclists and harriers, but this idea was abandoned when, as Joan writes: "The reason for the cancellation seems farcical in this day and age. 'Amateur' athletes some of whom receive many thousands of pounds in appearance money and prize money, are not allowed to compete against amateur cyclists, because it would endanger their amateur status." Meanwhile in Oxford, Tony Wirdnam a B.C-C.A coach was to repeat his popular training session this autumn at the Oxford Boys School.

During September, northeast stalwart Doug Morton gave the details of a series of six handicap events, which were to be sponsored to the tune of £200, by Sunderland Machine Design Consultancy Ltd. Langbaurgh Council, would enhance the North East Championship series with an additional £250 for trophies, which was all very encouraging news.

A 'What's On' column in *Cycling Weekly* of mid September, declared: "Gould set for fourth victory in Three Peaks." and continued to predict that the course record holder Tim Gould was set for his fourth win in this race and that organiser John Rawnsley had "selected 200 riders he thinks are capable of completing the gruelling climbs." The next week, the same magazine, had a full page picture (still only black and white) by David Worthy capturing the competitors tackling the hazardous descent of Ingleborough with the report by Colin Willcock saying: "Tim Gould made his own little bit of cycling history on Sunday when he won the Three Peaks cyclo-cross for the fourth successive year and did it in style, winning by a whopping 12½ minutes. The ACE Racing Team rider from Wirksworth in North Derbyshire joined Harry Bond and Eric Stone as a four-time winner, but neither of the others managed it in successive years."

After over three hours of endeavour Gould won from Mick Hammond (Advance Reprographics) and Mick Bradbury (Polytechnic C.C.) How racing over these peaks has changed was shown when Gould swopped to his road bike, complete with a rear disc wheel, for the last road section, saying afterwards, "if you have got the equipment you might as well use it." Both John Rawnsley and Neil Orrell both completed the course for an amazing 27th time. For the first time a woman covered this renowned course and the lady brave enough to break old taboos was Janice Theis of the North Wilts. R.C. Ian and Nick Craig of the V.C.Oldham took the unusual father and son team award. The first of the mountain bikers to try their luck in another discipline was Vincent Edwards of the Leicestershire R.C. Six national squad riders were in the best field gathered together for many years. The mountain bikers and women were started 10 minutes ahead of the main pack to enable them to get a clear get-away. The team award went to the two Gould brothers, plus Steve Barnes of the ACE R.T.

Another family affair was taking place during the Festival R.C. Pearson Scramble at Shirley Hills, with Steve Douce (Raleigh/Banana) winning from Barrie Clarke, with his brother Graham Douce back in fourth spot.

David Baker, riding for Great Britain, travelled to the 'European Challenge' event at Hohnat in Austria. The race winner was Dutchman

Martin Hendricks (Panasonic) from Poland's Edward Piech. Baker riding well to gain third spot, after leading from the start, and then keeping very close contact with the eventual first and second riders. The quality of David's ride can be judged by those who finished behind him, including world professional champion, Klaus-Peter Thaler and former world champion Albert Zweifel. This result meant that Baker was now second to Piech in the series, with G.B. leading the team section. The other G.B. riders qualifying being Clarke seventh, Gould 13th and Barnes 26th.

Back home, Robert Dane (Paragon R.T-Gazelle) was busy winning the Royal Sutton promotion held alongside Spaghetti Junction. Chris Young was victorious at the Macclesfield Wheelers event, where organiser Brian Brogan described Young's performance as "Faultless", and Stuart Marshall continued his winning ways by taking the Gainsborough Aegir event at Morton in Lincolnshire, although he still had his eye on higher things by saying, "I would like a place in the World Championship team."

The Smirnoff Scramble this year saw the Continental riders relegated to seventh, eighth, ninth and tenth placings, by a group of determined British riders, led by National Champion Steve Douce, Chris Young and David Baker, with the help of Barrie Clarke, Robert Dane and Tim Gould. It was not a smooth race though, as Keith Bingham reported in *Cycling Weekly*, "Cruel fate won in a thrilling Smirnoff International Challenge at Harlow, Essex, on Sunday, as British Champion Steve Douce (Raleigh/Banana) snatched victory from a super-fit Chris Young who looked to have it all sewn up with 500 yards to go ... Lady Luck had blessed Young by dealing his rival Douce a fall and a puncture after half distance." After the race had finished, Young described the last agonising section: "Just before the underpass with 500 yards to go this twig jammed in my gears." His pause enabled Douce to catch him and overtake, to win by a mere nine seconds.

November saw Joan Edwards covering topics both important and light-hearted in her 'Crosstalk' column. She reported that Nick Carter, the organiser of many events at H.M.S. Dryad, had in recent years been beset by problems associated with security: "Although no B.C-C.A rule exists, it has become common practice for all but major (Category A) events to have entries on the line." Security at navy bases had to be tight, meaning that they needed to know who was on their premises, so that entries on the line were not possible. On the lighter side she reported that British Summer Time meant that the training sessions called 'Twilight Tuesday' at the Magnet Centre Birmingham, needed to use the lighting provided by the 'Spaghetti Junction' motorway, so that those training could see their way in the darker areas.

This year the Beauvale C.C. at Nottingham promoted the National Juvenile Championships. A big plus for them was that their own Christopher Perry, at only fourteen, took the title winning by over two minutes from Jason Shackleton of ABC Centreville, who took the silver medal and John Pemberton (Bolsover Wheelers} the bronze. Eighty-eight hopefuls had started and the riders were soaked by the incessant rain, which typically only stopped when all the racing had finished. First girl home was Rachel McGhee of the Elizabeth C.C. and the team award went to Kimberley Comp. A paragraph in a report by Bernard Thompson in *Cycling Weekly* talks of a future champion: "Roger Hammond (Hounslow & District Wheelers) got a slow start, but went through after one full lap in eighth place, then showed remarkable experience for his 13 years in pulling back two places in lap two and hanging on grimly to his sixth place to the finish, to claim the under 14 years award." Little did he know just how this lad was to make his mark, not only in British cyclo-cross but to continue his career as a professional road racer and multi-champion.

Lewis Hall, a B.C-C.A coach, reported he had had a good response from *Cycling Weekly* readers who were interested in qualifying for the National Junior Squad. Those interested were encouraged to turn up to a training day, which involved a physiological test, running, cycling speed and technique. Dr. Richard Wood the Medical Officer would also give a talk on sports injuries.

Coalville Wheelers gave an unusual gift to every starter in their event, a box of eggs! This was thanks to the generosity of their sponsor 'Golden-Lay' who also provided a £500 prize list. Good prizes were definitely in the news at this time, for the Macclesfield Wheelers with their ANC Super-Cross were advertising it as the 'Richest of the Winter.'

Meanwhile, at Gansigen in Switzerland, Steve Douce (Raleigh-Banana) was finishing seventh behind Beat Breu, who had been a stage winner in the Tour de France, with Albert Zweifel taking second and Pascal Richard (Fra) third. Douce's placing was far better than it appears at first glance, because not only did he have the misfortune to pull his foot out of his toe-clip at a vital moment, but only two weeks before, in the Smirnoff Challenge he had injured his leg and as *Cycling Weekly* reported: "He was unable to train all week and he fainted after stitches were removed from his shin on Thursday." Added to that he had a stomach bug that had also affected the whole British team.

The Area titles again threw up winners, both familiar and little known. A roadman from Sussex, Dave Brooker (V.C.Etoile) took the South of England title held at Crystal Palace from Graham Douce (Wembley R.C.), with the Veteran title going to Mike Bradbury of the Poly C.C. The Eastern championships were held at Mistley in North Essex, where Stuart Marshall of V.C. Lincoln won the senior title only a few miles from Wivenhoe, where he had taken the 1982 Juvenile title. This time, the Juvenile winner was Glen Palmer of the Alford Wheelers.

In the Midlands it was Steve Knight (Halesowen A.C.C.) who took advantage of Tim Gould being away racing in Sardinia, to take the title by almost a minute from J.Snodin of Melton Olympic. Further north, it was Chris Young who outclassed all, to win by over 2½ minutes from F. Salmon (Oldham) in the North of England Championships. Young declared afterwards in *Cycling Weekly*: "Just my kind of course – I got some good training in."

Over in Wales, they were holding their own championships, and it was Tim Davies of C.C. Abergavenny who outrode Robin Everson (R.A.F. C.C.). At the finish he was over a minute clear, with the bronze medal going to A. Matthews, also of the Abergavenny club. Nearly 40 riders competed but one, Maurice Broadbent, had travelled all the way down from North Wales, a worthwhile journey because he went home with the Veteran's title.

Not only was Steve Douce away racing in Sardinia but a team of British riders were also racing on the island. Some with great success, David Baker took a win from Steve Barnes making a British one-two, with Robert Dane seventh, Barrie Clarke eighth, and Tim Gould sixteenth.

The main sponsors for the National Championships were Holdsworth, with their familiar 'Holdsworth Orange' on the cover of all the programmes, the same as the National Trophy Series programmes this season. When you have won the British title four times, then you have good reason to know your capabilities. Steve Douce (Raleigh/Banana) explained his tactics to the crowd after donning the Champion's jersey once more, with Keith Bingham of *Cycling Weekly* reporting: "He had not taken the lead at the start because he didn't want the amateurs sitting on his wheel. It was a ploy to let his opponents squabble for the lead between themselves before he relieved them of the responsibility for good." The silver medallist Tim Gould (Ace RT} and Chris Young (Paragon RT) bronze, both had to stand on the podium listening to this put-down from their tormentor.

The Holdsworth Company may have sponsored these championships for the first time, but the venue was the tried and trusted Sutton Park in Birmingham. David Baker and Steve Barnes, who shared the bottle of Champagne afterwards in celebration, backed up the winning team Ace RT led home by Tim Gould. A solid log wrapped in soft material and dubbed the 'Limbo-pole' had to be negotiated on every lap, but at first, this proved to be very controversial as it was bolted at a metre high, and took its toll in bruised backs, with one machine getting entangled. Before the senior race there was an attempt to remove it by disenchanted riders and their supporters, with even Bob Thom the junior world team manager objecting, but even his pleas fell on deaf ears, so it remained in place. Tall David Baker arrived at the obstacle on one lap with Barrie Clarke, but on feeling his kidneys "squeezed" he eased and Clarke raced on. The Raleigh/Banana team took full advantage of Douce's win by taking out full pages of adverts in the cycling press celebrating his fifth title win.

In contrast to the senior event, the Junior title race was a thrilling affair. Lee Wright of the V.C. Lincoln Metheringham club took his second national jersey and gold medal by over two minutes, from Lee Ferreday (Bolsover Wheelers) and Mark Bolt (Manchester Wheelers), both of whom were near to blows, after the former put the other into the tapes when fighting it out for the silver and bronze medals. Wright, though, was not without his problems for as the officials turned their backs the youngsters raced off and had to be called back, then as they restarted, he broke a pedal and lost a shoe plate, so had to exchange bikes at the first of the pits. After the awards had been made, Ferreday told *Cycling Weekly*'s Keith Bingham, "Together we could have got a lot closer to the front. At the finish he (Bolt) jumped me and I wasn't having him come past me. I'd made the race. I was tempted halfway through the race to hit him. But I didn't. I thought better of it." A quite an extraordinary admission of the will to win, that these youngsters had.

January's end saw the World Championships held in atrocious conditions. "SWISS DOUBLE IN SEA OF MUD" was the heading to Dennis Donovan's report in *Cycling Weekly*. They were held in Hagendorf, Switzerland, with all the pre-race predictions washed away in the rain and mud. Out of the nine individual medals, the home country won four; the gold and bronze in the Professional event, silver in the Amateur and another gold in the Junior title race. As Donovan explained: "Most of the problems were due to the course being designed with snow in mind, but in this mild winter unseasonable rain had fallen for three weeks." There were many protests that riders could only negotiate the run-ups by pulling themselves up on the crowd control ropes.

Professional Pascal Richard (Swiss) became champion by pursuing his own version of riding in a bath of mud, from Adri Van Der Poel of Holland (runner-up for the second time) with Beat Breu winning the bronze medal. Steve Douce started well, lying either fifth or sixth early on, but as Donovan reported "However, he was having breathing difficulties with a nose bleed which caused him to choke, as blood ran into his throat." So although he gave of his best, he was hampered and could only finish seventeenth.

Czechoslovakian Karel Camrda won the Amateur title from Roger Honegger of Switzerland by 35 seconds, with the Dane Henrik Djernis in third. Tim Gould was the best of the G.B. team when he finished in ninth; this was the highest placing by a British senior rider for many years. He told Dennis Donovan afterwards, "I had a reasonable start, I picked my way through to eighth place ... It was a different fitness to that needed for the Three Peaks, even the World Champion packed." Second of the Brits was Chris Young (30th) who described his ride, "I went forward for the first two laps, then backwards." David Baker was very disappointed finishing in 37th spot saying: "I don't like the mud any more." But it was the cold that got to Barrie Clarke (42nd) "I shivered for half an hour afterwards, I couldn't feel my knees or toes."

The Junior title race also produced a home winner in Thomas Frischknecht, with Mike Muller of West Germany in silver and yet another Czechoslovakian rider, Daniel Reh the bronze medallist. The first G.B. rider home was Ian Wright in 18th, with Lee Ferreday (28th), Christopher Layhe (32nd), and Mark Bolt back in forty-fourth. It was divulged afterwards that British Junior champion Wright had been suffering from back pain for a while and had to sleep on the floor to get relief. A French doctor told him that his right leg was shorter than his left, not as he had been told earlier, when he had been given the wrong information, with support to his wrong foot!

On the official side during 1988, Harry Gould was made the Chairman of the Executive set up to plan for the World Championships that the B.C-C.A wished to promote in 1993. Harry explained, "Events saw us seize the opportunity to promote them in 1992, which did lead to some unanticipated severe problems."

Jim Court, in his 'Chairman's Jottings' in the N.W.C-C.A Annual included this item: "On the official side I stood down as National

Chairman ... Harry Gould, initially acting as North Area Representative on the National Committee, rapidly seems to have taken on the role of National Mediator (or is it holder of coats for fights?)"

Season 1988/89

Steve Douce was in top form by late October, winning the first Holdsworth National Trophy Series event held at Wolverhampton. The event was reported by Keith Edwards in *Cycling Weekly*: "After the race Douce explained that he was struggling with his running following a road season that ended with the Nissan Classic. The organisation by the Wolverhampton Wheelers was immaculate, including the marshalling by Percy Stallard." (another of those very early 'cross stalwarts.) The Smirnoff International Race was blessed by sunshine, which picked out Douce in his bright Raleigh/Banana colours, he suffered first a broken chain early on and then he punctured! From then on his sheer class overcame all the other riders, including an impressive list of Europeans, to win from Chris Young (Paragon R.T.)

Up in Scotland, Martin Coll (ACT. RT Peugeot) was performing a unique double, by winning the Scottish title race only three months after winning their National Road Race Championships. The course was at Dundee's Balgay Park and was described as "Demanding, Tricky and Scary" by the riders. He won by just three seconds from G. Barr (Glasgow Wheelers) with S. Halan of the VC de L'Avenir in the bronze position.

Others with early season fitness included Mark Farrow (Norwich ABC), who took the victory in the Wolsey R.C. event from Tony Wilkins (unsponsored) and Chris Gooch (Leo R.C.). The last two named are still very much involved in cyclo-cross administration, just two of the many who are putting back a great deal of their time into the sport they have enjoyed for so long. It was also good to note the name of a past super champion John Atkins putting something back into the sport with the John Atkins Cycles Training Cross Events.

Barrie Clarke of the Wembley A.C/Testers team was another early season winner in the Finsbury Park C.C. event, with D. Booker (Festival R.C.) taking second place. Another Festival R.C. rider, Dave Rosbotham, was also busy winning the Dursley R.C event at Stroud, Gloucestershire.

The cover of the 1988/89 Handbook was quite different to any previous production. It had a green border, with the badge of the Holdsworth Company prominently displayed combined with the words "Holdsworth Helping Carry Cyclo-Cross Forward." The book consisted of 96 pages, the Treasurer's job was now in the hands of Betty Bewley, and Press Officer was that faithful servant of the Association Keith Edwards, with Mrs Joan Edwards turning her hand to being the General Secretary. Geoff Mayne became Development Officer and the new post of Grants and Sponsorship Officer was Mrs G.Wreghitt.

At this time the Wessex Area were advertising a mini bus trip to the World Championships in the New Year at Pont-Chateau, in France. The cost would be £45, which included the price of staying at a hotel and meals, but entries to the races were extra.

The National Juvenile Championship was held in Wales for the first time, with the course being in the Parc Cwm Darran, near Bargoed in the Rhymney Valley. An unusual feature of this course was that it was on a reclaimed coalmine. *Cycling Weekly* described the race as an "Exiting race-long battle" which ended in a win for 14-year-old Roger Hammond (Dr Challoners Grammar) who out sprinted Richard Thackray (Nabwood School) and the defending champion Christopher Perry of Kimberley Comprehensive. Sixty under 16s lined up, all dreaming of glory but after the first three laps, it was Hammond who led on the flat and Perry over the lumps. As Perry led out, he crashed among the trees, leaving Hammond to win. Afterwards Hammond said: "I had to use a high gear on the flat section. It was hurting a lot."

Joan Edwards thanked "the clerk of the weather" in her 'Crosstalk' column for providing a sunny dry start to the early season events. She also told of a scheme where, "ATB's (All Terrain Bicycles) now known universally as 'Mountain Bikes'" were being provided for schoolchildren to gain an idea of racing, but she did not name the schools.

An in-depth interview by Robert Garbutt in *Cycling Weekly* with Steve Douce, indicated that he might give up cyclo-cross at the end of the season: "While I am racing up and down a muddy field, my team-mate Chris Walker is enjoying the sun in Barbados and Chris Lillywhite is in Florida." During the year he had broken a finger in March and a collarbone during the Milk Race, but he was out riding his mountain bike complete with his shoulder strapped up, only four days after the accident. Garbutt then explained: "He is now in his 14th season, having first raced when he was 11."

Ten nations competed in the 'Falcon Nations Cup' held in Sutton Park, during December. Stodgy mud hampered all the riders, although Steve Douce (Raleigh/Banana) seemed impervious to the conditions as he took the laurels with yet another fine win. Second home was Milosslav

Kvasnicka of Czechoslovakia, who chased hard all the way to the finish. Keith Bingham's report in *Cycling Weekly* told of Chris Young's sterling ride as Britain's top amateur on the day to take third: "Young's was the ride of the race for the home supporters, as he jumped from seventh to third overall. Young rode a determined race over a course not to his liking. He had terrible difficulty at the log obstacles where riders had to 'bunny hop' and not lose speed. He slowed to a crawl each time, and had to churn his wheels in the thickening mud to get back the time lost." As a footnote, to show how hard the racing was, the reigning amateur World Champion could only finish in fourteenth. After this third event of the series, the leader remained Bruno Le Bras of France, second overall was now Kvasnicka with G.B's Young in third, the next British rider was Barrie Clarke down in ninth.

Glen Coltman (Leicestershire R.C. Medella) unexpectedly beat Graham Douce (Wembley R.C) in the Macclesfield ANC Spectus Supacross over Christmas. Coltman described his win in *Cycling Weekly* as "A career best win" and quipped: "When I hit the ground (in a crash) I found one of my ears had a foot stuck in it – my own foot." However, he made no mistake in the sprint, which he won by three lengths.

The headline in the next week's magazine, "Douce Shrugs Off 'Flu to Score Sixth Title Victory." was followed by a report by David Taylor on the National Championships, which were held once more at Sutton Park. Steve Douce's Raleigh/Banana team manager, Paul Sherwen, had advised his man not to start due to his low condition, but he was delighted to shake his hand after the win. Only three seconds separated him from Barrie Clarke (Wembley R.C.) the best amateur. Tim Gould (Cycles Peugeot) was a further 23 seconds back, to collect the bronze medal. BBC T.V cameras were there to record the action, as 100 riders battled it out in the mud and slippery conditions. Late on, there were just three leaders, David Baker, Clarke and Steve Barnes, but then Douce arrived. By the last lap it was Clarke who led Douce with a ding-dong battle for victory. At the very last log jump, Douce took the advantage to take the chequered flag and the glory for an impressive sixth time.

Lee Ferreday (Brook C.C) made the race winning attack on the last lap of the National Junior title race to win the gold medal. He had been involved in a race-long battle with John Pemberton (Bolsover Wheelers) and Roger Hammond (Wembley R.C), who finished in the silver and bronze medal positions. Ferrreday took the silver the previous year and the 18 year old was delighted to move up to the top place on the podium.

Pemberton, two years younger, was back at 10 seconds and at just 14, came Hammond, who was described in *Cycling Weekly* as "A Star of the Future."

Early February was the date of the Inter Area Team Championships. In the archives the small pink programme lists the seven teams involved and the prize list shows a £100 first prize for the winning team. Many top riders were involved and the teams riding make interesting reading: Yorkshire, London, Midlands, the North West, the Combine Services, Lincolnshire & Humberside, and Wales. Two teams had 18 riders, the North West and the Midlands, however it was the smaller team of Yorkshire who took the laurels, amassing 22 more points than the London team.

Another programme in the archives shows that all the top riders were down in Southampton racing in the final round of the Holdsworth National Trophy Series. The programme listed many of the hard working officials involved, with Norman Shelmerdine as the Chief Commissaire, Gordon MacDonald Chief Judge, and Geoff Greenfield as the Organiser.

For the first time in several years the G.B jerseys were in with a shout in the Professional World Championships held at Pont-Chateau in France. David Baker finished an excellent eleventh, which was the best professional placing by a British rider since John Atkins gained seventh place back in 1969. Tim Gould finished a respectable 19th and we are left to wonder what might have happened if Steve Douce had not crashed out in the first 100 yards. It was Danny de Bie of Belgium's day as the winner of the Rainbow Jersey, with a run-away win from Adri van der Poel of Holland, who for the third time took the silver medal, with France's Christophe Lavainne, taking third.

Britain's Baker had made his supporters hearts flutter, when at one point he stormed into the lead, it was only for a short while but very inspiring. De Bie had his own technique for jumping the planks; he hopped them, complete with his bike! Afterwards, despite Douce being taken to hospital by helicopter, it was found that he had not broken his arm. However the four times champion Albert Zweifel who crashed at the same time, did have a broken finger, so could not complete his 21st and last championship race.

Roger Honegger of Switzerland was the filling in a Czechoslovakian sandwich, when he finished third in the Amateur title race. Ondrej Glajza proved to be the winner, with his countryman Radomir Simonek second, with yet a third Czech, P.Hric in fourth. The G.B riders didn't find the beautiful sunny day and clear blue skies to their liking, Chris Young was our best man in 27th with the other G.B members coming in close behind, Steve Barnes in 29th, Stuart Marshall 32nd and Barrie Clarke 35th. Clarke was carried off afterwards saying: "I told Bob Thom that I was hot before the start, and he gave me a bottle, but I was told by a commissaire that I couldn't have it ... I drank gallons afterwards. I felt giddy and the doctor had me carried off on a stretcher."

The Junior title race saw three national champions vying for the top spot in the closing stages, Holland's Richard Groenendaal held out to win from Emmanuel Magnien the French champion, with Italy's Christian Bertotti in third. The race was run off at an extremely fast pace, which found the British riders once more wanting, although at one point Andy Layhe was racing with the group that sprinted for the bronze medal, however he crashed on the last lap and had to be content with 13th spot. His twin brother Chris was 21st, Lee Ferreday 27th and John Pemberton 35th from the 46 finishers. Andy Layhe told *Cycling Weekly*: "I never realised that I was the first Briton, the atmosphere was brilliant."

Joan Edwards put down some of her own personal impressions of the above world championships in her column in the same magazine, starting with the weather: "First – Days of blue skies, hard early morning frost, followed by glorious sunshine. Second – The crowds, thousands line anything from two to four deep all round both sides of the circuit. Third – The course – Superb, except for the complete absence of mud, it was a mechanic's paradise. And Fourth – The disappointment of our junior and seniors to find starting places, allocated according to 1988 team placings, and both started with eight rival teams lined up in front of them."

Joan also included a short biography of Ralph Digges, with an interesting insight into a career that has touched many in cyclo-cross: "Although short-listed for a pre-World War II Olympics, Ralph rode time-trials from five to 25 miles, took part in the occasional cross-country race, and early in the Forties competed quite successfully in those. A somewhat horrific motorcycle accident put an end to his cycling, but not long after he became interested in coaching and took the approved BCF course ... That was the start of something big. For years now Ralph advised and helped scores of riders at all levels. He has managed cyclo-cross world championship teams, and for his long-standing efforts in 'cross was made a B.C-C.A Life Member. He was later honoured by the Olympic Torch Trust for services to sport, the second cyclo-cross official to do so, being preceded by Ron Atkins. He was awarded the Birmingham Division Gold Badge of Honour, two weeks ago."

This year saw the appearance of the first edition of an excellent magazine, Yorkshire Crossways. It was edited by 'Scoop Brogan' and was packed with interesting articles, some of which were "What about a coach in every town?" "How coaches function" and "Anyone want to ride Mountain Bike events in summer?" This edition also had another article of note, called "Art of Cyclo-Cross Construction" outlining many of the places the writer had organised events: "Several schools, a power station, a motor racing circuit, a greyhound stadium, a garden fete as well as public parks, common land and farms." Going on to warn, "always obtain permission" he went on to give an example of what can happen: "I had a telephone call from an irate secretary of a gravel company…he had heard mention of the event over his car radio, and had obtained my name and address from the police. It took me several minutes to placate him … eventually he agreed to let the event proceed."

Another fine Area publication, the North West C-C.A. Annual carried a letter from George Robinson (the National Development Officer), outlining that Coaches' Conference this year was to be held at Great Barr, Birmingham. He wanted to encourage more Assistant Coaches to move up, and to take the Coach's exam, then moving into launching a Senior Coaches Award. When qualified, they would look very smart, and dry too, as they would be provided with new waterproof jackets and tracksuit tops in royal blue and red.

The A.G.M this year, took place on Saturday 4th March and started at 12 noon, afterwards there was a Dinner at 8 00 p.m. Reg Ward and Tony Lynch had made all the arrangements, tickets were £10 each, and there was a late bar and a Disco.

During 2008 Harry Gould explained how the B.C-C.A had planned ahead: "By the 4th year (of the 4-year plan) our income was £56,501, expenditure was £80,145 and the Sports Council grant more than made up the shortfall to leave the B.C-C.A with a surplus that it was allowed to keep." As to the Second 4-Year Plan, Harry explained, "The submissions for this Plan were required to be considerably more detailed, with broken down budgets required for what had merely been headings in the facts shown above, plus full details on admission costs."

Looking forward to the 1990's, the B.C-C.A was now financially healthy, with excellent officials, ready to go forward and equipped to tackle the challenges ahead.

19

Baker and Young are Champions, events are hit by snow and blizzards

Season 1989/90

Red was the dominant colour of the handbook with an advert for 'Falcon Cyclo-Cross' on the cover. Among the photographs inside, was one of five smiling schoolboys with cups and medals, all members of the V.C. Lincoln- Metheringham Car Sales Club, winners of the previous year's Juvenile National Team Championships. 121 events are listed, including more races for ladies and mountain bikers. New officials were T. Haigh as Sports Aid Foundation Grants Co-ordinator and L. Hall as Coaching Development Officer, but one post remained open, that of Sponsorship Officer. A very encouraging sign was the increase in the number of coaches, up to eighteen with eight assistant coaches.

Good news was reported from the Wessex Area, where their Newsletter for November outlined: "The number of riders taking part this season are well up on last year and with many new names from the Oxford area and riders of ATB's who rode the First Southampton Mountain Bike Challenge, we can look forward to a great season."

The programme for the Macclesfield Wheelers 'Supacross' held at the end of December, had race director Colin Clews emphasising the club's commitment should be for the enjoyment of all. A full programme of events of all types was listed, but the race that caught the eye, was the Pro/Celebrity Madison, which had a very impressive list of names among the 12 teams listed. They came from cycle sport and beyond, including Hugh Porter (4 times World Pro. Pursuit Champion) teamed up with Melanie Grivell (G.B ladies T.D.F team), John Herety (ex pro rider and team manager) with Neil Storey of Aristor Records, Phil Liggett (T.V presenter & much more) with Paul Sherwen (ex pro rider & team manager), Pat Liggett (G.B team soignuesse) who was teamed with the

1988 Pro Road Race Champion Steve Joughin and lastly Theresa Coltman (G.B. ladies R.R. squad) with Dave Rayner the Under 23 winner of the 1988/89 Milk Race. This must have been an ideal event for the autograph hunters, although Hugh Porter did not get away with just riding for he was also the race commentator. The question arises, how did he manage to commentate at the same time as riding?

Over the Christmas/New Year holiday period it was Midland Champion Steve Knight (Halesowen A.C.C.) who was to pull back a five-minute handicap to win the Coventry R.C.Easyglide Grand Prix on Kenilworth Common on Boxing Day. Junior Andy Layhe (Kenilworth Wheelers) took second spot and Gary Coltman overcame not only the 5-minute handicap from scratch, but the extra handicap of two punctures to ride into third spot in the 50-man field. Then in the New Year's Eve event at Macclesfield, it was Chris Young (Every Ready-Goldstar) who started 1990 with a convincing win in the popular Spectus Systems Supacross, behind him came Robert Dane (Crown Graphics-Chafes) and Gary Coltman also now riding for the Every Ready Goldstar team.

The Open Titles this season were held in early January. "Baker Grabs Title; Douce Only Third After Crash" were the headlines over an article by David Taylor in *Cycling Weekly*, for Baker (Cycles Peugeot) had ended the five-year reign of the Raleigh-Banana professional Steve Douce. Steve Barnes, the amateur from the Ace R.T club also arrived ahead of Douce to claim the silver medal, with the former winner back in third, after a bad crash where he hit a concrete post that left him with a broken frame. On this day, Baker was in a class of his own and Taylor wrote: "The Cycles Peugeot professional has been racing non-stop since last April, mixing mountain bike events with road racing, criteriums and cyclo-cross. On Saturday all his hard work paid off ... Even a fall on a muddy right turn did not throw him off his stride. He recovered, and back on his bike into the last half-mile." It was to be an exciting sprint for third place: "Young came off Douce's rear wheel as the pair came up through the crowds that thronged the finish. For the moment it looked as if Douce may be baulked by the spectators, but no, Douce was more than a match for Young and the last place on the podium was his, as he easily passed the 1984 champion." Barnes, at 25, also led his Ace R.T to the team prize backed up by Julian Gould and Andrew Shore.

The events were once more held at Sutton Park, Birmingham with Roger Hammond (Wembley R.C Testers) adding yet another gold to his growing total by winning the Junior title, with Richard Thackray (Bradford Olympic) riding to the silver medal, followed by Chris Perry

(Chesterfield Coureurs) to take the bronze. *Cycling Weekly* carried this report of Hammond's stately progress: "Hammond, not 16 until the end of the month, had a lonely ride breaking away as the flag dropped to send the 58 starters on their way."

A smart programme had been produced for this event with the word Falcon spread across the front cover, with the history of the company in words and pictures on the back page. Inside was a list of officials with Peter Towey, Clive Murden and Keith Simpson the Chief Commissaires. Stalwart of the B.C-C.A Keith Edwards the Course Director plus Jim Court, Alison Court, Joan Edwards, Maria Waugh, June Bayliss and John Burney also heavily involved in this promotion.

The selection for the coming world championships were announced after this days racing by the National Team Manager Bob Thom. For the Professional race David Baker, Steve Douce, Chris Young, and Fred Salmon with first reserve Tim Gould, who had not started the nationals due to a knee injury. The four man amateur team was to be Steve Barnes, Barrie Clarke, David Brooker and Tim Davies with Stephen Knight as first reserve. The juniors to go were Richard Thackray, Chris Perry, John Pemberton and Jake Elliot with Mark Rusby and Stuart Blunt as reserves. It is not clear why Roger Hammond was not on the list, unless he was too young to qualify.

David Taylor reported the exciting finish to the World Professional Championship in *Cycling Weekly* thus: "In a finish worthy of a Tour de France stage or Classic road race, Holland's Henk Baars won the World Professional Championship on Sunday afternoon as the temperature soared into the sixties at Getxo." His description of the rest of the race for medals on this early hot day in Spain continued: "The sprint for second place was so close that it needed a photo to decide it, surely the first time ever in the world cyclo-cross championships." This close finish resulted in Adrie van der Poel making it at Dutch one-two, his fourth silver medal at this standard in cyclo-cross, with the bronze medal going to Bruno Le Bras of France. This time the G.B. riders acquitted themselves well, with David Baker finishing a creditable 12th with Steve Douce following in 13[th.] Baker saying afterwards, "Everything went all right, it was so fast, just like last year, but I have no complaints." Fred Salmon finished 33rd but Chris Young, who was suffering with a heavy cold, is not recorded as finishing in the account.

Andreas Busser of Switzerland won the Amateur event on the Saturday, just 19 seconds clear of Miroslav Kvasnicka (Czechoslovakia) and the bronze medal went to Thomas Frischknecht, who had been Junior Champion in 1988. This time the British were well down the result sheet, with Steve Barnes being the best finisher in 21st place, Barrie Clarke 32nd. Tim Davies 37th and David Brooker down in 38th. Barnes said at the finish: "We have no excuses, we rode as hard as we could, it was so fast, before we knew it the race was over. We are used to racing for an hour and 10 minutes, today the winner took just 48 minutes." Davies also commented: "We have so little practice in racing as a group, we have got to learn the technique, and to add to that you have got to go where the racing is, Switzerland and Belgium, and I am willing to go and do that."

Time and time again over the years, the G.B. riders complained that the speed at these championships was too high, or the distance too short. Yet back in Britain the events continued to carry on in their own particular British way. It seems that our riders at this time were in a cleft stick, racing the British way all year then having to adapt another way for the World Championships, as they always had done since the formation of the Association.

In the Junior Championships, Holland provided the winner in the form of Erik Boezwinkel. The pre-race favourite had been Jerome Chiotti of France but he was attacked by Boezwinkel, who stayed clear to win by 12 seconds. Niels van der Steen, also of Holland, took the bronze medal. John Pemberton was the first home of the British riders in 16th, with Chris Perry in 26th, Jake Elliott in 34th, and Richard Thackray down in 39th spot. A Great Britain jersey was however seen at the head of the race, when Pemberton led the whole pack away from the start and was still in 12th when the big mass of riders stormed out of the Velodrome. Young Pemberton told reporter David Taylor of *Cycling Weekly*: "I was under geared when it came to the sprint, I had hoped to get 14th but my gear was too small. It was faster even than last year in France, I had the most trouble on the hill, they just rode up it so fast." In a later edition: "As far as back-up goes, the riders could not ask for more. The assistance that the National Squad gets from sponsors- Wolverhampton Partners in Progress, The Sports Council, The Sports Aid Foundation and Andrews Heat for Hire, plus 13 others add up to one of cycling's best sponsorship deals."

Joan Edwards, this time, wrote about the hazards and surprises of being a supporter travelling to see the World Championships in Getxo. She and her husband Keith had planned to travel by ferry from Plymouth to Santander, but their ferry was holed up in the Spanish port by severe weather in the Bay of Biscay. So after frantic phone calls, spaces were found on a coach trip being run by Euro-Links. On board they found the B.C-C.A Chairman Ray Brogan and other National officers already installed. The long trip, gave lots of time for many informal 'committee' meetings, which Joan described as "including the drivers!"

During late February the same magazine announced: "Coventry will soon have a permanent cyclo-cross course within the city. The circuit is to be constructed at the Coventry Wheels site – 14 acres of land set aside for wheeled sports by the City Council in the Bell Green area. A BMX track was already in use, but the cyclo-cross course would be built by voluntary workers, mainly from the Coventry C.C. David Tomes was in discussion with the council on this ambitious development."

The A.G.M this year on March 3rd at the Connaught Hotel, Wolverhampton had some very important posts that needed filling if the Association was to run smoothly. The changes in the election of officials that took place at the A.G.M were that Jim Court took over as Membership Secretary from Reg Ward and June Gilbert replaced Madeleine Jewell as the Handbook Secretary. However no replacement was found for Chris Wreghitt as the International Racing Secretary.

One of the decisions made at this A.G.M was that the B.C-C.A would promote its own ATB championships during the coming season. The decision was taken because "It follows the increase in the number of mountain bike riders taking part in cyclo-cross events and the number of ATB events being promoted by affiliated clubs on cyclo-cross courses", reported *Cycling Weekly*

Following on from this decision, the March issue of the Wessex Newsletter had a full-page entry form for the B.C-C.A Mountain Bike Cross Championships. These were to be held under B.C-C.A rules and were to take place on May 20th at North Walham, Hants with the Wessex C.C.A the promoters, by doing so the season was extended into the late spring. In the May issue the editor wrote: "I am pleased to inform you that Wessex have won the award for the highest number of clubs that have affiliated last season to the B.C-C.A this is the second time we have achieved this … The total of riders to date this season is 1,373 that is for senior and juvenile riders, and with the Mountain Bike Championships to come it is certain to be a record year." And on the same theme: "It is being mooted about that riders would like a Mountain Bike Cross League in the summer, have you any ideas? Do you like the idea?"

Another request was for Wessex courses to be made as hard as possible in order to compare with those in the Midlands and North of England and at the end of the piece was this light-hearted quip, "Say no to drugs and trip out on lactic acid."

As the sport dipped its toe into the nineteen-nineties, many changes were taking place in equipment. Two large changes were the development in shoes and clip-less pedals. Shoes had changed for good, with many varieties now on offer. But clipless pedals were taking longer to catch on. They were being used by the road and track riders, although looking back at photos of 'cross riders, very few had taken to them yet.

Season 1990/91

David Baker (National Senior Champion) appeared on the cover of the new handbook. The National Team Manager's position was in new hands, with Brian Cossavella taking on the job. The number of events listed had dipped slightly to 111, the first event being held as early as June, the Wigan Wheelers Oliver Somers Cycles event. Two training days are also listed, one in August organised by John Rawnsley, the Dales Training Day, and a High Peak Training Day run by Dave Halman. Unusual names for events were still turning up, showing that special touch of imagination that only cyclo cross organisers come up with. The 'Kirby Kross', the 'Cooper Cross' (promoted by Phil Cooper), the 'Xmas Cross', 'Fancy Dress Charity C.X.', the 'Coal Tip Cross', the 'Valentine Cross' and even a 'Wine and Dine Cross', all of which were designed to make events catch the eye and cause amusement.

As more doping of cyclists and athletes was being discovered, so the number of rules and banned items increased and this was reflected in the handbook. Under 'Drugs & Stimulants' were two and a half pages of rules and under 'Banned Substances' 95 items under various headings. These were followed by other sections such as Blood doping, Local anaesthetics and Corticosteroids and a warning that "Many of these drugs appear either alone or as mixtures in medication."

Joan Edwards in her September 'Cross Talk' wrote:

Another cyclo-cross season looms ahead. Buoyant with news of a 69 per cent increase in participation last season and the success of the bid for the 1992 World Championships, the sport is certainly on a 'high'. It is interesting to see how the sport has adapted to the emergence of mountain bike riders. Two seasons ago they were accepted with some reluctance, now they are part of every cyclo-cross promotion, with more events being organised by affiliated clubs solely for ATB adherents, on cyclo-cross courses. Not only are organisers willing to adapt, but also several are looking at new ways of presenting 'cross ... I know very little about activities North of the Border. However, it is apparent that for at least 28 years there has been a flicker of interest in cyclo-cross that has not been developed to its full potential. In 1962 there was a Scottish C-C.A affiliated to the B.C-C.A, but the S.C.U saw fit to stamp out the enthusiasm. In more recent years riders have made occasional forays to the South, and thanks mainly to the Glasgow United Club, Scotland has been represented in the National Senior Championships.

She also went on to outline the amazing achievements of John Rawnsley: "You have to be a man of strong character to organise a race for 30 consecutive years. You have to be a man of strong physique to ride the Three Peaks race at all. You have to be a super-fit man to run 72 miles passing over 42 of the highest peaks in the Lake District inside 24 hours."

In another 'Cross Talk' Joan also remarked on long-term promotions with "We are quite used to time trial and, more recently, road race promotions going back many decades, but cyclo-cross appears to be catching up. In this season's handbook I note the 50th Reading Wheelers promotion preceded two weeks earlier by the 36th. Dinedor Scramble Wheelers organised by the Gannet C.C. Eddie Thompson was the organiser then as he is for this year's promotion."

Race programmes were now being produced to a very high standard, one of which was for the B.C-C.A National Trophy Series, with full colour covers and also printed on high gloss paper.

Maryon Wilson Park, in South London was the site of David Baker's triumph in the first round of the B.C-C.A National Trophy Series on the last Sunday of October. David Taylor in *Cycling Weekly* reported the start with these words: "Baker was in a class of his own on the undulating park circuit, beating Barrie Young (Every Ready-Halfords), Tim Gould (Cycles Peugeot) and Steve Douce (Raleigh) in that order. The honour of being first amateur fell to Steve Barnes (ACE RT) who was also sixth overall."

The 31st Smirnoff Challenge International held the next week saw David Baker continuing his winning ways, by dominating the race. This time it was Stuart Marshall, riding for G.B.Amateurs who came in second with Barrie Clarke in third. The British riders held off the Continental contenders so well, that the first of them to finish was P.Schovaerts of Belgium back in sixth place.

Chris Young (Every Ready/Halfords) won the biggest first prize ever at a British cyclo-cross, £1,000, as he crossed the line in the National Championships. They were held on a Harlow course, with the Yorkshire man riding on his own for two thirds of the race, showing off his superiority on the day. As usual in cyclo-cross nothing ever goes completely smoothly, for despite taking advantage of Steve Douce slipping to the ground on a greasy section, Young then found he had a leaf lodged in his gear, leaving him with only three gears to select from. However a change of bikes meant he was on his way once more. The next two to finish were both Raleigh team riders, Douce having pressed on to gain the silver and defending champion David Baker, still a victim of 'flu, coming in for the remaining spot on the podium. Young would have been unsponsored, but both Ever Ready and Halfords extended his contract for two months, which proved a very wise move, for they gained excellent publicity from his win. When asked by William Fotheringham for *Cycling Weekly* what he was going to do with the prize money he said: "I don't know what I will do with it, perhaps I will give some to my father for petrol money."

Cycling Weekly headlined their report on the National Junior Championships with "Champion Hammond Dominates Juniors", and followed up with: "Totally dominant, are the only words which can be used to describe Roger Hammond's defence of his national junior cyclo-cross title at Harlow. Only 10 riders were able to stay within one eight-minute lap of the flying Wembley R.C/Testers junior."

This report was accompanied by a photograph of Hammond showing him crossing the finish line, sitting up, with eyes closed in relief, hands spread wide in triumph. In the silver spot came Richard Thackray (Bradford C.R.C.), then Hammond's team mate Stuart Blunt, who raced in for the third place. The main opponent to every rider though, was the amount of mud, which hampered all the competitors, although Hammond overcame it with supreme ease.

A snapshot of the other race winners during this period shows that in the southwest Andy Shaw (Plymouth Corinthians) was winning in the CS Dynamo event. Fred Salmon (Cycles Peugeot) was top man in the Middleton C.C. event, Tim Davies (C.C Abergavenny/Owen Construction) proved the winner in the Royal Forest of Dean and in Yorkshire Jake

Elliott (Dinnington R.C./Ideal Travel) was victorious in the Association race series.

Frozen ground and a freezing east wind with a mostly flat course, meant that racing was very fast indeed during this year's World Championships, held at Gieten in Holland. With Radamir Simunek making history in the Professional event, by becoming the first winner of a full set of titles, Junior, Amateur and now Professional rainbow jerseys. Three riders were still in the hunt for victory during the final stages of the last lap, then Frenchman Bruno Le Bras took a wrong line, and it was left to the others to sprint for glory. Dutchman Adri Van der Poel's best efforts were not enough, and he was second once again, the Czechoslovakian dual champion was therefore triumphant.

The British riders were once more unable to stay with the fast pace with Steve Douce finishing 15th, Chris Young 18th, Barrie Clarke 23rd and Nick Craig 28th. Steve Douce had turned in one of his usual consistent rides, saying afterwards to *Cycling Weekly* reporter William Fotheringham: "I couldn't get going, couldn't get my feet in the clips easily once they had frozen … It was too fast, but it was a good race. I have never been so fast before. I got in a group with Chiappucci (a Tour de France hero) He stormed down the road each time but wasn't so good at the running."

In the Senior Championship the gold medal and the honour of wearing the Rainbow Jersey, went to Thomas Frishneckt of Switzerland. The freezing temperatures, making the course hard, and super-fast, also affected this event. Henrik Djernis of Denmark took the silver medal and the Italian Daniele Pontoni claimed the bronze. This time the British riders were certainly not in the hunt, Stuart Marshall finishing in 44th, Jake Elliott in 49th and Steve Barnes back in 51st. Their efforts must have been almost invisible, because *Cycling Weekly* did not even give them a mention in its race report. They did have more than their share of bad luck, for Stuart Marshall found that his forks had broken and Barnes and Elliott were held up by a crash in front of them on the very first corner!

The temperature for the Junior event may have been minus 10°, but the racing was red hot, with the title being decided by a fierce five man sprint. The result of which was a win for Ondrej Lukes of Czechoslovakia, from his countryman Jiri Pospisil and Dariusz Gil of Poland who took the silver and bronze medals. Roger Hammond was the top placed Brit in 11th. He put on a fine early display by being in third spot until the leaders hit the sand on the first lap, he then led the second group only metres behind the leaders for the next lap. Richard Thackray finished 27th, Stuart Blunt 34th and Richard Bruce 41st and a consolation for these young riders was that it allowed time for improvement before the 1992 World Championships, on home ground at Leeds. One footnote to this event was that Leeds had sent over a Councillor and a Police Superintendent to observe the way a crowd of 20,000 was handled.

During February, snow caused blizzard conditions, making Britain appear more like Siberia. With more snow forecast and transport brought to a near standstill, the decision was taken to cancel the final round of the National Trophy Series. This was thought to be only the second time that a national event had had to be cancelled since the Association was formed. John Burney told *Cycling Weekly*: "We could well have held the event, but we did not feel this would have been fair on those riders in overall contention who were unable to compete because of travelling difficulties."

In the North Western C.C. Annual Jim Court reported in his 'Chairman's Jottings' that there had been a promising increase of 12% in membership of the N.W.C-C.A during the past season. He also wrote in another article about the Tuesday evening training sessions, proving an interesting insight into these evenings run under the experienced eye of Ian Small at Belle Vue. Jim then went on to describe Ian as "the Guru, Ian Small knows a thing or two, having been at the top of the sport for an awful long time and now being National Junior Squad Coach."

The evenings consisted of a jog round the cinder track, then stretching exercises, and then another jog. It was all wound up with a special subject, such as 'Starting', 'Carrying the bike', 'Riding a plank, or under the limbo pole'. All this was topped off with a handicap race, which often included the "Black Hole", as it entered an area where the floodlights didn't.

20

Hammond wins a World Title in Leeds

Season 1991/92

The topic of coaching was in the air in the September issue of the Wessex Newsletter, which printed an impressive list of the coming winter coaching and training courses. Every Wednesday from October to December there were to be sessions at both the Mountbatten cycle track in Portsmouth and the Southampton track. Also on the subject of training, the Yorkshire Crossways magazine had an article: "Y.C-C.A bikes for hire to novices – there are 8 cyclo-cross bikes available for hire, if not being used for training, for Try-it sessions." They had bikes sized 21½" to 23" with hire charges of £2.50 per weekend. All refurbished with new mechanisms, handlebar levers and new chains with money from Grant Aid for their upkeep.

Darrell Bradbury in another article pleaded for Starters to stamp their authority on events, by making sure that starts were fair. He asked for a start line that all competitors should keep behind, "because otherwise well organised events can have problems." There was also a reminder of the new rule on headgear: "All competitors shall wear protective head gear which confirms to the U.C.I requirements (current accepted standard- SNELL and ANSI) whilst racing or training."

For the second year running the handbook was priced at £2.00. The cover displayed the details of a very special year for Leeds, which was to be the venue of the Championnats du Monde de Cyclo-Cross, returning to Britain on the 1st/2nd February 1992.

When it came to winning with style, then Nick Craig (Cycles Peugeot) was the man, with an impressive winning gap of nearly seven minutes in the Three Peaks this year. Second man home was Ian Ferguson (Helwith Bridge Alers), next rider home was Steve Barnes (Ace R.T) with a enormous time gap of over 19 minutes. Craig became the third member of the Cycles-Peugeot team in a row to win this gruelling race. He also completed a unique father/son winning combination; his father Ian had been the winner, way back in 1963. Ferguson almost posted a unique achievement for himself, because as a top runner he had won the running edition of this race earlier in the year. He was also riding a very basic bike and only weeks before had lost a finger in a work accident. The course had been revised this year, which caused organiser John Rawnsley to say, "I wish we had used this course years ago." The junior winner was Richard Thackray, who left straight afterwards to ride the Mountain Bike World Championships, emphasising how these two cycling disciplines were very interchangeable.

Hail and rain battered the 80 riders just after the start of the Smirnoff International Challenge, the course at Harlow was usually fast, but this deluge instantly turned it into a quagmire, causing all the riders to slip, slide and fall as they fought the difficult conditions. Added to this a bitter wind caused discomfort to both riders and officials alike. The winner was Steve Douce (GB Professionals/Dawes) with Jo Martens of Holland second with just a 9 second gap and Steve Barnes finishing as both the first amateur and the third rider home.

Other race winners during this period were, Jason Shackleton (ABC Centreville) at Kirkby Stadium, Peter Middleton (NW Off-Road Club) in the St. Helens C.R.C. CMA Cycles event. The windswept Tunstall Hills near Sunderland was the sight of the Houghton C.C. event, where Kevin Sabiston (Team Orange) triumphed, but down in East Grinstead it was a mountain biker, Stephen Dennis of the promoting club, who beat the entire group of expert 'cross riders to take the victory, yet another sign that mountain bikers and their machines, would have to be taken seriously.

Controversy marred the result of the Selby C.C. event during November, because it turned into what the magazine *Cycling Weekly* headlined as a "Handicap Farce". The reason for the dispute was that the Isostar-Columbia professional Robert Dane was placed in the front group of this handicap race; while his fellow pros were in the scratch group, back at two minutes. After the inquest into what went wrong it had Dane saying: "I was a bit upset about it, to be honest. It looks like I am going for the wins, which isn't the case." Chris Young was also less than happy with his £10 prize for second place, saying: "I know I've got a contract now, so the prize money isn't important to me, but even so."

The last weekend of November was to be the one and only time a race would be held over the forthcoming World Championship course at Leeds, before the promotion itself. But it was the Continentals who showed the way to ride it, with three Swiss, two Dutch, a Frenchman and a Belgian, all coming in before the first British rider, Chris Young (Scott –Diamond Back). The winner of this trial run was Dieter Runkel of Switzerland who was quoted as saying: "I am very happy with the course. I have done two junior and two senior world championships and this compares very well." Luke Evans, a reporter on *Cycling Weekly* described the new course as: "The going was fast, but slippery on some of the downhill off camber turns, and clogged with mud in the wooded run-ups." Barrie Clarke was to rue his decision to ride, when he crashed at the hurdles, breaking a bone below his knee, although all those who tested the course gave it the 'thumbs-up'.

Lance Ravenhill (Sapphire R.C.) repeated his win of only two seasons before, by taking the victory in the National Veterans title at Sherdley Park, St. Helens. The leading trio were two minutes clear of the 54 riders at the bell, meaning that all the medals were still 'up for grabs'. But it was Ravenhill who passed under the flag first, ahead of Stewart Towers (V.C. Bradford) with Ian Jewell (Festival R.C.) in the bronze medal position. Evergreen Mick Ives took the Grand Vet (50-54 class) by coming in fifth, with Ian Small (Zodiac R.C.) arriving in ninth for the Master Vet (55 plus) award.

Writing in 'Cross Talk' in the New Year edition of *Cycling Weekly*, Brian Furness looked back to: "The decision at last year's A.G.M to introduce a National Amateur jersey at this weekend's senior championships must be welcomed by the top riders in the unpaid ranks, given the domination of the title by professionals in recent years." He then went on to show that the professionals had not had it all their own way during the 15 years since the title went 'open'. The amateurs had won eight of them, and the professionals only seven. He continued: "The move to an open championship in 1977 was surely motivated by the dwindling number of professionals competing at the time." It is interesting to see the word 'unpaid' still being used as late as the nineteen-nineties, a term looking back to a time when gaining money from sporting prowess was not considered the thing to do. Further on in his article, he explains that the B.C-C.A had intended that there would be a 'Demonstration' event for veterans at the coming World Championships, as recognition of International Veteran racing. This was rejected by the U.C.I. He went on to add: "Last month's B.C.F. A.G.M passed a motion which effectively calls upon the U.C.I to recognise the legitimacy of vets racing." The above shows that the B.C-C.A was leading the world in this area.

"Baker is King" declared *Cycling Weekly* over the report of the Open National Championships. This year they were sponsored by the General Portfolio Company, and took place at Harlow in Essex. *Cycling Weekly* continued: "Raleigh professional David Baker, now recovered from illness, stuns opposition with a murderous pace to win the richest-ever U.K pro-title." Behind Baker came Tim Gould (Cycles-Peugeot) for the silver medal at 24 seconds, then Chris Young (Scott-Diamond Back-BMK) at another 7 seconds for the bronze. The next place was taken by the six times national champion Steve Douce, who was left "gasping in their wake." The reference to Baker being ill referred to him being able to compete in only four events this season due to a blood disorder, making his win even more remarkable, going away £1,500 richer, after holding off all the pre-race favourites.

Reporter Luke Evans, spoke to some of the riders afterwards, showing more light on the racing: "Tim Gould's double booking at the surgeon, a few days before the title race, gave him the chance to ride ... If further repairs, (are needed) then he will miss the World Championships." Evans also interviewed Chris Young who said: "I couldn't have put any more in. I was getting blurred vision at the end and I got tangled up in the tapes at the start."

The first winner of the newly awarded Amateur jersey (since 1977) was Peter Stevenson, a Private Member, who also had problems before the start, which had a slightly comical ending. He was told that he could not ride in his 'foreign' club jersey, but his mechanic's T-shirt, was deemed acceptable if it was worn inside-out over his club jersey. The silver was taken by Jake Elliott (Dinnington R.C), followed by Stuart Marshall of the V.C. Lincoln for the bronze.

The Junior Champion, Roger Hammond (Wembley R.C.-Testers) led from start to finish to take his third National Championship jersey in only three rides. Next man home was Matthew Guy (Southport R.C.C) at over a minute, and then at a further 55 seconds came Richard Bruce, for the bronze also in Hammond's club.

At last, the long awaited weekend of the 1st and 2nd of February 1992 had arrived, all was set for a great weekend of racing at Roundhay Park, Leeds. But the main question was would it all be ready? The course had to be altered on the Friday before the weekend, because both the French and Dutch teams had had bad crashes on the frozen surfaces when they were descending the frightening drop just before the run-up staircase. This caused much concern to those team managers and they voiced their worries to the organisers. The area was soon sorted out but the small bridge also had to be rebuilt, a step had to be removed and a levelling out of the surface. The organisers and their team of helpers had to work very hard to put all these items right, because the racing started the next day.

The course was described in *Cycling Weekly* as: "The 2.9km Roundhay Park circuit may look innocent enough, with its road based start and finish and long grassy riding sections, but underneath, in the run-ups and the tricky technical sections in the wooded areas, there lurks a course with real bite."

"CHAMPION" was printed in 1½" high letters as *Cycling Weekly*'s salute to Roger Hammond becoming the Junior World Cyclo-Cross Champion. It followed up by describing the electric atmosphere of expectancy and the delight of the British crowd when he had won: "Tears flowed in the packed-out finishing enclosure as the Union Jack was hoisted up between two Czech flags, after a fairytale race which saw Hammond romp away from the field on the first lap, carried along on a Mexican wave of support around the barrier lined circuit." Afterwards an emotional Hammond told the *Cycling Weekly* reporter: "It was one of those days, when I couldn't push hard enough on the pedals. Everything was on my side today. I blew on the last lap but by then it was alright … I promised myself not to be frightened – I was the oldest rider there and I could dictate the pace." Behind Hammond came Vojtech Bachleda of Czechoslovakia at 20 seconds, followed home at a further 29 seconds by his countryman Jan Faltynek. Hammond had had his own worries when he punctured and had to ride half a lap on a flat tyre. "I probably wrecked my Dad's racing wheel doing that," he said. The next G.B. rider to finish was Matthew Guy, one of the youngest riders on the day at just 16 years who arrived in 29th position. Next came Richard Bruce in 34th with Richard Thackray a further three places back in 37th. So once more, the junior riders had come up trumps, adding to the triumph of Stewart Marshall in 1986 and the silver of Robert Dane in 1984 and fourth spot by Chris Young in 1982.

A determined Mike Kluge (Germany) had come to Leeds to add a third professional Rainbow Jersey to the two he already held, and in front of the large crowd he achieved his aim with a superb display, riding away from all the favourites which included the defending world champion Radomir Simunek and the consistent Adri Van der Poel. After several laps Kluge, Camrda (Czechoslovakia) and Van der Poel (Holland) checked each other out and Kluge decided the moment had come and he was away on his own. His last lap was more of a victory lap, as he had time to wave to the crowd on his way to win by 28 seconds.

David Baker rode the strongest of the British, remaining with the leading nine throughout the race and finally finishing in that position, at only one minute forty seconds down. None of the other G.B riders were ever in the hunt, Steve Douce finished down in 25th place, next came Chris Young in 26th and then Nick Craig came in a further two places back in 28th. Douce and Young both spoke to *Cycling Weekly* afterwards, neither making any excuses, with Douce saying: "It was so hard today, it wasn't just hard, it was also so fast. There were a lot of riders struggling today who shouldn't have been." The estimated crowd on the Sunday for the Junior/ Professional events was 25,000.

The Amateur Championship saw twenty-five year old Daniel Pontoni of Italy live up to his reputation as a rider of real talent, being already four times the Italian Champion. The Swiss rider Dieter Runkel led early on, with the former champion Thomas Frischknecht (Swiss) who was riding tactically to help his countryman. Then Pontoni put on the power and with his bike handling skills he just drew away to finish 46 seconds clear of Runkel, with Frischknecht in the bronze medal position.

Richard Thackray was the first of the British to finish in a disappointingly low 38th place. David Brooker followed him in 42nd then it was Stewart Marshall in 44th with Carl Thompson back in 52nd at one lap. Their reasons for not being able to challenge the leader for higher placings seemed to echo the reasons that the G.B squads have given over many years. Stewart Marshall was the exception because he was suffering with a heavy cold, and started feeling unwell. Thompson told a reporter at *Cycling Weekly*: "I would say it was the hardest I have ever ridden ... It was just too fast, we couldn't keep up." Brooker repeated a similar line, "It was fast, but it was strength-sapping with the running."

The programme for these championships was of a large format in full colour including a photograph of HRH The Princess Royal, whose letter of support was printed beside it.

BUCKINGHAM PALACE

This will be only the third time that Great Britain has hosted the World Cyclo-Cross Championships in forty years.

During that time major changes have taken place within the sport but the basic requirements of fair play, good sportsmanship and above all, enjoyment of the sport by the participants still prevails.

The British Cycling Federation, the British Cyclo-Cross Association and Leeds City Council have all worked closely together to ensure that visiting competitors, officials and spectators should thoroughly enjoy our British hospitality and the 1992 World Championships.

Anne

There were also photographs of the U.C.I Comite' Directeur which included all the usual faces and a few less well-known ones, and a page outlining the history of cyclo-cross.

As a closing item to this momentous weekend and an insight into the size of the task that had been undertaken to produce these wonderful championships, here are some extracts from a letter which appeared in *Cycling Weekly*:

I should like to offer my personal and grateful thanks to you all, far too many to name. You can all take great satisfaction in contributing to what the world's T.V and press are hailing as a superb spectacle.

Some of you turned up on the day; some laboured during the preceding week, unloading cabins, driving in the 3,000 stakes for the course, putting out signs, building the podium and painting the starting grid. Some toiled even longer. I've had working parties in the park since last March, building the several flights of steps and five bridges, which unlocked key areas of the course. Help has come from all directions, marshals in their 70s, timekeepers, runners aged 10-plus (who did a superb job), mums and dads of ex-riders, wives of friends and clubmates

I would also like to acknowledge the enormous support I have received from the championship organiser Tony Haigh and his family, from my wife and family, and George Masson, chief marshal ... It has been a once-in-lifetime experience and I am just beginning to enjoy it.

Thank you all

Peter Milsom

Course Director, World Championships, Leeds

With all the glory of such a wonderful Championships, it is very easy to forget or even not realise just how much work goes on behind the scenes to achieve such a promotion. Harry Gould explains some of the background behind this unforgettable February promotion:

The B.C-C.A promoted the Championships on behalf of the B.C.F, and the U.C.I only recognised the B.C-C.A through the B.C.F. I formed the Executive with hard working volunteers who I could trust and the finances were in the capable hands of the B.C.F's Norman Shelmerdine. He was a very wise choice ... We put in our nominal application to promote in 1993; some years notice is required as standard and I began the process of attracting venue candidates. Alan Rushton's company at the time was working with Leeds City Council to develop the city's recognition worldwide and a small number of my Executive met him in secret to establish if the B.C-C.A would work with Leeds City Council to promote our World Championship. Politics was involved here as the Council had bigger plans beyond the Cyclo-Cross World Championships, which had not to be disclosed. After much discussion, agreements were reached, Alan Rushton and some of his staff joined the Executive as did Officers from Leeds City and a full B.C-C.A /B.C.F application went into the U.C.I to promote in 1993 at Leeds. The U.C.I met the application with obvious joy, as the international reputation of Great Britain at promotion was undisputed! ... The U.C.I then had a problem. They had agreed that Spain would promote in 1992 but Spain was trying to back down. At first we were concerned at the possible shortage of time but Leeds for other reasons were keen for 1992 and that is why we promoted in 1992.

Harry continued

I will not go into all the problems we had to overcome due to the date change but the major one was that the Championships had to have full terrestrial television. We had written agreement with the B.B.C for 1992 ... Mother fortune then shined on us! Whilst the U.C.I.'s contract with us stated that International T.V. had to be provided, it was the first year of their new contract and it did not say who had to pay! Their contract now states clearly who pays! We had to ensure that there was no loss and perhaps the best idea that enabled this to be achieved was that as soon as we knew it was going to be Leeds, we contacted the leading hotels for them to quote how much they would charge us to take all rooms for the week of the Championships. We took out a contract with one for every room in the hotel and for another to be the press residential centre for a shorter period. We then quoted room rates and food etc, to all the countries coming to the U.C.I Conference held for that week, more than filled every room and made a very substantial profit whilst at the same time being congratulated by the U.C.I for providing rooms at one of the best hotels in Leeds at low prices. The Championships were a success. We had a British World Champion. We repaid in full the Sports Council Grant (politically a very wise move for the B.C-C.A) and made a tiny profit which the B.C-C.A sent to the B.C.F!

The B.C.F was not in a position to be able to finance these Championships, nor to sustain any loss whatsoever, so a Limited Company was set up to accept all matters regarding the promotion.

On a personal note, and a postscript to the successful World Championship weekend. Maureen and I still have a cardboard case from one of the large fireworks used in the celebration after the medal presentations. It stands on our bookcase as a memento of a great event.

In this year's edition of the N.W.C-C.A. Annual Ian Small reported in the 'Race Review' article, that the area was disappointed that two of their early events had not appeared in the 91/92 handbook. The 'High Peak Trial' which had been going for 20 years and the 'Three Towers' event which had been missed out, but that did not stop the 'High Peaks' organiser and half a dozen friends keeping the event alive by riding the course as a group rough-stuff ride.

Once more the topic of there not being enough judges and commissaires was being aired, with the plea being repeated in the Wessex Newsletter for March with the hope that Wessex would hold coaching sessions within three months.

Season 1992/93

The euphoria after a British Junior winning a World Championship had not died down by the time the new season's handbook came out, for on the cover was a photograph of Roger Hammond winning his Championship jersey. He also appears on the back page with the other medal winners.

The cover price tucked away in one corner was now £2.75p an increase of another 25p. A full-page advert on the inside cover catches the eye with a lightweight racing mountain bike. This was a reflection of how many more cyclo-cross stars were turning to mountain bike racing, as the British were finding they could compete well with the Americans and other nations in this discipline. David Baker, at present the British cyclo-cross champion, had converted well taking the bronze medal in Canada. Others that were also moving over to flat-bar racing, were Barrie Clarke, Tim Davies, Nick Craig, Tim Gould and junior Matthew Guy.

This topic also came up in early September, when the National squad met at the Alderley Stadium, Wolverhampton, where National Coach, Lewis Hall, put the slightly smaller squad (due to international racing) through their paces. The morning was devoted to a performance test, then after lunch it was sprint practice. Brian Cossavella the team manager was also present, noting that those who had raced on the mountain bike circuit during the summer stood out in the fitness stakes.

Writing in his 'Cross-Talk' column in *Cycling Weekly* Brian Furness expressed this view about the National Trophy series: "This will be the 30th season that the National Trophy has been contested, but amazingly it has produced only eight different winners in that time. Douce, Baker and Chris Wreghitt can all boast four times a piece, but the record is 12 victories by John Atkins, including eight in a row in the seventies." An achievement which will surely never be bettered.

Fred Salmon (Team Peugeot-Look) was in near perfect condition for the Three Peaks, and in winning, smashed the new course record by a massive margin. There had been a fear that thick fog would cover the high peaks, but this proved groundless as the summits were all clear. A total of 190 started but by Ingleborough, Salmon was two minutes clear of Chris Young (Scott Diamond Back) and Ian Ferguson (Helwith Bridge Alers). Salmon then just rode away from then on to win by 3 minutes 23 seconds. As he finished he felt physically sick, but he soon felt better when told that his time was a very impressive 13 minutes faster than the previous record. Young who came in second won the prize as the highest placed first timer, although he sounded cautious when asked by *Cycling Weekly* if he would ride again, replying: "If I had the time, and the road season is out of the way."

The programme for this 32nd edition of the race was a neat production, with a picture of Richard Thackray and Ian Holmes leaving Ribblehead Viaduct in a previous event. The prize list showed that the winner would receive £150, plus the Norman Thornber Trophy and a Gibbsport jersey, with second prize £100, and a countdown to 30th place. There were also prizes for first Amateur, Junior and Veteran at Senior, Grand and Master plus Father & Son Team and Veteran team and three primes, all in all an impressive prize list.

A noticeable change to the look of riders at this time was that more 'hard-shell' type helmets were being worn, many rejecting the old style open bar type, with some professionals being paid to wear the new designs and some sponsored clubs were having them supplied. The main visual effect at the start of a race was all the colourful helmets massed together making a fine sporting sight.

This is a good time to remember the grassroots of the sport, for the very heartbeats of the B.C-C.A are the standard weekend races which carry on in 'B', 'C' and 'D' class events run throughout the season. Whatever the weather the events continued, with competitors finishing so covered in mud that riders were almost indistinguishable from each other. Returning after a shower, with muddy racing clothes now tucked away in their sports bags, they could meet old friends as the tea urns whistled away and homemade cakes were consumed. In village halls around the country they would discuss the race, applaud the victors and plan to do the same thing all over the again next week.

Some typical riders and races were: Mark Farrow (Rennrad Club-Team Drill) who took three out of four rides this season, and therefore won the Aerobicentre Series at Bedfords Park, Romford with Ipswich B.C. riders, Ross Monaghan and Tim Butler taking the next two series places. Noel Clough (Eagle Trans) led all the way in the Hades R.C. event. Then in the third round of the Notts & Derbys League it was Jez Franklin (De Montfort/Rage On) who came out tops in the Ashfield R.C. race. Other races at this time were the Axholme Wheelers event, with Mick Daley (Cherry Valley R.T.) getting clear at the finish to win and in North Suffolk Gary Baker (Condor Cycles) turned on the gas to beat everyone at the Mildenhall C.C.Dairytime race. Women racing in cyclo-cross were still not getting the press coverage they deserved but some ladies making their mark were Isla Rowntree (Uvex-Reynolds) Marysia Holubecki (Ace RT) and Ruth Garnwell (Macclesfield Wheelers).

December was the time for the Annual Area Championships, where the new champions were to win their laurels. Six weeks forced lay-off due to an operation didn't prevent Nick Craig (Peugeot/Look) from making a remarkable comeback, returning to his winning ways in the North of England Championships held at Sherdley Park, St. Helens. The Welsh title won by Julian Winn (Extreme C.C.) for the second time at Pontypool Park, where he overcame the handicap of two punctures against a 50 strong field. The V.C. Lincoln- Metheringham Cars rider Stuart Marshall went one better, when he completed a hat trick of wins in the Eastern Area Championships.

Meanwhile, Frankfurt was the venue for Roger Hammond to take a fine win in a Junior International, where he simply rode away from the 80 other riders, which included both Britain's Matthew Guy and Robert Thackray. All three had to battle against riders from Germany, Switzerland, Czechoslovakia and Holland. In the senior event at the same venue, Steve Douce rode into eleventh spot behind the World Champion Mike Kluge. Gary Foord riding in his first race on foreign soil in a G.B. jersey finished twenty-fifth.

"Let's Work Together to Kick Doping Out of Sport" was the slogan prominently placed on the cover of the December 1992 issue of the Wessex Newsletter. It was punching home the message that doping was not acceptable in cyclo-cross. Also among the various articles was a note that Wessex now had 10 cycles being maintained by Peter Hargraves Cycles with Glen Longland transporting them to various venues.

To say that Steve Douce (Saracen) won the National Championship title for a sixth time is just too simplistic, for it cannot begin to describe how up and down his battle to gain back the title was. The event was headlined in *Cycling Weekly* as "One of the most exciting national cyclo-cross championship races in years." The course at the Aldersley Stadium, Wolverhampton, was exceptionally fast due to the frost in the ground, with many riders hitting the deck on the twisting circuit. A stretch of sheet ice was to be the villain in deciding who won in the end.

Roger Hammond was riding his first senior championships, wearing his junior World Champion rainbow jersey. He took the race lead early on, despite carrying a cut above the eyes and strapping on his right wrist after a training crash. Slowly riders dropped back until only Steve Douce and David Baker (Team Raleigh) were left to battle out for glory. They were both involved in a spectacular tumble on the back straight, when Douce slipped and Baker went straight over his handlebars trying to avoid him. When they remounted again, it was Douce who led with only half a lap to go yet there was still only inches between them. Approaching the final section Baker took the wrong line and the aforementioned sheet ice brought him crashing down, leaving Douce to glance round and press on to victory. Baker recovered enough to limp over the finish line with a sore back and a splitting headache.

Gary Coltman stepped forward to collect his team-mate Baker's medal, just as he was stretchered off to the hospital for an X-ray on his skull. Third place and first amateur prize was won by Peter Stevenson (Middridge CRT). Douce showed his sportsmanship when replying to a question from

Cycling Weekly: "I am very pleased to win especially after losing the title for three years –but obviously I would have preferred to win in a different way." The Junior Title was won by one of the favourites, Matthew Guy (Stars & Stripes) in a race that also had more than its fair share of spills on the greasy surfaces. Robert Thackray (Bradford Olympic) took the silver at almost a minute back, and Andrew Siers (Royal Sutton C.C) was also well clear of the any chasers for the bronze medal.

It seems amazing now to realise, it was only at these championships, that a Women's Demonstration Championships event was held for the first time. The event was very successful and it was promised that a fully recognised championship would be promoted the next year. The Midland C.C.A presented the medals at their own cost as they had promoted it. Twenty-six riders lined up out of an entry of thirty-two, and the super fit Caroline Alexander (unsponsored) used her mountain bike racing experience to take an early grip on the race. She won from Isla Rowntree who came in for the silver medal at just over a minute and a half. Next of these pioneers to arrive was the inexperienced Michelle Bergstrand (Leeds MTB) who took the bronze. A marker had been put down, and female cyclo-cross would have a higher profile from now on.

Corva, in Italy, was the venue for this year's World Championship and for the first time in 26 years the professional victory ceremony would echo to the French national anthem, as Dominique Arnould had won the gold medal. His battle for victory was a three-way thriller against the defending champion Mike Kluge and Dutchman Wim de Vos. The race was off to a blistering start, which left the British riders and many others gasping in the wake of the flying three. The course included farm fields, up and down steep bankings, with ditches and wooden hurdles to test the riders. In the cold dry conditions Kluge was away and clear on the last lap, when on a bumpy bank his chain derailed and Arnould flew past to win.

An unusual sight was that each of the first three to the line punched the air knowing that they had all played their part in a great cycle race. Steve Douce was once more the best of the British, this time in a respectable 17th spot, but well below his hopes for a top ten placing. Telling *Cycling Weekly*'s Rupert Guinness afterwards: "I had bad luck today, because I stacked both frames before the race, on the poxy jump (ditch). I had to use my third bike all the way around. And then snapped a wheel as well." Chris Young came in at 24th saying: "People say give it a rest, but I like doing it. So I'll be back for sure."

Denmark provided a little bit of history in the Amateur event when Henrik Djernis won the title, for he was already the World Mountain Bike champion and also the first Dane to win a cyclo-cross gold medal. It was particularly poignant, as last year his country lost two of their top riders and a team manager in a car crash. Second home was Germany's Raif Berner, and then came Daniele Pontoni of Italy for the bronze. Roger Hammond riding on his 19th birthday, received several presents he did not want, first when his tubular tyre rolled off not once but twice, then he had to change bikes four times, and to add to his woes, he crashed, injuring a finger on his left hand and after all those incidents he finished a disappointed 46th. However, he was still ahead of the other British, who were well packed together Steve Blunt in 48th, James Norfolk in 49th and Gary Foord in 51st. Afterwards Hammond confided to *Cycling Weekly*: "On the last lap I found it too painful to use my back brake because I injured my middle finger on my left hand. That made it a little dodgy."

In the Junior race many crashes dominated the event, because of the tricky and slippery conditions from the overnight ice and frost. Kamil Ausbuher of Czechoslovakia, already his country's national champion, won the gold 38 seconds clear of his compatriot Jaromir Freide. The bronze medal went to a Frenchman with a Spanish sounding name, Miguel Martinez. Of the British youngsters, Matthew Guy rode well, being at one point in sixth place, but finally dropped down to finish eleventh. Robert Thackray came in 20th, Andrew Siers 34th and Lee Mosley 36th. Lee had had a reoccurrence of back trouble during the race, suffering badly by not wearing his special corset. So bad were some of the crashes that two riders went straight to hospital, one having to be airlifted away by helicopter.

Brian Furness writing in his column 'Cross-Talk' in *Cycling Weekly* said that the Inter-Area championships were still important in the cyclo-cross calendar: "The championship was first staged in the early days of the B.C-C.A but discontinued in the mid Sixties. It was revived in 1983 when John Rawnsley decided to try something different … Since then the championships have been staged annually and hosted by six of the Association's 10 areas. In terms of performance Yorkshire has been the dominant force, taking the title no less than eight times."

Mountain bikers were not the only ones to be attracted to cyclo-cross from outside the sport. The North Eastern C-C.A Handicap League event at Redcar, proving the point when Cliff Featherstone from the Cleveland Triathlon Club overcame a handicap penalty of three minutes, and turned it into a two and a quarter minutes clear win over the local cross-cross specialists. Talking of mountain bikes brings us to Steve Douce who found that being sponsored by the mountain bike manufacturer Saracen could have its disadvantages, for when he came to renewing his pro contract, he did not want to be tied to mountain biking racing only.

February saw Jason Shackleton chalking up a hat-trick of titles riding for Elevated R.T when he won the North Western C-C.A League, but in the end it was very tight, as he topped the table by just one point, ahead of Brian Green of the Oldham Century R.C. Flipping through the pages of the North Western C.C.A publication Annual, a few results stand out, with the 'Juvenile Top 50' showing Nick Enston of the Rhyl R.C. topping that list. The 'Senior N.W.C-C.A. Team Table Top 20' listed the Zodiac C.R.C 'A' as top team, but perhaps the most impressive of all was the result for the N.W.C-C.A League, which listed 238 riders, with Jason Shackleton (Elevated R.T.) as its champion. There was even an 'Under 12s Top Thirty' list with Paul Kinsella of the Zodiac C.R.C topping this final table. Jim Court in his 'Chairman's Jottings' which he describes as "aimless ramblings" writing about the lack of judges: "This does highlight the need for more new judges to come forward – we will train you, it's not too hard and is very rewarding." On another topic, he comments: "An element of bad language also crept into the racing – not a scene we wish to encourage."

Richard Fenn was the editor of another very well produced Area magazine called Yorkshire Crossways, of which there are just two copies in the Archives. The 1992/93 edition carries a tribute to and profile of, John Rawnsley entitled, 'A Man For All Seasons', and going on to say: "He built up over the next 30 years the best association in the country … and the Three Peaks was his brainchild." The edition also outlines the numerous cyclo-cross coaching and circuit training that were to take place over the coming months at Keighley, Leeds and Sheffield. The next copy outlined that the future was bright in Yorkshire with an impressive 44 juveniles and 31 under 12s having competed during the past season.

The Annual General Meeting this year was held at a new venue, the Regency Hotel in Solihull on March 27th. The final event of the day departed from the tradition of an evening dinner as the organisers decided to go for a buffet at noon instead.

For the year-end Harry Gould outlined the 1992/93 finances: "Income was £38,026, Expenditure was £93,940 and the Sports Council Grant was £58,625 leaving the B.C-C.A again with a small surplus." Then came the Third 4-Year Plan, with similar details as previous being required, although there had been better planning, growth in promotions and rider participation.

21

Alexander becomes the first
Women's Champion

Season 1993/94

£3.00 was now the price of the new handbook, which had a photograph of Steve Douce riding flat out down a wooded path on the cover. There were now 124 pages, all packed full of information on races, rules, lists of winners and general topics, including nine black and white photographs of British champions. The B.C-C.A. also produced an excellent booklet this year, called 'Cyclo-Cross Rider's Handbook'; it was supported by the Sports Council and covered in a straightforward way, almost everything that a rider needed to know about the basics of how to start riding cyclo-cross.

Fred Salmon, the Peugeot Cycles professional, overcame the awesome descent of Ingleborough with both tyres completely flat, to win the famous Three Peaks race for the third time in four years. He had only just recovered from a bout of Shingles he had suffered during the summer. His ride was of the classic attacking style, by just riding away from the opposition, ascending Ingleborough and after a hair raising descent had to change bikes. In second place came Nick Craig (Diamond Back) and then the pre-race favourite, Ian Ferguson (Helwith Bridge Alers). The winning team was Bradford Olympic and James Taylor (Beeston R.C.) the fastest junior. Three times winner and multi-champion John Atkins also rode, as did his son Darren. Atkins senior, finishing just ahead of old rival Vic Barnett, said when interviewed by *Cycling Weekly*: "It has changed a lot but I've enjoyed it immensely."

Brian Furness, the B.C-C.A Press Officer, looking ahead to the next World Championships, outlined the changes that were about to take place. The Senior Championships would now to be open to both Professional and Amateurs, the first time they would race together since 1966. Brian then went on to say: "All this means that Britain's leading amateurs cannot afford to measure their success, simply by their standing within their own category – they need to compete with the likes of Steve Douce and David Baker if they are going to make the British team. However, the National Squad is a youthful one, and the goal of world championship selection has previously helped to keep them in the sport."

Another change was that only five riders could be selected for this one open race as against the four riders who used to qualify for each of the two races. There was also much debate at the time between countries, about who could and who could not qualify as amateur. Other changes taking place because of the U.C.I were a new Cyclo-cross World Cup Series and a Points Ranking for riders. The most controversial change of all was the new Rule 3 by the U.C.I saying: "Cyclo-cross races can take place all year round." This was at a point when all disciplines of cycle sport were beginning to overlap their seasons into that of cyclo-cross.

This December saw Roger Hammond, now with V.C. Bad, showing his superiority by winning the third round of the National Trophy Series by a clear 2¼ minutes from Barrie Clarke (Raleigh). In the junior race on the same day it was James Taylor (Beeston R.C.) who sprung a surprise by beating Brian Curtis of the Festival R.C. In third spot came the series leader Robert Thackray, who was riding with an injured Achilles tendon. Matthew Guy, the pre-race favourite, had started to drive to the event, but returned home as a previous arm injury was causing him so much pain, despite being x-rayed earlier, no bones were found to be broken. Les Lloyd (Didcot Phoenix) and Caroline Alexander were both winners who retained their overall leadership in their categories.

James Norfolk riding for V.C. St. Raphael/Waites, finished 1993 on a high note after a bout of flu, when he bounced back to win the second of the Crabwood C.C.'s Christmas Series of races, held at Tatchbury Mount Hospital at Calmore. A Christmas holiday mix of thick mud and frosty sections greeted the racers in the Belper R.C. event, which was promoted in Shipley Country Park. David Baker (Raleigh) proved to be the top man by winning from his team-mate Adrian Timmis, (the former Tour de France rider) and Julian Gould (ACE R.T.).

Ian Spensley the North Eastern C-C.A. Secretary had a cunning ploy to make sure the riders kept in the festive spirit in the Hades Fancy Dress race on Boxing Day at the Gateshead International Stadium. All riders not wearing fancy dress outfits had the cost of their entries doubled. No cyclo-cross has ever had such a strange sight at the finish as this race.

The first and second riders to cross the line were dressed as two of the 'Three Kings' followed by 'Batman', who in real life were Vince Potter (Bradford Olympic-Paul Milnes Cycles), Alan Nixon (Reading University C.C.) and 'Batman' was really Rob Colledge.

In Kent it was Stuart Blunt (Wembley R.C.-Dauphin Sport) who had most of the festive cheer, when he won the 25th edition of the Gemini B.C's Festival Cross. It was held at the Outdoor Activities Centre at Footscray, where Blunt resisted the challenge of Peter Rice (Army C.C.) by exactly one minute. Further South in Southampton, it was Barrie Clarke (Team Raleigh) who raced away from a 50 strong field with Brian Curtis (Festival R.C.) but Clarke won despite a puncture early on.

When the new Open National Champion was crowned at Southampton, it was Roger Hammond riding for the Invicta R.C. Dale/Farm team who took the chequered flag by 14 seconds from Nick Craig (Diamond Back). The day had dawned bitterly cold, which lasted all day. The course gave each type of rider a chance to prove himself with mud, grass and woods and a real speed section on the low banked cycle track. Four times the 87 riders surged forward and four times Jim Court the Commissaire brought them back, finally firing his gun for a clean getaway. Hammond continued to put the pressure on the other riders, until his power finally saw him clear and alone in the lead. There was a moment of near disaster, when he collided with a spectator in the wooded section but he remounted very shaken and continued his relentless progress towards the title. The bronze was taken by a former champion Steve Douce who was now unsponsored.

The new Junior Championship was decided early on, when Brian Curtis (Festival R.C.) surged ahead on the opening lap and was never challenged from that moment onwards. James Taylor (Beeston R.C.) arrived at the chequered flag just over a minute after Curtis to claim the silver medal, and then Richard Allaway (Fat Tracks) took the bronze. The new champion said in *Cycling Weekly*, "I hope I've ridden myself into the world's team with this." and Allaway said, "Something happened to my cleat – I couldn't get my foot in on the last lap." A footnote to these championships, following new regulations for juniors by the U.C.I., was that Matthew Guy and Robert Thackray, (who were now both 18 years old) and had been racing against seniors all season, would now be included in the Junior World Championship squad.

At long last the women cyclo-cross riders in Britain had their own championship, and the first winner to be crowned was Caroline Alexander of the Louis Garneau team. Her performance was well worthy of this momentous occasion for British cyclo-cross. She was never challenged, catching rider after rider, until half the field had been lapped. She finally finished over three minutes clear of the unsponsored Sally Hibberd, with Isla Rowntree (Black Country Wheelers) riding into the bronze medal position on this auspicious occasion. It is interesting to note that there were 24 finishers in this women's race, which compared very favourably with the 28 finishers in the Junior race and Caroline Alexander's time was only 3 minutes 24 seconds slower than Brian Curtis's race winning time over the same distance. So the move to a true Championship had been accomplished.

For the World Championships an estimated crowd of over 20,000 gathered along the sandy course at Koksijde, in Belgium. They became absolutely ecstatic, when their man Paul Herijgers won the senior title; he was now 32 years old and already the National Champion. There was talk in the press, that the course had been specially prepared for home riders but this comment has been put forward before about previous venues over the years, but nothing was ever proved. Herijgers arrived at the chequered flag alone; having dropped Dutchman Richard Groenendaal on the penultimate lap, with in third spot another Belgian Erwin Vervecker.

Roger Hammond started on the first rank of the grid, but he was soon involved in a crash, where a handlebar to caught him in the leg. Although he was otherwise unhurt, his chance of a high placing had evaporated. He did however finish as the first of the G.B riders in 33rd, with Chris Young 36th, arriving just ahead of Peter Stevenson 37th, then came Stuart Blunt back in 56th.

Hammond commented afterwards about the change of format to Open events to *Cycling Weekly*: "The thing is that if you have riders like me who are competing against older professionals and I wasn't the youngest rider in the field, there were guys nine months younger than me and I can see a drop in interest in riders of that age. I mean, what is the point in coming to the World Championships at 20 to ride against top professionals? The sport needs an 'espoirs' category to keep young riders interested, otherwise I can see a lot of riders stopping at National level."

In the Junior race the strongest rider was Gretienus Gommers of Holland, who was the rightful winner, followed by the defending champion Kamil Ausbuher of Czechoslovakia, with next over the line Ben Berden of Belgium. The British riders were led home by Robert Thackray in 22nd at just over three minutes, then came Matthew Guy 24th, Brian Curtis 29th,

Richard Allaway 44th and James Taylor in 51st. Thackray had been riding well in 13th until a crash in the sand caused his brake and gear mechanism to malfunction.

The enormous gap in the investment and therefore the prowess by the cycling nations involved, can be best gauged by the fact that the Hungarian team were strung out on the sprint to the dunes on the first lap and as they were all riding in trainers this did not help them either. There were also other Eastern Block teams riding with inferior equipment, such as Mafac centre–pull brakes, and many were still riding with toe-clips and straps on ancient road frames with close clearances, yet despite these disadvantages they put up very reasonable performances

Just because the world championships were over, did not mean the season was finished, for *Cycling Weekly* reported the winning of the Oxonian C.C event with these words: "Fireman Mike Bell doused the hopes of his rivals with a runaway–win on the Great Haseley course on Saturday. Bell, riding for London Fire Brigade C.C. finished a busy night shift at his Clerkenwell Station in time to drive out to rural Oxfordshire." Meanwhile up in Yorkshire, Chris Young having newly returned from the razzmatazz of the world's, won the Brook C.C 'Giant Bicycles Cross', which was the final round of the Yorkshire C-C.A points series.

The life of a cyclo-cross rider in 1994 was well illustrated when Young outlined his next few weeks. Coming up soon was two weeks training in Tenerife, then his first road race of the season, then straight into the Mountain Bike season, all showing how much of an all rounder a cyclo-cross rider had to be in order to earn a good living.

At the A.G.M held at Kegworth, Leicestershire, there was no report from Mrs. J. Gilbert, the Handbook Secretary, however it was noted that handbook sales profit was approximately £1,200. A vote of thanks was recorded by Jim Court to the retiring President Bob Thom, in appreciation of his work for the Association. Joan Edwards then became the Association's first Lady President. There was another vote of thanks, this time it was to E. Bewley who had retired as the National Treasurer. Jim Court was then voted in as Chairman, a position he continued to hold until the merger with British Cycling. Darrell Bradbury became the new Treasurer and Peter Stevenson the International Racing Secretary. There were no less than 57 amendments to the rules to be debated, with L. Hall explaining the various rule changes, which included the new coaching system. He also outlined the problems encountered following the late notification of the change in Junior qualification for the 1994 World

Championships. At the end of the meeting Keith Edwards proposed a vote of thanks to J. Gilbert for her hard work for the Association.

Jim Court's comments are always interesting, and in 'Chairman's Jottings' in the N.W.C.C.A Annual he both informed and kept his readers interested with such comments as: "At the last National A.G.M I took on the reigns of National Chairman of the Association with all its worries as well as retaining my position on the North West committee. Among the things to be sorted were the impending retirement of three major officials, the General Secretary Joan Edwards who had served the sport for many years giving many unpaid hours to the sport, the Treasurer Betty Bewley who had turned a balance of a few hundred pounds to several thousand and ultimately the President himself, Bob Thom, a respected figurehead for many years."

After all the years that the B.C-C.A had been sending British teams to the Senior World Championships, they were still getting similar results or even poorer, over recent seasons. This was despite all the improvements that had been made during the intervening years, but the specialist cyclo-cross countries had moved even further ahead.

Season 1994/95

The smiling face of Roger Hammond, resplendent with his B.C-C.A. championship jersey and medal, holding the Championship cup, looks out from the cover of the latest Association handbook. A big change in this issue is pictures of ladies racing, including Caroline Alexander, the first National Women's Champion and Women's National Trophy Series winner and of Isla Rowntree the runner-up in the Woman's National Trophy Series and Bronze medallist in the Championships.

Yet another lady made her mark in cyclo-cross this year, for Mrs Joan Edwards became the first lady National President. The post of National Treasurer is in the safe hands of Darrell Bradbury, with Peter Stevenson now the International Racing Secretary being based at Ghent in Belgium.

The August issue of the Wessex Newsletter revealed that the number of both senior and junior riders had been down during the 1993/94 season but that the under 12s had bucked the trend by increasing their numbers slightly. This small but well produced magazine, almost always included both a photograph on its cover and batches of photographs of riders in the centre pages. Looking through the Area magazines lodged in the archives it is amazing how much voluntary work is done in the name of the sport and how so many people were putting their efforts into the B.C-C.A.

Steve Douce, although still unsponsored, was out to prove that he was fit early, by retaining the Greenwich Trophy race, which he had won not only last year but back in 1979 as well. It was V.C.Elan who promoted this race, now in its 23rd year and held in the first week of October at Maryon Wilson Park in the Charlton area of London. By mid October, the new season was well under way, with some of the less publicised races such as the Kirkby Kross Series, where Stephen Cook (Wigan Wheelers) scored the win and at Hetton Lyons Cycle Park, Houghton-Le-Spring, where Vince Potter (Bradford Olympic R.C.) led from the off right through to the chequered flag to win the Middridge C.R. event. Over in the East, it was Ben Paton (Octagon V.C.) who was to take an early season win in the Godric C.C. event, the Broome Heath Scramble at Bungay in Suffolk, which was being run for the 29th time. In the Midlands, the torrential rain called an early halt to racing in the Ratae R.C. event. With ten minutes to go, the lap scorers' sheets and the judges' notes were quickly turning into soggy papier-mâché but Martin Seddon (ACT RT-Peugeot) was a delighted, if drenched victor.

In an interview with Phil O'Conner in *Cycling Weekly*, Steve Douce revealed that his life as an unsponsored rider was "not proving very stressful at the moment." Although he was going to move further north to ease the travel to events. He continued: "You spend so much time at weekends stuck in traffic on motorways, it's just a waste of your life." In the same interview Roger Hammond said he was interested to hear of the introduction of a championship for 19 to 23 year olds next January, with the event being the precursor to a full scale world championship which would provide a stepping stone to the senior open title. Hammond also proved he had a different approach to traffic problems: "I'm handy for Heathrow and travelling time can be less than driving to an event in the North of England."

Early December saw the third round of the B.C-C.A National Trophy won by Roger Hammond who built a lead early on. This added to the two other wins he had accumulated out of the four races in this series, and therefore establishing an unbeatable position. The course at Braunstone Park, Leicester, proved a slippery, soggy test for all, with crashes galore even by the top riders. The 78 strong field had to ride a stream swollen by overnight rain to a depth of bottom bracket level, but Hammond overcame these hazards to win from Steve Douce and Gary Foord (Scott International).

Over the Christmas period events were being run all over the country, such as the Coventry R.C. 'Easy Glide' G.P., the Middridge CRT, 'Fancy Dress' events and the Crabwood C.C. races at Southampton held on Boxing Day. Then on the 27th, there was the Gemini 'Festival Cross', the Macclesfield 'Supercross' or the 'Tatchbury Mount Cross' for riders to try. These events all seemed to be designed to help those overeating during the festive season to instantly burn off their excess calories. If that didn't do the trick, then on New Years Day there was the Coalville Wheelers, Crabwood C.C. Colchester Rovers or the South Western R.C. events to choose from.

The 'Circuit of the Moor' in the first week of the New Year had a massive field of ninety-six brave enough to face the starter, only days after the winter holidays. Gary Foord (Scott-International), Britain's only winner of a Grundig World Cup mountain bike race last year, led the wholesale charge as they set off into continuous rain. He was to go on to win from Steve Knight (Halesowen A & C.C.) the first of the amateurs, at just over one minute down.

A new name was to appear this year on the National Open Championship trophy, after one of the most exciting races for years. It was Barrie Clarke (Raleigh) who surged ahead in the last half mile of the race to take the victory. The main sponsors were Dawes Cycles, and it was organised by the Royal Sutton C.C, with support from the Birmingham City Council on the Sutton Park course. Clarke was the only man able to ride, where others had to run. His was a very popular win, not only with the large crowd, but with the other contenders, as Martin Ayres found out and reported in *Cycling Weekly* after interviewing Steve Douce, who had just gained the silver medal: "If I had to lose I'd rather it was to be Barrie than anyone else." Ayres himself described Clarke as "one of the nice guys of cycling sport." Afterwards Ayres gained this comment from the new Champion: "I've always been there or thereabouts, but never won until today, I was flying … I've been following Peter Keen's training programme, my training has been more structured."

The bronze medal went to Nick Craig (Diamond Back), giving the professionals all the spots on the podium. Next man in was James Norfolk (V.C.St.Raphael) who had swept past Roger Hammond on the final lap to be the first amateur finisher. One hundred riders had faced the starter, with former champion David Baker (Team G.T.) leading early on but he faded when a rib injury began to take its toll

The second edition of the Women's Championship race saw the "deceptively fragile Caroline Alexander once again showing steely determination and strength to retain the National Women's Title". That was how Martin Ayres in *Cycling Weekly* described Alexander winning her second title from Louise Robinson (Raleigh) by just over two and a half minutes, with Isla Rowntree (Black Country Wheelers) arriving for her second bronze. Alexander now riding for the Klein team took the lead before half a lap had been completed and was never headed again: "I had no problems – except when my chain came off, and I was quickly able to put that right." she told *Cycling Weekly*. Robinson had been a late convert to the sport, despite being the daughter of the legendry Brian Robinson, the first Briton to win a stage of a Tour de France.

Gavin Hardwicke (Long Eaton Paragon/Double A Cycles) proved to be one of the first of the new generation of young riders to take a title; all three on the podium were first year juniors. Hardwicke was a run-a-way winner after the first lap, high-speed sort-out. Jack Lambeth (R.T Elite) rode into the silver medal position and Danny Connolly (Bronte Wheelers) took the bronze. Cyclo-cross had gained Hardwicke as one of the growing number of riders coming from mountain biking, and after the race he told *Cycling Weekly*: "I enjoy mountain biking more, but seem to get better results in 'cross … I'd have preferred to have gone clear later but in an event like this when the opportunity comes you've just got to grab it."

This was a purple patch in the coverage of cyclo-cross by *Cycling Weekly*, for these championships included three pages of reports and pictures, added to this there were four pages of pictures on both inside and outside covers.

The World Championships held at Eschenback in Switzerland tested all categories of riders. Twenty–eight year old Dieter Runkel, brought delight to the home crowd, when he took the lead half-way through the third lap, powering along on the running sections where others were drifting backwards, he arrived alone and blew kisses to his home country crowd as he took the first Open/Elite rainbow jersey. Holland provided the silver medallist Richard Groenendaal, who was followed home by another Swiss, Beat Wabel. On lap three the British were grouped together at over three minutes but still on the same lap as the leader. At the finish Gary Foord arrived in 31st position, at the very moment Runkel was climbing the podium to receive the accolades of the crowd. Second of the British to finish was Barrie Clarke in 35th then came Steve Douce in 36th, followed by Nick Craig 39th and Peter Stevenson at 1 lap.

In the new race for Espoirs (19 to 22 year olds), Britain had put great hopes in Roger Hammond riding to a top placing, but the pre-race favourite was Jiri Pospisil of the Czech Republic who showed that his top billing was not exaggerated as he won alone 24 seconds clear of Patrice Halgand of France. The next rider home delighted the packed crowds, for it was the Swiss rider Thomas Steiger. Once more the G.B. riders found themselves at a disadvantage, for they were seeded as the ninth nation, and allocated the fourth line on the grid, this was despite Hammond being highly ranked. Adding to their woes, they were all delayed when there was a big pile-up just after the start. However Hammond, with his speed and dexterity, managed to advance up to sixth and then fifth, but at the finish he had slipped to sixth. Behind him James Norfolk and Stuart Blunt had climbed up to 11th and 15th but Richard Thackray finished near the back in 36th, with Matthew Guy having to retire. When he got his breath back, Hammond told *Cycling Weekly*: "I'm disappointed, I didn't know how they worked out the starting grid." Robert Thackray then explained: "I was right behind the crash and went over everyone. I ended up with somebody's bars caught inside my chainstay." Matthew Guy was also disappointed, saying: "I pulled out at the end of the second lap. I haven't trained since the nationals because of illness. There was nothing in my legs at all."

The moment Stefan Bunter crossed the line and then stood on the lowest step of the podium in the Junior Championship, the delighted Swiss supporters knew they had gained a medal in each event. The winner being another the Czech Republic rider, Zdenek Mynar, with Guillaume Benoist of France taking the silver. Freezing temperatures and heavy drizzle greeted these young men when they battled for the title, weather perhaps more to the liking of the five British riders, but it was not to be because they finished with R. Allaway in 24th, B. Curtis in 29th, A. Moorhouse 42nd, J. Lambert 50th, and G. Hardwicke in 51st.

What could be done to improve the lowly results still being produced by Great Britain in recent years at World Championships? Mid February saw Peter Cossins investigate the problem in an article in *Cycling Weekly*, interviewing top riders and officials to try and get an answer to this question. He entitled his piece, 'Good News Bad News'. Gary Foord stated: "I don't know how it is that we can have four or five riders challenging at top level in Mountain Biking, but we are getting nowhere on the 'cross scene ... British team manager, Simon Burney admits that several other teams were surprised by the lowly finishes of riders who could be guaranteed to be right in contention if the setting had been a Grundig World Cup race." But it could it have been the courses that were the real problem. British Cyclo-Cross Association Press Officer Brian Furness believes this could be part of the problem. Cossins also asked younger riders their opinions: "James Norfolk, 11th in the Espoirs race, agrees that the unfamiliarity of the World's courses is a factor, cyclo-cross on the Continent puts the emphasis on speed." He also interviewed Nick Craig, an older rider who expressed the view: "We can run well up-hill because that's not too different from riding with short steps and the feet digging in. Some of the guys looked like top-class cross-country runners. I know that Roger Honegger, for example, does a lot of work on the running track."

Simon Burney believed that money was the answer, as did Craig, explaining that "Overseas, 'cross riders have more resources at their disposal." Furness then added: "Ideally what we need is sponsorship for the national squad so that we can do more foreign trips." The conclusion seems to be that many facets of the sport did need to be looked at; more money and a change in courses would both help, as would changes in training. Added to that, is the fact that several of the top riders were turning to Mountain Bike racing for their livelihoods during the summer, it was all a very challenging problem for the B.C-C.A officials to get a grip on so that Britain could gain more success at future World Championships.

The 1994/95 A.G.M was held once more at Kegworth, near Derby, in March where the General Secretary's report covered the past season which had been a "moderately successful one ... The National Trophy series also produced some excellent racing from record fields." However he also said: "On the negative side, it was frustrating to see the opening months of the domestic season peppered with event cancellations, more than at any time than in recent years. Reasons were various: withdrawal of permission or 're-evaluation of recreational policy' by landowners, increases in charges and even, unforgivably, the organiser forgetting to book the venue." Then on membership he said: "In the first year in which the duties of Membership Secretary have been absorbed into the remit of the General Secretary, I am pleased to report a further 2% increase in the number of affiliations."

Jim Court continued with a warning: "Our various programmes are currently generously funded by the Sports Council, however the imminent restructuring of that body is likely to lead to a fundamental change in the way that governing bodies are financed in the United Kingdom." A table was produced showing club affiliations, at this time Midlands was top with 81, then North West 67, London 66 making the top three, then came Yorkshire 54, followed by Essex and Wessex tied with 33, then South West with 25. The final two were Lincs. & Humberside 19, and one called Direct with 3, making an impressive 438 total.

While on the subject of figures, an interesting table was produced showing all the participation count from 1985/86 season to this year and is reproduced at the end of this chapter. It shows an increase in overall numbers from 1,504 to 5,380 but perhaps the most surprising figure is that the professionals only increased by one from 13 to 14.

There was much discussion at the A.G.M about the "clarification on the officer's disappointment with riders' attitudes" regarding "the problems of getting top riders to participate in World Cup races" with no real resolution.

Jim Court, once more writing in his 'Chairman's Jottings' in the North Western C-C.A Annual, reported: "This year, has I think probably been one of the worst for cyclo-cross weather that I can remember. The washing machines must have worked overtime and it is a wonder more riders were not laid low with pneumonia … My own race at Woodbank Park, had to be abandoned as it took on the appearance of a gigantic swimming pool." He also found space to congratulate the local riders: "It was therefore left to our ladies to provide the only Gold (medal) as Clare Gross took the new title of National Juvenile Women's Championship by a street, and she still has another year to make it two."

In the same magazine is an article by Diane Evans, called 'Stay on the Right Side of the Judge" describing racing from the official side of the barriers.

Riders must wear a helmet while warming up on the course. It seems to me that some of the lads do not have very good memories, as we say it to some, every time they ride. It is just as easy to fall off while warming up, as it is whilst racing and, honestly, I do care about people hurting themselves, even if you think I don't … Riders are asked to put their numbers on the left which means they are always on the right side of the judges. It's in your own interests for the judges to see your number as otherwise you will be missed off the result sheet.

She then concluded with a plea that all judges at cycle races must agree with:

Please don't hassle the judges after the race finishes as we are trying our hardest to get the result out as quickly as possible and yes, we do make mistakes (only sometimes) but can do without somebody, after they finished 10th, as their dad said so or that he's just ridden for an hour and wants his result now. We have just stood for 5 hours and we would equally like to get finished.

Reading the above, all cyclo-cross judges across country must have been saying 'hear-hear' to that!

22

Success at the Worlds is elusive

Season 1995/96

During September, reigning champion Richard Thackray was still being sidelined by a back problem, so his elder brother Robert (Bradford Olympic R.C) took his opportunity to win the Team Sheffrec event, the opening round of the Yorkshire Cyclo-Cross Association's points series. The first of six events promoted by the Oxonian C.C. saw George Richardson (Coventry Olympic Squires Engineering) riding a mountain bike finishing the stronger in a tussle with Carl Thompson.   Mountain bikes were also dominant in the Charter Bash with Darren Howarth (Rusland Velo) lapping all but three of his closest rivals to take the win, although Martin Smith in second did ride a 'proper' cross bike in this Barrow Central Wheelers race.

At 146 pages this season's handbook was the thickest yet, with a photograph of Barrie Clarke in his Team Raleigh jersey on the cover. Twelve black and white pictures were intersected among the many races listed. One page has all the B.C-C.A trophies and a magnificent list it is, many are named after riders or officials, with the others presented by companies. Scanning across the trophy names it seems that all the history of the B.C-C.A. is there. There is the 'Swatkins', the 'Adrian Longland', the 'Ralph Digges', the 'Maurice Turner' plus 'The Arthur Gamble'. Then those named as memorial trophies such as, 'The Ray Richards Memorial', 'The Sgt.H.J.Colley, V.C.M.M. Memorial' and 'The Gill Wreghitt Memorial'. Added to these are company donations, such as the 'T.I. Reynolds Shield', 'The Halfords' and the 'The Findus' trophies.

Entry fees had climbed steeply over the years and had now upped again, ranging from £4.00 to £5.00 for Seniors, Vets and Junior riders. Juveniles and Women now had to pay from £2.00 to £5.00. There were several events listed as 'Mountain', with some indicating they would put on extra races for women, if there were enough entries.

The National Trophy Series this year were all supported by various Leisure Services, each round being supported by its own council. Greenwich first off in October, followed by Wolverhampton in November; December saw Leicester sponsoring the event and the final of the series took place in Hambleton, Northallerton with their Leisure Services coming up with the money.

During early October, Brian Furness wrote in his column 'Cross Talk' in *Cycling Weekly*: "The rearrangement of the road calendar has meant that it is more difficult than usual to register the fact that the cyclo-cross racing season is with us ... the campaign is already underway with more than 30 events already completed." Some of these were, the Don White's Cycles event promoted by YelloVelo. Where Mick Daley (Cherry Valley R.T), after a race long battle with Don Buckle (Brook C.C), won by just 10seconds. Meanwhile at West Kingsdown, in Kent, Ian Taylor (Redhill C.C) who had had a very successful mountain bike season, returned to cyclo-cross to win the Dartford Wheelers race.

Brian Furness in another 'Cross Talk' during December described the difference between British and the Continental countries as regards this sport. Brian went on to explain that whereas the B.C-C.A promoted an event in all 10 Areas every week during the season but "French cross activity is dotted around pockets in the north of the country; in Spain it is almost exclusively confined to the Basque Country; even in Switzerland the majority of races take place in a small area to the south-east of Zurich. You would be lucky to find more then one meeting on any given weekend in any of the main European countries."

The Association's preparations for the World Championships at Montreuil near Paris in February needed reversing, when the event organisers cancelled a pre-worlds race on the championship course. The event had first been scheduled for October then December, before being axed. A second cancellation was also a disappointment as it was a Madison for both Women and Veterans, which would have given both categories experience.

Roger Hammond, while trying to find his top form for the under-23 espoirs worlds race, travelled to Hombrechtikon in Switzerland at Christmas. "It was certainly worth going, but not brilliant" was how he described his ride for 19th place. Other Brit's racing abroad were the former national juvenile champion James Allaway who finished 2½ minutes down (22nd) on winner Bart Willems of Belgium; Gavin Hardwicke (national champion) took 26th, James Perry 29th, Philip Evans

31st, Matt Buckingham 38th were other GB riders in this World Cup race. Danny Connolly was a non-finisher, after snapping his chain. Junior Team Manager Ian Small told *Cycling Weekly*: "They all gained valuable international race experience."

Chaos reigned on Boxing Day, when just after the start of the Crabwood Cross No1 event, a fast start caused a mass pile-up just as the riders left the Southampton Sports Centre stadium after two laps of the track. National Champion James Norfolk (Extreme C.C/Specialized) thought his chances were gone when another competitor rode into him and his tyre punctured. But Norfolk rode on to win on this very cold day with a hard frost, from Ian Taylor (Redhill C.C) who had also been delayed by the mass crash. Taylor took revenge in the Crabwood's No 2 event when the thaw had set in, making the going muddy. Norfolk had been the victim of another crash this time but after a tough World Cup race in Belgium, admitted his form was "up and down" and "I didn't have the power."

Crashes were also the dominant feature of the Coalville Wheelers Cross on New Years Day. A double winner over the holiday period, Carl Sturgeon (O Rangers), after gashing his knee required hospital treatment afterwards but bravely finished second behind Steve Knight (Halesowen A & C C) with Stuart Blunt also a victim of a crash. Both Knight and Allaway were featured in stunning action shots in *Cycling Weekly*, captured by Phil O'Connor.

For the seventh time a reigning cyclo-cross champion lost his crown; this year it was Nick Craig (Diamond Back) who relieved Barrie Clarke (Raleigh) of his title. Hammond (South Western R.C) led at one point by 20 seconds and looked on his way to the title, but he reckoned without the guile of the two experienced professionals who worked steadily up to him, then pounced when he cracked. What some considered was the biggest crowd ever at a National Championships, saw a fast paced race over the Sutton Park course, once more promoted by the Royal Sutton C.C and sponsored this year by Dawes Cycles. Hammond was finally caught with less than a mile to go to the flag and in the run to the line had to settle for third. Craig explained his move up to the top spot on the podium, to *Cycling Weekly*: "I have changed my training. I've not used a pulse monitor once this winter – I've done it all on feel."

Danny Connolly (Bronte Wheelers/McManus& Poole) was described as "built like a rugby league forward" but still finished well clear of any rivals to take the Junior title, only 12 months after taking the bronze. Jack Lambeth (R.T Elite) took the silver for the second year running.

Next came James Allaway (Dawes R.T) who had made a classic start, which lasted for only just over a lap and in the end he had to settle for the bronze. It might all have been so different if Lambert hadn't unshipped his chain at the start, leaving him in last place losing 30 seconds before he even got going. The now well established women's title race had forty starters, but only two fought it out for the honour of the gold medal, Caroline Alexander (B.M.W /Klein) already a double winner and Deb Murrell (Team Saracen). In the end Alexander won calmly and well clear, but acknowledged to *Cycling Weekly*: "In the past I just turned up and rode. But now the championships are getting so much more competitive that I did put in some short fast sessions in preparation." Isla Rowntree (Black Country Wheelers) came in once more to take the bronze medal, well clear of any chasers. The women were racing for the same prize list as the juniors, the winner gaining £150 with £120 for second and £100 for third. Looking at the championship programme it also shows that the Senior Champion took home £500, second £400, and third £300 with the prize money going down to 20th place.

The two Allaway brothers both riding for Dawes R.T were ready to ride for G.B at the World Championships but honed their form at the Dursley R.C Cross. Richard the winner from Tom Locke (Team Bike Bristol) and I.Langdon his team mate, with the younger Allaway, James, coming in 4th.

After more than ten years of trying Adri Van Der Poel finally won the Pro Cyclo-cross Championships, at 36 the Dutchman added a gold to five silvers. He was followed home by two of Italy's best, in Daniele Pontoni and Luca Bramati. Held at Montreuil in France, only 57 riders completed the course with Barrie Clarke the best Briton 44th, Peter Stevenson was next in 50th, just one place ahead of Stuart Blunt. British champion Nick Craig and Chris Young were just two of the 17 who abandoned.

The Espoirs race, for under 23 year old riders, saw Miguel Martinez make France happy by winning. He was only 20 but after being involved in a crash with Britain's Roger Hammond he kept calm and went with the breakaway and just out sprinted Patrick Blum of Switzerland to take the title. Zdenek Mlynar of the Czech Republic came in next for the bronze medal. Hammond finished in 19th, then came Matt Guy in 23rd with the other GB riders Richard Allaway in 47th and James Taylor 62nd. Afterwards Martinez told the press that it was "the 253rd win of his career", an amazing total for someone so young.

Switzerland added a 54th cyclo-cross medal to its amazing total in this cycling discipline, when Roman Peter took the Junior title from Spain's Gaizka Lejarreta. The G.B riders again tried their best but were clearly not in the same race with Jack Lambeth being the best in 28th position, followed by Danny Connolly 41st, James Perry 43rd, S Bayliss 51st and J.Allaway 55th.

The B.C-C.A did not send any riders to the new Juvenile (under 16s) Championships in Germany won by Bjorn Schroder of Germany. Lewis Hall, the B.C-C.A coach believed it "unfair to impose the stress of a world title race on juveniles." This season's trip to the world championships was a disappointment, after the junior successes of a few years back .It was now time to go back to the drawing board in order to gain the world medals that the Association desired.

The Inter-area team championships were held at Bramcote Park, Nottingham. Tim Gould led the Northwest to a surprise win over Yorkshire, with the winners for the past two years, Midlands, relegated to third place. Gould riding for Team Schwinn, a professional, scoring his second individual win in two years. The event was promoted by the Notts & Derby Cyclo-Cross League, backed up by Nottinghamshire County Council. The North West team manager Stuart Johnson was jubilant at the win, saying to a *Cycling Weekly* reporter: "It's been a long time coming, but well worth waiting for." Tim's brother Julian Gould crashed into a tree at speed requiring the fire brigade to stretcher him off the hillside to hospital for an x-ray. The women's title went to the Midlands, led home by Isla Rowntree. The Midlands also came out on top in the Junior team event with Russell Taylor leading home a one-two-three.

Chairman Jim Court, in his report said: "At a time when other cycling organisations are reporting a downturn in membership it is pleasing to report that the affiliations for the last year at least remained the same as the previous year ... The Executive has spent a lot of time this year in considering the way forward in relation to membership issues, bearing in mind the abolition of the professional class, the changing face of clubs and the formation of Racing and Trade Teams ... The Executive considered moving straight to individual membership but felt this would destroy some of the appeal of cyclo-cross."

In the report by Brian Furness, as General Secretary, he reminded the meeting that it was now time to present a new four-year plan to the Sports Council. "In particular we shall need to address the two areas which the Sports Council has identified as priorities for all recognised sporting bodies, namely the participation of young people and the pursuit of excellence." Treasurer Darrell Bradbury explained that: "The overall expenditure was all within the budget forecast ... there was a surplus at the end of the year of £7.595 bringing the overall surplus to £56,937.20.

Season 1996/97

An agreement between the B.C-C.A and the Welsh Cycling Union had been in place for many years, so perhaps now is the time to cover this subject, for in March this year there was a new agreement. The control of cyclo-cross in Wales was vested in the Welsh Cycling Union and clubs wishing to take part in cyclo-cross would affiliate to the B.C-C.A. 50% of the affiliation and sponsorship fees would be paid back to the W.C.U. The W.C.U was also entitled to one representative on the Association's Executive Committee.

Nick Craig's determined face stares out from this year's handbook but members looking through it for any change of Officers would find the only one, Harry Gould was now listed in the new post of Director of Coaching and Competition. However, some National Official positions did change, Andy Thompson was now Coaching Development Officer and Bob Hayward was now in the post of Youth Development Officer. Gordon Macdonald stayed as Medical Control Officer and Geoff Shergold as Equipment Officer. New jobs listed are Sports Science & Medical Officer, Dr. Chris Butler, National Trophy Co-ordinator, John Burney. Events Committee of Keith Edwards (Chairman) with John Burney and Isla Rowntree members. There were now eleven Life Members: J. Atkins, R.F.Atkins, I.Dodd, Mrs.J.Edwards, H.Gould, G. Greenfield, T.Haigh, P.Milsom, J.Rawnsley, Mrs. B. Richards and R.P.Ward. The number of events in this handbook rose to 124, with a noticeable rise in the number of separate events for under 12s, Juveniles, A.T.B.s and Junior/Women.

The minutes of the Executive Committee meeting in September, show that a letter had been received from the English Sports Council inviting a representative to discuss the enhancement services to be offered to cyclo-cross. They also received letters from the British Horse Society outlining their opposition to remove bridleway anomalies. The minutes also reveal that B. Furness and G.Macdonald would attend the Dope Control Conference in London during October.

In a 'Crosstalk' column in *Cycling Weekly*, National Coach Martin Eadon reminded riders that the outdoor centre near Matlock offered "excellent grounds for cross training" and that 25 cyclo-cross and road race riders had made the most of a pre-season get together. He also covered the thorny problem of lack of success at the world championships.

All too often our riders complain that their preparation for international events has been inadequate and the blame has been put on a lack of international competition. However, what is already becoming clear is that very few riders seek expert advice on physical and mental preparation … In my reference to seeking expert advice it has become clear that few riders have a coach or mentor during the cyclo-cross season …. With the help of Andy Thompson and Bob Hayward I am optimistic that by the end of the season all riders on the national squad will have found a local coach.

"The worst conditions for years couldn't stop Andy Peace (Pace Satellite T.V) scoring his second consecutive win" were the leading words in a *Cycling Weekly* report of the Three Peaks race. Very heavy rain overnight caused the many local streams to flow downhill to provide the riders with a quagmire to race through. The rain continued to fall throughout the day, with all the peaks shrouded in thick cloud, despite the constant strong winds. Peace was a "man with a mission" as he raced onwards hardly hampered by puncturing on each of the three descents. He was followed home by Robert Jebb (Helwith Bridge Alers) and then Chris Young also of Pace Satellite T.V. The prize list was a massive £2,200, and John Rawnsley explained that little of the money had come from sponsorship, as he wished to keep it as close to a typical Dales event as possible. Few of the 216 starters were put off by the inclement weather which was also a trial for the brave spectators.

The first round of the National Trophy Series was held at Sutton Lawns, Sutton in Ashfield, Nottingham. The series had splendid programmes with a photograph of National Champion Nick Craig on the cover of each edition. The Commentator on these events and many other important races during this period was a man who did know what it was like to ride in the mud and cold, Hugh Porter M.B.E. The National Trophy Series included Juveniles, Veterans, Women, Juniors and Seniors and were therefore excellent events to race against the best in the country in various venues. Talking of programmes, one in the archives for the North of England Championships at Sewerby Hall, Bridlington, has the large letters 'Cyclo-Cross' at the top with snow dripping from the letters, perhaps a weather forecast!

During the month of October, there were many races for cross riders to choose from. On one Saturday there was a choice of three events, then on Sunday riders were spoilt for choice with eleven events, each with many categories to choose from.

"The return of Roger" was the headline in *Cycling Weekly* over a report of the London Open Championships. He had just arrived from Australia "to score a crushing victory". Hammond spoke after winning by almost a minute from Barrie Clarke: "Riding as a professional really opened my eyes. As an amateur you can get away with things, like being a little overweight, but not now. I'm working hard to shed more weight and make certain I don't get unfit during the winter."

Yorkshire had an emphatic win in the Inter-Team Championships held at the Morfa Stadium in Swansea, after taking a back seat for the last three years although they had held the title for a decade before that. The Pace Racing team of Richard Thackray, Chris Young and Ian Taylor with the help of Danny Connolly rode Yorkshire to the win. Thackray was described as "Masterful" by *Cycling Weekly* as he ignored the miserable wet conditions. "The course suited me, it was a typical Yorkshire day" as the heavy rain washed away the mud at his feet. Isla Rowntree led the Midlands West team to victory in the women's event, soloing away from her sister Sally with her mother Carolyn completing the winning team. Isla said afterwards: "It must be the worst day we've had for cross this season." A look at the programme for the Inter Area Team Championships shows just how far women's racing had progressed over the years with four teams taking part. Both London and Wales having six representatives, the North Eastern three riders but the North Western fielded eight. It is also noticeable that the young Nicole Cooke was listed in the full Wales team, as was Katherine Hibberd for the London team.

An article in *Cycling Weekly* by Tim Clifford and Brian Furness outlined the hopes of the British riders at the coming World's: "The squad has gained much needed experience and will at least start with a better grid position than at Montreuil." For the Espoirs he said: "The British challenge is led by national champion James Taylor … Robert Thackray and Gavin Hardwicke both making their World's debut, while Phil Evans is selected for the first time … James Perry and his team-mate are at their second World's."

The reports of the World Championships in *Cycling Weekly* were accompanied by excellent colour photographs. The races took place in

Munich, Germany and the weather for the Junior race had turned warmer by 5°C than the practice day, and thus the circuit turned into a "slide zone." As *Cycling Weekly* put it: "It made for great entertainment, albeit a comedy of errors…. a guaranteed crowd-pleaser." Leader after leader came crashing down to allow another leader to emerge, but in the end it would be David Rusch of Switzerland who would cross the line first ahead of two sprinting figures S. Toffoletti (Italy) and S. Weigold of Germany who were to finish in that order. Despite a full-page report on this race there was no mention of G. B riders, so little did they feature. Their finishing places being 30th J.Perry, 33rd S.Bayliss, 36th D.Booth, 46th R.Taylor and in 50th D.Bowater.

Belgium gained a one-two in the Espoirs Championships with Sven Nijs and Bart Wellens, *Cycling Weekly* calling Nijs's win "stunning". The dominant two tested each other, with Nijs faster over any obstacles but Wellens faster on the flat. Finally it was Nijs who triumphed with C.Morel of France in the bronze medal placing. The British riders once more having no impact on the outcome. The G.B riders were placed B. Curtis 37th at almost 6 minutes, followed by R. Thackray 44th, P. Evans 45th, J.Taylor 53rd and G. Hardwick back at one lap.

Italy produced a fine winner of the Elite World title in Daniele Pontoni, who led almost all the way. The course was by now very rutted and was drying out, but the riders soon threw caution to the winds, to judge by the blistering pace at which the race began. Pontoni was joined by Luca Bramati and *Cycling Weekly* described their progress as, "The azzurri were going, quite frankly, like bats out of hell." Both riders crashed on slippery sections but recovered to race on. At the line Pontoni was the winner by just 23 seconds from a sprint between his compatriot and a very fast finishing Thomas Frischknecht (Swiss) riding with straight handlebars, who just pipped Bramati to the silver medal. Once more the G.B riders arrived well down the result sheet with S.Knight in 26th, B.Clarke in 32nd, then P.Stevenson 41st, B.Blunt 45th and J.Norfolk in 47th.

It is important to point out that racing always continues after the World's right across the country. At venues such as at the Leicestershire R.C event where the Ace R.T-Muddy Fox duo of Dean Bennett and Martin Seddon took the first two places. Graham Sheldon (Swansea C.C/ Schnoo) was the winner for third time running at the Rhondda Valley Cross. There were also races at East Grinstead where the Sussex riders were contesting their own county championships, James Richardson of Sports Coaching proved to be the winner. Russell Parkins (Rennrad Club

Norwich) was an easy winner in the Shaftesbury C.C. Cross staged at the Brentwood course in Essex.

General Secretary Brian Furness outlined the past year's events at the Association's Annual General Meeting. He covered many topics, notably

If the picture at the top of the tree looks promising, the scene nationwide suggests that there is still no room for complacency. The latest overall participation figures for 1995-96, show another small decrease, although the loss of a well supported summer series in London to MTB rules probably accounts for a large chunk of this ... The next few weeks will be pivotal ones for the Association. Not only will we learn of our Sports Council funding ... But we also hope to attract National Lottery Revenue Funding for our World Performance Plan, designed to create future World Champions.

Jim Court also drew to the meeting's attention to the fact that the media had not reported the success of Lindsay Clarke and Judith Shakeshaft in gaining gold and silver medals at, as he put it: "the belated debut of the U.C.I World Masters Cyclo-Cross Challenge at Mol in Belgium. Sixteen British competitors made the trip, making us the best representative nation after the host country. The promotion attracted around 125 competitors in total, which allowed for some good competitive racing in the three male age bands. The women's competition attracted only two entries, both from Britain, but at least Lindsay Clarke and Judith Shakeshaft were rewarded for their enthusiasm with gold and silver medals, and for Lindsay a World Masters Championship jersey."

In the Development Report by Brian Furness he outlined "Two years ago, the North Eastern Area took a look at its league structure and recognising that small fields represented a wide range of abilities, opted to rearrange the season." This meant that they now had "a marked rise in participation, as even those without a realistic chance of making the weekly prize list now have seasonal targets to aim for in their own league competitions." So was this the way forward?

At the rear of the report is a table showing a Participation count, which makes interesting reading. It shows that the under 12s racing grew from 160 in 85-86 to 637 in the 95-96 season. Seniors racing upped their numbers from 661 in 85-86 to a maximum of 2,785 in 91-92 then a slight downturn to 2,376in the last total counted in 95-96.   But the women's total showed the greatest increase from 16 in 85-86 to 375 in 95-96, and that is in all categories.

The North Western C-C.A Annual for this year, again edited by Ian Small, included an article by Ken Matthews of the Kirkby C.C telling of the time when he promoted 13 events in 12 weeks. Each was held on a Saturday, 12 were for the B.C-C.A and the other was for the English Schools Cycling Association. "What do you want?" was the title of Jim Court's page, where he asked riders to write to him: "On the one side the National and International issues swallow up large amounts of the Association's money but we must be seen to perform at a high level, since the Sports Council supports a high proportion of our budget and therefore has some bearing through its policies on our way of working." He also went on to put forward some ideas as to why the number of entries in the North West was slightly down this season. Cost, asking if it was the prices of entry fees, the price of petrol or family commitments? Or perhaps it was the Registration Cards that were introduced this year to cut out the number of non-affiliated riders. He added to these reasons, the League Programme, Race Distances, Courses, Facilities or even Development.

The Fourth 4-Year Plan as explained by Harry Gould, "In effect over the period of this plan, the B.C-C.A was told by the Sports Council that it would no longer receive the grants to which it had been accustomed unless the B.C-C.A merged with the B.C.F and the grants would be received by the B.C.F. but 'ring fenced' for Cyclo-Cross. Of course this caused much unrest."

23

Events abandoned due to weather;
Craig topples Clarke and
Knight becomes Champion

Season 1997/98

In the handbook it was noticeable that the name of Keith Edwards did not appear in the list of officials, almost the first time since the Association was formed. Martin Booth was now the Events Committee Chairman and Harry Gould continued as Director of Coaching. Members looking closely at the address of Peter Stevenson, the International Racing Secretary would see that he had moved from Gent to Zevergem but still based in Belgium. All age categories were listed for the coming season as follows:

Under 12	born in 1986 or later
Youth	born 1982 to 1985
Youth – Under 14	born 1984 or 1985
Junior	born 1980 or 1981
Senior	born 1979 or earlier
Under 23	born 1976 to 1979
Veteran	born 1957 or earlier
Senior Veteran	born 1948 to 1952
Grand Veteran	born 1943 to 1947
Master Veteran	born 1938 to 1942
Grand Master Veteran	born 1937 or earlier

One has to wonder if those early enthusiasts ever dreamed that there would be so many riders still racing at such advanced ages, although they may have been even more surprised to see such young riders competing almost every week.

There was to be no hat trick for Andy Peace in the Three Peaks as his team-mate, Chris Young, had his own idea of how victory could be attained. Peace had already won the Three Peaks running race three times, so was keen to add another win in the cycle race. The Pace Racing duo set out rapidly and attacked each other on their best terrain but in the closing stages it was Young who put a disappointing mountain bike season behind him, to win in a record breaking time. Although it did include having to make three bike changes along the way. Third to arrive was Robert Jebb to make it a Pace Racing Satellite T.V team one-two-three. First Veteran home was the experienced Graham Schofield of Helwith Bridge Alers, the club name comes from the fact that it is based at the local pub. The women's winner was a rider competing in only her third cyclo-cross race, Mari Todd, riding for Scotland's Midlothian R.T, she had to overcame a slipping chain to arrive in under 4 hours in 63rd position. Organiser John Rawnsley once more successfully completed the course, to add to his amazing record of finishing it every year since 1961.

The Hillingdon Circuit's first cyclo-cross event of the season saw Matt Fuller (Dartford Wheelers) victorious in the senior race, promoted by the Twickenham C.C./Stairmaster club. Other early season events were the Dartford Wheelers Cross where Stuart Blunt (Ace R.T) was the winner for the second year running, and the Calder Clarion event where Robert Thackray led a one-two-three with his club mates from the Bradford based club Paul Milnes R.T. This was another period of excellent coverage with many splendid full page action photographs and several reports of even the smaller promotions every week in *Cycling Weekly*.

By November other riders were making their impact, including Mick Bell (London Fire Brigade) the winner of the Redhill Scramble and Julian Winn (Cwmcarn Paragon) who took over the lead on the fifth lap to win by a clear minute, in the M&P Cycles Cross at the Morfa Stadium, Swansea.

For national coach Martin Eadon's floodlit evening cyclo-cross events on Wednesdays at St. Andrew's Rugby Club, most of the light came from the club floodlights, but it was supplemented by additional lighting provided by a grant from Rugby Borough Council who were keen to promote cycle sport.

Ipswich was to be the new venue for the National Trophy Series this year and a new series leader was found in Carl Sturgeon (Team Orange) who took over at the top of the points table from the early season leader Barrie Clarke of Team Raleigh. He had retained his form from racing mountain bikes all summer and this showed when he held a three second gap at the bell. He raised his arms aloft as he crossed the line just five seconds clear of Garry Foord riding for Scott International. Afterwards, Sturgeon said to *Cycling Weekly*: "I just couldn't get going quick enough at the start ... I was having some bike trouble early on." The junior winner was Daniel Booth and the women's victor once more was Isla Rowntree, who said afterwards: "It's getting a habit, finishing in front of Louise (Robinson) and Jenny (Copnall)." But Copnall just said, "We have been here before."

The North of England Area title was won for the seventh time by Chris Young (Pace Racing Satellite T,V) who first won this event fifteen years previously. The ladies winner was the very fit Caroline Alexander of Team Richey. The Midlands title fell to Steve Knight (Peugeot 406/Michelin) but Ian Taylor (unattached) returned south to his home area to take the South of England championships, with the South of England women's champion being Jenny Copnall (Bikepark/ Raleigh). Julian Winn rode well to take the Welsh title, Liz Slater (Builth & District C.C) was the women's winner. In the Youth's title event Lewys Hobbs was the victor with a young Nicole Cooke riding for Cardiff Ajax finishing second, ahead of the other boys.

During December, Barrie Clarke of Team Raleigh regained the yellow jersey as leader of the National Trophy Series despite Nick Craig (Diamond Back) winning round three of the series held at Braunstone Park in Leicester. "Craig, Clarke and Stuart Blunt (Ace R.T) dominated the 12-mile clash after breaking clear just before half distance. Blunt matched the two experienced professionals until the final lap, when he was tailed off to finish third." These were the words by *Cycling Weekly* to describe this action packed event. In the Women's National Trophy race it was Caroline Alexander riding for Team Ritchey who won by nearly two minutes from Jenny Copnall (Bikepark/Raleigh), with Lindsay Clarke (Terry Wright Cycles) battling through to gain third. The overall junior leader was Daniel Booth of the Ace R.T and in the Veteran's race it was Pete Smith an unattached rider, who took advantage of the series leader Cliff Featherstone taking a break from the competition, to not only take the win but the overall leader's jersey.

Among his other wins during this period, Craig in devastating style, took the Royal Bank of Scotland Supacross held in Macclesfield. Although Carl Sturgeon (Team Orange) went one better, by completing a hat trick at the annual Coventry R.C's Boxing Day handicap and in Kent Stuart

Blunt led from start to finish to win the Gemini B.C event, at Foots Cray Meadow, a race he first rode ten years previously.

Storms and gales hit many southern events over the Christmas and New Year period with the Crabwood race abandoned because of concerns about trees falling on the course. With all races being cancelled in the London area, the Colchester Rovers event at Mistley, Essex had an influx of top riders including Olympic mountain biker Gary Foord who took the victory. The Gateshead area was much luckier with the weather conditions and junior James Bushby (KHS) took full advantage in the fancy dress event promoted by Velo Club 167. While many other competitors rode in some very odd attire he rode on to claim victory over the veteran Cliff Featherstone.

"Craig topples Clarke" were the headlines over a report in *Cycling Weekly* on the Senior National Championship race. Craig removed the reigning national champion, making it a record ninth exchange of titleholders in a row. Lap by lap Craig gained ground on the field to win by just over half a minute, having time to freewheel past the chequered flag ahead of the pre-race favourite Barrie Clarke, with Steve Knight (Peugeot406/Michelin) arriving almost a minute back in third. Hammond the 1995 champion in seventh place was overheard muttering dark thoughts about the route planners, saying later to *Cycling Weekly*: "I hit a log at 30mph and saw my whole life pass before my eyes." Craig, however, in an interview said: "It was a superb course – very well drained and fast, considering the rain we've had."

James Taylor (Giant/ESP) took a second win in the Espoirs title race, with Brian Curtis (Team Corridori) following him home for a repeat second place. The race for the gold and silver was settled very early on but the outcome for the bronze was far from clear cut, although in the end it was Danny Bell of V.C Lincoln who moved up from 10th last year to take the third spot. Saying afterwards, "I was just hanging on … I opened a gap when Phil Evans fell on a log."

Caroline Alexander took her 5th title in a row, remaining the only winner of this Women's Championship. Alexander took control of the race on the second of the five laps, by extending the gap on Isla Rowntree, but after the bell she began to fade and Louse Robinson came through to take the silver medal from Rowntree who had never been off the podium since the championships began. The Champion had suffered a serious crash last year but told *Cycling Weekly*: "I've been in the gym working with weights, on both my upper body and legs."

"Dramatic win for junior Morley." was the title over an article covering the Junior Championships. Last year's silver medallist Tim Morley (Raleigh M-Trax/Pearsons) had his chain snap just before half distance and Daniel Booth took the lead and was on his way to the gold medal when he encountered misfortune, his forks snapping as he rode through the wooded section. He was then overtaken by the trio of Morley, Cox and Taylor. Booth having changed his bike, was off in pursuit, but Morley was on his way to his first title with Booth finally taking silver. Cox derailing his chain still managed the power to out sprint Taylor to gain the bronze and so ended an exciting race where the spectators could not afford to take their eyes off the action.

It is interesting to note the number of entries for these championships, thirty-six juniors lining up, thirty-two women, forty-two under 23 men and eighty senior men with an added list of another twenty hopeful reserve riders.

After winning the National Senior Championship Nick Craig turned down a chance to ride at the World's in Denmark by saying: "It might seem that I'm being awkward, but I'm not. I've got a big mountain biking season coming up, and my sponsors will be looking for me to do well in the early-season events. If I ride the World's, I'll damage my chances in mtb racing." Fourth finisher Carl Sturgeon also declined the trip with "I'll be concentrating on mountain biking." Their words showed that the draw of the money in MTB racing was proving very attractive to the top cross riders during this period. The B.C-C.A selectors therefore picked 5 riders to go to each of the Elite, Espoirs and Junior races,

The World Championships were held on the Hindsgavi peninsula near the Danish town of Middelfart. The Belgian duo of Mario De Clercq and Erwin Vervecken powered away early to take the number one and two spots. The Danish crowd were delighted when their champion Henrik Djernis hove into view, seemingly to take the bronze, but he sat up a few yards from the line just as Daniele Pontoni made a last gasp effort to take the medal. His lunge was not enough as he fell off his bike face down then skidded across the tarmac in a daze. It was the final straw for Pontoni who was still under a cloud after testing positive for cocaine and needed special dispensation to race, and was very angry indeed to miss out on a medal.

The British riders finished well down in places they had been used to filling over the last few years. Having tried their best, they fell short of breaking through into the higher echelons with S.Knight in 30th, B.

Clarke 37th, P. Stevenson at one lap in 46th and S. Blunt also finishing at one lap.

It was a Belgian one-two in the Espoirs race, with Sven Nijs establishing a lead early on and finally winning from his team mate Bart Wellens by almost half a minute. Wellens had a tough job to claim the silver medal from the Czech Petr Dlask. The younger G.B riders also fell short of their hopes, with James Taylor being the first to finish in 45th, at just over 5 minutes down, then D. Bell in 51st, R. Young 54th and B. Curtis in 55th.

Top spot on the podium for the Junior race went to Michael Baumgartner of Switzerland. In this race the G.B riders were in the action early on but in the end it was the Continentals who were to take the honours in the race for the line. Second home was S. Toffoletti of Italy and the bronze went to D.Commeyne of Belgium. First GB rider home was D Booth in 15th at 35 seconds, T. Morley in 24th, M. Robinson 34th, P. Dixon 37th and R. Taylor in 42nd.

The atmosphere as usual was noisy and happy, with drums, cowbells and flags of every nation involved, including a few Union Jacks being waved with great gusto when Daniel Booth lay second and Tim Morley sixth in the Junior race. Beer tents with grown men in dyed hair and odd costumes blowing horns of every type and note, floating above this medley was a 'blow-up doll' on a 15 foot pole, just part and parcel of every cyclo-cross world championships

Chairman Jim Court started his A.G.M report with:

The last year appears to have been dominated by politics, both within the sport and dealing with the Sports Councils ... the membership must realise that we can only progress by achieving closer relationships with the BCF. This does not necessarily mean that we must merge with the BCF and lose our identity – this cannot happen without the agreement of an Annual General Meeting – but it does mean that we must seek ways of working together on matters of mutual interest ... This is already happening on a number of issues and we will be involved in the BCF's own reviews of the way we operate. The registration card system went into its second year and appears to be working satisfactorily, with riders getting used to carrying their card with them.

Jim also touched on another topic: "One worrying item, though, was the number of fairly serious crashes which occurred during the year. There would appear to be a great need to ensure that courses move with the times. Races are being conducted at a greater speed and consequently the courses must be designed to match this speed with the necessary safety factors."

General Secretary Brian Furness's report declared: "There have been many highlights to the 1997-98 cyclo-cross season: a succession of close finishes in the Junior Trophy series … Most incredible [highlight] was perhaps the fact that the Notts & Derby Cyclo-Cross League, with 184 counting riders over 17 races, managed to come up with a tie for overall first place." Then he went on to record the stresses and strains of running the B.C-C.A. "However, if the racing programme has provided me with less diversion than in the past, it is because the view from 'the office' over the last twelve months has been largely dominated by the increase in bureaucracy engendered by the new working practices of the national sporting agencies."

He went on to explain how problems over the World Performance Plan funding, meant that poor communication on the part of the Lottery Unit had led to the B.C-C.A having had their application rejected. Furness also mentioned how the Anti-doping controls were being operated. "Over the course of the 1997-98 season 27 tests were carried out on 21 different riders, including three foreign competitors and riders in the National Women's Championship. All tests produced negative results: no banned substances was detected in any of the samples." He also thanked Medical Control Officer Gordon Macdonald and Tony Wilkins who had been acting as his deputy.

In the Coaching and Competition report, Harry Gould stated that the Sports Aid Foundation had funded six riders to the tune of £3,000 in addition to grants obtained at Area level. He carried on to outline details of the World Performance Plan: "Peter Keen is planning to ask the U.K Sports Council to fit cyclo-cross into cycling's World Performance Plan. If successful, Lottery Funding would begin hopefully from 1st September and with the announcement early in February of the intention of the U.C.I to get cyclo-cross recognised as an Olympic sport, the chances of funding get better." Also in this report was a section on 'Manufacturer's Support' which told of how the B.C-C.A was having difficulties in gathering together sufficient equipment to create a National Squad on the lines of the Dutch Rabobank team.

The 'Executive Summary' for 1997-98 started with a paragraph outlining the way ahead for the B.C-C.A being determined by outside influences with, "the beginning of what is seen as a transitional period for cycling administration in England and the United Kingdom. The Sports Councils see as the ultimate objective the integration of existing organisations into a single governing body for competitive cycling, and have identified the pathway towards achieving this outcome as one of amalgamation into the revised framework of the British Cycling Federation."

Then in the 'Membership and Licensing' section is this comment:

The philosophies of the two organisations are very different in this area ... Firstly, (the B.C-C.A) to maintain control over all cyclo-cross competition in England (with agreements in place with Wales and Scotland) and avoid the formation of splinter organisations ... The current B.C.F membership and licensing system is seen as a barrier to potential participants.

Then comes a paragraph entitled, 'Image of the British Cycling Federation':

Notwithstanding the process of change which is taking place within the B.C.F, there still remain at grass roots level profound reservations over the Federation's ability to gain the confidence of its current and potential membership. Its membership administration is seen as overly bureaucratic, costly, overstaffed and unresponsive to its member's concerns. There is a lack of trust over its financial acumen, and its long-term viability is viewed as uncertain in the light of the potential costs of counter-litigation.

All strong and forceful stuff which continued with worries expressed about the way the B.C-C.A had carefully looked after its finances and it was concerned that "the provision of racing activities will be eroded"

A look at the balance sheet this year shows that the 'Overall Financial Summary' showed a total income of £57,704, which was less than the estimate. Expenditure was also down at £132,277. with a projected actual deficit of £8,823 despite an English Sports Council Grant of £11,750.

AREA	1997/98	1996/97	1995/96	1994/95	1993/94*	1992/93	1991/92
Midland CCA			£3,743.55	£3,339.35	£2,444.75	£1,346.50	£895.50
East Midlands CCA	£2,462.00	£3,029.10					
West Midland CCA	£1,245.00	£1,321.45					
North Western CCA	£1,395.00	£1,283.65	£1,104.15	£1,268.20	£1,595.00	£1,203.00	£999.50
Wessex CCA	£930.60	£850.00	£852.55	£850.85	£1,020.00	£721.00	£729.50
South Western CCA	£443.00	£395.00	£357.85	£357.00	£615.40	£294.50	£390.00
London CCA	£925.20	£1,115.70	£1,364.35	£2,348.95	£1,152.60	£1,134.50	£1,253.50
North Eastern CCA	£908.00	£797.30	£683.40	£480.25	£434.35	£226.00	£227.50
Yorkshire CCA	£1,271.00	£1,394.90	£1,165.80	£1,074.40	£1,496.00	£752.00	£785.00
Eastern CCA	£1,110.00	£879.00	£579.70	£684.25	£584.80	£400.50	£447.00
Welsh CCA	£254.50	£461.50	£807.25	£694.20	£555.10	£447.00	£388.50
Lincolnshire CCA	£1,017.00	£1,121.85	£799.85	£808.35	£704.65	£350.50	£346.50
Other (SCU)	£105.00						
TOTAL	£12,066.30	£12,649.45	£11,458.45	£11,905.80	£10,602.65	£6,875.50	£6,462.50

*Increase in levy rate

ADMINSTRATION ANALYSIS 1997/98

	Telephone	Postage	Printing	Stationery	TOTAL
Members' Services	£423.56	£468.96	£333.25	£113.15	£1,338.92
National Programme	£280.71	£948.72		£103.74	£1,333.17
Coaching & Competition	£1,242.33	£536.29	£73.17	£130.17	£1,981.96
Development	£185.39	£426.55	£1,328.70	£106.46	£2,047.10
TOTAL	£2,131.99	£2,380.52	£1,735.12	£453.52	£6,701.15

Season 1998/99

There was a new smart design for the handbook with two colour photographs on the cover, one of Tim Morley the 1998 National Junior Champion and the other of Nick Craig the National Senior Champion. The price was now £3.50 and the number of pages 160. The six National Officers remained the same. A whole page is taken up with a picture of a comic Viking character riding a bike under the slogan 'Cross is Cool' and on the opposite page is listed the outline of the 'Impruve Initiative' under the headline "Investing in the future: Attracting young people to cycle sport." The first paragraph outlines the aims of the scheme and looks to the future. "It is evident that there are hundreds of thousands of young people who own bicycles but are either unaware of, or not attracted to, organised cycle sport. Their priority is to have fun on their bike rather than tackle the rigours of a specific cycling discipline. The B.C-C.A's pilot 'Skills Award' recognised this by offering a series of non-competitive challenges which are both fun and encourage the development of riding skills." This scheme was certainly forward looking and a very ambitious idea for the Association to take on.

Gordon Macdonald, the editor of the Wessex Newsletter, expressed a desire to step down from that post and as the Wessex C-C.A Treasurer, as he had been in the post since 1975. He was yet another example of the long serving unpaid officials who had given service to the B.C-C.A through their local Associations.

During September Carl Buckle (Ace R.T) was busy winning the Sleaford Wheelers Cross by drawing away on the fourth lap from Carl Thompson (Elmy Cycles) and Matt Buckingham (Race Scene), and in the same month Ian Taylor (CS Pendle) was the victor in the Bronte Wheelers event held at Oakbank School, Keighley. There were lots of cross training sessions planned for October. In Yorkshire there was the 'training and skills' coaching session at East End Park, Leeds with two more floodlit training sessions, one at the St. Andrews Rugby Club, Rugby, led by National Coach Martin Eadon, which had a note that mtbs were welcome. The second held at Glenburn High School, Skemmersdale run by Ray Pugh, who also welcomed mountain bike riders.

Two established 'Scrambles' were still drawing the riders during this period, the Silcoates Scramble was going strong after 10 years, where Chris Young (Marie Curie-Pace Satellite T.V) triumphed again as he had in the very first race of the series. Young did not have it all his own way, for he was challenged strongly by Paul Dixon of the Race Scene team who finished in second place. In the 25th edition of the Mildenhall Riverside Scramble it was the early season dominator of Eastern C.C A. events, Greg Simcock (Elmy Cycles) who held off the challenge of Nick Ainsworth of the local Newmarket & D.C.C.

"Belgian raiders thwart Brits" was the way *Cycling Weekly* heralded its report of the Nottinghamshire International race where Belgian rider Peter van den Abeele won by almost two minutes from Barrie Clarke, the Raleigh professional. Close behind in third spot was another Belgian, the former world champion, 38 year old Danny De Bie. Three British riders vied for the fourth place, Steve Knight, Stuart Blunt and Tim Gould but in the final sort-out it was Knight who took fourth to retain some pride for the home based riders. Van den Abeele said afterwards, "I was third here last year, so today was my first win in Britain."

The London Open Cyclo-cross Championships saw the on-form Stuart Blunt (Ace R.T) take the title convincingly. Blunt had also won the Kent

R.C. event only 24 hours earlier but this did not slow him, as he won the championship jersey by almost a minute from George Richardson of Team Sabre.

Exactly 100 riders started round 11 of the Notts & Derby League series, held on a course at Bramcote Park, Nottingham promoted by the Beeston R.C. With Tim Gould racing for almost the last time in his Schwinn/Toyota team colours, he drew away each lap from his chief rival Carl Sturgeon (Team Raleigh) to win by 38 seconds at the flag. In the women's event Sharon Chamberlain (Ashfield R.C) was triumphant.

This year there were several festive names used by promoters, some of which were the: 'BJW Canford Cracker', the Christmas Fancy Dress Cross, the Coventry R.C. Boxing Day Cross and the Mossley Christmas Cross. Also over the Christmas period there was the 21st running of The Circuit of the Moor held on the Brickyard Farm course, promoted by the Matlock C.C. on the Bank Holiday Monday, which saw the unattached rider George Richardson take an impressive win.

Over this period the standard of race programmes was continually rising, all the National Trophy and National Championship programmes were being printed with full colour covers. Others, such as the Royal Bank of Scotland Supacross had twenty-eight pages packed with information, riders' photographs, a course map and adverts. Most were being produced by hard working unpaid club officials giving up their own time to give events an air of class.

Some excellent photographs of the race action on the icy course at the National Championships in Sutton Park, Birmingham were produced this year. Steve Knight was seen held aloft by his supporters after winning the Senior crown, from Nick Craig and Barrie Clarke. It was a case of a local hero takes the spoils, after a bronze and silver, he was now entitled to wear the white jersey with the red and blue bands. Although Craig took command early on, it was a ding-dong battle between him and Knight until the last lap, when 32 year old Knight attacked to take the win.

David Bowater of Black Country Wheelers romped away with the Espoirs title race to win by 30 seconds from Paul Oldham (Hope Technology), the battle for the bronze being fierce until Gavin Hardwicke of the Beauvale C.C. rode clear of Daniel Booth of the Belgium club Sportgroep Koksijde.

Shaun Snodden, the pre-race favourite, proved his supporters to be right, when he took the Junior Title by almost a minute from Ben Saunders (Hargroves Cycles) and Paul Lally who was riding for the unusually named KHS/AXO team. Snodden described his mid- race mishap to *Cycling Weekly*: "I was doing about 20 mph (when he crashed) and went down really hard, hurting my knee ... I think there were a few people who didn't expect me to get up."

Martin Booth (Black Country Wheelers) successfully defended his veteran's crown with what *Cycling Weekly* described as "a powerful display on a demanding course at Aldersley Leisure Village, Wolverhampton." All season Booth had been dominant in Vet's races so this win was no surprise. At the start, the massive bunch of 117 riders launched themselves off in the quest for the medals. In the final crossing of the line, the lap scorers recorded the experienced past champion Les Lloyd (Didcot Phoenix) coming in to take the silver medal, with first year veteran Mick Daley (V.C Lincoln) taking the bronze.

The women's race saw Isla Rowntree become the star, this lady had done a medal-winning ride in every women's championship since they were created. But this time it was the gold medal that finally hung around her neck as she stood on the podium. Beside her was her team mate at Team Raleigh, Louise Robinson with the silver medal and bronze winner Lindsay Clarke of the Keyprint team. Rowntree's ride had been far from smooth, as she said when speaking to the press afterwards: "I was in panic when my tub rolled off. I started to run, then someone shouted and told me I would be better off riding and losing less time." She only caught Robinson with 500 yards to go, but with a big effort she overtook to win by just 3 seconds.

The Youth Championships produced another exciting sprint, with Philip Spencer (Matlock C.C/Wards Shoes) just getting the edge by one second to take the title from Chris Skinner (V.C Norwich).The bronze medal being won by Robert Upex (Team Manchester). The event had a rather bizarre start when the starter's gun went off accidentally a full three minutes early, this left some riders still in track suits as the main field shot off. The top girl (who arrived in seventh place) was Nicole Cooke riding for Peugeot 406/ Michelin, collecting her third title in this age group. Afterwards she spoke of her troubles at the start to *Cycling Weekly*, which made her ride even more remarkable: "I still had two tops on when the gun went off ... One caught in my front wheel and I was last away from the start ... I overtook 40 riders during the first lap."

Near arctic conditions prevailed during the World Championships held at Poprad, Slovakia, with temperatures down to minus 12°. In the Elite event Mario De Clercq retained his Rainbow Jersey with a last lap attack which left his team mate Erwin Vervecken in the silver place for the second year running, and Holland's Adri van der Poel had to be content with the bronze. *Cycling Weekly* described the efforts of the G.B riders as "Meanwhile Britain had a weekend to forget ... Unlike most of the British team, Knight was able to stay upright on the icy, rutted course with its awkwardly cambered bends ... Barrie Clarke could only remember riding in such severe conditions once before, in Czechoslovakia 12 years ago ... The difference this time was that we were better prepared, with thicker skinsuits, headbands, gloves and other means of keeping warm." Steve Knight did gain some pride by finishing 21st in the Elite race and Clarke punctured on the second lap but his final placing is not recorded in reports.

The hot favourite for the Espoirs race was the Belgian Bart Wellens, and he did not let his supporters down, as he won the title by over one and a half minutes from his team mate Tom Vannoppen. The next man in was delighted, as he was the first U.S.A rider to gain a World cyclo-cross medal, Tom Johnson had been with a small group of U.S riders living in Europe out of their own funds. The only G.B rider listed as finishing was Tim Morley; David Bowater, Phil Dixon and Gavin Hardwicke all being pulled out after being lapped.

The U.S.A seemed to have picked this championships to emerge into the limelight of World cross, when Matt Kelly powered ahead of Sven Vanthourenhout to take the Junior title race. Holland's Thijs Verhagen took the third spot, but the British finished much further down the list this time. British Junior Champion, Snodden "looked tentative from the start" said *Cycling Weekly*. Ben Saunders was to give his team helpers a worrying moment when he crashed heavily within sight of the pits. The final positions being P.Lally 46th, Snodden 47th (after his chain snapped on the last lap), R. Bowater 57th and then D. Cox. It seems the U.S.A had learned how to move forward but Britain had slipped back. Although Shaun Snodden explained afterwards, " I really suffered with the cold."

Ian Small produced yet another fine edition of the N.W.C.C.A Annual including the usual pages of photographs of riders and results, plus interesting articles by Jim Court (their Chairman) and Neil Orrell. In Jim's article "Should Courses be Faster?" he gave an insight into the thoughts that some officials were having for the coming season: "The controversial debate on what constitutes a good cyclo-cross course, I believe that the course is a major factor in determining whether an event is successful or not … International Cyclo-cross has changed dramatically over the last few years with races becoming faster – almost off-road criteriums." He goes on to say that such courses in this country are rare and that those hoping for success at World Championship level must race abroad to sharpen their speed. "Also, I can promise you that the National Championships for all categories, to be held at Ipswich next year, will be quick – no, very quick – and any one without basic speed will be suffering." He closed his case for faster courses by saying: "Perhaps we should seek out new fast training courses."

The Agenda for the A.G.M held on Saturday 6th March at Park Farmhouse Hotel, Isley Walton, included the report by Jim Court. "Last year I urged greater co-operation with the BCF in order to further the sport … I can assure you that a great deal of progress has actually been made. The Executive decided against full integration at this time, mainly because we were still some way away from agreement on the key issues of membership and fees."

Then followed a 'Report from the Executive Committee' that included: "There has been much debate in recent months over the ongoing discussions between the British Cyclo-Cross Association and the British Cycling Federation, and understandable concern over where this process is leading. Not all such debate has been well-informed, and the purpose of this report is to clarify the situation to date and to outline proposed future action … To address these issues (joining all the differences) we sought discussions with the BCF, and it should be emphasised that the approach was made by the BC-CA and has never at any time led to a situation where the BCF has sought to 'take over' the BC-CA , as some have surmised." This was a closely typed three page report of the detailed discussions between the two bodies and ends with "Our more immediate decision, however, is a simple business one. We need to continue our dialogue in order to maintain the investment which cyclo-cross currently enjoys, and to seek ways of finding future investment which will allow cyclo-cross to achieve the real potential which I am sure that all who love and work for the sport feel that it deserves."

24

Louise Robinson wins a World silver, The Three Peaks reaches 40 and transition lies ahead

Season 1999/00

September saw many letters and e-mails travelling backwards and forwards between the B.C-C.A and the B.C.F. Some were very strongly worded but the B.C-C.A felt there so was much at stake that they could lose out if they did not get the negotiations right.

New plans to improve the standard of events throughout the country were addressed in issue number one of Cross Communiqué. It was sent out during October, with Colin Clews stating in his editorial: "This is believed to be the first such newsletter produced for cyclo-cross commissaires ... the purpose has been to seek to ensure consistency of application of the regulations for competitors, and to raise standards generally within our premier events."

Green was the main colour for this year's edition of the handbook and after holding the price steady for several years, a new copy this year would now cost £4.00. Previously we noted the number of banned substances had increased and the rules governing them. This year the rules now covered ten and a half pages and the banned substances and methods were listed in five categories – Stimulants, Narcotics, Anabolic Agents, Diuretics and Peptide Hormones. The next seven pages then lists nearly 150 banned items including many detailed explanations about banned practices, although cyclo-cross was not being swamped by the scandals and whispers affecting road racers.

The President Mrs Joan Edwards and Chairman Jim Court now headed the 'Executive Committee'. These are then followed by six 'Members' - Martin Booth, Keith Edwards, Harry Gould, Steve Grimwood, Clive Tiley and Tony Wilkins. Meanwhile Steve Douce had stepped down from National Office, leaving the Management Committee for Coaching & Competition as Harry Gould (Chairman) with Martin Eadon, Bob Hayward and Geoff Shergold.

A feeling of how far apart the two bodies, B.C-C.A. and B.C.F, were at this point can be gauged by the wording in a e-mail from Peter King: I have a strong feeling that we will never reach a point at which cyclo-cross can come under the umbrella of the BCF until we ask BC-CA to write the terms and conditions. The content of your e-mail, including comments about openness and implied criticism of much of what we do and the way that we do it, leave me in little doubt about that.

It is not, of course, surprising that those who have been used to a 'free affiliation' sport and have only recently accepted grudgingly a £5 fee should be resistant to paying £10. Unfortunately those at UKS (UK Sport) and ES who have, in the past, been prepared to fund the administration of BC-CA to permit it to subsidise the free/cheap 'sport for all' philosophy are not prepared to do the same for the BCF ... The BC-CA framework cannot 'slot in under the BCF umbrella' without changes ... We are clearly fundamentally at odds over Coach Education, the BCF will definitely NOT support any initiative which trains and supports coaches.

An Executive member's comment to this letter was: "It appears that Mr. King/BCF are no longer on the same planet as the rest of us." It appears that the two bodies were still very far apart, but during this period of intense negotiations by cycle sport officials, racing throughout the country was going on as usual with many riders completely oblivious to all the hard work being done on their behalf.

The last weekend of the old year saw several sporting events cancelled due to snow but many cyclo-crosses still went ahead. With those that were held, the wins were spread across many riders, Carl Sturgeon (Team Raleigh) winning the 12th round in the Notts & Derby CX League event, racing in the colours of the new Midlands Area champion. Another champion, this time the National Junior Shaun Snodden, was busy winning on the Boggart Hole course in North Manchester, in the Mossley CRT promoted race. Meanwhile the Shaftesbury C.C's cross, held at the Thriftwood Scout Camp, Brentwood, saw Greg Simcock of Elmy Cycles taking the victory from his team mate Carl Thompson.

The next weekend the weather was even worse and riders were battling through five inches of snow and over sheet ice in the Abergavenny Cross held at Great Betws Farm. The race time had to be shortened because of the severe conditions, with George Richardson (Cycles Clements) clear by two minutes from junior Rayan Bevis (Builth) Nicole Cooke not only won the women's race but came fifth with her brother Craig being the top Youth.

On the 6th January, Keith Edwards circulated a letter, entitled "Future of Cyclo-Cross Sport in this Country" which is in the archives:

I think I can justifiably claim to be the person who initiated the formation of the British Cyclo-Cross Association nearly 50 years ago. [He then went on to outline the path he took to bring cyclo-cross to this country, much of which we have covered within earlier pages.]

The need for an overall governing body for cycling has been apparent for many years. I enclose copies of two letters, one twenty years old, one ten, showing efforts made by the B.C-C.A and my club to bring this about.

In 1989 my wife (BCCA Secretary at the time) and I were invited to the BCF head office in Kettering to discuss the formation of a governing body for mountain-bike racing .On our arrival we found other organisations represented – some small, some non-competitive – plus a Sports Council representative ... Our proposal fell on deaf ears as we were later informed that the Sports Council and the BCF had decided to form a separate governing body.

That body experienced several changes of name before finally merging with the BCF ... We have promoted three World Championships – 1973,1983 and 1992, and but for the problems of the BCF in recent years would most likely to have had the 2001 promotion ... May I urge all those concerned to give serious consideration to the proposals to be put forward by the BC-CA Executive Committee, in order to ensure that the future of this discipline of cycle sport, which caters for all ages, is safeguarded.

Yours sincerely,
Keith Edwards

A powerful letter in favour of the amalgamation of the two bodies.

"Hammond's Suffolk Punch" was the headline over a picture of a smiling Roger Hammond crossing the finish line at the National Championships, punching the air in delight. The *Cycling Weekly* report went on: "Seven national championships packed into two hectic days produced some high-speed racing and closely contested finishes in the British Cyclo-Cross Association's title meeting at Ipswich over the weekend ... The meeting – based on heathland and wooded tracks surrounding Foxhall Speedway Stadium – proved a champions' graveyard. With new title holders crowned in every category." The thought of seven championships being won and lost during one weekend must seem amazing to all the old timers.

Hammond turned the clock back six years when he crossed the line wearing his Collstrop jersey 36 seconds clear of Barrie Clarke (Team Raleigh) and Carl Sturgeon (Lutterworth C.C.) He would then swap that trade jersey for the Senior Championship one. Afterwards Hammond told *Cycling Weekly*: "It's always good to have a championship jersey, but the real bonus is the 100 U.C.I points that go with it ... They'll put me into the first three or four rows of the grid in the World Championship, which is always important. I've been starting World Cups six or seven rows back and had to spend half the race battling to get forward."

Only 56 competitors started out of an entry of 76, the smallest field for an Open Senior championship for many years. The winning team for the second year running was the local team of Elmy Cycles, Greg Simcock, Russell Parkins and new-comer Dean Barnett.

Three riders contributed to a thrilling U 23 race, Tim Morley of Team Corridor/Specialized, who took the victor's laurels by the least possible margin from Daniel Booth (Sportgroep Koksijde) and the third of the trio Phil Dixon riding for Peugeot 406/Michelin. Morley was out of the blocks the fastest and soon gained 20 seconds. Booth described his last minute thoughts to *Cycling Weekly*'s Martin Ayres: "I knew from my road racing I was probably the strongest sprinter ... Now I'm looking for a top 20 place at the World's."

Louise Robinson riding for the Stourbridge C.C was just too strong and fast for the up and coming young multi-champion Nicole Cooke, winning by over 3 minutes. It looked as if Susan Clarke (Letchworth Schils) was set for the bronze medal until she tumbled on an icy corner, then the excitement increased as Diane Moss passed by, only for the fallen Clarke to chase back, pass Moss and claim the medal. Robinson summed up her win with "To be honest my main objective is the Olympics and that's what I'm training for."

The result of the Junior race gave Liam Killeen (Team Y2K) the gold medal, from Matthew Kipling (Merlin Cycles), followed home by Philip Spencer of the Matlock C.C. Killeen said afterwards: "This is the first one I've prepared for properly." Killeen wasn't sure about riding the World's by stating: "I want to concentrate on mountain biking."

When it came to the Veteran's race, it was Peter Stevenson based in Belgium who travelled home to take the spoils. Stevenson riding for Middridge C.R.T. added this title to the national title he won in 1992. He blew the race apart after only 10 minutes leaving a 'flu hit Martin Eadon (Ace R.T) in his wake. The final result showing that Andrew MacDonald of G.A Cycles team had gained the bronze medal. Vic Barnett (Welland Valley Wheelers) became the over-50 champion, with the runner-up Mick Ives (who also took the over-60's prize), the bronze medal going to Chris Gooch of Team-Clean.

The other titles went the way of Les Allen (Team Valley) who took the Youth title. Under 15 years Karl Elliot, Under 14 years Sammy Cotton, Under 13 years Jon Mozley and the Champion Girl Nikki Harris. *Cycling Weekly* reported: "Riders praised the 2.6 kilometre course, which featured flat terrain enlivened by three sets of hurdles, 500 metres of surfaced roadway and a short run-up."

Looking at the programme for the National Championships, it is interesting to see how many competitors were taking part and the prize values. On the Saturday morning there were 35 Veterans over 50 who were competing for a top prize of £50, with the 'Master', 'Grand Master' and Super Veterans racing for £10 prizes each. Later there were 51 Youths lined up, with the winner gaining £50, plus first girl £15, 1st under 14 £15 and the 1st under 14 Girl £10. Saturday afternoon saw 52 riders battling for the Veterans championships where £100 was on offer. Then the Under 23 men where 28 were competing for the £100 prize money.

At 11a.m. on the Sunday it was the Women's race, where 27 ladies lined up for a £60 first prize. Next came the 20 Junior men vying for £60. The last race of this championship weekend was the Senior Men's event with 76 riders lined up for the £500 on offer. Each champion also took home one of the coveted white jerseys with the blue and red bands, a medal and a trophy.

Eight years had passed since Britain won a medal at the World Championships. This year Louise Robinson returned Britain to the podium and would bring back a silver medal across the channel from St. Michelsgestel in Holland. Robinson took second place after the German road star Hanka Kupfernagel had taken the rainbow jersey 57 seconds clear of all rivals, and in third spot came Daphny Van den Brand of the home country. Two items of history were made with this result, firstly, the German became the winner of this inaugural running of a Women's World Championship, then Robinson herself set a new mark by becoming the first daughter of a Tour de France stage winner to win a cyclo-cross world medal. Forty women lined up for the first edition of their title race and Britain was left with great hopes for the future when 16 year old Nicole Cooke rode into a fine 18th place after puncturing. Britain was also placed fourth in the team race when Helen Macgregor came in 29th and J.Copnall 31st with the four British women finishing on the same lap as the winner, with Susan Carter at one lap, after her chain wrapped into a tangle, in 36th. Many of the British fans wished the men could gain similar results in their events.

Bart Wellens, the defending world champion led a complete clean sweep of the medals in the Espoirs (under 23) race followed home by his Belgian teammates, Tom Vannoppen, and Davy Commeyne. The British came in further up the result list than the previous year with Phil Dixon in 19th and Tim Morley in 24th after being pushed into the barriers. National Champion Daniel Booth had a good start until he had a tyre roll off resulting in a final placing of 33rd. In 40th came Shaun Snodden and James Perry in 58th. G.B. was placed 6th in the team event.

The Junior race turned out to be a two man battle between Belgium's Bart Aernouts and Walker Ferguson of the U.S.A. Aernouts finally took the victory by 15 seconds, with the Czech David Kasek taking the bronze. The British started from way back in 11th placing on the grid, Liam Killeen had to change bikes due to slipping gears, finally finishing 17th, a commendable ride by a mountain biker new to cyclo-cross. Phil Spencer arrived in 28th, saying afterwards to *Cycling Weekly*: "My front mech. snapped on the way to the start and I hopped on to my spare only to find the left pedal was coming unscrewed." He was followed in by Chris Skinner in 37th, M. Kipling 48th, and R. Bowater 58th.

Once more the Elite race proved a disappointment to the British supporters, but Richard Groenendaal sent the Dutch supporters away delighted, by winning the senior title in style. Taking the lead from the start, lap after lap he extended the gap to add another Rainbow jersey to the Junior one he had won in 1989. Mario De Clercq took the silver medal, followed by his Belgian team mate Sven Nijs who claimed the bronze.

On a day when 15 riders were lapped and eliminated, all three Britons completed the race. Roger Hammond arrived in 17th.place, having given his supporters hope early on, when as he told *Cycling Weekly*: "I felt great, I had a good start and sat on the back of the group." Then he got stuck in a muddy patch and hit the ground, when he remounted he had lost contact with the fast moving leaders, finishing a deeply disappointed rider. Matt Ellis sprinted in with a group to take 31st saying afterwards: "I snapped my STI (brake/gear lever) and lost about 10 places." Stuart Blunt completed the trio of Brits by coming in 39th.

The Association continued to join together for talks with the B.C.F, Road Time Trials Council, Scottish Cyclists' Union, Welsh Cycling Union and the Road Records Association to agree Anti-Doping & Ethics Policy. This year they would add Child Protection in their deliberations for obvious reasons.

There was a strong plea for someone to come forward as the new secretary, in the April edition of the Wessex Newsletter: "Geoff Greenfield our long serving Secretary is looking to retire and we require a replacement and it will be a hard act to follow, but this post needs to be filled." Research shows he became Wessex Secretary in the 1974/75 season, making it an amazing 26 seasons of service, and he was their Treasurer before that.

Season 2000/01
After hundreds of hours of discussion a final agreement was made on 29th July 2000 between the Association and the Federation. This agreement outlined the "Constitution & Management, Membership & Licences, Regional Administration, Finance and General Provisions."

This important change for the B.C-C.A was signed:
On behalf of the B.C-C.A.   On behalf of the BCF:
Mrs J.Edwards (President)   B Cookson (President)
J. Court (Chairman)   R.E Howden (Vice Chairman)
D. Bradbury (Treasurer)

So we come to the final look at the annual handbook, its shape has remained almost the same throughout the life of the Association. It is entirely appropriate that this one should be the largest yet at 168 pages. Every page was packed full of information, with110 events listed and everything anyone might need to know about how to compete in cyclo-cross. It was also interspersed with 10 photographs, showing most of the Association Champions and Series winners. The final list of the Executive Committee, Officers, Officials, Trustees and Auditors is littered with the names of those who had put in dozens of years service for the sport they love, from the President Mrs Joan Edwards downwards. The final list of Life Members also reflected the number of committed people involved, J.Atkins, R.F.Atkins, J.Court, I.Dodd, Mrs.J.Edwards, H.Gould, G.Greenfield, T.Haigh, P.Milsom, J. Rawnsley and Mrs B. Richards. Some other observations on this handbook are the number of events listed for Under 9s, Under 10s, Novice Women, Youth/Women. All categories not even dreamt of at the creation of the Association. Riders were racing longer and longer into their dotage, with the creation of the Super Veteran class a few years ago.

The front cover had a new heading, the 'British Cyclo-Cross Handbook', reflecting the new change of name. Also on the cover were colour pictures of Roger Hammond, Lee Allen and Louise Robinson. Readers turning to the first page might be surprised to see that for the first time in many years there was a 'Chairman's Introduction.' As this is an important year in the life and closure of the Association we repeat the full text here:

Chairman's Introduction

The year 2000 marks another milestone in the history of cyclo-cross in Britain. Nearly 50 years after the formation of the British Cyclo-Cross Association, the Annual General Meeting took the decision to work in the future within the framework of the British Cycling Federation.

As a first step, we have adopted the brand name of 'British Cyclo-Cross' for the coming season. By the time the season commences the integration should be well under way with the BCCA budget incorporated into that of the BCF. However, the operation of cyclo-cross events will, on the whole, remain unaltered for the current season with fees remaining unchanged. Looking to the future though, any club or team already affiliated to the BCF, or rider who is already a BCF member, will actually pay less for their racing from next season. In addition, all BCF clubs will be entitled to compete in cyclo-cross.

On the elite front, we are staging five rounds of the National Trophy this season, all of which will be eligible for UCI Ranking points.

We now look forward to a bright future, using the opportunities available to us as part of the 'British Cycling' family. But, one thing of which you can be certain, cyclo-cross will continue to be run by cyclo-cross enthusiasts for cyclo-cross riders.

Jim Court

Chairman, British Cyclo-Cross Association

The first of October 2000 was a momentous day for all those who had been involved in any way with the Three Peaks race, as with this event it reached its 40th edition. The programme was full of atmospheric photographs and portraits from the early days of the race until the present day, including one of each winner.

It may seem ironic that the 40th anniversary edition of this famous event should once more be won by an international fell runner who took to cyclo-cross. Rob Jebb (Ronhill RT) had been threatening to take the victory for seven years and today he stood on the top spot on the podium. Nine past winners were amongst the 271 riders (a record number) who lined up for this classic promotion by the Bradford Racing C.C on a glorious day of sunshine after the early mist had disappeared. Tim Gould (RATS) finished second at 4¼ minutes, then it was debut rider Ian Wilkinson (Team Y2K) who managed to outride many experienced Three Peaks riders to take the third placing. Afterwards *Cycling Weekly* gained this reaction from Tim Gould: "I couldn't keep up with Robert on the running sections ... My preparation has been hampered by a leg injury."

Organiser John Rawnsley had won the very first race and amazingly had completed every race since. Kevin Watson, the first rider ever to complete the course, had the honour of presenting the prizes to the winners, most of whom had not been born when he did his ground breaking epic ride. He admitted to still riding a few events on the road when he could manage time off from being a Doctor. In this anniversary event there were no fewer than six awards for veterans, an idea not envisaged 40 years ago. The classes being Veterans, Senior, Grand, Master, Grand Master and Super Veteran. The fastest Woman was Sue Thomas (Scott UK) with the Women's Vet being Ann Hobbis of the organising club.

The first win in the National Trophy Series went to Stuart Blunt (Team Corridori/Specialized) He gained the maximum points in this series, now expanded to five races, leaving his closest rival Matt Spencer before halfway. The Junior was last year's defending winner Phil Spencer (Elmy Cycles) and the Women's winner Louise Robinson led from start to finish to take the victory. When they had all got their breath back, *Cycling Weekly* gained these views, Blunt saying "I'm well chuffed with that ... I'd been telling all my mates I was to win, so it's a relief that I have." Robinson commentated: "That makes up for last year." and Spencer said "I was going alright today, but I'll have to see how the series fits in."

November saw the Yorkshire C.C.A points series promoted by the Drighlington B.C at Birstall in West Yorkshire. Training was taking a step up this month, with reports of good sessions taking place at Basildon in Essex, where the Eastern Counties League organiser Steve Gregson reported many new riders taking part. New events were also being promoted by such as the Brecon Wheelers, who staged a race on a new course at the Brecon Leisure Centre. The Midlands series leader Darren Atkins of MI Racing /Peugeot 406, (son of the former multi-champion) proved the strongest yet again by winning the Black Country Wheelers event at Oldbury.

The Collstrop professional, Roger Hammond returned to these shores once more during December to take the lead in the National Trophy Series, with a win in the city where he won his Junior World Championship jersey nine years before. Chris Young of Team Marie Curie, at ten years older, took second place with J.Bryan (Ace RT) coming in for third. By winning the junior event Chris Skinner took over the yellow jersey from his team mate in the Elmy Cycles team, Phil Spencer. Louise Robinson scored her third win out of four in the series with the help of her famous father working hard in the pits. Just before Christmas the North Eastern C.C.A League saw Carl Sturgeon (Ace RT) win the last round of the year in what *Cycling Weekly* described as "an awesome display of cross skills to win."

The capacity for promoters to think up zany names for events over the Christmas/New Year period remained unabated. There was the 'Crow Christmas Cross' promoted by the New Forest C.C , the 'Southall Xmas Shopping & Curry Cross', (which sounds like hot stuff) at the Hillingdon Cycle Circuit. The Yorkshire C.C.A. was promoting the 'Christmas Fancy Dress Cross' and on Boxing Day there was the 'Fun Team Relay Cross' promoted by the Middridge CRT near Houghton-le-Spring. For those who had a better than expected holiday there was the 'Hangover Cross' promoted by the Coalville Wheelers at the 'Travellers Rest' at Griffydam in Leicestershire. Boxing Day saw 60 riders lining up for the guaranteed £400 prize list, plus primes every lap, on offer in the Coventry R.C handicap. The organisers claiming that this was the longest established event still run on the same course.

After Christmas it was Louise Robinson who grabbed the headlines by finishing second in the World Cup event held at Zeddam in Holland. The race started on an uphill section, but unfortunately Robinson just could not get out of the pack. The course was very hard and included a stretch of 104 steps to run up, although it was here where she overtook many riders to finally finish with only Daphny van den Brand ahead of her. "I'm pleased with second, but I was disappointed with my start ... I've beaten Daphny this season ... We raced for five days over Christmas in Belgium – so we could have given the crowd a really good race."

Six championship titles changed hands on the famous course at Sutton Park, but one rider Roger Hammond, did retain his senior title. Hammond won the gold medal by just 13 seconds from Steve Knight of MI Racing, with the bronze medal going to Matt Ellis of Sett Valley Cycles. Sickness had hit Hammond the week before and afterwards he cast doubts on riding the World Championships at Tabor in the Czech Republic, when speaking to Martin Ayres of *Cycling Weekly*: "It's a long way to go if I'm not going to perform at my best, so why should I take the place of somebody who can perform well there?"

"Cooke roasts the seniors" was the heading over the Women's title race report. The race ended in a dramatic finish, it was a two woman race from early on, although the drama started on the second lap when Louise Robinson crashed in the quarry. She was up quickly and onto Nicole Cooke's wheel, then Robinson's gear lever jammed but she was not about to give up. She closed metre by metre until at the line the World Junior road racing champion, riding for Cardiff Ajax, just held off the advancing Robinson (Stourbridge C.C) by a mere 4 seconds, with the bronze medal going to Sue Thomas of the Team Y2K team. So Cooke became at 17 years the youngest ever winner of the Women's title.

Last year's Junior Champion Liam Killeen, upped his game so much that he ran away with the Under 23 title. Tim Morley also moved up, by taking the silver medal after his bronze last year although still suffering with a back sprain and had been a doubtful starter. Shaun Snodden of the Ace RT arriving at chequered flag at just over 1½ minutes for the bronze medal. The under 16s title went to Sammy Cotton of Team GT, and Martin Booth of Ace RT-Alan won the Veteran's title for the third time. In the Over 50s race it was Chris Gooch of Team Clean who took the victory.

With the end of this event another career came to a close, for Keith Edwards retired as a race organiser. *Cycling Weekly* covered his retirement thus: "Fond Farewell to Edwards" it also described how Edwards and his wife Joan had been deeply involved with the sport and the formation of the Association back in 1954. *Cycling Weekly* also covered the last event of the championships: "At the end of Sunday's racing. Edwards was persuaded to take top spot on the podium and receive the gift of a GB team-issue fleece jacket from newly crowned champion Roger Hammond."

Tabor in the Czech Republic was the site of the World Championships this year, with snow and sub-zero temperatures. The Czech's made it clear that they were not only up to the task of organising but also winning, by making a clean sweep in the Junior event, claiming two medals in the Espoirs race and a silver in the Elite race.

Louise Robinson confirmed her claim to being Britain's top cyclo-cross rider on the world stage, with a sixth placing behind Hanka Kupfernagel of Germany, who seemed little hampered by the arctic conditions. Robinson started on the second row of the grid with Nicole Cooke, as National champion, taking the front row spot. Robinson saying: "Two girls cut across me at the start, and that was it." Cooke who finished 7th said, "I was comfortably ahead of Louise, but then on the run-up I just couldn't get a grip at all." Isla Rowntree claimed 15th place and Sue Thomas 20th, altogether a very good result by the ladies.

Sunday saw the snow melt in the higher temperatures and the Czechs took full advantage by taking all three medals. The British coming in with P.Spencer 35th, J.Aveyard 36th, C.Cooke 55th, and M.Russell 61st. Ewin Vervecken took the Elite crown for Belgium, from Peter Dlask at one second. Britain's Matt Ellis took 16th, Stuart Blunt, 34th and Steve Knight 36th. Roger Hammond had to retire after a crash, when a Czech rider took the wrong line, bringing Hammond down, then he had other problems with his shoe.

After the Elite race, Team Manager Martin Eadon told *Cycling Weekly*: "Roger (Hammond) broke something, Matt (Ellis) snapped his chain, Dave Collins rolled a tub, Steve Knight had a puncture. The mechanics were fantastic, they were really under pressure … The whole thing's been very good. Obviously we're disappointed not to get a medal, but it's probably overall the best team performance we've ever had." He also carried on to say , "we're funded through the B.C.F If we were to become a Winter Olympic sport who knows what would happen."

In the Espoirs race, won by Sven Vanthourenhout, *Cycling Weekly*'s report did not even mention the British riders, although Tim Morley did finish 42nd, P.Dixon 46th and S.Snoddon in 49th.

Perhaps now is a good time to record a list of the last officials still organising the local Area Associations, continuing to work hard in the background keeping local cyclo-cross running smoothly year in year out.

Eastern C.C.A.:	Secretary Ian Poole.
	Treasurer Neil Pears (who was recorded as being the Treasurer of the old Eastern C. C. League back in the 1971/72)
Lincolnshire C.C.A.:	Secretary / Treasurer Joe Vaughan
London C.C.A.:	Secretary Paul Tunnell.
	Treasurer Kristin Durant
East Midlands:	Secretary Vacant c/o Tony Wilkins
	Treasurer Julian Gould
West Midlands:	Secretary Mrs Kim Burgess
	Treasurer Gordon Siers
North Eastern C.C.A.:	Secretary Graham Bell
	Treasurer Jim Sunley
North Western C.C.A.:	Secretary Gina Upex
	Treasurer Ian Small
South Western C.C.A.:	Secretary Clive Tiley
	Treasurer Kit Bohin
Wessex C.C.A.:	Secretary Geoff Greenfield (first record -ed as treasurer of the Wessex C.C.A. in 1967/68, what an amazing record!)
	Treasurer Ian MacDonald
Yorkshire C.C.A.:	Secretary Mark Gill
	Treasurer Richard Lebeter

At this time there were also sixty-six Senior Coaches and five Honorary Coaches. Doping was still a growing problem throughout cycle racing and this was reflected in the coverage in this last handbook, which included sixteen pages of regulations and banned substances. Although the title on the cover of the handbook was 'British Cyclo-Cross', the A.G.M held on the 9th March 2001, at the Kegworth Hotel in Leicestershire was still listed as 'British Cyclo-Cross Association Annual General Meeting'.

The very last events recorded in this handbook were:
Tuesdays 15th, 29th MAY and 12th, 26th June,
Bristol Springs/Summer Series

These events were for most categories, Under 12s, Youth, Sen/Jun/Vet and Women

The entry fees were, Under 12s Free, Youths £2.50 and the rest £6.50

This last promotion shows how the list of categories had expanded over the past 47 seasons. If those pioneers had looked at just this one promotion, it would demonstrate how the sport now stretched far into the summer.

With this last entry the British Cyclo-Cross Association finally ceased to exist in name, although the majority of officials continued to put their brains and their backs into the task of getting on with running the sport of cyclo-cross. This change of name did not mean that they would stop doing their very best for the competitors.

The final list of Trustees in the handbook is shown as D. Bradbury, J. Court and Mrs.J.Edwards. Others would come forward under Chairman Jim Court, after the sad death of Joan Edwards, to look after the remaining funds and to look at ways they could remind people about the spirit that was the B.C-C.A.

Perhaps the question to ask now is, how would the sport go from here? Could 'British Cycling' now produce a World Elite cyclo-cross champion, or was the sport in Britain destined to remain on the sidelines? Only time can give an answer, however, one thing is for sure, throughout the coming seasons, come gales, snow, mud or sun, riders of all ages will be out training and riding for glory. With enthusiastic officials giving up their time to make sure that races are run efficiently and with style, presenting the sport in a professional way. Now at last is the time to wish all involved in cyclo-cross, good luck and long may the spirit of being just that little bit different continue, ready to believe what a great sport they have in their hands and to look forward to the future.

Appendices

APPENDIX ONE

Officials

The following lists are as found in the yearly Handbooks. Other officials may have been appointed, co-opted or even removed at different times.

Season	President	General Secretary	Treasurer	International Racing Sec.
1954/55	R. Atkins	no record	no record	no record
1955/56	no record	no record	no record	no record
1956/57	R. Atkins	K. Brock	K. Edwards	A. Emery
1957/58	no record	no record	no record	no record
1958/59	no post listed	K. Edwards	R. Atkins	no post
1959/60	no post listed	K. Edwards	R. Atkins	P. Hoban
1960/61	no post listed	K. Edwards	R. Atkins	P. Hoban
1961/62	no post listed	K. Edwards	R. Atkins	P. Hoban
1962/63	no post listed	K. Edwards	R. Atkins	P. Hoban
1963/64	no post listed	K. Edwards	R. Atkins	P. Hoban
1964/65	no post listed	K. Edwards	R. Atkins	P. Hoban
1965/66	no post listed	K. Edwards	R. Atkins	M. Dyason
1966/67	K. Edwards	R. Richards	R. Atkins	J. Rawnsley
1967/68	K. Edwards	R. Richards	R. Atkins	N. Billington
1968/69	K. Edwards	R. Richards	R. Atkins	N. Billington
1969/70	K. Edwards	R. Richards	R. Atkins	N. Billington
1970/71	K. Edwards	R. Richards	R. Bull	R. Fowler
1971/72	no post listed	R. Richards	R. Bull	R. Fowler
1972/73	no post listed	R. Richards	R. Bull	R. Fowler
1973/74	no post listed	R. Richards	R. Bull	J. Morris
1974/75	no post listed	R. Richards	R. Bull	J. Morris
1975/76	no post listed	R. Richards	S. Rooker	J. Morris
1976/77	P. Fretwell	R. Richards	S. Rooker	J. Morris

Season	Membership Secretary	Chairman	Handbook Secretary	Press/PRO
1954/55	no record	no record		
1955/56	no record	no record		
1956/57	no record	no record		
1957/58	no record	no record		
1958/59	no record	K. Brock		
1959/60	no record	P. Lovell		
1960/61	no record	P. Lovell		
1961/62	no record	P. Lovell		
1962/63	no record	P. Lovell		
1963/64	G. Ingham	P. Lovell		
1964/65	G. Ingham	P. Lovell		
1965/66	G. Ingham	P. Lovell	R. Hesling	
1966/67	R. Atkins	P. Lovell	R. Hesling	
1967/68	J. Marshman	P. Lovell	K. Bonner	
1968/69	J. Marshman	J. Dickenson	K. Bonner	J. Morris
1969/70	R. Bull	J. Dickenson	J. Marshman	J. Morris
1970/71	R. Bull	J. Dickenson	J. Marshman	R. Ward
1971/72	S. Cauvain	J. Dickenson	I. Dodd	R. Ward
1972/73	S. Cauvain	J. Dickenson	I. Dodd	R. Ward
1973/74	R. Fowler	J. Dickenson	I. Dodd	R. Ward
1974/75	J. Court	J. Dickenson	I. Dodd	R. Ward
1975/76	J. Court	J. Dickenson	I. Dodd	R. Ward
1976/77	J. Court	I. Dodd	R. Ward	Mrs J.Edwards

Season	President	General Secretary	Treasurer	International Racing Sec.
1977/78	P. Fretwell	R. Richards	S. Rooker	J. Morris
1978/79	P. Fretwell	R. Richards	S. Rooker	J. Morris
1979/80	no post listed	R. Richards	S. Rooker	J. Morris
1980/81	B. Thom	R. Richards	S. Rooker	J. Morris
1981/82	B. Thom	R. Richards	S. Rooker	J. Morris
1982/83	B. Thom	R. Richards	Mrs J. Gilbert	J. Morris
1983/84	B. Thom	R. Richards	Mrs J. Gilbert	J. Morris
1984/85	B. Thom	R. Richards	Mrs G. Wreghitt	J. Morris
1985/86	B. Thom	R. Richards	Mrs G. Wreghitt	B. Cossavella
1986/87	B. Thom	R. Richards	Mrs G. Wreghitt	C. Wreghitt
1987/88	B. Thom	Mrs J.Edwards	Mrs G. Wreghitt	C. Wreghitt
1988/89	B. Thom	Mrs J.Edwards	Mrs E. Bewley	C. Wreghitt
1989/90	B. Thom	Mrs J.Edwards	Mrs E. Bewley	C. Wreghitt
1990/91	B. Thom	Mrs J.Edwards	Mrs E. Bewley	
1991/92	B. Thom	Mrs J.Edwards	Mrs E. Bewley	B. Cossavella
1992/93	B. Thom	Mrs J.Edwards	Mrs E. Bewley	B. Cossavella
1993/94	B. Thom	Mrs J.Edwards	Mrs E. Bewley	C. Paton
1994/95	Mrs J.Edwards	B. Furness	D. Bradbury	P. Stevenson
1995/96	Mrs J.Edwards	B. Furness	D. Bradbury	P. Stevenson
1996/97	Mrs J.Edwards	B. Furness	D. Bradbury	P. Stevenson
1997/98	Mrs J.Edwards	B. Furness	D. Bradbury	P. Stevenson
1998/99	Mrs J.Edwards	B. Furness	D. Bradbury	P. Stevenson
1999/00	Mrs J.Edwards	B. Furness	D. Bradbury	no post listed
2000/01	Mrs J.Edwards	B. Furness	D. Bradbury	no post listed

Season	Membership Secretary	Chairman	Handbook Secretary	Press/PRO
1977/78	J. Court	I. Dodd	R. Ward	Mrs J.Edwards
1978/79	J. Court	I. Dodd	R. Ward	Mrs J.Edwards
1979/80	J. Court	I. Dodd	R. Ward	Mrs J.Edwards
1980/81	J. Court	I. Dodd	R. Ward	Mrs J.Edwards
1981/82	J. Court	I. Dodd	R. Ward	Mrs J.Edwards
1982/83	J. Court	I. Dodd	R. Ward	Mrs J.Edwards
1983/84	J. Court	I. Dodd	R. Ward	Mrs J.Edwards
1984/85	J. Court	I. Dodd	R. Ward	Mrs J.Edwards
1985/86	J. Court	I. Dodd	R. Ward	Mrs J.Edwards
1986/87	R. Ward	J. Court	Mrs M. Beagley	Mrs J.Edwards
1987/88	R. Ward	R. Brogan	Mrs M. Beagley	M. Brown
1988/89	R. Ward	R. Brogan	Mrs M. Jewell	K. Edwards
1989/90	R. Ward	R. Brogan	Mrs M. Jewell	K. Edwards
1990/91	J. Court	R. Brogan	Mrs J. Gilbert	K. Edwards
1991/92	J. Court	R. Brogan	Mrs J. Gilbert	
1992/93	J. Court	R. Brogan	Mrs J. Gilbert	B. Furness
1993/94	J. Court	J. Court	Mrs J. Gilbert	B. Furness
1994/95	no post	J. Court	no post	B. Furness
1995/96	no post	J. Court	no post	B. Furness
1996/97	no post	J. Court	no post	B. Furness
1997/98	no post	J. Court	no post	B. Furness
1998/99	no post	J. Court	no post	B. Furness
1999/00	no post	J. Court	no post	no post
2000/01	no post	J. Court	no post	no post

Season	Coaching Advisor	National Coach	National Team Manager	Coaching & Development Officer	Director of Coaching
1969/70	K. Edwards				
1970/71	R. Digges				
1971/72	R. Digges				
1972/73	B. Moss				
1973/74	M. Ives				
1974/75	K. Edwards	G.Greenfield	J. Morris		
1975/76		G.Greenfield	J. Morris		
1976/77		G.Greenfield	J. Morris		
1977/78		G.Greenfield	no post listed		
1978/79		F. Westell	R. Thom		
1979/80		no post listed	R. Thom		
1980/81			B. Moss		
1981/82			J. Morris		
1982/83			J. Morris		
1983/84			J. Morris		
1984/85			J. Morris		
1985/86			G. Shaw	K. Edwards	
1986/87			G. Shaw	K. Edwards	
1987/88			R. Thom		
1988/89			R. Thom	G. Mayne	
1989/90			R. Thom	L. Hall	
1990/91			B.Cossavella	L. Hall	
1991/92			B.Cossavella	L. Hall	
1992/93			B.Cossavella	no post listed	L. Hall
1993/94			no post listed	C. Paton	L. Hall
1994/95			no post listed	T. Wirdnam	L. Hall
1995/96			no post listed	T. Wirdnam	L. Hall
1996/97		M. Eadon	S. Douce	A.Thompson	H. Gould
1997/98		M. Eadon	S. Douce	A.Thompson	H. Gould
1998/99		M. Eadon	S. Douce		H. Gould
1999/00		M. Eadon	no post listed		H. Gould
2000/01		M. Eadon	M. Eadon		H. Gould

Season	Sports Aid Foundation Grants Co-ordinator	Racing Secretary	Youth & Coaching Development Officer	Chairman of Coaching Committee	National Trophy Co-ordinator
1980/81				R. Digges	
1981/82				B. Watson	
1982/83				B. Watson	
1983/84				B. Watson	
1984/85				B. Watson	
1985/86					
1986/87					
1987/88					
1988/89	Mrs G.Wreghitt				
1989/90	T. Haigh				
1990/91	T. Haigh				
1991/92	T. Haigh	A. Hill			
1992/93	T. Haigh	J. Burney			
1993/94	T. Haigh				J. Burney
1994/95	T. Haigh				J. Burney
1995/96	T. Haigh				J. Burney
1996/97	T. Haigh		B. Haywood		J. Burney
1997/98	T. Haigh		B. Haywood		J. Burney
1998/99	H. Gould		B. Haywood		J. Burney
1999/00	H. Gould		B. Haywood		J. Burney
2000/01	H. Gould		B. Haywood		J. Burney

Season	Clerical Officer	Medical Officer	Medical Control Officer	Medal Sales/ Distribution	Equipment Officer
1985/86	Mrs J. Edwards				
1986/87	Mrs J. Edwards				
1987/88	Mrs J. Edwards				
1995/96		Dr.C. Butler	G. Macdonald	R. Bacon	
1996/97		Dr.C. Butler	G. Macdonald	R. Bacon	G. Shergold
1997/98		Dr.C. Butler	G. Macdonald	R. Bacon	G. Shergold
1998/99			G. Macdonald	R. Bacon	G. Shergold
1999/00			G. Macdonald	R. Bacon	G. Shergold
2000/01			G. Macdonald	R. Bacon	G. Shergold

LIFE MEMBERS				
1968/69	R. Atkins	Mrs J. Edwards	K. Edwards	P. Lovell
1973/74	R. Richards	Mrs B. Richards		
1977/78	J. Dickenson			
1978/79	J. Atkins			
1983/84	R. Ward			
1985/86	R. Digges			
1986/87	I. Dodd			
1990/91	G. Greenfield			
1992/93	T. Haigh	H. Gould	P. Milsom	
1993/94	J. Rawnsley			
2000/01	J. Court			
LIFE VICE PRESIDENT		1986/87 R. Richards		

APPENDIX TWO

Champions

SENIOR CHAMPIONS

Year	Venue	Champion	Club	Second	Club	Third	Club
1955	Welwyn Gd City	Alan Jackson	De Laune CC	Alan Winters	Warwickshire RC	Don Stone	34 Nomads
1956	Halesowen	Alan Jackson	De Laune CC	Don Smith	Midland C & AC	Mick Weston	Coventry RC
1957	Brands Hatch	Don Stone	34 Nomads	Alan Jackson	De Laune CC	Paddy Hoban	34 Nomads
1958	Bagshott Heath	Don Stone	34 Nomads	Barry Spence	Wolverhampton Whs	Bill Radford	Elizabethan CC
1959	Bolton	Barry Spence	Wolverhampton Whs	Alan Winters	Solihull CC	Ken Knapman	Southern Velo
1960	Baddesley	David Briggs	Saracen RC	Don Stone	Croydon RC	Alan Winters	Solihull CC
1961	Cobham	John Atkins	Coventry RC	Mike Wilkinson	Southport RCC	David Briggs	Solihull CC
1962	Tingley	John Atkins	Coventry RC	Mike Wilkinson	Southport RCC	Keith Mernickle	Middx Clarion
1963	Harlow	Mick Stallard	Wolverhampton Whs	John Atkins	Coventry RC	Keith Mernickle	Middx Clarion
1964	Wolverhampton	Mick Stallard	Wolverhampton Whs	Keith Mernickle	EG Bates Cycles	Mick Ives	Coventry CC
1965	Leeds	Mick Stallard	Wolverhampton Whs	Keith Mernickle	EG Bates Cycles	Harry Bond	Ellis Briggs –Simplex
1966	Birmingham	John Atkins	Coventry RC	Roger Page	Edgbaston RC	Dave Wren	Edgware RC

AMATEUR CHAMPIONS

Year	Venue	Champion	Club	Second	Club	Third	Club
1967	Birmingham	John Atkins	Coventry RC	Dave Wren	Edgware RC	John Barnes	Morden CRC
1968	Crystal Palace	John Atkins	Coventry RC	Roger Page	Edgbaston RC	Dave Wren	Edgware RC
1969	Coventry	Barry Moss	Solihull CC	Roger Page	Solihull CC	Eric Stone	Matlock CC
1970	Crystal Palace	Olly Nagle	Coventry RC	Daryl Brassington	Coventry RC	Roger Page	Solihull CC
1971	Manchester	Daryl Brassington	Coventry RC	Roger Page	Solihull CC	Chris Dodd	Coventry RC
1972	Leeds	Chris Dodd	Otley CC	Roger Page	Solihull CC	Vic Barnett	Welland Valley Wh
1973	Sutton Coldfield	Chris Dodd	Coventry RC	Graham Collyer	GS Barossa'	Richard Travis	Solihull CC
1974	Liverpool	Jeff Morris	Polytechnic CC	Chris Dodd	Coventry RC	Alan Williams	Archer RC
1975	Sutton Coldfield	Jeff Morris	Diddington RC	Chris Dodd	Coventry Olympic	Phil Allison	Brook CC
1976	Sutton Coldfield	Jeff Morris	Diddington RC	Phil Allison	Diddington RC	Tony Lyne	Gannet CC
.							
1992	Harlow	Peter Stevenson	Private member	Jake Elliott	Diddington RC	Stuart Marshall	VC Lincoln
1993	Wolverhampton	Peter Stevenson	Middridge CRT	Roger Hammond	VC Bad	Gary Foord	Wembley RC
1994	Southampton	Roger Hammond	Invicta RC	Stuart Blunt	Wembley RC	Matthew Guy	RT Italia
1995	Sutton Coldfield	James Norfolk	VC St Raphael	Matthew Guy	Private member	Roger Hammond	South Western RC

PROFESSIONAL CHAMPIONS

Year	Venue	Champion	Team/Sponsor	Second	Team/Sponsor	Third	Team/Sponsor
1967	Featherstone	Keith Mernickle	Ryall/Weldwork	Mick Ives	Mottram/Simplex	Mick Coward	Witcomb Cycles
1968	Croydon	Mick Ives	Bantel-Mercian	Dick Goodman	Carlton BMB	Keith Mernickle	Ryall/Weldwork
1969	Coventry	John Atkins	Marsh & Baxter	Keith Mernickle	Ryall/Weldwork	Mick Ives	Bantel-Mercian
1970	Crystal Palace	John Atkins	Marsh & Baxter	Keith Mernickle	Chris Barber	Eric Stone	Tower Cycles
1971	Manchester	John Atkins	TI Carlton	Eric Stone	Tower Cycles	Keith Mernickle	Chris Barber
1972	Leeds	John Atkins	TI Carlton	Daryl Brassington	Coventry Eagle	Keith Mernickle	Chris Barber
1973	Sutton Coldfield	John Atkins	TI Carlton	Keith Mernickle	Chris Barber	Eric Stone	RBM
1974	Liverpool	John Atkins	TI Carlton	Daryl Brassington	Falcoln-Tighe	Keith Mernickle	Chris Barber
1975	Sutton Coldfield	John Atkins	TI Carlton	Keith Mernickle	Chris Barber	Barry Davies	Ron Kitching
1976	Sutton Coldfield	Keith Mernickle	Chris Barber	John Atkins	Viscount-Shimano	Chris Dodd	Bantel
*							
1992	Harlow	David Baker	Team Raleigh	Tim Gould	Cycles Peugeot	Chris Young	Scott-Diamond Back
1993	Wolverhampton	Steve Douce	Saracen Cycles	David Baker	Team Raleigh	Chris Young	Team Orange
1994	Southampton	Nick Craig	Diamond-Bk Karrimor	Steve Douce	BCCA Professional	Barrie Clarke	Team Raleigh
1995	Sutton Coldfield	Barrie Clarke	Team Raleigh	Steve Douce	BCCA Professional	Nick Craig	Diamond Back

SENIOR OPEN CHAMPIONS

Year	Venue	Champion	Club/sponsor	Second	Club/sponsor	Third	Club/sponsor
1977	Sutton Coldfield	John Atkins	Viscount-Shimano	Keith Mernickle	Chris Barber	Ian Jewell	Chris Barber
1978	Sutton Coldfield	Chris Wreghitt	GS Strada	John Atkins	Viscount-Shimano	Eric Stone	Ron Kitching
1979	Sutton Coldfield	Chris Wreghitt	GS Strada	Phil Alison	Altrincham RC	Eric Stone	Ron Kitching
1980	Sutton Coldfield	Chris Wreghitt	GS Strada	Barry Davies	Trumanns Steel	Paul Watson	Coventry Olympic
1981	Sutton Coldfield	Chris Wreghitt	GS Strada	Chris Ledger	Altrincham RC	Eric Stone	Benotto
1982	Sutton Coldfield	Chris Wreghitt	GS Strada	Paul Watson	Anglia Sport	Martin Springer	Bournemouth Arrow CC
1983	Sutton Coldfield	Steve Douce	Bedouin CC	Chris Wreghitt	GS Strada	Chris Young	Burnley CRT
1984	Sutton Coldfield	Chris Young	Burnley CRT	Steve Douce	Bedouin CC	Steve Barnes	Seacroft Wheelers
1985	Sutton Coldfield	Steve Douce	Wembley RC	Chris Young	Paragon RT	Steve Barnes	Brook CC
1986	Sutton Coldfield	Steve Douce	Tshirt-Dauphin-Nico	Chris Young	Paragon RT	David Baker	Paragon RT
1987	Sutton Coldfield	Steve Douce	Tshirt-Dauphin-Nico	David Baker	Paragon RT	Tim Gould	Ace RT
1988	Sutton Coldfield	Steve Douce	Raleigh-Banana	Tim Gould	Ace RT	Chris Young	Paragon RT
1989	Sutton Coldfield	Steve Douce	Raleigh-Banana	Barrie Clarke	Wembley RC	Tim Gould	Cycles Peugeot
1990	Sutton Coldfield	David Baker	Cycles Peugeot	Steve Barnes	Ace RT	Steve Douce	Raleigh-Banana
1991	Harlow	Chris Young	Ever Ready- Halfords	Steve Douce	Raleigh RT	David Baker	Raleigh RT
1992	Harlow	David Baker	Team Raleigh	Tim Gould	Cycles Peugeot	Chris Young	Scott- Diamond Back
1993	Harlow	Steve Douce	Saracen Cycles	David Baker	Team Raleigh	Peter Stevenson	Middridge CRT
1994	Wolverhampton	Roger Hammond	Invicta RC	Nick Craig	DiamondBk- Karrimr	Steve Douce	BCCA Professional
1995	Southampton	Barrie Clarke	Team Raleigh	Steve Douce	BCCA Professional	Nick Craig	Diamond Back
1996	Sutton Coldfield	Nick Craig	Diamond Back	Barrie Clarke	Team Raleigh	Roger Hammond	South Western RC
1997	Sutton Coldfield	Barrie Clarke	Team Raleigh	Steve Knight	Halesowen C&AC	Steve Knight	Evans Cycles
1998	Sutton Coldfield	Nick Craig	Diamond Back Racing	Barrie Clarke	Diamond Bk Racing	Barrie Clarke	Peugeot406/MfRacing
1999	Sutton Coldfield	Steve Knight	Peugeot406/MfRacing	Nick Craig	Team Raleigh	Barrie Clarke	Team Raleigh
2000	Ipswich	Roger Hammond	Collstrop	Barrie Clarke	Team Raleigh	Carl Sturgeon	Lutterworth Cycle Ctr
2001	Sutton Park	Roger Hammond	Collstrop	Steve Knight	Mf Racing	Matt Ellis	Soft Valley

UNDER 23 CHAMPIONS

Year	Venue	Champion	Club/sponsor	Second	Club/sponsor	Third	Club/sponsor
1996	Sutton Coldfield	Roger Hammond	South Western RC	Matt Guy	Ace RT	James Taylor	Brook CC
1997	Sutton Coldfield	James Taylor	Giant-Gripshift	Brian Curtis	Team Corridori	Gavin Hardwicke	Shocktech/C'tal
1998	Sutton Coldfield	James Taylor	Giant-ESP	Brian Curtis	Team Corridori	Daniel Bell	VC Lincoln
1999	Sutton Coldfield	David Bowater	Black Country Whs	Paul Oldham	Hope Technology	Gavin Hardwicke	Beavvale CC
2000	Ipswich	Daniel Booth	KVV/Sporty Koksijde	Phil Dixon	Peugeot 406/Mil Rac	Tim Morley	Corridori/Specialized
2001	Sutton Park	Liam Killeen	Team Y2K Trek	Tim Morley	Team Y2K Trek	Shaun Snodden	Ace RT

JUNIOR CHAMPIONS

Seasn	Venue	Champion	Club	Second	Club/sponsor	Third	Club
1966/7	Featherstone	Phil Norfolk	Bradford RCC	David Cartwright	VC Central	Mike Girling	Crabwood CC
1967/8	Denton	Chris Dodd	Coventry RC	Roger Meer	Birmingham RCC	Paul Paddock	Wolverhampton Whs
1968/9	Hessle	Chris Dodd	Coventry RC	David Goddard	Humber Velo	Barry Dixon	Humber Velo
69/70	Wolverhampton	Peter Williams	Longslade School	Barry Dixon	Humber Velo	Brian O'Hare	Birchfield CC
70/71	Wolverhampton	Jeff Morris	Polytechnic CC	Andrew Jones	Royal Sutton CC	Phil Allison	Sheffield Phoenix CC
71/72	Cleethorpes	Jeff Morris	Polytechnic CC	Steve Atkinson	Calder Clarion	John Metcalf	Halesowen C & AC
72/73	Bagshot Heath	John Fenwick	Consett Wheelers	John Metcalf	Crabwood CC	Paul Edwards	Royal Sutton CC
73/74	Sutton Coldfield	Martin Springer	Crabwood CC	Peter Brookes	Crabwood CC	Paul Drury	Coventry CC
74/75	Colchester	Martin Springer	Crabwood CC	Mervyn Cartwright	Wolverhampton Wh	Paul Drury	Coventry Olympic
75/76	Norwich	Simon Hawkes	Bristol RC	Chris Wregitt	Coalville Wheelers	Martin Eaton	Rugby Velo
76/77	Poole	Steve Davies	Coventry RC	Michael Davies	Wreake Valley CC	Simon Armitage	Bradford RCC
77/78	Kenilworth	Chris Wharton	Wolverhampton Wh	Tim Broadhead	Solihull CC	Kevin Carr	Selby CC
78/79	Harlow	Chris Wharton	Halesowen C & AC	Mike Bell	CC Orpington	Chris Ledger	Norton Wheelers
79/80	Eastway	Paul Watson	Coventry Olympic	Steve Douce	VC Elan	Chris Ledger	Brook CC
80/81	Northallerton	Steve Douce	VC Elan	Mark Noble	Halesowen C & AC	Chris Young	Bradford RCC
81/82	Wolverhampton	Mick Hammond	Bradford RCC	Chris Young	Bradford RCC	Steve Barnes	Seacroft Wheelers
82/83	Bingley	David Baker	Norton Wheelers	Mark Rigby	Brook CC	Stuart Marshall	VC Lincoln
83/84	Sutton Coldfield	Paul Dixon	Mirfield CC	Robert Dane	Brook CC	Michael Bradley	Solihull CC
84/85	Sutton Coldfield	Paul Dixon	Mirfield CC	Stuart Marshall	VC Lincoln	Michael Bradley	Solihull CC
85/86	Sutton Coldfield	Steve Noble	Seacroft Wheelers	Nick Craig	VC Lincoln	Martin Maskell	Glendale CAC
86/87	Sutton Coldfield	Ian Wright	VC Lincoln	Nick Craig	VC Elina	Martin Maskell	Glendale CAC
87/88	Sutton Coldfield	Ian Wright	VC Lincoln	Lee Ferraday	VC Oldham	Mark Bolt	Manchester Wh

Season	Venue	Champion	Club/School	Second	Club/School	Third	Club/School
88/89	Sutton Coldfield	Lee Ferreday	Brook CC	John Pemberton	Bolsover Wh	Roger Hammond	Wembley RC
89/90	Sutton Coldfield	Roger Hammond	Wembley RC	Richard Thackray	Bradford Olympic	Chris Perry	Chesterfield Couriers
90/91	Harlow	Roger Hammond	Wembley RC	Richard Thackray	Bradford Olympic	Stuart Blunt	Wembley RC
91/92	Harlow	Roger Hammond	Wembley RC	Matthew Guy	Southport RCC	Richard Bruce	Wembley RC
92/93	Wolverhampton	Matthew Guy	Stars & Stripes	Robert Thackray	Bradford Olympic	Andrew Siers	Royal Sutton CC
93/94	Southampton	Brian Curtis	Festival RC	James Taylor	Beeston RC	Richard Allaway	Fat Tracks
94/95	Sutton Coldfield	Gavin Hardwicke	Long Eaton Paragon	Jack Lambeth	RT Elite	Danny Connolly	Bronte Wheelers
95/96	Sutton Coldfield	Danny Connolly	Bronte Wheelers	Jack Lambeth	RT Elite	James Allaway	Dawes RT
96/97	Sutton Coldfield	James Perry	NW MTB Centre	Tim Morley	Sutton & Croydon	Daniel Booth	Ace RT
97/98	Sutton Coldfield	Tim Morley	Raleigh M-Trax	Daniel Booth	Ace RT	Oliver Cox	Double A Cycles
98/99	Sutton Coldfield	Shaun Snodden	Ace RT	Ben Saunders	Hargroves Cycles	Paul Lally	KHS/AXO
99/00	Ipswich	Liam Killeen	Team Y2K	Matthew Kipling	Merlin Cycles	Phil Spencer	Matlock CC
00/01	Sutton Park	Phil Spencer	Elmy Cycles RT	Jordan Aveyard	Cycle Force 2000	Craig Cooke	Cardiff Ajax

YOUTH CHAMPIONS

Season	Venue	Champion	Club/School	Second	Club/School	Third	Club/School
19645	Birmingham	Geoff Shaw	March End Sec Mod	M O'Connor	Lordswood Tech	Vic Fullard	March End Sec Mod
19656	Croydon	Geoff Shaw	Bilston College	Vic Fullard	March End Sec Mod	Colin Browning	Cardinal Newman
1966/7	Wolverhampton	Barrie Elson	Wolston High School	Bob Russell	Forest Hill CC	Ray Pinder	Cauldon Castle Coventry
1967/8	Oldbury	Alex Hook	Daventry School	Barrie Churcher	Merry Oak Soton	Dave Goddard	Jarvis HS Hull
19689	Chingford	Peter Williams	Longslade School	Eric Smith	Beauchamps School	Neale Jauncey	Arden HS
69/70	Sheffield	Paul Wood	Foxwood School	Phil Chant	Bexley-Eritti Tech	Richard Lawrence	Herbert Carter Sch
70/71	Southampton	Geoff Williams	Brook CS Sheffield	Steve Jolley	Culceth HS	Nicholas Wood	Longslade School
71/72	Sutton Coldfield	Paul Edwards	Bishop Vesey GS	Charlie Jackson	Penwortham CS	Martin Springer	Glen Eyre CS Soton
72/73	Sheffield	Andrew Bagnall	Wellington GS	Paul Drury	Cauldon Castle Cov	Martin Springer	Glen Eyre CS Soton
73/74	Grimsby	Chris Wraghitt	Loughborough GS	Gerald Taylor	Castle Man Haverhill	Adrian Longland	Wyvern S'hampton
74/75	Coalville	Martin Eaton	Lawrence Sheriff	Robert Egglington	Droitwich	Andrew Sawyer	Broadstone
75/76	Southampton	Andrew Sawyer	Poole GS	Steven Davies	Finham Frn Coventry	Chris Boyce	Whitley Abbey Coventry
76/77	Kirkby	Kevin Carr	Sherburn HS	Dave Miller	Grove CS	Mike Bell	Kenmal Moor
77/78	Cambridge	Andy Palmer	Highams Park School	Chris Ledger	Rowlinson CS Sheff	Nigel Gilbert	King Ed V11 Sheffield

Year	Venue	Champion	Club/Sponsor	Second	Club/Sponsor	Third	Club/Sponsor
78/79	Eastway	David Wootton	Bereton Wheelers	Steve Douce	VC Elan	Barry Smallworth	Clarence Wheelers
79/80	Poole	Steve Lewis	Leamington Manor	David Hobson	Rowlinson CS Sheff	John Tonks	Smestow CS
80/81	Leyland	John Tonks	Smestow CS	Mike Gilby	Northallerton GS	Richard Hodges	Emerson Park
81/82	Sutton Coldfield	Nick Noble	Marlwood	Mark Cottrell	Farrngdon	David Baker	Dinnington CS
82/83	Colchester	Stuart Marshall	Yarborough	Dean Booth	VC Lincoln	Nick Bradwell	Kindersport CRT
83/84	Bournemouth	Steve Noble	Leeds	Guy Pearson	Nork Park	David Warner	Kenilworth
84/85	Lincoln	Nick Craig	New Mills CS	Ian Wright	Askern CC	Simon Hempsall	Brook CC
85/86	Stockport	Simon Hempsall	Chesterfield Crs	Ian Wright	VC Lincoln	Gareth Gimson	Wilsthorpe CS
86/87	Coalville	Phil Hinchcliffe	Barnsley RC	Paul Maven	Houghton CC	Andy Oldham	Walton Le Dale HS
87/88	Eastwood	Chris Perry	Beauvale RC	Jason Shackleton	Sidall HS	John Pemberton	Dene Court Sch
88/89	Bargoed	Roger Hammond	Dr Chaloners	Richard Thackray	Natwood	Mark Rushby	Sowerby Bridge
89/90	Southampton	Roger Hammond	Dr Chaloners	Lee Mosley	Hemsworth HS	Edward Holland	Boston GS
90/91	Northallerton	Robert Thackray	Salts GS	Brian Curtis	Cream HS	Darryl Gooch	Leo RC
91/92	Wigan	Matthew Jeuncey	Royal Sutton CC	Steven Cooke	Wigan Wheelers	Kevin Duckworth	Blackburn CTC
92/93	Verwood	Tom Crewe	Colstons Bristol	Gavin Gledhill	Ossett	Phil Neale	Henry Harbin
93/94	Wakefield	James Alleway	Fat Tracks	Mark Lloyd	Didcot Phoenix CC	Danny Connolly	Bronte Wheelers
94/95	Nottingham	Russell Taylor	Beeston RC	Tim Ireland	Hull Thursday RC	Lloyd Tommony	Unattached
95/96	Swansea	Russell Taylor	Brook CC	Daniel Booth	Ace RT	Matthew Robinson	Keighley Velo
96/97	Chesterfield	Mark Proudman	Raitrae RC	Shaun Snodden	Giant-Gripshift	Peter Middlehurst	Octagon VC
97/98	Durham	Richard Bowater	Black Country Whs	Tom Fowler	Cyclesport Midlands	Nathan Harman	Woolwich CC
98/99	Wolverhampton	Philip Spencer	Melton CC	Chris Skinner	VC Norwich	Robert Upex	Team Manchester
99/00	Ipswich	Lee Allen	Team Valley	Robert Spragg	Red Kite Cycles	Michael Jolley	Oldham Century RC
00/01	Sutton Park	Sammy Cotton	Team GT	Ben Crawford	Palmer Park Velo	Ed Perry	Victis RCC

WOMEN'S CHAMPIONS

Year	Venue	Champion	Club/Sponsor	Second	Club/Sponsor	Third	Club/Sponsor
1994	Southampton	Caroline Alexander	Louis Garneau	Sally Hibberd	BCCA Professional	Isla Rowntree	Black Country Wheelers
1995	Sutton Coldfield	Caroline Alexander	Klein USA	Louise Robinson	Team Raleigh	Isla Rowntree	Black Country Wheelers
1996	Sutton Coldfield	Caroline Alexander	BMW/Klein	Deb Murrell	Team Saracen	Isla Rowntree	Black Country Wheelers
1997	Sutton Coldfield	Caroline Alexander	Team Ritchey	Isla Rowntree	Black Country Whs	Louise Robinson	Team Raleigh
1998	Sutton Coldfield	Caroline Alexander	Team Ritchey	Louise Robinson	Team Raleigh	Isla Rowntree	Team Raleigh
1999	Wolverhampton	Isla Rowntree	Team Raleigh	Louise Robinson	Team Raleigh	Lindsay Clarke	Black Country Wheelers
2000	Ipswich	Louise Robinson	Stourbridge CC	Nicole Cooke	Peugeot 406/MI R	Susan Carter	Keyprint
2001	Sutton Park	Nicole Cooke	Cardiff Ajax	Louise Robinson	Stourbridge CC	Sue Thomas	Letchworth – Schtis / Team Y2K Trek

YOUTH WOMEN'S CHAMPIONS

Season	Venue	Champion	Club/School	Second	Club/School	Third	Club/School
94/95	Nottingham	Clare Gross	Oldham Century CC	Clare Bishop	Brough Wheelers	Hannah McCuaig	Belper RC
95/96	Swansea	Clare Gross	Ace RT	Nicole Cooke	Cardiff Ajax CC	Katy Middlehurst	St Ives CC
96/97	Chesterfield	Nicole Cooke	Cardiff Ajax CC	Katy Middlehurst	Octagon VC	Hazel Wakefield	Derwent Valley ATC
97/98	Durham	Nicole Cooke	Cardiff Ajax CC	Hazel Wakefield	Derwent Valley ATC	Kimberley Walsh	Huddersfield RC
98/99	Wolverhampton	Nicole Cooke	Peugeot 406/MI R	Hazel Wakefield	Derwent Valley ATC	Lorna Webb	Royal Sutton CC
99/00	Ipswich	Nikki Harris	Double A Cycles	Amy Hunt	Merlin Cycles	-	-
00/01	Sutton Park	Nikki Harris	Team Cycleweb	-	-	-	-

VETERAN CHAMPIONS

Season	Venue	Champion	Club/Sponsor	Second	Club/Sponsor	Third	Club
70/71	Alexandra Pal	Tony Summerfield	Elizabethan CC	Mick Florence	Solihull CC	Jim Blankley	Calder Clarion
71/72	Coventry	Alan Winters	Solihull CC	Jim Blankley	Calder Clarion	Tony Summerfield	Elizabethan CC
72/73	Wakefield	Roger Page	Everwarm	John Rawnsley	Bradford RCC	Jim Blankley	Calder Clarion
73/74	Cannock	Roger Page	Solihull CC	John Rawnsley	Bradford RCC	Mick Florence	Redditch R & PCC
74/75	Stockport	Roger Page	Hereford Rebores	Mick Ives	Coventry Olympic	Harry Bond	Bradford RCC
75/76	Malvern	Roger Page	Hereford Rebores	Harry Bond	Bradford RC	Mick Ives	Coventry Olympic
76/77	Bungey	Graham Button	Falcon Cycles	Mick Ives	Coventry Olympic	Bill Radford	Elizabethan CC
77/78	Loughborough	Graham Button	Harry Quinn Cycles	Mick Ives	Coventry Olympic	Tom MacDonald	Bronte Wheelers
78/79	Baginton	Roger Page	Hereford Rebores	John Rawnsley	Bradford RCC	Alan Winters	Coventry CC
79/80	Bingley	Roger Page	Hereford Rebores	Harry Bond	Bradford RCC	Alan Winters	Coventry CC
80/81	Maidenhall	Harry Bond	Bradford RCC	John Rawnsley	Bradford RCC	Mick Ives	Coventry Olympic
81/82	Baginton	Mick Ives	Coventry Olympic	Graham Button	Telford CC	Ian Small	Zodiac CRC
82/83	Knaresborough	Mick Ives	Coventry Olympic	Graham Button	Telford CC	Steve Burton	Calder Clarion
83/84	Greenwich	Graham Button	Telford CC	Mick Ives	Coventry Olympic	Ian Small	Zodiac CRC
84/85	Coalville	Mick Ives	Coventry Olympic	Lance Ravenhill	Coventry Olympic	Ian Small	Southern Velo
85/86	Sheffield	Mick Ives	Coventry Olympic	Ian Jewell	Southern Velo	Lance Ravenhill	Coventry Olympic
86/87	Alexandra Pal	Mick Ives	Coventry Olympic	Barry Davies	Wyvern CC	Lance Ravenhill	Sapphire RC
87/88	Southampton	Mike Bradbury	Festival RC	Lance Ravenhill	Sapphire RC	Mick Ives	Coventry Olympic
88/89	Bedale	Mick Ives	Coventry Olympic	Lance Ravenhill	Sapphire RC	Stuart Johnson	Zodiac CRC

Year	Location	1st	Club	2nd	Club	3rd	Club
89/90	Birmingham	Lance Ravenhill	Sapphire RC	Mike Bradbury	Festival RC	Ian Jewell	Festival RC
90/91	Croydon	Ian Jewell	Festival RC	Paul Bennett	Ross Wheelers	Lance Ravenhill	Sapphire RC
91/92	St Helens	Lance Ravenhill	Sapphire RC	Stuart Towers	VC Bradford	Ian Jewell	Festival RC
92/93	Lancing	Les Lloyd	Didcot Phoenix CC	Ian Jewell	Festival RC	Dave Lloyd	Didcot Phoenix CC
93/94	Oxford	Les Lloyd	Didcot Phoenix CC	Dave Lloyd	Didcot Phoenix CC	Ian Jewell	Festival RC
94/95	Nottingham	Les Lloyd	Didcot Phoenix CC	Roy Hunt	Bolton MTB	Dave Lloyd	Didcot Phoenix CC
95/96	Swansea	Cliff Featherstone	Derwentside CC	Andrew Russell	Keighley Velo	Andrew Russell	Keighley Velo
96/97	Chesterfield	Cliff Featherstone	Derwentside CC	Martin Booth	Ace RT	Steve Bennett	Team Orange
97/98	Durham	Martin Booth	Ace RT	Roy Hunt	Ace RT	B Wood-Anderson	Matlock CC
98/99	Wolverhampton	Martin Booth	Ace RT	Les Lloyd	KHS/Alexa	Cliff Featherstone	Derwentside CC
99/00	Ipswich	Peter Stevenson	Middridge CRT	Martin Easton	Didcot Phoenix CC	Mick Daley	VC Lincoln
00/01	Sutton Park	Martin Booth	Ace RT Alan	Paul Gilbert	Team Hed	Andrew MacDonald	G A Cycles
						Nick Kinsey	De Laune CC

VETERAN 50+ CHAMPIONS

Year	Location	1st	Club	2nd	Club	3rd	Club
99/00	Ipswich	Vic Barnett	Welland Valley Whs	Mick Ives	Peugeot 406/Ml Rac	Chris Gooch	Team Clean
00/01	Sutton Park	Chris Gooch	Team Clean	John Atkins	Coventry RC	Vic Barnett	Welland Valley Whs

APPENDIX THREE

National Senior Rankings

This system of producing a list of rankings for Seniors was introduced on a trial basis in 1995; it was based on the U.C.I World Rankings. The system is rather involved, covering a 24 month period. The points values awarded, vary according to the standard of the race, from 100 points for the winner of the National Championship down to 30th place, to 6 points for the winner of a Category C event down to 5th place.

Position in 1996-97 Handbook from previous season
1 Barrie Clarke	Team Raleigh	449.0 points
2 Nick Craig	Diamond Back	378.0
3 Roger Hammond	South Western R.C	341.3

251 counting riders

Position in 1997-98 Handbook
1 Barrie Clarke	Team Raleigh	543.2 points
2 Steve Knight	Halesowen C & A.C	413.4
3 Stuart Blunt	Ace R.T	381.4

322 counting riders

Position in 1998-99 Handbook
1 Barrie Clarke	Team Raleigh	414 points
2 Steve Knight	Peugeot 406	409
3 Stuart Blunt	Ace R.T	366

247 counting riders

Position in 1999-00 Handbook
1 Steve Knight	Peugeot 406MI Racing	457 points
2 Barrie Clarke	Team Raleigh	317
3 Stuart Blunt	Ace R.T	300

250 counting riders

Position in 2000-01 Handbook
1 Roger Hammond	Collstrop	349 points
2 Barrie Clarke	Team Raleigh	340
3 Steve Knight	Peugeot 406	315

253 counting riders

Note that Barrie Clarke was never ranked lower than second during this period.

APPENDIX FOUR

British Cyclo-Cross Trophies

The Swatkins Trophy. Awarded annually to the winner of the National Senior Championship

The Adrian Longland Trophy. Awarded annually to the winner of the National Junior Championship

The Europa Shield. Awarded annually to the winning team in the National Senior Championship.

The Joan Edwards Trophy. Awarded annually to the winner of the National Under 23 Championship

The Ralph Digges Trophy. Awarded annually to the winner of the National Women's Championship.

The Maurice Turner Trophy. Awarded annually to the winner of the National Veteran Championship

The Gordon MacDonald Trophy. Awarded annually to the winning team in the National Veteran Championship

The Halfords Trophy. Awarded annually to the winner of the National Youth Boys Championship

The Arthur Gamble Trophy. Awarded annually to the winner of the National Youth Girls Championship

The Findus Trophy. Awarded annually to the leading under 15 rider in the National Youth Championship

The Notts & Derby Trophy. Awarded annually to the leading under 14 rider in the National Youth Championship

The Ray Richards Memorial Trophy. Awarded annually for a single meritorious ride

The Sgt. H.J.Colley V.C., M.M. Memorial Trophy. Awarded annually to the rider adjudged to be the most improved of the year

The Gill Wreghitt Memorial Trophy. Awarded annually to the leading rider in the Senior National Trophy Series under 20 years of age. (From 1996-97 leading Under 23 rider).

The T.I. Reynolds Shield. Awarded annually to the club or school with the highest aggregate points total in the B.C-C.A Youth Award Scheme.